FRONT BURNER

FRONT BURNER

AL QAEDA'S ATTACK ON THE USS *COLE*

COMMANDER
KIRK S. LIPPOLD, USN (RET)
Former Commanding Officer, USS *Cole*

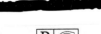

PublicAffairs
NEW YORK

Published in the United States by PublicAffairs™,
a Member of the Perseus Books Group

PublicAffairs books are available at special discounts for bulk purchases in the U.S. by corporations, institutions, and other organizations. For more information, please contact the Special Markets Department at the Perseus Books Group, 2300 Chestnut Street, Suite 200, Philadelphia, PA 19103, call (800) 810-4145, ext. 5000, or e-mail special.markets@perseusbooks.com.

Book Design by Pauline Brown

Typeset in 12 point Adobe Garamond Pro by the Perseus Books Group

The Library of Congress has cataloged the printed edition as follows:

Lippold, Kirk S.
  Front burner : al Qaeda's attack on the USS Cole / Kirk S. Lippold. — 1st ed.
    p. cm.
  Includes bibliographical references and index.
  ISBN 978-1-61039-124-5 (hardcover : alk. paper) — ISBN 978-1-61039-125-2
(e-book) 1. USS Cole Bombing Incident, Aden, Yemen, 2000. 2. Cole (Ship).
3. Qaida (Organization) 4. Terrorism—Yemen (Republic) 5. Terrorism—United
States. 6. Yemen (Republic)—Foreign relations—United States. 7. United States—
Foreign relations—Yemen (Republic) I. Title.
  VA65.C57L56 2012
  363.325'93598354—dc23

                                                                    2011049048

First Edition

10 9 8 7 6 5 4 3 2 1

Mom, Dad, and Kelly
Through a family's love all things are possible

L   J   N

CONTENTS

ACKNOWLEDGMENTS

FIRST AND FOREMOST, a ship is a reflection of its crew. In a singular moment in time, USS *Cole* and its crew became part of the Navy's history and long heritage of unswerving devotion to our nation and the freedom of its citizens. The war on terror started with us. All the sailors of USS *Cole* chose a life of consequence in service to the nation and are heroes for what they endured that horrific day and in the weeks that followed. Those who lost their lives will always be remembered in our thoughts and prayers. It is my honor to have been given the unique and humbling opportunity to command the officers and crew of USS *Cole*.

The writing of *Front Burner* has been a long overdue, painstaking process, not just of capturing in writing the heroic acts of a crew as they saved USS *Cole* and their shipmates, but also a reckoning for me in facing up to what happened to my ship and crew as the sole accountable officer—the Captain. For years I pecked away at the story, constantly outlining and reworking the project in my mind. It wasn't until after retirement that I felt ready to begin addressing the challenge in earnest. For years, people throughout the Navy, Department of Defense, FBI and NCIS, and elsewhere gave me information, paperwork, documentation, pictures, confidential insight into conversations, and material that slowly allowed me to flesh out the larger and more detailed picture of what really happened before, during, and after the attack. To each of those who quietly contributed but must remain anonymous, you have my deepest gratitude and thanks.

Immediately after the attack, I was quietly encouraged to retire and—like many in the military who had undergone a unique experience—pump out a book and leverage the experience for financial gain. My sense of dedication and desire to continue to serve the nation thankfully stopped me from giving in to that temptation to make an insincere career change. While I gave serious consideration to writing in 2002 when my career appeared derailed, thanks to some very sage advice and counsel from a great friend and Naval Academy classmate, Rear Admiral Frank Thorp, USN (Ret), I chose to forego a book then and instead continue my military service. The *Front Burner* I might have written years ago would never have measured up to the book it is today.

I also owe a great deal to another classmate, Captain Stephen Metz, USN (Ret). Reacquainted again when he was selected to oversee the demanding task of reconstructing USS *Cole*, Steve also became my most stalwart and vocal source of encouragement for continuing my career following the attack. I will always appreciate his friendship and unwavering support as a sounding board for my ideas, frustrations, and plans for the future.

As time went on and especially following retirement, there was a growing sense that what had happened to USS *Cole* and the crew was being lost; not just relegated to history, but truly lost, with no actual accounting of what happened. Over the years, the crew and I were approached by a number of interested authors, but none pursued the project past the talking stage. The pressure to write began to hound me more and more. Why I felt that I had to be the one to capture the event, in my own words and from my unique vantage point as the CO, remains unexplained even to myself, but I felt that without that perspective, the full scope and context of how the Navy reacted to the event would never receive the full examination it needed. The attack on USS *Cole* was an act of war. It was also an inexcusable intelligence failure on the part of the U.S. government. Sadly, neither the Navy nor the nation did anything to respond and the wheels of the nation's destiny were set into motion, culminating in the attacks of September 11 eleven months later.

When I finally did decide to capture that moment in our nation's history, I quickly realized that, as a naval officer, I did not really know how to write a book. I felt overwhelmed and not up to the task. Thanks to Captain Mike McDaniel, USN (Ret), and some brilliant historians at the Navy's History and Heritage Command, specifically, Randy Papadopoulos, Robert Schneller, John Sherwood, and Jeffrey Barlow: they convinced me that I had what it took to write a book. I will always be particularly thankful to Randy, who became my first editor and gave me those initial frank critiques that helped form the basis of what eventually became *Front Burner*. I will always be grateful for their faith and confidence in me to do what few have done successfully in making history come alive.

As I began to write, the telling became the reliving, and with it came the familiar anxiety that accompanied the experience itself. Many times, I pushed away from the desk unable to write another word. Reliving the challenges and horrors of the event minute by minute, second by second sometimes proved too much to deal with. Still, I kept at it—the story had to be told.

While this is my story, it is by no means the definitive account. More can and should be told by those who feel drawn to share their perspective and experience with others. Before my journey into writing began, I had been introduced to Peter Osnos, the founder of PublicAffairs. For this telling, he paired me with a superb journalist, Bruce Nelan, who showed an amazing capacity to draw out the story in a series of interviews that I used extensively in writing my account. Throughout my fits and starts putting pen to paper, Peter showed a remarkable and unwavering confidence in my ability to write a powerful account of the attack. His patience over the intervening years is a testament to his commitment. While my ability to survive the attack may have come from years of at-sea experience, it is because of Peter that *Front Burner* is finally a reality for people to share in.

It wasn't easy, though. I will never forget his comment to me after I turned in the initial draft. "Kirk, here's the reality of your situation. You have given us a great narrative that has superb documentation, and you are a very good naval officer, but that doesn't necessarily make you a good storyteller!" While both of us got a good laugh, it was through his introduction to his friend Craig Whitney, a retired foreign correspondent and editor, that *Front Burner* truly came alive. It is through Craig's unsurpassed skill and ability that he could take my lengthy prose and deftly help me craft it into the story you will soon read. It may be my story but it is his skill in the art of writing that showed me how to bring out the events surrounding USS *Cole* in a way that puts that life-changing event and its searing images at the forefront of history and the war on terror.

I also learned that no finished book is the work of just a few individuals. I owe a great deal of thanks to those who helped me make the book a successful reality in the unfamiliar world of publishing, including Susan Weinberg, Brandon Proia, Jaime Leifer, Anais Scott, and Collin Tracy. I also owe a great deal of thanks to Theresa Yates. Her skill as a transcriptionist and her ability to listen to sometimes very emotional and powerful descriptions of what happened to individual crew members as they recounted and shared their experiences with me gave her a profound insight into what happened to us.

In an insightful moment of introspection, I came to realize that had I not been given the tools gained over eighteen years of experience, there was no way I could have led my crew through that event. Those experiences were best learned from the commanding officers I was privileged to serve under throughout my career, including Captain Robert Powers, USN, Captain Andrew Fosina, USN, Captain Carl Anderson, USN, Rear Admiral Phillip Dur, USN, Vice Admiral John Morgan, USN, Captain Lyal Davidson, USN, Captain John Russack, USN, and Captain Paul Schultz,

USN, all retired. Without their leadership and astute experience to guide me in how to manage and lead, I would have never been able to keep my crew motivated and ship afloat when the burden of command weighed most heavily on me.

In command of USS *Cole*, I was also blessed with a phenomenal squadron commodore, Captain Mike Miller, USN (Ret), whose confidence in me put the pieces in place for our future success and survival in an unforeseen combat scenario. I will always be grateful for his quiet and incisive counsel and hands-off approach to leading the COs in Destroyer Squadron Twenty-Two. His relief, Captain Gary Holst, USN (Ret), also gave similar latitude in leading the COs in his charge.

USS *Cole* is afloat today thanks to the myriad forces that came together after the attack to support our survival. In particular, I am grateful to two of my squadron mates, Rear Admiral J. Scott Jones, USN, and Captain Matthew Sharpe, USN, who provided for my crew, supported visits to their ships of not only the crew but the investigative teams as well, and were kind enough to allow me the opportunity to share my thoughts with them when they visited the ship. To all those who participated in Joint Task Force Determined Response, know that each of you had a hand in history and should be proud of your contribution in keeping USS *Cole* from becoming a trophy for the terrorists who sought its destruction. Bravo Zulu and well done.

It also cannot go without mention that without the dedicated work of the Federal Bureau of Investigation and Naval Criminal Investigative Service, the terrorists would never have been held accountable for their heinous act. In particular, Don Sachtleben, Mark Whitworth, Tom O'Connor, Kevin Finnerty, John Adams, Cathy Clements, and Mike Martz made contributions above and beyond the call of duty both on USS *Cole* and in the years that followed.

Captain Barbara "Bobbie" Scholley, USN (Ret), Chief Warrant Officer Frank Perna, and the divers of Mobile Diving and Salvage Unit Two faced the difficult task of recovering our shipmates with a steely resolve as they also ensured that damage to USS *Cole* was properly assessed in preparation for making the ship seaworthy to leave port. Ken Baggett and the volunteer shipyard workers from Norfolk Naval Shipyard also demonstrated an uncanny ability to adapt to our circumstances, and with gritty determination helped us keep USS *Cole* afloat. Each of them is a hero in their own right for their contribution to history.

Lastly, there is one person who stood beside me from before the moment of the attack until *Front Burner* was complete, Nicole Segura. As the person closest to me, she has truly kept me grounded and focused on never losing sight of what it means to serve the nation and honor my crew. Her friendship and support helped me appreciate and enjoy some of the highest moments of service and get past the darkest moments of my life. Nicole gave me the encouragement to stretch myself and grow beyond what I thought possible.

Now, with *Front Burner* a reality, it is my hope that a crew of heroes who survived the crucible of combat will at last be recognized for what they did to live up to the example of USS *Cole's* namesake, Sergeant Darrell S. Cole, USMC, who was posthumously awarded the Congressional Medal of Honor for conspicuous gallantry in the battle of Iwo Jima.

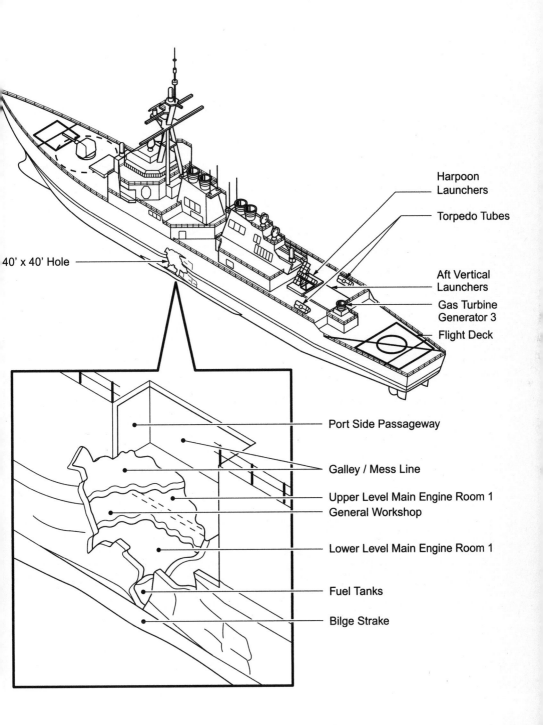

40' x 40' Hole

Harpoon Launchers

Torpedo Tubes

Aft Vertical Launchers

Gas Turbine Generator 3

Flight Deck

Port Side Passageway

Galley / Mess Line

Upper Level Main Engine Room 1

General Workshop

Lower Level Main Engine Room 1

Fuel Tanks

Bilge Strake

USS *COLE*—KILLED IN ACTION

In Memoriam
May their sacrifice for our freedom
never be forgotten

Kenneth Eugene Clodfelter
Hull Maintenance Technician
  Second Class
21, Mechanicsville, Virginia

Richard Dean Costelow
Electronics Technician Chief
  Petty Officer
35, Morrisville, Pennsylvania

Lakeina Monique Francis
Mess Management Specialist
  Seaman
19, Woodleaf, North Carolina

Timothy Lee Gauna
Information Systems Technician
  Seaman
21, Rice, Texas

Cherone Louis Gunn
Signalman Seaman
22, Rex, Georgia

James Rodrick McDaniels
Seaman
19, Norfolk, Virginia

Marc Ian Nieto
Engineman Second Class
24, Fond du Lac, Wisconsin

Ronald Scott Owens
Electronic Warfare Technician
  Second Class
24, Vero Beach, Florida

Lakiba Nicole Palmer
Seaman
22, San Diego, California

Joshua Langdon Parlett
Engineman Fireman
19, Churchville, Maryland

Patrick Howard Roy
Fireman
19, Cornwall on Hudson, New York

Kevin Shawn Rux
Electronic Warfare Technician
  First Class
30, Portland, North Dakota

Ronchester Manangan Santiago
Mess Management Specialist
  Third Class
22, Kingsville, Texas

Timothy Lamont Saunders
Operations Specialist Second Class
32, Ringgold, Virginia

Gary Graham Swenchonis, Jr.
Fireman
26, Rockport, Texas

Andrew Triplett
Lieutenant (junior grade)
31, Macon, Mississippi

Craig Bryan Wibberley
Seaman
19, Williamsport, Maryland

USS *COLE*—WOUNDED IN ACTION

Short of being killed, there is no sacrifice greater than those who bleed for the freedom of their nation, for they know the price of war.

Disbursing Clerk Third Class Adedeji O. Adewunmi

Electronics Warfare Technician First Class (Surface Warfare)
Melvin L. Alston

Information Systems Technician First Class (Surface Warfare)
Larry D. Bloodsaw

Chief Gas Turbine System Technician (Surface Warfare)
Mark P. Darwin

Mess Management Specialist Third Class Joseph C. Davis

Electronics Technician Third Class Russell E. Dietz

Operations Specialist Seaman Timothy S. Eerenberg

Ship's Serviceman Second Class (Surface Warfare) Craig B. Freeman

Electronics Warfare Technician Third Class (Surface Warfare)
Johann Gokool

Fire Controlman First Class (Surface Warfare) Douglas J. Hancock

Chief Gunners Mate (Surface Warfare) Mark A. Hawkins

Fire Controlman Third Class Jason S. Hayes

Senior Chief Fire Controlman (Surface Warfare)
John M. Henderson

Boatswain's Mate Third Class Frederick H. Ings

Chief Boatswain's Mate (Surface Warfare) Eric S. Kafka

Mess Management Specialist Third Class Elizabeth Lafontaine

Fire Controlman First Class (Surface Warfare)
Tremane N. Lide

Gas Turbine System Technician First Class (Surface Warfare)
Margaret K. Lopez

Senior Chief Gas Turbine System Technician (Surface Warfare)
Keith A. Lorensen

Seaman Apprentice Edward T. Love

Gunner's Mate Third Class Kenya N. McCarter

Gas Turbine Technician Second Class Robert D. McTureous

Ship's Serviceman Third Class Paul P. Mena

Gas Turbine System Technician Fireman Raymond A. Mooney

Gas Turbine System Technician Fireman Andrew A. Nemeth

Damage Controlman Fireman Sean H. Powell

Operations Specialist Second Class (Surface Warfare)
Tiffany N. Putman

Chief Quartermaster (Surface Warfare) Michael O. Russell

Postal Clerk Second Class (Surface Warfare) Isadore B. Sims

Hull Maintenance Technician Third Class Jeremy W. Stewart

Seaman Kesha R. Stidham

Chief Electrician's Mate (Surface Warfare) Fred C. Strozier

Storekeeper Second Class (Surface Warfare) Sean L. Taitt

Fire Controlman First Class David K. Veal

Chief Fire Controlman (Surface Warfare) Jeffrey M. Vinneau

Lieutenant Denise D. Woodfin

Operations Specialist First Class (Surface Warfare) Alonzo W. Woods

Introduction: Nightmare

ON THURSDAY, OCTOBER 12, 2000, the guided-missile destroyer USS *Cole*, DDG-67, under my command, was attacked while refueling in the harbor of Aden, Yemen, by two suicide bombers who were members of the al Qaeda terrorist network of Osama bin Laden. Because U.S. intelligence had no idea that an al Qaeda cell was present in Aden and planning an attack, we were taken completely by surprise when what we expected to be a garbage-removal barge approached the port side of our ship and blew up. The devastating explosion blasted a hole through the hull amidships, destroying one of the main engine rooms as well as the galley where scores of *Cole*'s crew were gathered for lunch. The explosion killed seventeen sailors, wounded thirty-seven others, and took the ship out of action.

If not for intelligence and military failures, the tragedy might have been avoided. As it was, the Navy, my ship, and I were left unprepared to deal with a new kind of terrorist threat that should have become apparent by 1998 at the latest, as a series of coordinated attacks simultaneously destroyed U.S. embassies and killed hundreds of people in Kenya and Tanzania.

I do not wish to minimize or excuse my own failure as captain to prevent this tragedy. After I oversaw *Cole*'s return to the United States and turned over command to my successor, I wondered whether continuing a career in the Navy was the wisest choice for me, or if it was even possible. Yet despite my doubts, the highest leaders of my service, the chief of naval operations and the secretary of the Navy, repeatedly insisted that it would be wrong to hold me any more responsible than they and the rest of the chain of command were for what had happened to the ship and the crew. After they made that clear, on the day just before the inauguration of President George W. Bush in January of 2001, I was determined to keep working quietly within the Navy to try to ensure that such an attack could never happen again to another ship, another crew, another captain.

So in 2001, with the rank of commander that I had held while I was captain of *Cole*, I found myself assigned to the Strategic Plans and Policy Division of the office of the chairman of the Joint Chiefs of Staff, working on United Nations and multilateral affairs. The pace and scope of the work were beyond anything I had been exposed to in any of my previous jobs as a Navy surface warfare officer, but three years in a multiservice assignment was part of the preparation that Congress had mandated for all officers who would eventually be under consideration for promotion to the most senior ranks. The posting to one of the most coveted divisions of the Joint Staff was, to me, the clearest indication I had yet seen that the Navy understood the unusual circumstances of the terrorist attack against USS *Cole*.

During my first few weeks on the staff, one of my former commanding officers, Captain John Russack, whose executive officer I had been on the Aegis guided-missile cruiser USS *Shiloh*, contacted me to see how I was doing. He had gone to work full time at the Central Intelligence Agency after retiring from the Navy, and was now deputy to Charles Allen, a legendary figure and forty-five-year veteran of the agency whose position gave him responsibility for how the CIA collected intelligence worldwide. After John had mentioned our acquaintanceship, Allen became interested in talking with me about what the CIA knew about Osama bin Laden and how it had determined that it was al Qaeda that had planned, financed, and carried out the attack against my ship. Needless to say, I was also very much interested in meeting Allen and hearing why neither Central Command, which had operational control over my ship at the time of the attack, nor the Navy, nor USS *Cole* had been provided with the kind of information that would have better enabled us to protect ourselves. I also wanted to understand why, after American intelligence had developed evidence that al Qaeda was responsible for the attack on the ship—a classic act of war—and that high-ranking operatives tied directly to Osama bin Laden had directed it, no aggressive retaliatory action had yet been taken against any of them, though their whereabouts in Afghanistan, where the Taliban regime had given al Qaeda sanctuary, were well known. Almost a year after the attack, the Clinton and the George W. Bush administrations had left the issue on the back burner, as far as I could tell.

John and I were finally able to work out a date for the meeting, and I arranged to arrive late to work that morning.

I had never been to the CIA before this day. Driving from Alexandria, Virginia, to Langley, headed up the George Washington Parkway thirty minutes before sunrise, I could tell it was going to be a beautiful day. Without a cloud in the sky, the first glow of the coming sunrise painted the skyline of Washington, D.C., and the white marble monuments across the Potomac a pale yellow glow.

The moment I walked into the front entrance is burned into my memory. On the highly polished floor of the Old Headquarters Building, the CIA seal, inlaid granite measuring sixteen feet across, stood out starkly against everything else around it. The sight stirred my emotions and raised the hairs on the back of my neck. The security guard in the lobby directed me to a phone to call John, who said he would be down in a few minutes. As I waited, I walked around the lobby until I came upon a single gold star in reverse bas-relief in the marble wall on the south side, honoring the men and women who had given their lives for our nation while serving with the CIA's predecessor organization, the Office of Strategic Services. On the opposite wall were row after row of gold stars representing the men and women of the CIA who had made the ultimate sacrifice. I felt a close bond with these names—to me, the sacrifice of the seventeen sailors on

my ship just one year before was no different from the sacrifices memorialized here on these hallowed walls.

A few minutes later, at 0630, John picked me up and escorted me to
his sixth-floor office next door to Allen's. For the next thirty minutes we
sat, drinking coffee and catching up, until at 0700 sharp, we went into
Allen's office.

The first thing Allen did was apologize for the clearance level of the
material he was about to show me, since I had not undergone the extensive
background checks and polygraphs necessary for a CIA clearance. But for
the next hour and a half, Allen carefully walked me through what the CIA
knew about Osama bin Laden and his organization. He began with the
coordinated embassy attacks in 1998 and then walked me through the presumed timeline for the development of the plan of attack against my ship.
Some of the things I had learned from the FBI's criminal investigators—
including John O'Neill, George Crouch, and Ali Soufan, who gathered
evidence on the ship in Aden and at safe houses—such as the names of
the suspected masterminds and in-country facilitators of the attack, for
instance, were not included in the CIA briefing.

What I found most difficult to understand was why the CIA station
chief at the U.S. embassy in Sana'a, Yemen's capital, had been unable or
unwilling to ascertain that al Qaeda and other terrorist organizations operating in Yemen and throughout the region could pose a threat to ships
refueling in Aden. The embassy, of course, was a couple of hundred miles
north of Aden, but along with the ambassador, he was supposed to be the
in-country expert and, in my view, both had failed the crew and me. But
I bit my tongue. At our meeting, Allen and the others conveyed a strong
sense of urgently wanting to go on the offensive and bring to justice the
terrorists who had committed the atrocity against *Cole*, whoever and wher-
ever they were, and that was more important now.

As the discussion wrapped up, we briefly discussed how magnificently
my crew had performed in the aftermath of the attack, taking care of each
other and preventing the ship from sinking. I shook my host's hand and
said, "You know, Mr. Allen, first, thank you very much for taking the time
to go over all this with me. It means an awful lot for me to understand

what our country is doing to try to catch this guy. But, I don't think America understands. I believe it is going to take a seminal event, probably in this country, where hundreds, if not thousands, are going to have to die before Americans realize that we're at war with this guy."

Allen, a bit surprised, said, "Well, hopefully that'll never happen. I hope we'll be able to head that off before it does."

John then took me around the building to talk to some of his co-workers and look at more work relating to the attack on USS *Cole*. I decided my work at the Joint Staff could wait. John first took me to see satellite images of some of the al Qaeda terrorist training camps in Afghanistan and elsewhere that were under observation for any sign of preparation for more attacks.

It was about 0850, as we were walking through another office, that a news bulletin flashing across one of the television monitors caught our attention. The north tower of the World Trade Center in lower Manhattan had a gaping hole near the top, with dense black smoke and flames pouring out of it. The anchor reporting the story said there were now doubts about earlier reports that a private plane, a sightseeing plane perhaps, had gone off course and hit the building. I just shook my head. It was clear that only a large plane could cause so much damage.

The date was September 11, 2001.

JOHN AND I CONTINUED making our way along, he introducing me as the former commanding officer of USS *Cole* and I thanking everyone for what they were doing to keep our nation safe and accepting condolences on behalf of my crew and their families. We came to the office of Cofer Black, head of the CIA's Counterterrorism Center, the CTC. Waiting while he finished a telephone call, we continued to watch the unfolding scene in New York. Then, at 0903, with gut-wrenching horror, we watched as the second plane came into view on the television screen, banked to the left, and drove straight into the south tower.

In that instant, it was clear to everyone present that the United States was under attack. The office became a ferocious beehive of activity, with people running in and out of Black's office. We slipped in, were quickly introduced, and just as quickly slipped back out.

As we turned to leave, Black's office assistant took a phone down from her ear and yelled out, "John, is that Lippold with you? Mr. Allen wants to see both of you up in his office, now!"

When we arrived at Allen's sixth-floor office, I was in a state of shock as he motioned us in and came around from behind his cluttered desk. He walked straight up to me, put his arm around my shoulders, looked me in the eye, and said, "Kirk, I can't believe you said what you did this morning." As calmly as I could, I looked back at him and replied, "Well sir, I guess this is something I have suspected for eleven months—and the country is finding out about it the hard way this morning." Adding that I knew all of us were going to have a busy day and that I needed to get on the road back to the Pentagon, I left. Passing once more by the walls of remembrance in the lobby, I realized that our nation was now at war. And Osama bin Laden and al Qaeda were the enemy.

As I got back onto the George Washington Parkway, I called Nicole Segura, the person closest to me, on my cell phone. Hearing her answer, my emotions cracked. My voice tightened; I felt tears of anger and frustration roll down my face. I felt that I had failed my nation again. People were dying because of my inaction. I had chosen a path in life that should have enabled me to defend my country to the utmost of my ability. But as commanding officer of USS *Cole*, I had not been able to prevent those fifty-four crew members from being killed or injured on my watch, and I had remained publicly silent about the entire event. Now, as the Twin Towers burned in New York, I called myself to task for my silence. "I can't believe this is happening. It's my fault," I told Nicole on the phone. "I have kept my mouth shut for eleven months and tried to get my career back on track, and now look at what it has cost my country. I should have done something, anything to forewarn the Navy and the nation about this son of a bitch. Oh, God, why is this happening to me again?" It was my sworn duty to protect my country, and I had failed yet again.

As I got closer to the Pentagon, Nicole suddenly broke off the conversation. "Oh my God, Jim Miklaszewski is on NBC News at the Pentagon saying that it was just hit."

A calmness suddenly settled over me. It was a feeling I had not experienced since the attack in Aden. Nicole told me later that it was as if a curtain had come down on my emotions. I became very calm and measured, intensely focused on what had just happened and what I could do to help.

Through the front window of my car I could see the billowing column of black smoke rising into the clear blue sky. I told Nicole, "Yes, the Pentagon has taken a hit. You can see the smoke and flames. I don't know what happened. Call my folks and let them know I'm okay. I don't know when I'll be home. It's going to be a long day. Pack things up in case the city takes another hit and you have to get out of town."

No one knew how big or complex this attack might become. As I neared the Pentagon, I pulled onto the main highway, 395 South, and parked on the shoulder by Boundary Channel Drive. People evacuating the building on the Potomac side were just starting to reach the grass area. Flames shot into the air 100 to 120 feet above the building, and clouds of greasy, black smoke filled the air. Even from where I was, on the opposite side of the building from where the terrorists had crashed American Airlines Flight 77, I could smell burning jet fuel. A Virginia State trooper and two Arlington County police cars quickly joined me at the ramp. I introduced myself and offered to help them manage traffic flow.

Over the next few hours, the officers and I directed traffic to get emergency vehicles and ambulances to where they were needed. We also made the decision to stop buses and load them with Pentagon evacuees. The police told the bus operators to drive down 395 and stop as people needed, to get them closer to home. The Washington Metro rail system and its station at the Pentagon had shut down altogether.

Amid the horror, I ran into one of my co-workers, Commander Cathy Knowles, a brilliant, hardworking lawyer, walking up the road. Luckily, our office was exactly on the opposite side of where the aircraft had impacted. Relieved at having found me alive and well, she reported that everyone in the office had evacuated the building. "What are you doing?" she asked. "I'm out here directing traffic," I answered.

"I can't believe you," she said, with an astounded look. "With everything that has gone on in your life, here you are again out here doing things. We've all been told to go home and call tomorrow to see whether we go back to work or not."

"I'll be out here for the rest of the day, but I'll eventually get home," I replied. "Let me know what we decide to do tomorrow." I found some compensation for my feeling of inadequacy in just doing what was needed out there on the road, helping people.

Minutes later, a large black Ford Expedition with blue flashing lights roared by. Abruptly screeching to a halt as smoke curled up from the tires, the SUV backed up to where I was standing with police officers. The side window rolled down and there I found myself talking to one of the FBI agents who had been working the USS *Cole* criminal case: Special Agent Mark Whitworth, an explosives technician I had met in Pascagoula, Mississippi, after the ship returned to the United States. He asked the same question as Cathy: "What are you doing out here? Haven't you had enough of this stuff?"

I spent the next eight hours working with the police officers. Around 1700, the situation had quieted down considerably. Although the Pentagon continued to burn through the night, there was nothing more to do. It was time to go home, where, sunburned, tired, and emotionally exhausted, I found Nicole and gave her a big hug. We watched the news on television. I was dumbfounded at seeing the footage of the Twin Towers collapsing, even though I had heard over the car radio when it had happened.

As a professional military officer, my job was to protect my country. It had been a long eleven months since the attack on USS *Cole*. During that time, my crew, their families, and I had all silently watched as our political and military leadership did nothing in response. Could I have pressed harder for actions that might have prevented the appalling disaster of the day we had just lived through? I did not know. But I did know that now, our country would finally be ready to respond. We would take action at last to avenge these terrorist attacks and prevent a recurrence.

My nation was at war and, at that moment, my resolve to help defend it was stronger than ever.

1 | Destination USS Cole

GROWING UP IN CARSON CITY, NEVADA, in the 1970s, I never dreamed of becoming an officer in the Navy. My dream was to fly. As a teenager I would go the local airport about a mile from home just to sit on the edge of the runway and watch the planes. My father had earned a private pilot's license years earlier, but eventually let it lapse. Even so, I can still vividly remember the few flights I took with him.

A small parachute drop zone stood just off the airport, out in the middle of the sagebrush. I loved to watch the skydivers jump from small airplanes, then slowly drift to a solid landing in the gravel. When I turned sixteen, I asked my parents for permission to make a skydive: *No!!* I would have to bide my time until the opportunity came. When eventually I began skydiving myself, I found that looking down with eyes wide open as the ground rushed up at hundreds of feet per second gradually sharpened my ability to integrate and analyze inputs from all my senses—that or miscalculate the time for the parachute to open and break my fall. The capability would serve me well in the career I finally chose.

My father had moved the family to Nevada when he was offered the opportunity to become the first psychologist for the Nevada State Prison system. My mother, a schoolteacher, started work in 1970 for the Carson

City School District and continued teaching at the high school until her retirement a few years ago. My sister, Kelly, who is two years younger than me, also graduated from Carson High School, attended the University of Nevada, Reno, and is a schoolteacher today in California.

During my junior year, the opportunity to attend one of our country's military academies loomed larger and larger in my mind as an option to consider for college. Just prior to my senior year, I made a decision to become politically active and, in a giant leap, ran for Student Body President and won. In 1977, I received two appointments: one to West Point for the U.S. Military Academy and the other to Annapolis, to the U.S. Naval Academy. I had no real idea of what lay ahead for me, but the Navy seemed to offer the greatest flexibility in a choice of career and profession: at graduation, I could become an officer in the Marines or Navy. I could even become a pilot.

I earned my U.S. Navy gold military parachute jump wings while in Annapolis. However, when I obtained my commission as an ensign on graduation day in 1981, I chose to serve in surface combatant ships such as destroyers and cruisers—a career path that also required the acquisition and application of skills in air and submarine warfare—and went immediately to Surface Warfare Officer School in Newport, Rhode Island. At the end of the course that December, I was so anxious to report to my first ship that I drove straight from my graduation ceremony in Newport to a shipyard in Chester, Pennsylvania. I reported for duty in my service dress-blue uniform the next morning aboard the tank landing ship USS *Fairfax County*.

At the time, the ship was in dry dock. Walking up the "brow," as the Navy calls a gangplank, I had my records tucked under my arm and was ready to go to work. I was to serve as main propulsion assistant, in charge of about forty men who ran the six main diesel engines, three diesel generators, and the boilers and evaporators for making steam and fresh water, and managing the fuel and lubricants for all this equipment. I smartly saluted the ship's ensign, the U.S. flag flying over the stern, turned to the officer of the deck, and said, "Request permission to come aboard." When he responded, "Permission granted," my real career in the U.S. Navy had finally started!

Just before Christmas, we sailed down the Delaware River into the Atlantic and up the Chesapeake Bay to our home port of Little Creek, Virginia—a short at-sea period, but long enough for me to learn that a flat-bottomed tank landing ship can rock side to side with surprising power. Thankfully, motion sickness never bothered me and I was in seventh heaven on this great ship.

My first exposure to war came during a 1983 deployment to the Mediterranean. Our job was to support Marines in the multinational peacekeeping force that was sent into Lebanon to oversee the withdrawal of the forces of the Palestine Liberation Organization (PLO) and Syria from Beirut after the truce that followed the Israeli bombardment and partial occupation of the city in 1982. Undaunted by our presence, Christian and Muslim factions in Lebanon continued the civil war they had been fighting for years, and, anchored off the coast, we could see tracer rounds and rockets arcing back and forth in bloody street-to-street and building-by-building fighting.

Ship's officers routinely went ashore to get mail and provide the Marines with other supplies. On rare occasions, however, the Marines would take a small and select group for a tour of downtown Beirut and surrounding small towns. Finally, my turn came up. Going ashore by small boat, I was met by one of the officers from the artillery battery that we had transported here, and we went to the U.S. embassy compound. There I exchanged money and then toured the cities of Beirut and Juniyah. For me, Lebanon was a grand adventure. Dressed in a working khaki uniform, complete with flak vest and metal helmet, and issued a .45 caliber semiautomatic pistol, I found the drive around the city and countryside thrilling. I had no idea of the real complexity and dangers that surrounded me.

The day after we left for a port visit to Athens, on April 18, 1983, the Islamist terrorist group Hezbollah used a relatively new terror tactic, the car bomb, in a deadly attack on the embassy in Beirut. A van carrying about 2,000 pounds of explosives crashed through the front gates and detonated.

The force of the blast collapsed the front section of the building, including the office where I had changed money, and killed sixty-three people, seventeen of them Americans, and wounded over one hundred.

It was only the beginning of a string of deadly anti-U.S. attacks by Islamist groups. While we had already returned safely home in June, later that year, on October 23, 1983, an organization called Islamic Jihad rolled a Mercedes-Benz truck full of explosives into the U.S. Marine barracks compound at the Beirut airport and killed 241 Marine Corps and Navy personnel. The Marines had been expecting a water truck. Among the dead was a Naval Academy classmate and friend, First Lieutenant David Nairn, USMC. This new form of warfare had now become personal.

Throughout the period I learned about all the systems on the ship, and how each department—Engineering, Operations, Supply, Combat Systems, Deck, and Administration and Navigation—functioned and integrated to make it a combat-effective unit. I spent more time on the bridge, first as a conning officer, learning how to drive, or "conn" the ship, then, with time and growing experience, as officer of the deck (OOD), assuming the responsibilities of being the captain's representative on the bridge in a role that shaped my career. Since a captain cannot always be present on the bridge or in the combat information center, individuals must be qualified to "stand watch" on the captain's behalf for the operation and safety of the ship. Throughout the entire qualification process, an officer learns the accountability and responsibility each watch qualification brings with it, and the personal integrity it requires.

After just over a year and a half on the ship, I would undergo a series of oral examinations by a qualification board, who would then certify my readiness to the commanding officer. In the end, I earned my Surface Warfare pin and had it proudly pinned to my chest during a ceremony in the wardroom with all officers in attendance. Even with this milestone behind me, there was plenty of hard work to come.

In December 1984 I left the *Fairfax County* and in the spring of 1985, after attending Communications Officer School in Newport, I reported to one of the Navy's newest ships, USS *Yorktown*, an Aegis guided-missile cruiser, in Norfolk, Virginia. *Yorktown* was at the leading edge of Navy technology and shipbuilding prowess. The Aegis combat system, which integrates sophisticated anti-aircraft, surface-to-surface, and anti-submarine weapons, powerful radars, and computer-driven command-and-control complexes, represented an order of magnitude leap in the Navy's ability to protect an aircraft carrier battle group and to project power globally. Two months after I reported aboard, the ship deployed to the Mediterranean for what would prove to be the most exciting deployment of my early career.

At first, we enjoyed routine port visits along the coast of Spain, France, and Italy. We conducted numerous exercises with NATO allies and were occasionally shadowed by spy ships from the Soviet Union. Then, on October 7, 1985, Palestinian terrorists hijacked the Italian cruise ship *Achille Lauro.* During the course of the hijacking, the terrorists took a wheelchair-bound American tourist, Leon Klinghoffer, shot him, and dumped his lifeless body overboard.

Three days later, I was sitting in the combat information center as USS *Yorktown* and USS *Saratoga* raced to the southeast Mediterranean in an attempt to intercept the airplane the hijackers were using to try to escape justice. Early in the morning on October 10, F-14 fighter jets, launched from the *Saratoga* and monitored by the *Yorktown,* intercepted the aircraft and forced it to land at the Naval Air Station at Sigonella, Italy.

Because of the distance from the ships to the F-14s, I could barely make out the pilots' radio conversation as they made the intercept on the hijackers' aircraft. After the plane landed, both Italian and U.S. forces surrounded it and a standoff took place. Following some tense negotiations, the Italian authorities took custody of the hijackers. Unfortunately, the Italian government did not have the stomach to confront this new type of warfare, and after only a short period of imprisonment, freed the terrorists. In fighting terrorism, I learned, politics has too often preempted doing what was right, even when lives were at stake.

By Christmas 1985, the ship had settled into a seemingly regular routine of at-sea exercises and port visits, but it was only a matter of time until terrorism again reared its ugly head. On December 27, at the international airports in Rome, Italy, and Vienna, Austria, terrorists detonated grenades and used automatic weapons to slaughter eighteen innocent civilians and wound 138. USS *Yorktown* shortly got underway and over the next three months rigorously practiced combat operations, preparing to hold Libya accountable as one of the chief sponsors of those terrorist attacks. At the same time, in another bellicose act, Libya claimed the Gulf of Sidra as its territorial waters. Drawing a "line of death" at 32°30" north, the Libyan dictator, Colonel Muammar Qaddafi, proclaimed that any "unauthorized" ship below that line would be attacked. This was in clear violation of international law, and the United States refused to recognize the claim. The *Saratoga* battle group, operating with the aircraft carrier USS *Coral Sea*, conducted freedom of navigation operations in the Gulf of Sidra in January and February 1986, specifically to refute it, and again from March 23 to 29, with the carrier USS *America*'s battle group now joined. The Libyans, upset by these "unauthorized" incursions into their claimed waters, countered by firing SA-5 anti-aircraft missiles at U.S. jets. Over the next three days, the United States attacked land-based missile sites and missile patrol boats near our ships without the loss of any of our forces or personnel.

On April 5, 1986, as *Yorktown* and the rest of the *Saratoga* battle group were headed home across the Atlantic from deployment, a bomb exploded in a disco in Berlin, Germany. U.S. intelligence quickly found that Qaddafi was responsible, and on April 15, 1986, the United States launched aircraft attacks against Libya with both Air Force and Navy bombers. At last, the United States was finally willing to stand up and fight back against this particular state sponsor of terrorism. Unfortunately, it would also be the last time until 2001 that the United States would draw a line in the sand and send an unmistakable message that it would not tolerate terrorist attacks against our interests.

After leaving *Yorktown* in May 1987, I attended the Naval Post-graduate School in Monterey, California. With a Master of Science degree in Systems Engineering, my technical skills were honed to prepare for my next assignment as the operations officer to the USS *Arleigh Burke,* the Navy's first Aegis guided-missile destroyer. A new class of ship, its construction at the shipyard in Bath, Maine, proved surprisingly challenging. Designed to present a smaller cross section to enemy radar, it minimized the number of surfaces that met at ninety-degree angles, to decrease the reflected energy from a radar beam. Incorporating many of the lessons learned from Aegis cruisers such as *Yorktown*, the ship was outfitted with the latest Aegis phased-array radar and, for the first time, all the weapons the ship had were truly integrated into one seamless combat system. The Navy had not built a new class of destroyer in over twenty years, the last one being the *Spruance* class destroyer, which did not have an anti-air warfare capability—the ability to shoot down incoming missiles or aircraft.

The leadership of the surface warfare Navy handpicked Commander John G. Morgan, Jr. for this prestigious assignment as the commissioning commanding officer for the *Arleigh Burke*. His choice for executive officer had been a shipmate of mine on *Yorktown*, Lieutenant Commander Roger C. "Rick" Easton. As part of this crew, I knew I was in for a lot of hard work, but the chance to bring this new ship to life for the Navy was irresistible and I jumped at the opportunity.

After six months of learning how to be a department head, once more in Newport, I reported to the precommissioning crew of the ship in Norfolk, Virginia. On July 4, 1991, the Navy commissioned *Arleigh Burke* as the most combat capable ship in the world at the time. Almost two years later, we deployed to the Mediterranean Sea for operations to safeguard those vital sea-lanes of communication for our nation.

Mid-deployment, orders came transferring me from the ship to the flatlands of Kansas to learn how to speak "Army" at the U.S. Army's Command and General Staff College in Fort Leavenworth. An interservice assignment like this allows promising officers to learn in an open but structured educational environment how each service develops the procedures and concepts that guide its operations. More important, it allows some of the best and brightest of them to get to know each other and develop bonds of friendship.

Attendance at one of these schools builds the groundwork for an officer's eventual assignment to a joint staff, critical for a continued career. For me, it was a chance to learn how the Navy's thought process and outlook on problems differed from the Army's. From my perspective, the Army allowed as much initiative as necessary to accomplish a mission, provided you adhered to its defined doctrine and guidance. In the Navy, however, you can take as much initiative as necessary by following one simple golden rule: if there is no prohibition against something, then you are allowed to do it until told to stop. That concept proved a great source of amusement during tactical and operational discussions in the course and I delighted in challenging my classmates to exercise that same degree of unfettered initiative.

After Kansas came a set of orders to yet another dream assignment—as executive officer (XO) of an Aegis cruiser, USS *Shiloh*, home ported in San Diego, California. Since the ship was on deployment, I was unable to report aboard the day after graduating from the Executive Officer course, again in Newport; however, I did drive cross-country in four days, rested one day, then flew out a day early to meet the ship in Phuket, Thailand, in September 1994, as it returned from a six-month deployment to the Middle East.

Over the next twenty months, I would learn what it meant to be part of the ship's core leadership team, made up of the commanding officer, executive officer, and command master chief. Entrusted with the daily well-being, morale, and welfare of the crew, two very different but excellent commanding officers ran the ship, John Russack and Paul Schultz. To learn from their experiences and actions helped me understand how to succeed as a commanding officer myself.

Supported by a broad depth of talent in the department heads of *Shiloh*, I truly learned how to judge the strengths and weaknesses of officers and chief petty officers and integrate them into a cooperative and effective combat fighting team. This experience was different from my previous Navy jobs, aimed at mastering a single specialty. As an XO, the best lesson one can learn is the art of how to truly lead and manage a crew.

From USS *Shiloh*, it was off to company headquarters in the Pentagon, but even after I transferred off the ship I did not know the exact job I was going to next. In April 1996, the Bureau of Personnel recommended that I, along with several other officers, be interviewed for the position of aide-de-camp to the chief of naval operations. I was also interviewed for a possible appointment as executive assistant to the chief of legislative affairs, but finally was selected instead by Secretary of the Navy John H. Dalton, to be his administrative aide, and reported to his office for duty in August 1996. Administrative aides are highly visible officers, and the role can make or break careers. The job requires interaction on a daily basis with admirals, generals, assistant secretaries of the Navy, and other high-ranking Department of Defense officials, with all the sensitivity that this demands, but it also requires confidence and competence in keeping on top of myriad files, military programs, and documents. For me, it was the opportunity of a lifetime to see the inner workings of the military and civilian top echelons of the Navy and observe how decisions made at that level trickled down to the ships on the waterfront and affected the daily lives of sailors.

About one year after arriving in the office of the secretary of the Navy, I began to discuss my next assignment with the Bureau of Personnel. I had already screened for command at sea and now it was only a matter of actually being assigned to a ship. As with all my previous assignments, location did not matter as much as getting the best ship possible. For me, that meant an *Arleigh Burke*–class guided-missile destroyer.

I detached from the office of the secretary of the Navy in early February 1999 to begin the pre-command battery of schools required prior to assuming command. After some uncertainty about which ship I was in fact to get—my orders were changed three times—I learned finally that I would be entrusted with command of USS *Cole,* DDG-67, home ported in Norfolk, Virginia.

Launched in 1995, *Cole* was named after a U.S. Marine, Sergeant Darrell S. Cole, who was posthumously awarded the Medal of Honor for his exceptional valor on Iwo Jima in World War II. The ship was state of the art, with an AN/SPY-1D radar and combat system integrator for its surface-to-air and Tomahawk cruise missiles, anti-submarine torpedoes, and close-in defense weapons systems, including a five-inch gun and twenty millimeter close-in weapons system (CIWS), and a helicopter landing deck aft for a variety of helicopters, including those that could be armed with

Hellfire missiles and MK 46/MK 50 torpedoes. The ship was 505 feet long from stem to stern, 66 feet abeam at its widest point, with a displacement of 8,373 tons fully loaded, and carried a crew of around 300 sailors. Its four gas turbine engines, powering two propeller shafts, could move the ship through the water at more than 31 knots, more than 35 m.p.h. At the time, *Cole* was one of the most sophisticated and best armed ships in the U.S. Navy, capable of projecting power at sea and ashore to support our national interests.

While still at the Prospective Commanding Officer course in Newport, I studied the manning documents of the ship and found that none of the department heads were women. USS *Cole* had only recently been structurally modified to accommodate women, and had begun the process of integrating women into the crew within the past year. I firmly believed that leadership at the top set the tone throughout the chain of command and having a woman as one of my department heads sent a strong signal that I believed in their integration onto all naval combatants. Coincidentally, I had met an engineer officer attending Department Head school, also at Newport, Lieutenant Deborah Courtney. She had orders assigning her to another ship, but *Cole* was scheduled to get a new engineer officer, and a long-time friend and mentor of mine, Captain Ray Spicer, who had previously worked with her, had nothing but great things to say about her technical capabilities and professionalism. I dropped by her classroom one day, introduced myself, and asked if she would like to have lunch to discuss her future.

I explained my somewhat convoluted journey to receive orders to *Cole*, and then told her that she had a well-recognized reputation as an exceptional officer. A 1990 graduate of the Naval Academy, as a woman, she had originally been unable to become a surface warfare officer on combatants, but when Congress and the Navy finally changed that a few years later, she jumped at the opportunity and changed her career field. She had honed her skills as an engineer on her first ship, USS *Gettysburg*, an Aegis guided-missile cruiser, and now was quite content with her orders to another *Arleigh Burke*–class destroyer, *Donald Cook*. I thought her ambition would make her a great asset on a newly integrated ship, and when I explained why I wanted her to join me and how that decision would better serve both her and my interests, she asked if she could have a few days to think about it. Two days later, Debbie stopped me in the hallway and asked if the offer still stood. I told her absolutely yes, and later that day we coordinated with the Navy's Bureau of Personnel to get her orders modified to send her to USS *Cole*. I was thrilled with her decision.

On June 14, 1999, I drove onto the U.S. Naval Station in Norfolk, parked my car, and prepared to walk down the pier. After Washington duty, it was good to be back on the waterfront with the fleet and its sailors, smelling the salt air. I felt ready to take command and looked forward to the challenges that lay ahead. I met first with the captain I was to relieve, Commander Rich Nolan, a gregarious officer with whom I hit it off instantly. He offered me exceptionally candid and generous insights and recommendations about the crew and the ship's equipment, covering each department in detail. Our turnover, longer than usual, would last almost twelve days, offering me plenty of time to take stock of what I already knew: *Cole* was a great ship and continued to set the standard for excellent performance on the waterfront.

On June 25, I stood on the fantail in front of my family and friends and in a centuries-old, time-honored tradition, said to Rich the three greatest words a naval officer can say in a career: "I relieve you." That phrase signified the moment when total accountability and responsibility for a $1 billion national asset and the lives of almost 300 of our nation's finest sailors passed from one commanding officer to the next.

There was plenty of work ahead. USS *Cole* was part of the USS *George Washington* aircraft-carrier battle group, whose next combat-ready deployment would begin in about a year. My next job was to ascertain what additional training would be needed to get *Cole* combat ready. It was clear that this was a great crew, but there was a clear difference in the level where the crew perceived their training readiness (very high); where the destroyer squadron commodore, my immediate boss, viewed their performance (high, but not as high as they did); and where I assessed their capabilities (room for improvement). The ship and crew had a well-established reputation for being highly competent and capable, but like any crew, over time they had begun to rest on their laurels. I needed to take stock of their training level and performance and bring them back up to the high standards that had set *Cole* apart from other ships in the squadron.

My vision for the ship's future was taking shape. I would work to realize it with the help of two key advisors: the executive officer, then Lieutenant Commander John Cordle, the second-ranking officer aboard ship, and the command master chief, the senior enlisted member of the crew—who as I took command had just been temporarily appointed to that post—Master Chief Paul Abney. As I settled in to command, John was an absolute blessing for me. He was a surface warfare officer who had also been trained and qualified as a nuclear power officer on nuclear-powered aircraft carriers and thus had a thorough and extensive background in engineering. One of his greatest strengths for me was his calm demeanor, the perfect counterbalance to my own hard-driving and forward-leaning qualities. Master Chief Abney was probably one of the best technical experts in the Navy in the field of surface-ship sonar systems, and he was also a talented leader, always willing to try new approaches and to be innovative in his working relationships. Throughout Navy history, the rank of chief petty officer has always been considered the gold standard for enlisted leadership. According to most professional sailors, it is the chief petty officers who run the Navy, not the admirals. The command master chief position was crucially important on *Cole*.

Once I was in command, I asked John to distribute two important documents to each crew member. The first was my command philosophy, which outlined how I expected the crew to perform, establishing the benchmarks by which they would be measured: integrity, vision, personal responsibility and accountability, trust, and professional competence. On this list, integrity came both first and last. Like many commanding officers before me, I believed that unless all crew members conducted themselves with personal integrity guiding every decision, the temptation to compromise on performance and safety standards could lead to cutting corners and performance levels falling far short of their potential. The second document was the framework of my goals for the ship and crew, when operating the ship and interacting with each other as shipmates. It was specifically tailored to where we as a crew were in the training cycle and set both short- and long-term objectives for the next year to ready us for our next deployment and any operations we might undertake in the coming months.

There were some adjustments to be made at first: I was new to command, and the crew likewise needed time to learn what I expected. Building a reputation as a very aggressive and "to-the-point" officer, I knew the ship and crew could accomplish far more than they thought possible, and set about pushing them harder than they had been driven to date. Just a week after taking command, both crew and I learned just how heavily the burden of leadership could weigh on a commanding officer.

Gliding through the calm waters of the Atlantic off the Virginia Capes, *Cole* had coordinated an underway replenishment with a Military Sealift Command oiler. Underway resupply of fuel, stores, and food is standard Navy practice, the ship being resupplied maneuvering behind and then alongside the supply ship while both are steaming in a straight line ahead. The maneuvering requires precision and control, with the approach ship closing to the stern of the replenishment ship to between 300 and 500 yards, and sufficiently offset from its wake to be able to synchronize speed exactly with it and end up alongside about 140 to 160 feet away. Lines are then shot between the ships, wires and hoses hauled across, and then replenishment begins. The complex ballet requires that all members of the crew in the replenishment detail know exactly how to perform their duties, with constant vigilance and attention to safety. Both ships must keep precisely on course and speed, at a steady distance from each other.

Usually all this is done without incident. But I have always believed that an underway replenishment is the most hazardous peacetime activity Navy ships engage in at sea. History is replete with examples of ships colliding and personnel being injured or falling overboard, so every ship prepares a detailed underway replenishment watch bill, listing in detail each position that must be manned and by whom, with personnel specifically trained and qualified to perform those duties. There is no margin for error. Everyone has to know what to do in an emergency, and to be ready for one at any moment.

I had asked John and the senior watch officer and combat system officer, Lieutenant Commander Rick Miller, to make a series of checks at specific watch stations throughout the ship before we began the replenishment, though normally I would personally make them myself, starting in the after steering position at the back and working my way forward to the Combat Information Center, and then to the bridge. As this was my first underway replenishment as captain, it was more important to be on the bridge throughout to see how the watch team got the ship and crew ready.

The conning officer took a deep breath, checked the angle of approach one last time, and then spoke confidently into the microphone, "All engines ahead flank, indicate turns for 25 knots." The high-pitched whine of *Cole's* four gas turbine engines quickly increased. With 100,000 shaft horsepower driving it forward, the ship rose slightly and we gradually surged forward. The feeling of wind in our faces made everyone smile.

The approach was almost perfect in angle and would put us at about 150 feet lateral distance from the oiler once alongside. Just as the bow appeared to cross the stern of the oiler, the conning officer used relative motion and a seaman's eye to judge the distance and, without taking his eye off the distance between the ships, crisply ordered, "All engines ahead standard, indicate turns for 13 knots," deftly bringing the ship into position.

Soon the lines and hoses were across, the refueling rig was in position, and, very slowly at first, the refueling hose wriggled and jerked to life as the first few hundred gallons started flowing down the hose. Everything seemed to be going like clockwork. Our time alongside was estimated to be about forty-five minutes.

"XO, do we have the cookies ready to go?" I asked John. This was the start of a new tradition. Every time the ship would pull alongside an oiler for an underway replenishment, a bag containing a couple dozen hot, freshly baked chocolate chip cookies would be sent over to the commanding officer of the oiler to thank him for great at-sea customer service. At first, the crew thought this a pain and somewhat of a waste of time but soon, we found, the oilers we operated with over the year actually looked forward to the ritual, and so did *Cole's* bridge watch team, because the supply officer would also send a bunch of warm cookies up for the boatswain's mate of the watch to pass around.

Soon the reports from the engineers indicated our fuel level was at almost 98 percent. We had topped off our tanks and were ready to execute a standard maneuver called a breakaway. This procedure has the two ships disconnect the refueling hoses and cables attaching them together in a very precise and methodical manner to ensure the safety of the ships and the crew working the rigs.

After every refueling, both ships simultaneously practice what is called an "emergency breakaway," a fundamental safety skill in an actual emergency. The crew had done such a fabulous job with the refueling that I was sure my first emergency breakaway would be just as successful. After releasing the high-tension metal wire that kept *Cole* and the oiler at a proper distance from each other, and disconnecting the phone and distance line, we went to "flank speed," 31-plus knots, and the ship leaped forward. The wind began to roar across the bridge wing. The ships were still about 160 feet apart, and as our speed increased dramatically, the margin for error shrunk to almost nil. The gas turbine engines, with fully open throttles, screamed with a high-pitched whine. Seconds later, we were well ahead of the oiler, keeping a close eye on it to make sure nothing could go wrong—any errors in determining course or position could cause a disaster.

We set a course to continue moving away and within minutes announced that the refueling evolution was over and the regular watch team could assume the watch. I left the bridge and went down to my cabin, feeling very proud of myself and my ship: command at sea with the first underway replenishment now under my belt, without incident. It just doesn't get any better than this! I thought.

But quickly, I was brought down from this reverie by a knock on my cabin door: it was the XO, who asked, "Captain, do you have a minute for Rick and me to talk with you?"

"Sure. Come on in and have a seat," I answered. "Mind if I shut the door?" asked John.

With a question like that, and stern expressions on their faces, he and Rick, the most senior department head on the ship, couldn't be bringing good news. They weren't. Rick reported that when he had made his rounds before the maneuver to the section of the ship that controlled the rudders, he had found the safety officer and two other personnel asleep on the deck instead of properly carrying out their duties.

The fact that the senior watch officer had found personnel responsible for steering the ship neglecting their duties was a matter of grave concern. They could have left *Cole* critically vulnerable to a collision—and Rick had discovered them malingering just as the ship came alongside the oiler, with only 150 feet between them.

I asked John what he thought we should do. Like me, he was somewhat at a loss as to how to proceed but he did not want to overreact. I agreed, but ordered the XO to charge all three with violating the Uniform Code of Military Justice, by hazarding a vessel, among other offenses. This administrative process on ships is called captain's mast, or non-judicial punishment. I wanted it to send a definitive signal to the crew that no actions would be tolerated that endangered the ship or anyone on board.

The next week I met with the new commodore of our squadron, Captain Mike Miller. A very earnest and hard-working naval officer, he truly believed in letting commanding officers run their ships. While I was very concerned about how he might perceive the replenishment incident, I also wanted his guidance. "Well, Captain, how do think this came to happen and what do you think needs to be done to fix it?" he asked. I described my plan of holding not just the enlisted men but also the officer accountable for their mistakes. While knowing that taking an officer to captain's mast for this offense might end his career, I also knew that the safety of the ship and crew was paramount. This incident had crossed an inviolate professional standard of conduct and endangered the crew.

While initially uncomfortable with my decision to punish everyone, the commodore backed me 100 percent. Nevertheless he encouraged me to ensure that I was on sound legal ground before proceeding. One week later, I held my first captain's mast, first for the two enlisted personnel and then the officer. Quite frankly, the crew was stunned to see me actually punish an officer. Immediately after imposing the non-judicial punishment, levying a punitive letter of reprimand for the officer—who then felt he had no chance of making the Navy a career and later left the service—and a reduction in rate and pay grade, a fine, and a thirty-day confinement to the ship for the others, I separately met with the chief petty officers and officers to explain my rationale and decision. To both, I made it very clear that I would never tolerate anything endangering the ship or crew. All of us had an enormous responsibility to safeguard that national asset and ensure that it was maintained at peak operating condition in the safest manner possible. I would be unforgiving if this responsibility was not taken seriously.

Having affirmed in action the importance I had set forth in my command philosophy and goals and expectations for the crew, I had clearly established a benchmark for my expectations of professional performance. As the crew moved inexorably toward deployment overseas, they grew more comfortable with the goals for the ship and developed a sense of personal accomplishment in reaching them. During weeks of intensive training with other ships in our squadron from mid-October of 1999 to mid-February of 2000, despite the demanding drills and exercises needed for certification, I had no disciplinary issues requiring the imposition of captain's mast. The chain of command below me dealt with minor problems, and the officers and chiefs were able to resolve all of them before they reached my level, which for me was a tribute to the officers, chief petty officers, and senior petty officers running the ship.

Two events stood out that best captured the essence of how well the ship was operating. One of the most challenging exercises involved our towing another ship. It was an overcast day, and the wind had created a very difficult situation. As the ship to be towed drifted in the open ocean—we were down in the Caribbean—*Cole* had to maneuver in very close ranges of less than 100 feet to pass a towing line and then remain in position while the other ship safely rigged it in place. The winds kept blowing us away and I found it very difficult to hold our position. I finally decided only one more attempt would be tried and then I would stop the exercise for safety reasons. During this last attempt, *Cole* began to drift away again, and I ordered the ship to reverse engines in an attempt to not open the distance between us. Unfortunately, the towline slipped from the other ship, dipped into the water just astern of us, and in a matter of seconds wrapped around the port propeller shaft.

I ordered the engines stopped and immediately shut down to prevent any damage to the ship or injury to those on board who were working near the towline. We were in water shallow enough to drop anchor, and after we notified the destroyer squadron we waited for a diving team to fly out to the ship by helicopter to free the towline from the shaft. They were able to do that within two hours, and determined that no damage had been done.

While skill had prevented anyone from being injured, to my mind, we had also been extremely lucky. As we got the ship underway from anchorage and proceeded to the next exercise, I gathered the crew and the towing team to discuss the day's events. The first thing I made clear was that the responsibility for the towline's getting wrapped around the shaft was solely my fault as captain. It had been my judgment that had failed them, and we had been fortunate to not damage the ship or injure any crew members. In detail, we broke the exercise down into short time intervals and covered every aspect including communications, maneuvering the ship, wind and sea conditions, engineering actions, and the consequences of each decision. In the end, while it cost us the expense of replacing the towline, the experience created a more mature and experienced crew. It was better for them to understand the consequences of my decision to continue to press forward and complete the exercise despite clear indications that should have caused us to delay or cancel the exercise.

A few days later, late in the afternoon, after we had successfully completed the series of towing training exercises, we were told we could conduct another few hours of training with the other ship. I declined the offer and instead told the other ship we needed to conduct some internal training for the next few hours. Once that ship had sailed away, I told John, "XO, let's come to all stop and have the engineers shut down the main engines."

He raised his eyebrows, wondering what I was up to next, but the lightbulb came on as I told him, "Get on the 1MC [general announcing system] and get a boat in the water with a duty gunner's mate. It's time for the crew to enjoy their first swim call."

We were off St. Thomas. Swimming in the ocean in crystal-clear water with the sea floor 3,000 feet beneath is very different from being in the deep end of a pool where the bottom is only twelve or fifteen feet down. It is a beautiful and humbling experience. Looking up at the ship, feeling the immense power of the sea swells, makes you realize how small and insignificant you are in the larger scheme of nature. We had swim call for about an hour and twenty minutes. I took every safety precaution, managing the risks from many angles: a nearby boat contained a trained sharpshooter to guard against shark attack; all the ship's engineering equipment was set to keep anyone from possibly getting sucked underwater into an intake; and a rigorous check-in/check-out routine was in place to make sure that everyone who went overboard got back on the ship. The crew was thrilled by what for many was a once-in-career experience, and they talked about it for days afterward.

About this same time, I received a message from the Navy's Bureau of Personnel reporting that a permanent command master chief (CMC) had been ordered to the ship directly from the Senior Leadership School in Newport, Rhode Island. As was his nature, Master Chief Abney was graceful when I told him, and looked forward to turning his duties over to his relief. In November 1999, Command Master Chief James Parlier arrived on board. With a medical background as a fully qualified hospital corpsman, he had a knack for talking with the crew and soon took a keen interest in conveying their views to me.

When he came aboard he was hard charging and eager to do well in his new position. Initially, he had some hesitation about embracing the concept of being part of the CO-XO-CMC triumvirate running things on the ship. He had conceived of his role as being more a command representative of the crew than full-fledged member of the leadership team. Quickly though, he embraced being an integral part of my long-range vision for the ship and its crew.

He spent some time figuring out how he wanted to work with the XO and me, as well as lead the chief petty officers in being the real deck-plate role models and leaders on the ship. As the leading master chief on the ship, he had to assert himself not only in making sure the chiefs were doing their jobs and staying active with the crew, but in creating a bond with the chiefs so that they would approach him to confidentially relay any difficulties they were having up the chain of command. As good a ship as USS *Cole* was, crews always have a few folks who don't quite embrace the tempo of the organization and resist moving along as fast as they should. The command master chief's job is to keep those people and the chiefs supervising them motivated. Master Chief Parlier did just that by walking all around the ship and talking with the crew, on watch or down in their berthing compartments, rather than by sticking close to his office. He had his finger on the pulse of the crew's morale, and his insights were of priceless value to me.

The last change to the command team came in December 1999, when John was relieved as the executive officer by Lieutenant Commander John Christopher Peterschmidt. "Chris" Peterschmidt was an intense and extremely focused officer. We quickly hit it off and he seemed destined to be a perfect match for the ship. As we got to know each other better over the next few months, each of us realized that we had previously met in the Pentagon, where he had worked for the admiral in charge of the Navy's Surface Warfare directorate, which was responsible for the manning, training, and equipping of Navy ships and crews, while I was working for the secretary of the Navy.

As Chris and I continued to prepare the ship for deployment, we came to know each other's strengths and weaknesses and, with the command master chief, worked to make *Cole* the best ship on the Norfolk waterfront. Steady progress became our hallmark. There was about a 3 percent turnover of the crew every month, normal for the Navy, but we wanted to achieve something unprecedented in its scope and impact. Over the next few months, we wanted to qualify all enlisted crew members to man each of the watch stations on the sea and anchor detail—the stations that have to be manned when the ship is entering or leaving port. We hoped to qualify members of the crew who were not officers to be certified to perform every one of those duties by the time the ship's combat-ready deployment started, including positions normally filled only by experienced officers—officer of the deck, helm safety officer, after steering helm safety officer, and conning officer.

While filling these four critical roles may seem relatively easy, it actually took a great deal of coordination between the watch teams to free up the needed senior petty officers or chief petty officers to allow them the time and experience in the watch station to earn their added qualifications. This often resulted in extra work by other crew members standing additional watches normally filled by these personnel, but they accepted it with a professional poise that had become their hallmark. This goal would have far-reaching consequences for the rest of the crew in the not too distant future.

As part of the nuclear-powered USS *George Washington* aircraft carrier battle group, USS *Cole* was to be deployed to the Mediterranean and Middle East along with USS *Normandy*, an Aegis guided-missile cruiser; USS *Donald Cook*, like *Cole* an Aegis guided-missile destroyer; USS *Simpson* and USS *Hawes*, both guided-missile frigates; USS *Pittsburgh* and USS *Albany*, nuclear-powered attack submarines; and USS *Seattle*, a fast combat logistics ship. The battle group's aircraft wing was Carrier Air Wing 17, which consisted of various fighter, attack, electronic warfare, and surveillance aircraft, as well as helicopters.

Over the next several months, the ship completed the last two phases of training to be certified as combat ready. Throughout this entire period, the emphasis on damage control drills—exercises to prepare the crew to repair damage and handle casualties in the event of hostilities—continued unabated both in port and underway. *Cole's* damage control assistant, Lieutenant (junior grade) Nathaniel Fogg, had spent the last year pushing, prodding, and leading the crew to become experts in damage control techniques and capability. In retrospect, he cast the die for success in saving the ship after the attack that was to come.

2 | Deployment to the Middle East

THE FINAL PHASE OF TRAINING included force protection measures—security precautions—to be taken against unauthorized approach or boarding of the ship. The only contingency we trained for while based in Norfolk was a threat from ashore—unauthorized boarding by intruders coming from the pier while the ship was tied up in port. Although a broad spectrum of threats existed, especially in this new era of terrorist attacks, with limited resources and time the Navy had not incorporated how to defend against them into the training and intelligence programs for battle groups and ships preparing for deployment.

Prior to deployment of the battle group, the Commander in Chief of the U.S. Atlantic Fleet scheduled an anti-terrorism/force-protection exercise for May 3 to 5, 2000. The primary objective was to train shore and afloat commanders and personnel to operate and deploy forces under any threat condition. Specifically, the drill was "not designed as an inspection but rather an opportunity for commands to practice . . . procedures and assess capabilities to provide adequate protection for personnel, facilities and assets." During the exercise, we learned, unauthorized persons would try to get aboard every ship at least once during the week. How and when this would occur we were not told, putting everyone on edge, prepared for the worst. Typical for this type of exercise, the ships almost all focused on countering any incursion that might be made over their in-port quarterdeck, the position on the main deck at about the middle of the ship, between the two superstructures where the watch team was normally stationed.

Throughout the week, crews from each ship in the battle group were assigned to try to penetrate the security perimeter of others in the squadron by pretending to be crew members, or bluffing that they had been authorized to do work on board. Most of these amateur penetrations failed. But when ships faced more sophisticated types of intrusions carried out by Naval Criminal Investigative Service (NCIS) agents acting on behalf of the Atlantic Fleet staff, failure was the standard for almost every one of them.

In USS *Cole*'s case, the NCIS agents demanded access to the pier by showing an arrest warrant for the ship's navigator, Lieutenant Ann Chamberlain. When the watchstander responsible for maintaining security on the pier questioned their credentials or the validity of the warrant, the agents threatened arrest for interference with a criminal investigation and were allowed onto the pier. When questioned again at the bottom of the brow by *Cole*'s security watch, they again flashed credentials and threatened to have the watchstander arrested. Ultimately, they gained access to the quarterdeck area—which meant that the ship failed the intrusion exercise.

While this showed how vulnerable a ship could be to unauthorized access by a convincingly trained agent, that scenario seemed more akin to what ships might have faced from the KGB or the Soviet navy during the Cold War. As an exercise designed to train shipboard personnel to deal with terrorists, who would likely be armed with weapons or explosives, the drill was hardly realistic.

Notably, there was no training on how to respond to a suicide bomber entering the ship or using a car to ram through onto the pier and attack us by blowing it up. And at no time were any of the ships trained or prepared to defend against assault from the sea. There was no training in how to anticipate or respond to an attack by a boat in the harbor; all threats in the exercise were land based. By the end of the week, every ship had suffered one form or another of security breach and held training to teach the crew how to counter the perceived threat. At the conclusion of the exercise, the commander, Second Fleet, Admiral William J. Fallon, sent out a message to all twenty Second Fleet ships that had participated, specifically mentioning seven for "noteworthy performance." USS *Cole* was one of those ships. With the exercise complete and the lessons incorporated into our operating procedures, we looked forward to deployment with a sense of confidence that unwittingly set in place the circumstances for a tragedy.

As the date for the battle group's six-month deployment in late June approached, the commander, Rear Admiral Gary Roughead, had to select two ships from the squadron as "late deployers," leaving six weeks after the rest. That was because when it came time for the group to move from the Mediterranean to the Arabian Sea and Persian Gulf, different types of ships would have to stagger their departures and arrivals to mesh with the operational requirements of the Sixth Fleet and European Command in the Mediterranean, and Fifth Fleet and Central Command in the Middle East, where the tasks included inspections of ships entering and leaving Iraq, and readiness for contingency operations against Saddam Hussein's regime. Admiral Roughead chose USS *Cole* and USS *Simpson* as the late deployers.

We left about six weeks after the rest of the battle group, on August 8, 2000. As expected, it was an emotionally charged morning, with more than a few tears shed by the crew as well as by the loved ones they were leaving behind. When all the lines were pulled in from the pier, the ship sounded a four-to-six-second prolonged whistle blast, and, finally, USS *Cole* was underway with a fully qualified, all-enlisted crew manning every watch position—a new milestone in the Navy's history. Little did we know how soon and how much we would need these added skills.

The Atlantic was calm and sunny during our crossing, and we soon passed through the Straits of Gibraltar into the Mediterranean. Because of our outstanding performance in preparatory exercises we had been cleared to make port visits in Barcelona, Spain, Villefranche, France, Valetta, Malta, and Koper, Slovenia, in the Adriatic, before proceeding to the eastern Mediterranean to pass through the Suez Canal on our way to the Middle East. Now we were under the operational control of U.S. Naval Forces Europe and Commander, Sixth Fleet. Sixth Fleet rules allowed each ship to make its own determination of how many people should remain on board while in port. We decided to err on the side of caution and keep a third of the crew on duty at all times. Everybody else was permitted to enjoy liberty and see the world—which is after all why most had joined the Navy in the first place.

An additional requirement that had crept into the lexicon of overseas port visits was threat conditions. The Navy now had four threat conditions—Alpha, Bravo, Charlie, and Delta—with Alpha requiring the lowest level of protection, similar to what the ship would have had in Norfolk, and increasing degrees of security for the next three conditions up to Delta, the highest level of security to guard against an expected imminent attack. In the Mediterranean, *Cole* operated under Threat Condition Alpha Plus, which required increased security around the pier where the ship was moored and in the vicinity of the fleet landing, where the crew left the pier area and went into town on liberty. All measures were coordinated with local police in each port.

Everywhere we went, many of the crew understood how lucky they were to be Americans and wanted to give something to the community. Usually, about twenty to thirty crew members volunteered for community works projects, helping to clean up an orphanage, restore a local playground, or similar activities. They would always have a great time playing with the kids and more often than not they would play a soccer game at the end of the day. It was our way of quietly showing the U.S. Navy to be good ambassadors for the United States. We all also took advantage of the other ways of enjoying ourselves offered by a Mediterranean deployment. At each port visit, arrangements were made to eat at one of the best local restaurants or visit a winery for a tasting. The crew was also allowed to bring local wine and liquors onto the ship for storage in a cool space until we returned home.

Following a last port visit to Slovenia in early September, USS *Cole* conducted so-called presence operations in the Adriatic aimed at the government of Serbia, which had retained the name Federal Republic of Yugoslavia even though that country had dissolved in a brutal civil war that had seen the worst atrocities of "ethnic cleansing" in Europe since World War II. The Serbian regime, led by Slobodan Milošević, was still in the process of recovering from a NATO bombing campaign from March through June of 1999 that had halted the brutal repression of ethnic Albanians who had declared the independence of the province of Kosovo. Milošević had been warned that if any of his country's naval vessels entered the Adriatic, even within their territorial waters, their actions might be considered hostile and the United States would take appropriate defensive action to eliminate any perceived threat.

For the first time on our deployment, the crew was conducting real-world operations in support of U.S. strategic objectives. While we had certainly enjoyed being U.S. Navy diplomats during port visits, the crew now had a sense that this was what we had really been training for during the past year.

The tone of the ship immediately grew more serious and calm. We uploaded ammunition into the five-inch gun, readied surface-to-air missiles for immediate arming and firing, loaded torpedoes into the launching tubes, and charged their high-pressure air flasks to be ready for attachment on a moment's notice. Tomahawk cruise missiles were readied for launch on short notice. For several days we operated within areas designated for that purpose, downloading updates for the Tomahawk guidance systems with the most recent priority targets for any such emergency contingencies. With the primary mission of being air defense commander for all Navy ships in the area, USS *Cole* refueled at sea every few days. The ship was on a combat footing, ready for action.

Underway operations continued for the next two weeks, until early October. European Command had been reluctant to release *Cole* until the last minute in order to maintain a large number of Tomahawk missiles in theater to support all possible contingency requirements, in the Balkans or elsewhere. It was finally decided that *Cole* would pass from the operational control of Sixth Fleet and Naval Forces Europe to Fifth Fleet and Central Command on October 9. *George Washington* and *Normandy* departed Fifth Fleet and Central Command early, reporting into the European theater of operations to support the expanding pace of operations in the Adriatic and had arrived several days previously in preparation for *Cole*'s imminent departure. *Normandy,* which had been with the *George Washington* battle group that had left for the Middle East six weeks before us, assumed the air defense duties from us on October 6. That afternoon, we conducted our last underway replenishment in the Mediterranean from the USNS *John Lenthall,* which had transited the Atlantic with *Cole* and *Simpson* two months earlier. Upon completion, *Cole* was detached by the commander of the battle group. Our orders were to proceed, alone, through the Suez Canal into the Red Sea and then report for a briefing on our new duties with Naval Forces Central Command/Fifth Fleet in Bahrain.

Under normal conditions, a ship tries to sail at a speed that conserves fuel as much as possible. In *Cole*'s case, the best economical speed was around 14 knots. However, because of the delay in making the operational decision about when we would shift from one theater to the next, the timing of our arrival now required a high-speed transit of 25 knots, covering approximately 5,000 miles, and significantly increasing our fuel consumption. In order to keep our fuel reserves above the required minimum of 50 percent, we would need fuel even before we could reach Bahrain. Since the Navy was undergoing a decline in the number of active ships from just shy of 600 in 1986 to only 315 by 2000, there was only one oiler available for an at-sea refueling in the entire 2.5 million square miles of ocean in the Central Command's area of responsibility, and it was up in the Arabian Gulf. So a brief stop for fuel in a local port became our only recourse. Aden, at the southern tip of Yemen, and Djibouti, across the Strait of Bab el Mandeb in Africa, were the only two options. Naval Forces Central Command chose Aden because the intelligence available deemed the threat of terrorism in Djibouti greater than it was in Aden. Besides, Navy ships that refueled in Djibouti did not receive any priority to refuel and were put in rotating order with commercial vessels, sometimes sitting vulnerably at anchor for over twenty-four hours.

We were ordered by Fifth Fleet to conduct a "Brief Stop for Fuel"— as the Navy officially calls it—in Aden on October 12.

After racing across the eastern Mediterranean at 25 knots, USS *Cole* arrived on October 8 off Port Said, Egypt, the entry point for the Suez Canal the next morning. This also marked the transition to the Central Command area of operations, and our force protection security requirements changed. Where we had been under Threat Condition Alpha Plus, we were now moving up to the next step, Threat Condition Bravo. No one was about to take any chances as the ship went through the Suez Canal.

Most of the officers and crew, like me, had never made a deployment to the Middle East; consequently, we needed to be ready for anything that might happen. With that in mind, I had the crew set up our self-defense weapons. As we swung on the end of our anchor and waited to be called into the line of ships to enter the canal, the gunner's mates mounted four .50-caliber machine guns, two forward on the bow and two aft on the fantail and helicopter flight deck area. We also mounted two 7.62 mm machine guns on each of the bridge wings. The MK-38 25 mm chain gun on the starboard side of the ship near the quarterdeck area was similarly readied for action. Ammunition was placed in the small ready-service magazines near each weapon, locked up but available for immediate use. And the crew loaded twenty rounds of five-inch ammunition—artillery rounds five inches in diameter—into the ready-service magazine for the five-inch gun system on the bow. We also unlocked and readied a number of surface-to-air missiles in the vertical launcher tubes, forward and aft, and placed them in a condition that allowed the tactical action officer in the ship's combat information center to immediately insert a key and turn a switch to arm and launch them. To support missiles in flight, the fire control team would have to keep the AN/SPY-1D three-dimensional air-search radar operating despite the closeness to land.

Lastly, we briefed the security teams that would respond to a small-boat attack if one occurred while we were in the Suez Canal. They would remain in readiness on the mess decks and respond with weapons from the security lockers nearby. The crew set the highest condition of combat readiness and survivability with Material Condition Zebra in all compartments on the main deck and below, which meant keeping most hatches and doors closed so that the ship would be at the maximum level of watertight integrity if it sustained damage from an attack.

The transit passed without incident, and by 1700 on October 9 we were ready to resume cruising at 25 knots down the Red Sea to Aden.

Since we were headed back out into open waters, the threat condition for the ship allowed us to adjust our defensive posture to better reflect our surroundings. We stood down the alert for possible small-boat attack. A Secret message we had received during one of the port visits in the Mediterranean had said that a terrorist organization, possibly al Qaeda, operating in that area had been assessed to be targeting U.S. Navy ships for such attacks, and we had taken precautions at that time. But now that we had left the Mediterranean and passed through the Suez Canal into the Central Command area of operations, this threat was no longer viewed as relevant to the *Cole*.

Unbeknownst to us Naval Forces Central Command had taken that same message and readdressed it to all the ships operating in the region under its control, telling them to be mindful of the threat by al Qaeda and the possibility of a small-boat attack. In what was one of many seemingly benign intelligence shortfalls, *Cole* never received this significant reiteration of the message, since we were still operating in the Mediterranean under Sixth Fleet.

We stowed the .50-caliber and 7.62 mm machine guns and relocked the missiles. Although I left the twenty rounds in the five-inch gun magazine, the missile firing key was stowed back in the weapons safe in my cabin. As we sailed down the Red Sea, we took advantage of the time to continue to refresh and hone our war fighting skills. U.S. Navy ships, including *Cole*, would be operating off the coast of Iraq, where the prospect of a chemical warfare attack was very real. Consequently, over the next two days we simulated being attacked by chemical, biological, and radiological agents. The crew practiced donning their gas masks, and bulky and hot chemical-warfare suits, and went through the motions of detecting, disinfecting, and eliminating each of these threats to the ship and crew.

I knew that when we reached Aden, Threat Condition Bravo would require more security steps and greater coordination with local officials in port before the ship was moored. In early 1999, Central Command, then under U.S. Marine General Anthony C. Zinni, had negotiated a broad engagement policy with the Yemeni government in conjunction with the Department of State and the U.S. ambassador to Yemen, Barbara Bodine. Port visits by U.S. Navy ships sent a message of confidence in our hosts. This was also validated by the refueling contract the Defense Logistics Agency had negotiated, with Yemeni government help, with a local businessman. *Cole* would be the twenty-seventh ship to refuel in Aden. None of the previous twenty-six ships had knowingly encountered any threat.

Prior to each of the refueling visits, the ships were required to submit a force protection plan in advance for approval. *Cole* had not been given any information about logistics: the location or configuration of the refueling pier; the names of the Yemeni authorities or civilians involved with the arrangements; what force protection assets—police, harbor patrols, and the like—the Yemenis would provide; or whether they would allow the ship to deploy inflatable patrol boats with armed pickets if they were needed to keep potential trouble away. Under Central Command and Navy Standing Rules of Engagement in effect at the time, the ship could use force to defend itself only if it was attacked, shot at, or overtly threatened with weapons or met with other clear demonstrations of hostile intent. Supplementary measures could authorize more aggressive defenses, but for USS *Cole*, none were authorized in Aden. We were not provided with specific intelligence about the terrorist threat, though Central Command had classed the general level as High—that is, below Critical, the highest level, but above Medium, Low, and Negligible. Indeed, there was some confusion even about this, as we had been also told about a new four-point system that put Yemen's threat level at Significant, the second highest on a scale that began with High and continued through Moderate to Low.

The weapons officer, Lieutenant Joe Gagliano, who also had the collateral duty (that is, the part-time job) of force protection officer, worked with the strike officer, Lieutenant (junior grade) Robert Mercer, his force protection assistant, to draw up the force protection plan based on the most recent information we had about the port facilities in Aden. Since we had no confirmation of where we would actually be berthed and refueled, it was written for a worst-case, highest restriction scenario: a pierside mooring accessible to vehicles and foot traffic. It consisted of all sixty-two measures required in port for Threat Conditions Alpha and Bravo. We assumed that after arriving, we would adjust the security posture to fit whatever our actual circumstances turned out to be. With the delay in reporting to Central Command, the plan was submitted on October 7 to Commander, Task Force 50, the *Abraham Lincoln* battle group we would be serving with after the refueling, and was quickly approved without modification or comment, with no deviations authorized.

On October 8, USS *Cole* sent a standard unclassified message to the U.S. embassy's defense attaché's office (DAO) in Sana'a, requesting logistics support for the short duration of the refueling: a pilot and tugs to assist in entering the port and mooring the ship to the refueling pier; a hookup to provide drinking water for the crew; a connection to pump sewage off the ship to a shore-based waste facility; fuel delivery; and a request for details of any specific security arrangements needed. The supply requests were noted and referred to a local contractor to arrange with us upon arrival. There was nothing in response to the request for information about security arrangements.

In hindsight, it may seem obvious that I should have asked for more information before arrival, but it had been standard operating procedure by the Navy for decades to accept a lack of information and still make a port visit. Usually, upon arrival, the lists of unknowns would be answered by the port authorities without incident or issue. Rarely, if ever, were all the requests for information answered by the embassy prior to arrival. Such gaps in information were an accepted way of doing business overseas, even in a port in the Middle East operating under Threat Condition Bravo.

On October 11, the defense attaché's office acknowledged our request for logistics support and instructed the ship to coordinate services with the local contractor upon arrival. A lot of other important information was missing: at which pier the ship would moor; the number of tugs that would berth the ship; how and when the local contractor would board the ship to confirm fueling and other arrangements; on which side the ship could expect to moor; and the local security arrangements that would be provided by the Yemeni port authorities. Nor were official Navy channels much more helpful. Naval Forces Central Command, in the person of Vice Admiral Charles W. "Willie" Moore Jr., who was also the Fifth Fleet commander, had mandated through his staff that no information regarding any aspect of operations was allowed out of theater without their express knowledge and clearance. The headquarters staff was apparently very concerned about how the command was perceived, and the admiral wanted to ensure that all operations under his command appeared well orchestrated and that his staff was seen as being well in control of every U.S. Navy ship, aircraft, and submarine movement in theater. Communication was clearly filtered, to eliminate even the hint that anything adverse could be happening in theater. We would be briefed in depth on operations, intelligence, and logistics only after we completed the refueling and arrived in Bahrain on October 17, not before.

While I did not press Fifth Fleet or my chain of command, my apprehension increased as we entered an area of the world known for terrorist attacks. The odd nonchalance by Fifth Fleet and the new battle group commander, even with only generic terrorist threats that remained the same day after day in the message traffic, seemed strangely out of place. We would be essentially blind for seven days before pulling into Fifth Fleet headquarters in Bahrain for our in-depth regional intelligence briefings and updates. We would later learn of the clearest example of leaving USS *Cole* blind to a potential threat. Upon our arrival, the staff had planned to share the retransmitted message originally sent to only Sixth Fleet units in the Mediterranean regarding the al Qaeda small-boat threat to Navy ships operating in the Fifth Fleet area of operations. In the context of importance within the Fifth Fleet area of operations, we never received it prior to pulling into Aden.

Fortunately for the *George Washington* battle group, all the ships had been outfitted with a very basic e-mail capability used by the crew to correspond with home as well as effective communication between ships. At a speed of only 56 kbps (kilobits per second) and just one communications channel per ship, it was slow to say the least. I knew I could not take the ship blindly into my first Threat Condition Bravo port visit without *some* additional information. Although not officially sanctioned, I had been in contact with my good friend and squadron-mate the commanding officer of USS *Donald Cook*, Commander Matt Sharpe, who had arrived in the region two months before us. He was very sensitive to the fact that he was not supposed to tell me anything about how ships operated in the region until we had arrived in Bahrain for in-processing briefs from Naval Forces Central Command. He did, however, share unofficial information about the port and how we might expect to conduct the upcoming brief stop for fuel.

While *Cole* was in transit down the Red Sea, Matt and I exchanged e-mails. In his replies, he told me that I could expect to be berthed at a refueling "dolphin"—a pier out in the middle of the harbor in the northeast part of the bay, accessible from the city or from shore only by boat. Additionally, he told me that he had experienced a refueling rate of between 300 and 500 gallons per minute, which since we had requested 220,000 gallons would mean a long day before the ship was ready to go.

During the *Donald Cook*'s refueling, which had been done in August 2000, Matt told me, he had submitted the routine logistics request for a brief stop for fuel in Aden and encountered the same lack of information in advance. Nonetheless, he had pulled into port and then adjusted his routine to fit the circumstances, including his force protection posture. All had gone well.

On the evening of October 11, we passed through the Strait of Bab el Mandeb, rounded the corner of the southwest tip of the Arabian peninsula, and by 0200 on October 12, we were off the coast of Yemen, ready to enter port in the morning. We had to stay at least twelve nautical miles offshore, in international waters, until we got diplomatic clearance to enter port. During the night, we slowly steamed the ship back and forth in a small five-by-five-mile box and let the crew rest for the night. We were well below our 50 percent minimum for fuel, and messages from Naval Forces Central Command informed us that they were very anxious for us to get in and out of port as quickly as possible. Nothing from the staff or the stack of routine intelligence messages indicated that *Cole* should expect anything out of the ordinary.

3 | A "Routine" Refueling Stop

BEEP. BEEP. BEEP. October 12, 0415. I reached over and shut off the incessant noise from my alarm clock after only a few hours of sleep. Taking a deep breath to clear my head, I sat upright, stretched, and rolled out of bed. In my Night Orders to the officer of the deck, I had directed him to awaken me at 0500, the same time as reveille for the crew, but I preferred to be shaved, showered, and ready for the day before the call.

I called down to radio central and asked for the daily stack of messages transmitted to the ship overnight to be delivered to the bridge. Just sitting in my chair drinking hot coffee as the boatswain's mate piped reveille for the crew was the perfect way to start the day, and it promised to be a spectacular one. The temperature at sunrise was already in the eighties and climbing fast. A puff or two of cloud could be seen in the sky and outside Aden's harbor entrance the water was calm.

It was the first port the *Cole* would enter under Threat Condition Bravo. During the navigation brief the night before, and as part of our procedures for entering port, we had covered every aspect of our arrival, knowing we would have to adjust a number of procedures, from refueling requirements to force protection, during the first hours after our arrival as soon as the port authorities filled in the many unknowns the embassy and Fifth Fleet had left us with.

We were not scheduled to meet the harbor pilot until 0800, but I wanted to get into port early. From my perspective, if the refueling was going to last six to eight hours, the sooner we entered port and moored the ship, the sooner we could start and finish refueling. It would be easier and safer to get the ship underway again during daylight since we did not know the reliability of the harbor's navigation aids. I also wanted to minimize our vulnerability.

At 0549, the boatswain's mate of the watch announced, "Station the sea and anchor detail," which signaled the crew to take up their watch stations for entering port. We had received confirmation of diplomatic clearance to enter the port and steamed toward the harbor at 10 knots. The outermost buoy marking the harbor entrance was also the point where the harbor pilot was expected to board the ship and help navigate it into port. As we steamed toward it, the communications officer on the bridge pressed the transmit button on the bridge-to-bridge radio:

"Aden Port Control, this is U.S. Navy warship USS *Cole*, channel one-six, over."

There was no response. He tried again and again and got nothing. After twenty minutes and several more calls, finally he heard, "This is Aden Port Control. What time are you scheduled to come in?"

"Aden Port Control, we were originally scheduled to come in to port around 0730. We have arrived early. Would it be possible for the pilot to meet us early? We would like to come in and get moored as soon as possible to start refueling. Over."

After considerable delay—suddenly, they told us, our transmissions were garbled—they said, "The pilot is not here. You are going to have to wait. We'll get back to you, over."

It was frustrating for the watch team. They had been on watch now for almost two hours and the officer of the deck had to slow the ship to less than 5 knots, waiting for the Yemenis to get their act together so we could enter port. Finally, over an hour after the first contact the radio crackled to life with: "Navy warship *Cole*, request you enter the harbor channel. The pilot will meet you with two tugs in the channel and escort you to the refueling pier, over."

This was not going to work. Since the ship had never made a port call to Aden, we were unfamiliar with the harbor area and safety dictated that the pilot be on board prior to entering the shipping channel. "Aden Port Control, request the pilot meet us at the pilot buoy with tugs," the communications officer answered. "We will not enter port without a pilot, over."

Clearly, the port authority was not pleased with this development but complied, and around 0720, a small boat with two tugs behind it came chugging down the channel toward us, bringing out the pilot. It was already becoming clear that we would be entering the harbor and mooring later than scheduled. While not of great concern, it was another factor that raised the tension level. Being in port under Threat Condition Bravo, the less time the ship spent refueling alongside the pier, the less vulnerable we were to any security threats.

The pilot boat maneuvered alongside back by the flight deck, and at 0746 the pilot, Mr. Ibrahim, boarded USS *Cole* and was escorted to the bridge. He was a slightly built man with a gaunt face tanned by years in the sun. The heat of the day had already caused his clean but slightly wrinkled shirt to begin to spot under his arms. The conning officer stepped aside as he walked directly up to the centerline compass pelorus and confirmed the ship's heading.

As we headed up the channel into port, I asked him, "Captain, what side of the pier do you want to moor the ship?" "We will moor port side to," he curtly replied with a thick accent—with the left-hand side of the ship against the pier, in other words. I looked down onto the forecastle at the lines already laid out by the boatswain's mates, anticipating a mooring arrangement with the starboard side to the pier.

Fortunately, we would be mooring at the same refueling pier, an island structure in the northeast part of the inner harbor, that Matt Sharpe, the CO of USS *Donald Cook* had referred to in his unofficial e-mails to me. After the exchange with Matt, I already knew that I wanted the ship moored starboard side to the pier with bow facing out in the event of an emergency. Although it was only in the back of my mind, I was concerned that if *Cole* came under hostile fire or attack, I did not want to waste precious minutes turning the ship around in the middle of the harbor before being able to sail safely out to sea. Since *Cole* was 505 feet long and the pier was about 350 feet long, the bow and stern would stick out from both ends of the pier. Consequently, of the six lines we had available, four would moor us to the pier while the lines at the bow and stern of the ship would be made fast to mooring buoys using small boats that the pilot had already arranged to meet us near the pier. We could get underway even quicker by axing the mooring lines. In that event, those precious minutes would surely save lives.

Chris, as XO, was unhappy with the harbor pilot's determination to moor the ship port side to the pier, and told him so. I looked at Chris and without a word spoken between us, motioned him to back off. Remembering Matt Sharpe telling me how difficult it had been for him to convince the pilot to let *Donald Cook* moor starboard side to the pier, I knew this would have to be handled delicately. The pilot was offered hot tea (another key tip from *Donald Cook*), which he politely accepted. After he had sipped for a few minutes, I again approached him and said it would be much better if we could moor starboard side to the pier. Almost immediately, he lowered his head and began to shake it slowly side to side. I persisted, "If we twist the ship in the harbor now and use the two tugs you have brought out to us, it will save you time and money this afternoon. With the ship moored starboard side to, when we finish refueling, it will only take one tug to lift us off the pier, instead of two. If I have to moor port side to the pier now, I will need two tugs this afternoon to help get us off the pier and turned around in the harbor. With only one tug, we can leave quicker and get back to sea sooner. Also, since I did not know which side you would moor the ship, I already laid out my mooring lines on the starboard side." I motioned for him to step around from the front of the pelorus and look down to the lines laid out on the forecastle. After quickly glancing down at them, he looked up for a moment, rubbed the slight stubble on his chin, and checked the ship's heading again before he replied.

"OK. We will turn the ship and moor it starboard side to the pier," and with that, he contacted the tugs on his radio and told them he had changed plans.

Unfortunately, the tugs were clearly not experienced at working a ship like *Cole* next to the pier. What should have taken us ten minutes to get the ship tied up instead took almost an hour. The tugs could not keep the ship in place for more than a few seconds and allow us to tighten on the mooring lines without risk of parting them. After more than thirty minutes of sliding back and forth alongside the pier, I was finally able to convince the pilot to not have the tugs press against the ship while we worked with the line handlers on the pier. In short order, the line handling teams were able to get the first lines to the pier at 0851 and within about fifteen minutes the ship was finally moored.

One of the security measures in the force protection plan I had agreed to implement had been to launch an armed picket-boat into the harbor on fifteen-minute standby. I chose not to carry out that step because I knew that given the geography of the port and the island structure of the refueling pier, a boat not ready for immediate action would be of little use. In time, this decision would have a momentous impact on *Cole*.

By 0935 the crew was finished with the sea and anchor detail. As we stationed the in-port watches, the engineers began the detailed preparations to refuel. Since we would be stationing the sea and anchor detail again later that day to get back underway and leave port, the bridge was left operationally ready and most equipment was not stowed, as it would be for a normal in-port visit. Navigation charts were left out, navigation equipment—the alidades for each bridge wing pelorus—were left out, and the handheld bridge-to-bridge radio was left near my chair.

Walking down from the bridge to my cabin, I was looking forward to getting around the ship. I was not always successful, but at least twice daily I tried to visit as many of the crew's workshops and offices as was practical. Getting out of my cabin and away from the drudgery of paperwork was good for me and just being with the sailors always gave me a sense of pride in how well they were doing in keeping up the ship and working together as a team. As I walked into the central control station (CCS), the heart and nerve center of the ship's engineering plant, Lieutenant Deborah ("Debbie") Courtney, my engineer officer, had already signed and approved the watch bill and was now working to make sure everyone was completing the necessary checklists before we actually started pumping fuel. Seeing that everything was well in hand, I continued to walk around the ship and visit with the crew.

I arrived back in my cabin around 1000 and sat down at my desk. The main propulsion assistant (MPA), Ensign Andrew "Drew" Triplett, knocked on my door and asked, "Captain, do you have a minute to review the in-port refueling checklist?"

By now we were running behind schedule—something he must have been aware of. As he handed me the sheet he offered to speed up the refueling by having me sign the engineering report now, assuming that Debbie would also verify that the checklist was complete and find everything mechanically in order, especially the fuel valve alignment, so that we could start. I looked at him, smiled, and told him, "MPA, I know you are just trying to speed things up in an effort to get out of this port as soon as possible. Let's wait until the engineer is done with her checks, signs off on the checklist, and *then* I'll sign it."

Drew, one of my best officers and a true professional, let his head drop to his chest in mock and exaggerated disappointment, and walked out mumbling, for my amusement, "Every time we want to get some work done, procedures get in the way." He left to await the engineer officer as she finished her checks. Drew had joined the Navy as a young Fireman Recruit and had always been an exceptionally talented and hard working engineer. After thirteen years in the Navy, as a chief petty officer, he decided to become a limited duty officer (LDO), a technical specialist, with the rank of ensign. He was exceptionally well liked by the crew.

This was the last time I saw him alive.

Around 1025, Debbie knocked on the door to my cabin with the completed in-port refueling checklist in hand. As she left my cabin, I heard her calling the quarterdeck watch on the ship's wireless internal communication system, an internal walkie-talkie system, to inform them that she had permission from me to start refueling the ship. She asked them to hoist the Bravo flag, indicating the ship was conducting refueling operations, and announce over the 1MC general announcing system that the smoking lamp was out, prohibiting everyone from smoking or engaging in any activities that would produce flames or sparks. It seemed like a routine morning as I turned back to my desk and the mounds of paperwork that awaited me. At 1032 the announcement came that refueling had begun.

At 1040, the supply officer, Lieutenant Denise Woodfin, knocked on my door and asked for a few minutes to review some items with me. Denise told me that the Yemeni husbanding (logistics) agent, who had come aboard the ship via boat shortly after arrival alongside the pier, had made all the arrangements for the sewage removal and refueling operations requested in our logistics message to the embassy. The sewage barge, about twenty by forty feet in size, was already tied up to the port side of the ship near the back of the flight deck preparing to remove sewage and waste water. As any good businessman would do, the husbanding agent had made an additional offer to Denise to have three small garbage barges come out to the ship and remove all of our trash, plastic waste, and hazardous waste materials, for the very reasonable equivalent of about $150. He or his colleagues had made the same arrangement, for three garbage boats, for other Navy ships before us. Denise was quite pleased at the prospect of getting all this material off the ship at so little expense. She also foresaw the opportunity to reduce the amount of work when we pulled into Bahrain.

But I told her I didn't want to take up the offer, for several reasons.

First, I tried to run the *Cole* on a fiscally conservative budget and preferred to use as much of the appropriated money as possible for the crew in either purchasing tools to allow them to do their jobs better or items that would benefit them in other ways, like equipment and organizational clothing. The ship was scheduled to arrive back from deployment in February 2001. Norfolk at that time of year was usually cold and wet, and $150 could buy two foul-weather jackets for the boatswain's mates. It wasn't a large amount of money, but I preferred to spend it in the United States rather than in this small, hole-in-the-wall port. Second, none of the *Cole*'s storage areas was overflowing with any trash or other items. I also knew the growing collection of waste paper and metal trash could be disposed of for free that evening once we were at sea and far enough away from land. Additionally, there was more than enough storage capacity on the ship to last until we pulled into Bahrain in about five days for our in-theater briefings by Naval Forces Central Command/Fifth Fleet and, hopefully, some liberty. I had also been told that Bahrain had facilities available for visiting ships to remove their plastic waste and hazardous material at no charge.

Hearing my explanation, Denise politely rolled her eyes and smiled as she walked out of my cabin. I thought the issue was closed, but she returned at 1050, this time with the executive officer in tow. As they walked in, I asked, with some amusement, "I take it you want to discuss the garbage barges some more?" Both laughed as Chris began a lengthy explanation about why spending this $150 was a good investment in time and savings for the crew. From both of their perspectives it was well worth the money, even considering that the ship would need more foul-weather jackets in February. I looked at both of them, shook my head, and said, "OK, fine. Go ahead and bring the boats out to us. Let's pass the word and get everything off the ship." The $150 was not worth the minor battle this was shaping up to be. How long it was going to take to refuel the ship remained foremost in everyone's mind.

Denise had anticipated that the XO could get me to change my mind, and had already notified the quarterdeck that three garbage boats would be approaching the ship. Two of them had already crossed the harbor and were now alongside. One was back by the flight deck and fantail area near the sewage barge, collecting trash and hazardous materials; the other was amidships, directly below the area between the stacks, where it was collecting plastic waste being brought up from the plastic waste processing room under the mess decks.

Chris brought some good news. The refueling was going faster than we expected. "We're probably going to be done between 1230 and 1300," he told me. "I would like to start lunch early and get everyone moving through the line so we can get the sea and anchor detail stationed early in preparation for leaving port." Instead of the 300 to 500 gallons per minute that we had been expecting, we were getting closer to 2,500 gallons per minute. This huge difference in pressure had initially complicated the refueling operation, since that amount of fuel being pumped onto the ship so quickly was over-pressurizing the fuel tanks, threatening to cause a spill. The *Cole*'s engineers had to ask the Yemeni fuel workers on the pier to close down the valve to slow the rate to around 2,000 gallons per minute.

Chris had already discussed with the supply officer the possibility of opening the galley and mess decks early to feed the crew. Since we normally started feeding the crew around 1130, the supply officer quickly checked with the petty officer in charge of the noon meal, Mess Specialist Third Class Ronchester Santiago, in the galley and promptly determined that opening thirty minutes early would not pose any problems. Everything was lining up to allow us to leave earlier than expected.

I told Chris this was a great idea. He then left my cabin to go down to the quarterdeck to make the announcement, and said he would be in the classroom in the aft part of the ship holding a meeting of our welfare and recreation committee.

Around 1115, the sewage barge, shortly followed by the two trash boats, left the side of the ship and headed across the harbor to dump their waste. The quarterdeck watch and security personnel stationed topside had been told to expect the third boat to come out to the ship shortly to pick up any remaining material.

With the quiet hum of a ship at work in the background, I slid my chair up to the desk and turned back to the never-ending grind of paperwork in front of me. The smell of lunch being prepared for the wardroom wafted into my cabin and, despite the slight delay getting into port, the revised refueling schedule had buoyed everyone. Soon, *Cole* would be underway and back out at sea where we belonged and ships are safest.

4 | Attacked

S UDDENLY, AT 1118, there was a thunderous explosion. Eight thousand four hundred tons of guided missile destroyer thrust quickly and violently upward and to the right. Tiles from the false ceiling in my cabin popped out and landed on the floor. The coffee and water on my small round table tipped over, spilling onto the dark blue carpet. Everything that was not bolted down lifted off my desk and seemed to float twelve inches in the air for a split second before slamming back down with a dull thud. Around me, it felt like we had just been speared like a giant fish as the ship rose up and flexed back and forth, so quickly and violently that I had to pull myself out of my chair, stand on the balls of my feet in a crouched position, and grab the underside of my desk to keep from being knocked over. The *Cole* seemed almost to float slowly in a counterclockwise direction before settling back down in the water. All the lights went out and the emergency lighting came on. Everything rolled from side to side as the ship surged forward and backward alongside the refueling pier in an odd three-dimensional circular motion.

As soon as I gained my footing, I turned left toward my cabin door and staggered to the opening, holding the doorframe on either side. One emergency light from a battle lantern right above the door shone brightly towards the floor in front of me. Another, halfway down the passageway, glowed eerily in the dark, illuminating the path from the wardroom (the officers' mess) on the port side of the ship opposite my cabin.

Engineer Officer Debbie Courtney, who had been in her cabin working, came flying out of her stateroom, steel-toe boots untied, heading for the central control station to try to find out what had happened, looking wordlessly into my eyes as she ran by. A cloud of smoke and dust came rolling from the port side and down the passageway toward me. There was almost complete silence. No noise—not a fan, not an alarm, no announcements from the quarterdeck watch—just blaring silence. As the cloud washed over me, I could smell dust and the pungent odor of fuel, and something else—a repellent acrid and metallic tang that seemed to sink into my mouth and nose.

Lieutenant (junior grade) Jim Salter, the system test officer for the Aegis weapon system, came out of the stateroom immediately to my left and grabbed the doorframe. "What the fuck was that?" he asked me, and for a second he stared into the distance. Then he gasped "Fuel!" and took off down the passageway. He ran toward the refueling laboratory outside main engine room 1 to see if the fuel we were taking on had exploded during the refueling.

Instantly I knew that we had been attacked. How, by whom, and how badly we had been damaged I could not know. But as the ship was moored with the right side to the refueling pier, I knew that if fuel had exploded, either on the pier or inside the ship, we should have been shoved to the left. Instead, Cole had been violently thrust up and to the right. On the left side of the ship was the open harbor area around the pier. Something must have detonated on that side. I had to get down to that area of the ship and find out what had happened.

Quickly, I turned around and went back into my darkened cabin. In the small safe near the headboard of my bed, I kept the keys to all the weapons for the ship—missiles, five-inch gun, close-in weapons system, torpedoes, and so on, but also a personal weapon: a Sig Sauer P229 9 mm pistol and three thirteen-round clips of ammunition I had brought with me on deployment. At that moment I didn't know if we had been boarded, or if we would come under sniper fire, or anything else. I took the pistol in my right hand, grabbed a magazine full of ammunition and shoved it into the butt, chambered a round and decocked the gun before heading out of my cabin, two spare magazines clicking against each other in my left front pocket.

One deck below, outside on the starboard side of the ship next to the refueling pier, I glanced around. Not a single person was anywhere in sight—no one. The area in front of me, where the quarterdeck watch had been positioned—the officer of the deck, petty officer of the watch, and messenger, the "front office" of the ship in port—was deserted. Manned by three experienced watch standers, Storekeeper First Class Rodney Jackson, Ship's Serviceman Second Class Craig Freeman, and Ship's Serviceman Third Class Paul Mena, I knew they would not have abandoned their watch unless absolutely necessary. Already the crew had raced out to find out what had happened.

The ceremonial wooden podium that served as a desk for the deck log and held routine paperwork used by the watch team lay splintered and scattered across the deck. Thick black wires, still attached to the crossbeam of the mast—all that was left of our high-frequency radio antennas—were draped across the deck. Dirty black water was dripping down off everything. Small pieces of blackened debris lay scattered all around.

I did not know if this attack would be just the first of many. I didn't know if we were going to be, or had already been, boarded by someone carrying out this attack and now wreaking havoc throughout the ship. I had to get to the port side.

Holding my pistol pointed upward and ready to use, I ran around the corner towards the epicenter of the explosion, ready to die to defend my ship, my crew, and my country. A memory flashed to mind. On July 6, 1977, I had stood in the center courtyard, Tecumseh Court, at the U.S. Naval Academy, sweat running down the middle of my back, my hair closely shorn and my crisply starched and freshly issued uniform beginning to smell of the sweat of the unknown. "What have I gotten myself into?" I wondered over and over as my classmates and I stood in the still of the late afternoon sun to enter the U.S. Navy. Moments later, I swore an oath to my country, to support and defend our Constitution against all enemies, foreign and domestic. I was now committed to giving my life to defend my country. Those words spoken over two decades before were now stark reality as I took a deep breath and steeled myself to face what might be my own death.

As I reached the middle of the port side amidships area, on the left side at *Cole's* midpoint, Gunner's Mate Chief Norm Larson ran up, wearing an open flak vest and a Kevlar helmet, its chinstrap dangling loosely down his cheek. He and I stopped and stood still for a second. Locking eyes, I made a quick, sweeping gesture with my hand as if silently asking about the devastation surrounding us. Clearly, this was the center point of the blast. The deck was littered with debris. Measuring back about twelve feet from the back of the port brake—a semi-enclosed shelter used by crew members working topside in bad weather—and five feet from the side of the ship, the central part of the deck bulged up about eight inches into a slight peak. Several of the fiberglass lifelines that had lined the port side had been snapped off by the force of the explosion and lay limp on the deck in front of us or hung over the side.

Chief Larson placed himself directly in front of me. "Captain, you need to get down or get back behind something," he said, reaching out to try to tuck in the collar rank insignia on my coveralls. "Sir, you really need to take your khaki belt off and stop pointing at things. You could be a sniper target!"

"Chief, don't worry about me. I'm not a sniper target," I told him. "These guys don't operate like that. Let's get the focus off me and back out on the harbor. We cannot allow anyone else to get alongside."

The list to the port side was slowly increasing. The ship was flooding. Carefully, I leaned over the side of the ship and could see the top curve of what had to be a huge hole. Black and brown scorch marks sprayed out from the blast hole itself. Small pieces of black residue speckled the side of the ship. And the metal surrounding the hole was bent inwards in huge jagged shards from the force of the explosion.

Clearly, something had detonated alongside us. The ship's general workshop, the adjoining sixty-foot-wide main engine room 1, the galley one deck above where the crew had just been taking their lunch, and the chief petty officers' mess, were all in the part of the ship where I was standing. In the engine room were the two gas turbine engines that powered the starboard propeller shaft, as well as the two reverse-osmosis water processing units that made fresh water out of 24,000 gallons per day of seawater. The explosion had been so powerful that I knew almost everything in these and immediately adjoining spaces must have been destroyed or severely damaged, crippling the ship and killing or severely wounding anyone who had been in these areas.

But what could have done this? With my mind racing to explain the devastation in front of me, I could see four orange rafts in the water along the length of the port side. Questions burst into my mind, "Could these have been the vehicle for a bomb?" "How did someone manage to get these rafts alongside the ship with no one seeing them?" They were evenly spaced, from directly below where I was looking into the blast hole to the area back by the flight deck at the stern of the ship. The first raft, in the area of the blast hole, was mostly sunk and in tatters. The next two were deflated, lying flat on the surface of the water. The fourth raft, however, was fully inflated and gently rubbing and bobbing against the ship back by the flight deck and fantail area. Based on the limited evidence I had before me, it seemed as though the raft nearest me must have been the one that detonated and blew the hole in the side of the ship. The force of the explosion must have damaged the detonators on the two deflated rafts and caused them not to go off. In my mind, the fourth raft alongside the flight deck area now posed the greatest danger to the ship. It had to be full of explosives ready to detonate and cripple the twin rudders and propellers for steering and driving the ship, and if that happened we could not get underway and out of port. At the same time, I could see the crew streaming out onto the flight deck area, peering over the edge of the port side. They could all be killed if the raft exploded. I had to do something, fast.

Meanwhile, Chief Larson had issued *Cole*'s rapid response security team every weapon available: 9 mm pistols, M-14 rifles, twelve-gauge shotguns, M-79 grenade launchers, and ammunition. "Get everybody who isn't part of the security team back inside the skin of the ship," I barked out to him. He immediately passed the order to those on the flight deck, hollering, "We don't know what we've got out here."

The security teams began rounding up the crew and shoving them back inside. One of the wounded being attended to by other crew members was Fireman Raymond Mooney, his face covered with blood. He was lying in the aft passageway near the exit onto the flight deck when he saw Chris Peterschmidt, the XO. Calling out and grabbing him by his coveralls, he pulled him close: "Sir! I saw what happened! I saw what happened!"

Mooney told Chris that he had been stationed near the forward refueling station, on the harbor side of the ship opposite from the refueling hose connection from the pier. His assignment had been to watch for a fuel spill into the harbor. He had seen the two garbage barges slowly make their approach to the ship, he said, but since they were expected—these were the first two, and there was to be a third—he saw no reason to be concerned. Once the crew had loaded the boats up with trash and debris, both headed together back to shore. He was watching them cross the harbor when he saw a third boat coming toward the ship at high speed.

Mooney wondered at first why it was coming toward *Cole* so fast, but as it got closer, it slowed to make a steady approach about forty-five degrees off the port bow. He could see it was white, about thirty feet long, with red on the interior. There was an open well in the boat with a center console for the controls and although it looked clean, almost new, it also didn't look so different from the previous two trash boats. The security team member who was watching its approach with him also seemed unconcerned, Mooney said. From when they first saw it, it took about thirty-five seconds to come alongside. The two men in the boat then looked up at Mooney, waved, and smiled. He was surprised, and hesitated before waving back. The boat bumped solidly into the side of the ship and drifted slightly away from the side.

Then, Armageddon.

A huge red fireball vaporized the boat and both of the men. Mooney's vision went black, and a quick flash of intense heat blew by him. He raised his hands to his face and pulled them away, seeing what appeared to be only a few spots of blood.

Tearing off his headset, he jumped the eight feet down onto the deck from the refueling station. He ran across the front of the ship toward the starboard side and then down the starboard brake past the ship's small boats, past injured sailors lying on the deck, and back onto the flight deck. Two engineers he came across told him he looked in bad shape and should get to medical immediately.

Chris told two sailors to grab Mooney and get his wounds treated. Reaching a large medical box near the entrance to number 3 gas turbine generator room, they let Mooney sit down with a slump, and suddenly he was overcome with the most intense pain had ever felt in his life. His eyes were burning and he could barely see. The fireball from the explosion had caused flash burns to his face and eyes, now quickly swelling shut.

Chris relayed Mooney's account of the attack to the security team. One of the team's members found me within less than a minute, and corrected my misinterpretation of the rafts. "Captain, it wasn't those rafts alongside the ship that blew us up. It was another boat that came out from shore. We thought it was the third garbage barge. Those rafts are *our* rafts, look." He pointed to the now empty twenty-five-man life raft racks on the port side of the ship. Almost every one of the life rafts had been blown out of its fiberglass container.

So: we had been attacked by kamikaze terrorists. One of the most modern twenty-first-century destroyers of the world's most powerful navy had been successfully attacked by a technologically primitive, explosive-laden suicide boat. We might as well have been in 1945.

Chris had been below the flight deck, well aft of the explosion's epicenter, when it had happened. The force of it almost blew him off his feet. He set off toward the forward part of the ship to see what had happened, but was quickly overcome by smoke and ordered the watertight door leading forward closed to keep it from spreading aft.

Crossing over to the starboard side to try to continue forward, he saw crew members streaming back, fleeing the blast zone. Though he knew almost everybody aboard by name or by face, he was unable to recognize many of them, so much blood was streaming down their faces, arms, and hands. Some had been on the mess decks or standing in the mess line picking up their meals. There, at the focal point of the blast, the force of the explosion had shattered the plastic coating that kept the steel decks of the ship from rusting and blown it into the sailors like flechettes from a grenade. Chris also found sailors who had been outside at the moment of the attack almost unrecognizable because they were covered from head to toe with residue from the black, sooty wave of water that the explosion had washed up onto the ship. Their eardrums were ruptured and they were dazed and confused.

Despite his shock at the scene around him, Chris quickly got his bearings and fell back on the training provided by hundreds of damage control drills. The Navy trains repetitively for this very reason: during a crisis, people don't have time to think, they only have time to react, and everyone had to get to work immediately to save the ship.

The standard list of tactics, techniques, and procedures—manning general quarters stations, manning the repair lockers, closing all hatches and doors, assessing the damage to the ship—this is what everyone was thinking, as if each step had been indelibly imprinted on their brains. At this point, Chris did not know if the captain was killed, wounded, or incapacitated. He began barking out orders, and the crew organized itself to stop the flooding, stop the spread of smoke, prevent fire, and man the battle-dressing stations to treat the wounded. With the ship's communications system knocked out and the battery-powered backup system out of commission, all that could be heard were the shouts of crew members as they went to work to save their ship and shipmates.

Making his way to the central control station, Chris was shocked to come across one of *Cole's* leading damage control experts on the Damage Control Training Team, Gas Turbine System Technician-Mechanical Chief Mark Darwin, lying seriously wounded on the deck. Ships like *Cole* in the *Arleigh Burke*–class of guided missile destroyers were intended to have a chief petty officer in charge of the damage control division. However, chiefs with that kind of experience and leadership were scarce. Our ship had worked hard to train and educate other personnel, including Darwin, to fill the gap with their background and experience in the Engineering Department. Now, with him wounded and unable to directly contribute to the damage control effort, Chris began to seriously worry about our prospects for saving the ship. Kneeling down, he saw that Darwin was having trouble breathing. Some of his ribs had been cracked or fractured. In the past, Darwin and Chris had had a very contentious relationship—now all Chris wanted was to stay and give comfort. Even so, Darwin told Chris the best thing he could do for him was to keep moving and look after the ship and crew.

Topside, with Chief Larson standing by me, I now understood what had happened. My mind was clear and sharp. I told Larson, "I have got to get to the bridge to tell the Yemeni port authorities what's happened. Do not allow any more boats to come alongside the ship. We cannot afford another hit."

I walked up the port side, opened up a watertight door, and in the dark began to climb the stairs leading to the bridge. Why us? Why now? What did we miss that allowed this to happen?

As I opened the door and stepped onto the bridge, I came upon the Navigator, Lieutenant Ann Chamberlain, as well as my leading electronics technician, Senior Chief Pam Jacobsen and leading operations specialist, Senior Chief Al Trapani. I still held my 9 mm handgun at the ready as the three of them looked at me wide-eyed and asked what was going on. Although they were shocked by what I told them, I needed them to focus on getting me in touch with the Yemeni port authorities immediately. Without power on the bridge to operate the ship's bridge-to-bridge radio, used earlier to contact the Aden Port Authority, Ann found an alternative and passed me the hand held bridge-to-bridge walkie-talkie that operated on the same channel. As the operations officer, Lieutenant Derek Trinque, came onto the bridge from the port side. I keyed the radio.

"Aden Port Control, this is USS *Cole*, over."

"This is Aden Port Control."

"This is USS *Cole*. We have experienced an explosion amidships. I need your assistance, over."

"This is Aden Port Control. We understand. What do you need us to do?"

"Aden Port Control, request you stop all harbor movements until we know what has happened and we know the status of the security situation. I say again, request no ship movements in the harbor, over."

"This is Aden Port Control, we understand. We will not allow any ships to move in or out of the harbor. Is this correct?"

"This is USS *Cole*. Roger, that is correct."

"I need you to notify your local hospital. We have wounded on the ship and they will need medical treatment. Do you have a facility available, over?"

"Yes, yes, we have two hospitals. We will notify them and get ambulances down to the pier to take your wounded to them."

Time was of the essence, and the "golden hour" for saving those most seriously hurt was inexorably ticking away.

But when *Cole* pulled into Aden, I had made that decision not to put a picket boat in the water. As with any decision you make in command, even the best ones given the surrounding conditions can have effects that cannot be anticipated. In this case, the result was that the ship's boats were now not available for use at all. They were still in the boat skids on the starboard side of the ship. Since we were moored starboard side to the pier and without power, there was no way to lower them to the water, since we were too close and the large rubber fenders keeping us off the pier would have hemmed them in. So I had one last request for the port authorities.

"Aden Port Control, request you send boats out to the ship to take wounded ashore. Do you have any boats available to help do this, over?"

"Yes, we have boats available and will send them out to your ship."

"Aden Port Control, thank you, but I must insist that they approach the ship in the following manner. When they come toward the ship, they must not approach my port side any closer than 100 meters. They should stay clear of my port side, come around the stern of the ship, the back of the ship, and make a very slow approach to the back side of the refueling dolphin." I repeated the message to them again and added: "If you come any closer than 100 meters to my port side, I will shoot you. I repeat. Do not come any closer than 100 meters to my port side or I will shoot you. Do you understand?"

"Yes, yes, we understand. We understand. Do not come any closer than 100 meters. We will come around your stern to the back of the refueling pier. Yes we understand."

I placed Derek, the senior officer on the bridge, in charge, and told him we were changing the rules of engagement. If another boat approached on the port side and came within a 100-meter arc, it was to be considered a danger to the ship and given warning with the battery-powered bullhorn to stay away. If it continued to close on the ship, he was to direct the security team to fire a warning shot in the boat's direction. If it kept coming after that, the security team was to open up with every weapon available.

We were now listing at over five degrees to port and over one degree down by the bow, and I had to get to the central control station, the nerve center of the ship, to oversee the damage control effort. "Make sure the security teams know about the rules of engagement and don't let them accidentally shoot any of the boats coming out to take off the wounded; otherwise, we are screwed," I told him. He looked me square in the eye and said, "Got it, Captain."

On shore, Major Mark Conroe, the assistant defense attaché of the U.S. embassy to Yemen, soon got a vivid experience of what these instructions meant. He had been at the refueling pier while we moored the ship, making sure the arrangements made with the Yemeni firms to resupply *Cole* were working. Once refueling began, he had taken a boat and gone back into town. He was sitting at an outdoor café sipping coffee when he heard the explosion; the defense attaché, Lieutenant Colonel Bob Newman, in Aden on leave with his family, also heard it while playing with his children near his hotel swimming pool. Separately, they both made their way to the harbor to see what had happened.

As the first to arrive, about twenty-five minutes after the explosion, Conroe had commandeered a boat and, minutes after the attack, tried to make his way out to the ship. As he approached, he saw the sailors in the security force pointing a number of guns at his boat. If he had proceeded within 100 meters, he may well have been fired upon. He then made the wise decision to turn around and wait until he could communicate with us to approach. Back at the pier, he found Newman and briefed him on what had happened. Together they went to the port control office and were able to get through to *Cole*'s bridge team. Within another half-hour, they were on a Yemeni boat back to the ship. Newman had a cellular phone—a rarity back then—and was telling his office at the embassy in Sana'a that there had been an explosion of some kind on the ship when he suddenly interrupted himself: "Oh my God! We're coming around to the other side of the ship. There's a big hole in the side—maybe forty feet wide, right in the center of the ship. We're going to try and get on board. I'll call you later."

Reaching the refueling pier, Conroe saw me and yelled up to me to ask what he could do to help. By that time, almost an hour after the ex-plosion, our rescue and damage control efforts were in overdrive, and I told him we needed water for the crew as soon as possible; the temperature was in the nineties and the humidity was high, and without a fresh-water supply, there was the danger of dehydration. He said he would take care of it and left with the next boat in search of bottled water, returning about twenty minutes later with 240 one-liter bottles that were tossed up to crew members. "Keep bringing us water until I tell you to stop, and that isn't going to be for awhile," I said. "Tell every boat coming out here to bring more water."

Newman walked over the pier to get within speaking range and asked me, "Have you had a chance to tell Fifth Fleet what has happened to you?" There was no way to communicate with them. Radio central, with all the communications equipment on the ship, was without power, and so far we had been unable to restore it. Hearing this, Newman pulled out his cell phone, which had the global system for mobile communications

(GSM) capability, and held it above his head and yelled up to me: "I have the number to the Ops Center at Fifth Fleet. Do you want to use it to give them a call?" With an underhand motion, he tossed it in my direction.

As the phone tumbled through the air, I quickly flashed back to high school and the Naval Academy. "Lippold," I thought to myself, "you played two sports—tennis and golf. If there was ever a time in your life that you need to catch something, this is it."

It was a perfect toss, and I got it with relative ease.

After three rings, the Fifth Fleet Tactical Flag Command Center, in Bahrain, answered. "Fifth Fleet Surface Ops, Commander Schnell speaking, may I help you?"

"Yes, this is Commander Kirk Lippold, Commanding Officer of USS *Cole*," I said, speaking as clearly and slowly as possible. "I have an OPREP-3, Pinnacle, Front Burner Report." OPREP-3 is a military report used to inform the highest levels of command of a major event or incident; Pinnacle indicated that this would be a matter of national-level media interest; Front Burner signified a report of an attack on American forces—with the highest priority for transmission. An act of war, in other words.

"Are you sure?" the duty officer asked. I stared at the phone in disbelief. I had looked into the hole in the side of my ship and was standing amongst wounded still being evacuated off the ship. Oh, yes, I was sure.

In about a minute's time, I gave him an initial voice report detailing the attack and recounting how the boat, ostensibly a trash barge, had come alongside and detonated. Then I gave the status of the ship, what compartments were flooded, what I knew of the progress of the damage control effort, and, finally, the status of the wounded. Since we were still in the middle of triage, I omitted any report of crew members killed because that could be premature or inaccurate. I said I would report again when I had more information, folded the phone shut and slipped it into my left pocket, where it clanked against the two clips of 9 mm ammunition. I still felt a need for the pistol in the other pocket. At least now help was on the way.

5 | Saving the Ship

THE HOUR BEFORE THAT CALL had been horrific and life changing. When I walked off the bridge into the darkness immediately after the explosion, we were without power and slowly sinking into Aden harbor. It would be up to my crew to save the ship and take care of the wounded—and we would have to work fast.

What I discovered as I walked through the ship were the horrific results of the detonation of hundreds of pounds of high explosive. In about one ten-thousandth of a second, a rapidly expanding ball of gases sent a massive shock wave, traveling at over 25,000 feet per second, outward from the suicide boat. The initial expanding bubble slammed into the water around the rapidly disintegrating boat and suicide bombers. An incompressible fluid, the water instantly translated the force of the explosion in all directions downward and outward from its source in the boat.

Later investigations would reconstruct the sequence of events. Below the waterline of the ship the hydraulic energy from the explosion slammed downward into the seabed to form a crater about twenty feet across and four feet deep, then reflecting upward as a wave of energy focused toward the bottom of the *Cole* and its keel. The wave bowed the ship directly over the reflected blast area, and the ship rose almost ten feet before settling sloppily back into the water, gyrating drunkenly from side to side and surging forward and backward next to the pier.

The mooring lines tied to the pier and the fore and aft mooring buoys strained under the pressure of keeping the 8,400-plus tons of warship from breaking free from its moorings. None of them broke, but the strain flattened and scored small sections of the Kevlar lines where they rubbed back and forth in the chocks and around the bitts tying them to the ship.

The wave of dynamic energy that had not reflected downward spread outward as an immense pressure wave that impacted the side of the ship. The force punched through the half-inch steel hull and continued to expand inward. In less than three milliseconds, the blast wave surged through the engine room at its widest point, a sixty-foot-wide section in the middle of *Cole*. Instantly, main engine room 1, the galley, general workshop, mess line, chief petty officers' mess, and the port side passageway were transformed into unrecognizable and misshapen spaces of bent and jagged metal.

In moments, the general workshop disappeared. Energy from the blast pressure wave was transferred to sheet metal, a desk and computer, welding equipment, and steel storage racks as everything was blown through the air toward the quickly buckling bulkheads, which had separated the workshop from main engine room 1. A five-ton metal lathe for milling replacement parts sheared off its foundations and flew across the ship onto the starboard upper level of the engine room. Simultaneously, the pressure wave of expanding gases folded the steel walls up like wadded paper, leaving the engine room exposed to the brutal force of the explosion.

As the blast pressure wave crushed into the ship, the machinery in its path—the reverse osmosis water filters, local operating console and gas turbine modules for the 1A and 1B gas turbine engines, the number 1 high-pressure air compressor, and the starboard reduction gear that converts rapidly spinning gas turbine revolutions into turns of the propeller shaft—were all either sheared off their bases or twisted and crushed into almost unrecognizable, misshapen chunks of metal. A six-foot-long, four-inch section of pipe ripped away and became a deadly missile. Flying across the space and accelerated by the gases, it pierced the three-inch-thick reduction gear casing, stuck out for just a moment, then bent over to lie awkwardly twisted over on the top of the gear.

Outside, the ten-degree outward flare of the hull caused the blast pressure wave to radiate away from the ship for a split second before curling back over the top of the ship, causing overpressure damage to the superstructure and fittings topside. Each piece of equipment with a fiberglass dome or covering was damaged, including antennas for the AN/SLQ-32 Electronic Warfare set, the International Maritime Satellite dish, and the dome covering the forward MK-15 close-in weapons system (CIWS) antenna. The force of the blast pressure wave snapped an ultra-high frequency antenna off its mount and sent it arcing through the air to land with a metallic thud on the refueling pier.

By the time the explosion had run its course, main engine room 1 was destroyed and flooded. The galley directly above it was ripped into shreds and unrecognizable as floodwaters rushed into auxiliary machinery room 1, the supply office, and the reefer decks containing the refrigerator, freezer, and dry provisions storeroom. In auxiliary machinery room 1, water and fuel leaked through cracks in the bulkhead, while back aft, main engine room 2 was slowly flooding with an oily water and fuel mixture leaking from additional cracks in the bulkhead, as well as around the shaft seal for the starboard shaft, which had been damaged by the flexing of the ship.

Could the ship stay afloat with so much damage? That would depend on the crew and on me. Somehow, I had to save my ship and my crew.

After talking with the Yemeni port authorities, I knew I needed to get to the central control station, where damage control efforts should be well underway. Stepping off the bridge, my footsteps echoed loudly off the walls as, minutes after the explosion, I descended the "ladder," the stairs on the starboard side to the passageway to my stateroom two decks below. The only lighting came from battery-powered emergency "battle lanterns." My cabin was completely dark, but I ducked in and grabbed a Maglite flashlight from the top drawer of my desk. Then I went down two decks more to get to the control station.

Smoke and dust still hung in the stale, hot air. Looking aft through the starboard passageway that ran the entire length of the ship, I could see that normal lighting was working in the back third of the ship, from past the mess decks all the way back to the stern. Electricity was still available to the pumps in the engineering plant, which meant that the damage control teams should be able to control the inflow of seawater from the huge hole in our side.

I passed one of the damage control team members, Boatswain's Mate Second Class Martin Songer, who was surveying compartment after compartment and reporting what he found to the repair stations. He told me that repair teams were busy throughout the ship, and confirmed what I had seen from the main deck outside: the heaviest damage was in the area of main engine room 1. He quietly turned and went down the ladder toward auxiliary machinery room 1, the engineering compartment just forward of that engine room, to survey the damage with Machinery Repairman Second Class Rick Harrison, who was already in the space.

The farther back I went, the more sickened I was by what I saw. The thick bulkhead that formed the wall of the starboard side passageway bulged out of place. A little farther on, at the intersection of the passageway and the way to the mess line, the walls of Repair 5, one of the three main repair stations and the only one specifically outfitted with the material we needed to cope with damage to the engine room, had warped, its door jammed shut by the blast. To the left of the bent door and entrance, what was left of the mess line—the cafeteria counter where crew members were served their meals—appeared to be nothing more than a tangled and crushed mass of twisted metal. Along the mess line and in front of Repair 5, pools of blood collected on the deck. It was an absolutely heart-rending sight.

I continued aft in the starboard passageway and through the open watertight door. From the darkened passageway, I opened the door to the ship's main medical treatment area. Inside, it too was completely dark, without lights or power. That meant the ship had no ability to treat wounded except for two small battle dressing stations near the remaining

two repair lockers, Repair 2 up forward and Repair 3 under the flight deck
and the fantail at the back of the ship. The back doors of the treatment
area opened onto the mess decks and here, the area designated for mass
triage—part of the mess decks, where the tables could also be used to examine and treat wounded sailors—was itself a battle casualty. In the darkness, my flashlight played across glints of broken glass, shattered plates,
cracked serving trays, and knives, forks, and silvery spoons scattered in
front of me. Food was everywhere. I walked carefully through the debris
over to the port side passageway. The watertight doorframe just forward
of the mess line was twisted, the door hanging at an awkward angle.

Just beyond the door was total devastation: the heavy metal deck, the
floor of the mess line, where sailors had been sliding trays and getting servings of chicken fajita, had curled upward at about a sixty-degree angle,
jamming into the overhead. I went back into the mess decks and sought
another entrance from which I could step up into the mess line and the
area that used to be the galley.

Halfway across the forward bulkhead of the mess decks was a small,
unblocked passageway that contained the entrance down into the flooded
supply office and auxiliary machinery room 2. Stepping through, I found
myself standing at the edge of the blast hole itself. Sunlight came through
the gaping hole in the side, and outside I could see the harbor water and
floating pieces of debris. A jagged mass of metal, which must have been
the steam tables and other fixtures, had crushed against Master Chief Parlier's office next to the galley entrance and was jammed up against the
bulkheads that formed the wall of Repair 5, almost sixty feet across the ship
from the source of the explosion. From where I was standing, there was
no way I could get in.

What had been the galley, the kitchen, was no longer recognizable,
and the deck—the floor right above main engine room 1 and the general
workshop—had violently fractured into four sections. One piece had been
the one I had seen jutting up and cutting off the port side passageway.
While I did not yet know it, this piece had also severed the eight-inch fire
main that encircled the ship. A second shard of the deck had ripped forward

and slammed into the chief petty officers' mess, killing and injuring or trapping inside about two-thirds of my chief petty officers, the leading enlisted men on the ship, until rescue teams could succeed in cutting them out. A third piece of the deck had scooped up the galley equipment—ovens, griddles, sinks, and food preparation areas—and shoved everything violently toward the starboard side.

The fourth piece had peeled up and slammed back toward the forward bulkhead of the mess decks. That had crushed the stainless-steel serving line, where sailors were sliding trays and getting servings of chicken fajita for early lunch, and jammed the metal upward into the overhead. Now, in the devastation, I could smell an overpowering odor of fuel coming from what was left of the engine room, immediately below. Thousands of gallons of fuel had continued pumping into the ship at 2,000 gallons per minute for at least five to seven minutes after the attack, and it was now freely flowing into the gaping area left by the explosion and out into the harbor. And I could hear, down in the blast hole, in the middle of the thousands of gallons of fuel, the popping and crackling of live electrical wires. Great, I thought. Not only have we suffered a devastating explosion, now the ship could have a major fire on its hands. I had to get to CCS, and fast.

I turned back to the mess decks and walked by the scullery, and then back into the starboard passageway, where two sailors stood staring down at the deck. Between us lay the bloody and shattered remains of Signalman Seaman Cherone Gunn. Gunn was an eager and hardworking sailor with a sharp intellect who loved being in the fresh air and near the bridge when underway. When his time for a three-month rotation as a food service attendant came up, his professional demeanor and easy smile landed him in the wardroom, where the officers took their meals. He was well liked and clearly enjoyed the ability to exercise discretion with the sometimes unrestrained banter among the officers. Now he was lying there, the blue tablecloth haphazardly tossed over him only partially covering his body.

I snapped the fingers of my right hand at head level to grab his two shipmates' attention and, pointing with two fingers at my eyes to get them to look at me, told them, "Hey guys, focus. There is nothing we can do for him. I'm sorry, but he's dead." They shook off the daze they had been in and looked directly at me. I asked them where their emergency (general quarters) stations were, and both named them and started hurrying off. "Whoa, whoa, whoa," I told the second sailor. "Before you go to your general quarters station, I need you to do something for me. Go down to one of the aft berthing compartments and get a couple of blankets. Bring them back up here and let's get our shipmate covered and moved out of the passageway. Can you do that for me?" Calmly, he answered, "Yes sir, I can," and left.

As the sailor walked away to find blankets, the impact of that earlier decision to have the security teams push the crew back inside the skin of the ship because of the unknown security situation topside lay spread before me on the deck. Wounded crew members were haphazardly spread in random order on the deck as far as I could see. Some of the wounded were in the engineering office just off the passageway, and even more were scattered along the aft-most passageway that ran across the back of the ship.

Injuries were typical for an explosion of this magnitude: broken bones, shrapnel, cuts, scrapes, bruises, shock. The crew feverishly sought to stabilize and calm their wounded shipmates. Fortunately, there was no sense of panic, no uncontrolled fear. The crew before me so far had been amazingly calm and efficient as they moved along the passageway, doing what needed to be done to save their ship and shipmates. Even here among the wounded, I heard no raised voices.

I would have given anything to stop and look after every one of the wounded sailors I came across. But I could not. None of them could be saved unless the ship itself was saved. That had to be my number one priority.

As the executive officer, and not knowing my status, Chris got to CCS before I did. Communication with the crew was critical in these first few minutes. He picked up the microphone to make an announcement on the 1MC public address system, but it did not work. The back-up system was down as well. One by one, he attempted every method possible to try to communicate with the crew and the repair lockers. Nothing worked. Every circuit seemed to have been damaged or destroyed by the explosion.

By now people who had organized into small damage control parties were beginning to survey the damage. One by one, each group would come back into the engineering control station to report that USS *Cole* had a massive hole on the port side. The most telling description was when some said that it looked like a giant had taken his fist and punched through the ship. No one had ever seen this much damage to a ship before. For many it was almost incomprehensible.

A wave of debris had been blown from one side of the ship to the other, almost coming out the opposite side. This created a great divide inside the ship, making the port side impassable. Initially, even portions of the starboard passageway on the other side seemed blocked, and in order to go forward of the damaged area, personnel had to go up to the main deck, cross it above the damage, and then go back down inside. As time progressed, Chris continued to have a lot of trouble communicating to the crew members that were on the other side of this damage.

When I reached the central control station, I found Engineer Officer Debbie Courtney and her engineers to my left, reviewing the status of the only operating gas turbine generator, number 3. They were discussing the kilowatt power load on the generator, the number and types of pumps still running, and what other equipment they needed to get back online and operating in order to save the ship. The flat screen plasma displays and indication panels that normally showed the status of the alarms throughout the ship were just continuously scrolling data and no one could make any sense of the readouts.

To my right, the damage control assistant, Sean Dubbs, a brand new ensign who had finished specialized training a few weeks earlier and had been flown out to the ship while we were operating in the Adriatic less than two weeks before the explosion, was calmly plotting the damage control status reports. That team, working under Chris, was taking in information, analyzing what they knew against what needed to be done, and making decisions that could well determine whether we stayed afloat or sank at the refueling pier.

It was at this point that I made what I consider to be the smartest decision of my command tour: I kept my mouth shut. I didn't know enough at this point about what was going on or had been done to walk in and take charge.

Standing there in CCS watching the messengers delivering vital information to each of the two teams at work, I watched as Chris and Debbie continued to develop a better picture of the status of the ship. After silently watching what was going on for about thirty to forty-five seconds, I finally said, "Engineer, XO, when you two are ready, tell me what we've got." Seconds later, both were standing in front of me.

Chris then updated me on the damage to the ship as messengers from the repair lockers continued to report it. He reported that they had initially been unable to establish normal communications via the ship's internal voice communications system (IVCS). Falling back on the standard for shipboard communications since World War II, they had gone to the secondary system of sound-powered phones. This phone system requires only the power of a sailor's voice to vibrate a diaphragm, which transmits those vibrations through a drive rod to an armature centered in a wire coil, creating an electric current that is transmitted to a receiver, where the process is reversed and the voice can be heard. Even though this system is extremely reliable, they were only able to communicate with Repair 3; apparently the sound-powered phone system to Repair 2 was not working.

In an attempt to overcome this obstacle, Chris had ordered emergency communications wires, also known as salt and pepper lines, to be strung from the central control station to Repair 2. A team had been busy doing this when I walked in. Within a few minutes of my arrival, however, sound-powered communications were established and maintained with both repair lockers. While standing there taking reports, messengers from the repair lockers ran in and out of CCS with messages. Even with communications established, the most reliable form of communication, a sailor from a repair locker would be used for the near term to guarantee the flow of information.

The battery backup system—the alarm systems for the ship to sound general quarters and other emergencies—which was tied to the 1MC system, even the alarm indicator systems that could have shown the engineers in the command center where the ship might be experiencing flooding, fire, or smoke—all had failed. Without these systems, the crew did not have the benefit of anyone or anything to tell them what to do or what had happened to the ship. But they did not let that stop them from doing what they could see obviously had to be done.

In the immediate aftermath of the explosion the engineers had determined that none of the alarms could be relied on to provide accurate data, and they quickly came to ignore them. Every few seconds as I stood there, alarm indicator lights would start flashing and their associated aural annunciators would start ringing from random signals in the system. Each time, someone would reach out and immediately press a button to acknowledge and silence them without even bothering to determine their origin or cause. It was controlled pandemonium as everyone was trying to figure out what happened.

Debbie briefed me on the status of the engineering plant, including the generator and what pumps were online. Next she told me about the lack of firemain pressure, which would make it impossible to fight a serious fire if one broke out. Everyone in the central control station was on edge knowing that thousands of gallons of fuel had leaked into the area beneath the smashed galley and into the destroyed main engine room 1. If those areas could not be quickly and completely electrically isolated and the fuel flashed to a major conflagration, the ship would have almost no chance of staying afloat. She also reported that one of the two still functioning gas turbine electricity generators had shut down, for unknown reasons, and that power was out in the forward two-thirds of the ship. Chris confirmed that main engine room 1, the general workshop, and the fuel lab, which controlled the flow of fuel into the tanks during refueling, had all been destroyed and flooded. Two members of the crew who had been working in the lab with "Drew" Triplett at the time of the explosion, Gas Turbine Systems Technician-Electrical Second Class Robert McTureous and Gas Turbine Systems Technician-Mechanical First Class Kathy Lopez, had survived the blast, though severely injured, and had escaped by swimming out of the hole in the side of the ship into the harbor, where shipmates fished them out to safety. Triplett was still missing.

I already knew the galley had been destroyed, and now learned that water pouring into the ship had flooded auxiliary machinery room 2 just aft of main engine room 1, the supply office and supply support, as well as the reefer deck, where all the ship's canned and packaged food was stored. The refrigeration machinery and the computers that tracked maintenance records and personnel watch qualifications had also been inundated. Water was also seeping into main engine room 2, the largest single space on the ship, with the gas turbine engines that powered the port propeller shaft and other vital equipment. All around the starboard shaft where it passed through the bulkhead separating this engine room from auxiliary machinery room 2 and the flooded spaces forward, water was spraying in at high pressure.

The situation was dire. Debbie looked up and even though she knew the answer, asked: "Captain, are we going to lose the ship?" The engineers heard the question, stopped what they were doing, and listened.

"No, we are not going to sink," I said after only a brief pause. "If those are the only spaces we've lost, we are not going to sink." On *Arleigh Burke*–class destroyers like this one, it was possible to sustain flooding damage to all four of the main engineering spaces and remain afloat, if just barely. *Cole* had as yet lost only two of these spaces to flooding. "Let's get the flooding and shoring teams down there," I ordered, and the mood immediately changed. The sense of relief was almost palpable.

But bad news kept coming in. The repair lockers were reporting no firefighting water pressure, and Debbie and her engineers had shut down the pumps that pressurized the system. The ship would be in grave danger if fire broke out. Chris and Debbie were both aware of the live-wire problem in the ruined engine room and the galley, now full of water and fuel, and Chris had ordered aqueous film-forming foam liquid poured in to try to prevent ignition. Teams of sailors had dragged blue five-gallon jugs of it to the galley area and were pouring it down into the blast hole. Soon the repair locker teams were able to isolate and bypass the part of the firemain that had been severed. The fire pumps were restarted and, with the pressure successfully raised to the required 150-psi mark, damage control teams began spraying fire-fighting foam around the entire area damaged by the explosion. The imminent danger, it seemed, was past. The rescue and triage of wounded crew members and their treatment in hospitals was the next priority.

6 | Saving the Wounded

I LEFT THE CENTRAL CONTROL STATION knowing that the damage control effort was well in hand. Altogether, it was clear that the men and women of USS *Cole* were doing a noble and heroic job of saving their ship and their shipmates, one that would go down in the annals as one of the most distinguished such performances in the history of the Navy.

I stepped gingerly between the wounded lying on the deck, who were still being attended to by their shipmates. Walking forward again toward the mess decks, I found that the sailor who had been killed outright by the blast hitting the mess decks still lay in the passageway. He had been covered in a blanket and moved to the side. I paused for just a moment to consider the daunting hours ahead of us and then moved on.

Crossing through the dark mess decks, I reentered the small vestibule at the forward end that led to the mangled area of the mess line. Instead of going through, however, I went up the ladder to the watertight door that opened back onto the open area at the middle of the ship. The carnage of the injuries seen so far in the crew hardened my resolve to save them. No matter what my feelings were inside, now was the time to dip into that inner reserve of strength and be strong for their sake. As their captain it was my duty and obligation not to let them down.

For many of the crew, the blast and its immediate aftereffects had seemed like an eternity packed into a few short seconds. After the odd twisting and flexing of the ship slowed and *Cole* settled back into the water next to the pier, there was a deafening silence, followed by the thump of boots running through the passageways. Inside the galley, where so many had been getting early lunch when the blast came, it was almost pitch dark with thick, acrid smoke. Seconds later the screams and moans of the wounded echoed off the bulkheads.

Hospital Corpsman Third Class Tayinikia Campbell had just finished listening to the XO announce a few minutes before that the ship would finish up refueling early and get underway in about two hours. Standing in the medical treatment room, she was listening to the CD player as an RJ Kelly song thumped in the background. There with her was a young deck seaman, Eben Sanchez-Zuniga, who had just transferred into the Medical Division to learn the hospital corpsman profession. Suddenly the whole ship shook violently beneath them, the lights went out, and the CD player went dead. Campbell was thrown backward as the doors to medical flew open with an ear-splitting bang and smoke poured in. She and Sanchez looked at each other and instantly headed off to their emergency stations.

Petty Officer Campbell had taken only a few steps before she began to hear the voices calling, "I need a doc, I need a doc!" She turned and faced the devastation of the mess line and the smoke-filled confusion of the starboard passageway and hollered, "I'm right here!" She asked another sailor to take her keys to the aft battle dressing station where she had been headed and unlock it, but right now she needed to help the wounded at her feet. As she worked in the cramped space of the passageway, the wounded just seemed to keep coming from the area of the mess line, from inside the mess decks, and soon from inside the chiefs' mess. At one point, she remembered hearing herself ask out loud, "Where is my Chief? Where is Doc?" A hand touched her shoulder and she looked up to see Lieutenant Mikal Phillips, *Cole*'s gunnery officer, who had heard her question. "It's all on you, kiddo," he said quietly. They expected the worst, but unknown to either of them, "Doc," Hospital Corpsman Chief Clifford Moser, the ship's senior medical corpsman, had survived, but was working on other wounded sailors topside, in the center of the ship between the stacks.

Master Chief Parlier was also a medical corpsman, but as the senior non-commissioned officer on board, his duties as command master chief lay elsewhere, with helping Chris and me run the ship. Now, in the middle of a medical crisis, his skills once again turned toward saving lives. Just after the explosion, he had made his way from the back of the ship to as far as the barbershop when he saw Chief Mark Darwin, a gas turbine systems technician, lying on the deck with extensive injuries to his left side. Darwin had just finished eating lunch in the chiefs' mess when the blast picked him up and threw him through the air, knocking him briefly unconscious. When he came to, he heard groans and moans around him but could see nothing. The mess was completely dark, thick with acrid smoke and it was sealed shut by the wreckage. He was bleeding from his wrist and his left arm and shoulder did not seem to work. Taking a rag out of his coverall pocket, he tied it as best he could to stem the flow of blood. When it became possible, he crawled out into what had been the galley, over what felt to him like the bodies of dead or wounded sailors, until he was picked up and carried to the area near the back of the ship by the barbershop and Repair 3. Master Chief Parlier determined that Chief Darwin had broken bones in his left shoulder, broken left ribs with a possible punctured lung, and unknown internal injuries in his abdomen, besides the deep cut on his left wrist.

Someone hollered down at Parlier that there were more wounded in the starboard passageway near the back of the ship. He dashed up the stairs to the engineering office, where the most seriously injured were temporarily staged, and found lying on the deck in front of him the most seriously wounded sailor he had yet seen—Seaman Craig Wibberley. Wibberley had been standing in the mess line at the time of the explosion. In its aftermath he had severe injuries on his right side, and what Parlier judged to be life-threatening head trauma. His breathing was labored. Master Chief immediately ordered several other sailors nearby to help get Wibberley loaded into a litter for evacuation out to the flight deck. By this time, the urgency of getting the wounded attended to had overridden my initial concerns about topside security, and by the time they got Wibberley's litter out into the heat of the day, Master Chief was taken aback to see at least a dozen wounded crew members lying on the flight deck, being worked on by other crew members. "Airway, breathing, circulation!" he hollered out to them. "That's the most important. Monitor them, and if you need me to look at them, let me know." Master Chief began trying to treat Wibberley, assisted by Fire Controlman Chief Jonathan Walker. Parlier put his ear on Wibberley's chest and could hear that both lungs were rapidly filling with fluid. As the pulse began to weaken, Master Chief started cardiopulmonary resuscitation (CPR), but Wibberley's life signs were fading away. In the background, there were screams and moans, and other crew members crying out, "Corpsman!"

In Parlier's mind's eye, a memory flashed by as he recalled Wibberley only recently standing before the ship's Professional Development Board. While assigned to Deck Division, he had taken his time in deciding what career path he wanted to take in the Navy. After months of thinking about it, Wibberley submitted a request chit to start training to become an information technology specialist. As he stood before the board, he knew he faced an uphill battle to leave Deck Division. Billets for undesignated deck seamen like him had been undermanned by almost 30 percent since the beginning of our deployment, because of Navy-wide manpower shortages. At the end of the board's deliberations, however, he was unexpectedly rewarded with a compromise: as long as he could keep up on his work and watch assignments in Deck Department, he could start training with the information technology (IT) personnel in preparation for attending an advanced training school. In a flash, Master Chief Parlier remembered his smile and unending gratitude to the board members as he left the chiefs' mess that day. Now, all those hopes and ambitions were fading away as Wibberley struggled to breathe his last.

Finally, Chief Walker quietly spoke up. "James, you need to stop," he told the Master Chief. "You've got to look around."

Almost two dozen wounded needed his lifesaving skills. Now, for the first time in his life, Master Chief found himself before the most difficult of all decisions. By this point Wibberley had stopped breathing. Master Chief lifted his hands, sighed, said a short prayer over Craig Wibberley's body, and the decision was made.

Steeling himself to deal with the rest of the wounded, he turned to attend to the next most seriously wounded sailor, Electronic Warfare Technician Third Class Johann Gokool, who was screaming with excruciating pain. Gokool had been standing in the mess line near the point where the deck was violently ripped apart and was blown back along the passageway toward the starboard side of the ship. The force of the impact had had a brutal effect on his lower legs and feet. His boots were literally blown open and both feet were visible through gaps in the shredded seams. They appeared to be mangled beyond recovery and blood seeped out onto the deck between them. The sailors attending to him were preparing to cut off his boot, but Master Chief told them to stop and wrap bandages around the entire extremity. It was better to keep the injury contained than try to deal with it on the ship. Within minutes, Gokool's feet were wrapped and he was gently taken up the ladder to be staged in the amidships area for evacuation.

Master Chief then spotted a sailor leaning up against the bulkhead in a forward corner of the flight deck. Working over Operations Specialist Second Class Timothy Saunders was Seaman Sanchez-Zuniga, the corpsman trainee who had been with Campbell when the explosion hit. Saunders had a severe cut or gouge in the back of his left upper leg. Sanchez-Zuniga had already inspected the wound and wrapped it tightly to stem the bleeding. But even before Master Chief bent down to give Saunders a more thorough examination, he could tell that despite the apparently superficial wounds, his condition was grave. He was likely suffering internal injuries that they simply could not treat amidst this pandemonium. Saunders murmured, "Man, I don't feel good, Master Chief. I don't feel good." Master Chief just looked directly at him, "We're going to take care of you. Sanchez has done a great job. He's going to reinforce that dressing, we're not going to take it off, and we're going to get you out of here."

It was harder than the Master Chief had ever imagined it would be. But with every step he took, he was saving lives.

Standing in the mess line at the moment of the blast, Signalman Second Class Hector Figueroa had just placed his right hand on the Plexiglas menu board just outside Master Chief Parlier's office when he was stunned by the loudest noise he had ever heard in his life and felt a tremendous force pressing his eyeglasses into his face, and searing heat. He and the people around him were thrown through the air and slammed hard into the starboard passageway wall. "The kitchen must have blown up," Figueroa thought.

Staggering back upright, Figueroa ran toward the galley. He could see a body lying on the deck, staring lifelessly back at him. Behind the debris was another sailor, pinned under what looked like the remnants of the ship's oven, her left leg bent out at an impossible angle. "I can't do this by myself," Figueroa thought, and yelled out, "Wounded in the galley!" to get others to help. He heard a cry from somewhere lower down and, peering through the scuttle opening of the hatch that led to the ladder and the refrigerators one deck below, saw Mess Specialist Third Class Joseph Davis, standing unsteadily near the entrance. "My leg is broken," Davis said, and Figueroa saw that water was slowly flooding the space where he was. He slid through the scuttle hole, went down the stairway, and leaned over to wrap his arm around Davis's shoulders and try to pull him up toward safety.

Another sailor came up to Figueroa and told him Storekeeper Second Class Sean Taitt was trapped down in the supply office, a deck lower than the already flooding refrigeration deck. "Got him," Figueroa answered, and wriggled through the scuttle hole again and went down until he saw Taitt, a solid, muscular man who was one of the best weightlifters and workout hounds on the ship, standing unsteadily near the door to the supply office. "Shock, he must be in shock," Figueroa thought to himself. Water, now thigh deep, churned around their legs. He grabbed Taitt and then began lifting, dragging, and pushing him up two sets of stairs to the scuttle hole, where Figueroa was relieved to see Personnelman Third Class Nicole "Nikki" Lozano's face looking down. She offered to help, and together they worked Taitt up through the hole and out onto the mess decks to be treated for his injuries.

Fire Controlman Third Class Dyon Foster, who had rushed toward the source of the explosion to get to his emergency station, heard the cries for help and came to the galley. He looked at the mass of tangled equipment and saw two or three bodies in the wreckage, but there was no way to get to them from where he stood. He and another sailor, Gunner's Mate Third Class Kenya McCarter, saw that Hull Technician Fireman Jeremy Stewart, who had been working in the galley as a food service attendant, was alive but trapped in the wreckage of the steam tables. Stewart's right forearm was bent at a ninety-degree angle and he was in severe pain. With his left arm, he could reach down to his lower leg and feel metal pinning him to the deck. Stewart sensed movement next to his head and saw that Mess Specialist Seaman Elizabeth Lafontaine, who had been working in the galley with him, was regaining consciousness, but was in great pain. He tried to lift the metal off his legs but found it would not budge, and then felt his legs and realized they were both broken at mid-shin. Bones were sticking out from his lower left leg and his right leg felt like mush.

Foster and McCarter, joined now by Operations Specialist Second Class Jaja O'Neil, climbed over the metal and saw that they would need to get Stewart out first before they could extricate Lafontaine. Grabbing him by the upper arms and the belt loops on his pants, O'Neil got ready to pull. "This is going to hurt," Stewart heard, and answered, "I don't care, just get me out of this galley." Straining to lift the twisted metal off Stewart's legs, they succeeded in pulling him out and got him to a triage station, where Hull Technician Second Class Christopher Regal saw him. "Chris, you've got to save the ship," Stewart told him. Staring down at him in disbelief, all Regal could whisper in response was "Jesus Christ," when he saw how badly injured Stewart was.

Lafontaine, who had only recently reported to *Cole*, had just walked by the huge convection ovens near the middle of the galley when the blast went off. The deck beneath her feet buckled and tore to pieces, smacking her into the air and brutally tossing her sideways, almost horizontally. The oven sheared off at the base from its mountings, and pinned her beneath a mass of other debris. Lieutenant (junior grade) Jim Salter, who had made his way to the galley a few minutes after leaving me just after the blast, saw Storekeeper Senior Chief Joseph Pelly and Petty Officer Dyon Foster trying to free her and bent down to see what he could do to help. He could not immediately make sense of what he could see of her legs.

Lafontaine was on the deck with her back to the wall but pushed down by the debris on top of her and all around her. She faced the hole in the side of the ship, but her torso had been twisted slightly to the left by the displaced oven and other debris, near the smashed and buckled galley door. Her left leg was bent backwards and behind her at the femur, and the lower part of her leg was snapped and bent upward, with the bottom of her foot facing towards the ceiling. Her right leg, visible beneath the oven, was clearly broken in more than one place, and the lower part was crushed and bent at an odd angle.

As Salter peered into the darkened recesses of the galley, he saw the lifeless body of another sailor, Seaman Lakiba Palmer, folded over and leaning up against the far wall and covered by debris. Salter knew that time was not on the side of the rescuers.

Pelly and Foster, working feverishly to try to free Lafontaine, could not pry the metal off her legs. Foster was holding an oxygen mask a few inches from Lafontaine's face to keep her breathing. Jim Salter jumped into the middle of the effort. Each of the three grabbed pieces of metal to try to shove, bend, and pry them back. Lafontaine was in tremendous pain. Even the slightest movement caused her to cry out or scream every time the metal debris around her body moved even slightly. Jim, kneeling in front of her, kept calmly telling her to just hang on, they would get her out in only a few more minutes. When it looked to the three as if they had freed her enough to pull her out, Jim leaned in over her body, putting his chest in front of hers and told her, "Honey, I know this is going to hurt like hell, but grab onto my neck and hold tight when I lift you." The three rescuers looked at each other, and Foster and Pelly lifted and pushed upward on the debris. Lifting the debris just enough, in one smooth motion, Jim slid her sideways and upward. As her left leg straightened out, hit the deck, and slid grotesquely underneath him; she let out a series of blood-curdling screams. He reached beneath her shattered legs and cradled them as he

walked through the vestibule into the mess decks to lay her gently down
on a clear table near the rear entrance.

How Jim Salter came to be part of the rescue effort in the wreckage
of the galley speaks volumes. After blurting out to me his blunt reaction
that fuel had caused the explosion, he had hurried down the passageway
and then smelled the acrid stench of something like cordite, like the smoke
after artillery shells have been fired. His instincts and his training then
kicked in, and led him to help shipmates, too. Salter's mind absorbed but
did not understand why no alarms were going off on the ship to send the
crew to their general quarters stations. He also had an odd sensation that
no 1MC announcements had been made to tell the crew what had happened or what to do next. While he knew getting to the fuel lab might be
important, he also knew he had a more critical obligation to get to his
general quarters station.

Turning toward the forward part of the ship and proceeding that way,
up a port side passageway, Salter had passed the ship's administrative office,
rounded the corner, and entered combat system maintenance central
(CSMC). Light from the one or two battle lanterns cast hazy beams that
stared down at the deck to illuminate an otherwise dark space. There was
no power and only a couple of technicians had shown up, responding like
him to their battle stations.

Salter's primary technical expert on *Cole's* combat system and fellow
general quarters responder, Fire Controlman Master Chief John Henderson,
still had not arrived on station. The internal phone system for the ship did
not work and no one was communicating on any of the sound powered
phone circuits. After waiting just a few minutes, Salter announced that he
was going to go out into the ship and see what he could do to help. He also
told the other sailors who had arrived in the space that there was nothing
they could do there. He ordered them to leave and go see if anyone needed
their help at any of the repair lockers. Clearly, there was nothing more
they could do up there in the dark.

As he walked out of CSMC, Salter paused for just a second to once
again sniff the air. Something was just not right about that smell. Directly
in front of him was a ladder that went down one deck and stopped directly

in front of Repair 2. Looking down the ladder as he descended, he could see the Repair 2 team already getting equipment out of the locker as crew members decided to go out and investigate damage around the ship. The Repair 2 locker officer, Ensign Greg McDearmon, had not arrived, so Jim, with years of experience and shipboard training, stepped into his role of repair locker officer. Already, word had reached the locker that the chiefs mess was heavily damaged by the blast. A team from the repair locker was needed to break into the space and rescue many of the wounded chiefs. Salter quickly assessed who was getting equipped to go out as damage control investigators, who would form the team to rescue the chiefs, and who would remain behind at the locker to help coordinate any responses to damage that might be found.

In the middle of this action, word now came to them that there was a huge hole in the port side of the ship. That would explain the sideways list that everyone could feel worsening as they rushed about the locker. Seconds later, Greg arrived and Jim briefed him on the status of the investigators who were out checking for damage and a laundry list of what else needed to be done. Just as quickly as he had taken over, he was now free to examine what had happened to the ship.

Rather than walk out of the repair locker into a darkened ship, Jim instead left through the emergency escape scuttle in the overhead of the repair locker, which opened onto the forecastle just behind the forward vertical launching system magazine. He wanted to know more about this "hole" in the port side that had been reported to him and what the situation was topside.

As he crawled out of the scuttle into the bright sun, Denise Woodfin immediately confronted him. She was holding her right arm, which had been injured in the blast. Clearly, she was still dazed by the effects of the explosion. Not quite knowing what to do, she looked at Jim, "Hey, STO, I still have people down in the supply office and it's flooding."

Jim looked back at her as he decided what to do next, "I'll go down and see what I can do," he said, and with that, he turned and walked across the forecastle. Quickly he ducked through the forward door, down the starboard brake, and into the darkness of the ship. If there were sailors trapped below the waterline in flooding spaces, he knew what he had to do. As Salter walked down the starboard passageway toward Repair 5 and the mess line, it was still a whirlwind of triage and rescue efforts. The bulkhead around the door to the repair locker was oddly bowed out with the door jammed shut and denying access to the damage control teams. Turning down the mess line, he confronted the jumble of twisted and torn metal in front of him but nothing immediately registered in his mind.

He stopped and asked several sailors in the area if they knew about any crew members trapped in the supply office. Quickly Jim learned that the only people trapped down there, Petty Officers Davis and Taitt, had been rescued and were being attended to for their injuries. Instead, Salter heard a commotion coming from inside the galley and made his way down to the mess line, where he helped in the rescue of Seaman Lafontaine.

Of all the mess specialists and food service attendants who had been working in the galley to prepare the noon meal that day, Lafontaine and Stewart were the only survivors.

Petty Officer Campbell had been working to keep Stewart stabilized, urging him to stay focused and not close his eyes, when she learned that Chief Moser was working above decks, and knew she needed to tell him what was going on inside the ship. She walked up the ladder into the sunshine. As soon as he saw her, Chief Moser directed her to begin administering morphine to those in the worst pain, first among them Gas Turbine Technician Senior Chief Keith Lorenson. As the painkiller worked its way through his system and tense calm settled over Lorenson's face, Chief Moser continued triage, working on the most seriously wounded and prioritizing their injuries in the order they were to be evacuated from the ship.

It was now about half an hour after the explosion. Returning amidships from the central control station at that point, I walked up to Chief Moser and asked him: "Doc, what do you need from me?" His answer was, "Nothing right now, Captain, but we need to start getting them off the ship as soon as possible." I told him about my radio conversation with the Yemeni Port Authority and confirmed with Chief Larson that the rules of

engagement were now clear and that no one would shoot the Yemeni boats
that would be coming out to the ship to take wounded ashore. He said he
would guarantee it personally.

Master Chief Parlier had sent two critically wounded patients, Petty
Officer Timothy Saunders and Fireman Jeremy Stewart, to the amidships
triage area for priority evacuation. It was a setback to me to see, in the
third litter in that group, Senior Chief Lorenson. He was my most experienced gas turbine technician and the most senior enlisted man in the
Engineering Department. I had been counting on him as a mainstay in
helping us through this event.

Chief Lorenson had been sitting at a table in the chiefs' mess just forward of the entrance to main engine room 1 eating lunch, with the movie
Mission Impossible: 2 playing in the background, when smoke suddenly
filled the room with a sharp crack of glasses and coffee mugs shattering
on the deck, then complete silence. He found himself lying on the deck,
unable to move and covered by debris. He did not feel the blast or hear the
explosion, which trapped everybody there. A vision of a black-and-white
photo of his family that his wife, Lisa, had given him before *Cole* set sail
floated into his mind. In the minutes afterward, though he could not make
out shapes or see any of his fellow chiefs, he could hear shouts, moans,
and screams for help. Damage control personnel had arrived outside and
were swinging axes to chop a hole in the lightweight, honey-combed, com-
posite nomex wall in the port passageway to get personnel into the space
and begin to pull everybody out.

All Chief Lorenson could sense around him was that crew members
were moving around. He became aware of a foot near his head. Be careful,
he warned the rescuers, there were body parts in the area and they should
take care not to do more harm to those already wounded. He knew he
was bleeding from his right leg, and used his training to remove his belt
with one hand, slide it down to his inner thigh and wrap it tight around
his thigh to slow the bleeding. After some of his colleagues were pulled
out, he found himself in the dark alone, and feared he had been forgotten,
but the rescue personnel reentered the space and began trying to free him

as well. Mindful of the foot near his head, he told them to be careful of the person who was on top of him, because whoever it was had not moved since the explosion. This met with silence. When the rescuers finally started moving him onto a litter, he looked at his lower body and realized that the foot near his head was actually his own. He had suffered a compound fracture to his right femur and that leg had been wrenched violently up and across his body, with his foot resting on his left shoulder. He had as yet felt no pain, and when he told his rescuers to straighten out his leg, they were amazed at how calm he was.

Now he was lifting his head and motioning for me to come over to him. I walked over and knelt down, and he grasped my hand. "Captain, I don't think I am going to make it," he said in an unsteady voice. I saw that he was scared, afraid, but not panicked. "Senior Chief, I don't want to hear that. You are not going to die," I told him firmly. "I want you to think of Lisa and those two blond-headed kids of yours who want to see their Daddy again. You are going to be fine."

He looked back at me through the haze of the painkiller and said, "But Captain, I don't think you know how badly I've been hurt." I told him, "Senior, I know what happened. So, you have a badly broken leg; you're not even the first priority to leave the ship. You're going to be fine." But I was worried, not only for Lorenson but for his wife. Lisa Lorenson had become ombudsman for *Cole* just before I took command, filling one of the ship's most critical family-support functions. Ombudsmen keep the commanding officer informed about the general morale, health, and welfare of the ship's families by staying closely in touch with them and helping them deal with support agencies like the American Red Cross and the Navy-Marine Corps Relief Society. They circulate newsletters and maintain telephone trees for normal and emergency communications, and I had instantly taken a liking to Lisa and come to rely on her. But she was now going to be more concerned about her husband than about USS *Cole*.

As I started to get up, the Chief managed to say, "Hey Captain, thanks."

Now we needed to get him and the other seriously injured victims off the ship within the "golden hour," and we were already coming up on thirty minutes after the explosion. Designated for evacuation first was Petty Officer Timothy Saunders, whom Chief Moser had determined to have suffered internal injuries far more serious than the badly cut leg Seaman Sanchez-Zuniga had swathed in bandages. Now, morphine helped him cope with the pain, but he was lying in an evacuation litter on the deck and the heat of midday was debilitating, both for him and the rescue teams.

At this point, my navigation officer, Lieutenant Ann Chamberlain, who had come down from her general quarters station on the bridge, pointed out a problem. "Captain, we are evacuating all the sailors off the ship and sending them to hospitals ashore but we have no idea which hospital they are going to, what the diagnosis is on their injuries, or what they are doing to treat them. I recommend we send someone ashore to track them."

"Nav," I said, "that's a great idea. Who do you recommend?"

In a very matter-of-fact way she said, "Sir, I'll volunteer to go."

I was thrilled at her decision. Looking quickly toward the back of the ship to see the boatswain's mates still working on getting the brow into position to be lowered to the pier, I told her, "Great. As soon as the brow is down on the pier, I want you to be the first one off. Let us know how they're doing and if you need anything."

With a quick nod of her head she turned away, saying only, "OK, sir."

I was moved by the quality of leadership shown by this decision. She didn't ask, Where do I go, who will go with me, how do I get money if I need it, how do I get protection ashore? She took on the responsibility for figuring all that out and getting it done herself. And she knew that I trusted her to be able to do it.

When *Cole* arrived in Aden, we had not put a brow or gangplank down to the refueling pier. Aden was not a liberty port and no visitors were expected; there was no need for it, and because of the configuration of the refueling piping on the pier, a brow would have had to be positioned at the back of the ship, away from the quarterdeck watch, and would have required an armed guard on the refueling pier and another one on deck to verify the identities of people coming aboard. Now, looking for options, someone noticed a twelve-foot wooden extension ladder, like one you might use to paint the side of your house, lying on the pier. Crew members yelled down to the Yemeni fuel workers and motioned them to get the ladder, pull it out to its fullest length, and lean it out to the ship. A good boatswain's mate could rig this to get litters safely down to the pier, and an excellent one was standing near me, Boatswain's Mate First Class Randall Butte. Seeing what needed to be done, he soon had a team tying steadying lines to the top and bottom of the litter carrying the first injured sailor to be evacuated off the ship. With three sailors tending each of the two lines at the head of the litter and the Yemeni fuel workers tending the two lines tied at the foot, they lowered him, and quickly others as well, down to the pier, where the workers lifted them carefully to the boats that had begun to arrive at the back side of the refueling pier.

Soon the leading boatswain's mate, Boatswain's Mate Chief Eric Kafka, though injured himself, had managed to get one of the ship's heavy aluminum brows moved into position and lowered down to the pier so that all the injured could be led or carried quickly off the ship.

Derek Trinque had done his job well: *Cole*'s security teams, manning .50-caliber and 7.62 mm M-60 machine guns, closely tracked the boats as they came out to the pier, but knowing they were coming to take their wounded shipmates to be treated in hospitals, no one fired a shot in anger. Still, this didn't mean all was quiet either.

Suddenly the controlled pandemonium of the lifesaving efforts was loudly interrupted by two rapid-fire gunshots. I had been looking down at a wounded sailor in the middle of the triage area as a group restarted the resuscitation effort on him, and had just lifted my head to scan the shoreline. Everyone around me hit the deck thinking we had come under fire. Glancing quickly around, several sailors had thrown themselves on top of the wounded to protect them from further injury.

Standing there with my hands on my hips, I had mentally placed the shots coming from above me and to my left—the bridge wing. Spinning to look up there, Derek was already standing at the back edge with his hands in front of him yelling, "It's OK, Captain. We just had an accidental discharge, everything is OK." Looking back up at him, I just calmly hollered, "Are you sure?" "Yes, sir. Everything is fine, I've got it under control. Sorry," he yelled back down at me. By this point, everyone realized that the shots were ours and had already started to get back up and turn to the wounded once again. It was as if those two gunshots had barely broken our stride to save the wounded from their injuries.

At that point, I became aware of a struggle in the middle of the triage area, where three sailors were working feverishly giving chest compressions and mouth-to-mouth resuscitation to Electronics Technician Chief Richard D. Costelow, whom I remembered from his promotion to chief petty officer only three and a half weeks earlier, while we were in the Adriatic. We shared the same birthday, April 29. Despite their efforts, the team, working under Chief Moser, was losing the battle. The color had drained away from Chief Costelow's face, his fingers were ash gray, and his lips and fingernails were starting to turn blue.

Leaning over and placing a hand on his shoulder, I quietly told Chief Moser, "Chief, keep going as long as you feel you need to, but if the time comes, you have to make the call." "I think we'll be all right," he said, but a few minutes later, the team stopped working on Chief Costelow and slumped back, exhausted. He was now clearly dead. Chief Moser got up, his face twisted in anguish and anger, with tears streaming down his face. I turned to speak to him but as I did so, he turned away and tried to go back to work on the lifeless body. I reached out to try to comfort him, but he resisted me. Firmly, I reached out, grabbed his upper arms and looked into his tear-filled eyes. "Chief, we have a lot of sailors here who still need you to save their life. I need you to pull yourself together for their sake. Can you do it?"

He took a deep breath, looked at me, and with a cracking voice said, "Yes, I can, Captain. Just give me a minute," and walked toward the port side to compose himself. As he did, I turned back to the sailors who had tried so hard to save Chief Costelow and said, "I'm sorry you couldn't save him. You did the best you could. Let's get him moved over there and get him covered up. We'll take care of him later, but we need to keep going with saving these other guys first." They got up and gently moved him out of the way, covering him with a gray wool blanket.

Chief Moser was back in the middle of the triage area directing life-saving efforts within a minute. It must have been the most difficult decision of his medical career, but he was poised and in control, and I knew his professionalism would see him through and enable him to save other lives.

Without even a pause in the triage and damage control action, Chief Electrician's Mate James Newton came up to me with a couple of other engineering petty officers. He was a plankowner, or one of the ship's original crew members, when it was commissioned on June 8, 1996, and had served on board since then. Like Chief Costelow, he had been promoted to chief petty officer only three and a half weeks earlier. Since the leading chief for his division, Electrician's Mate Chief Fred Strozier, was seriously wounded and staged for evacuation off the ship, Chief Newton was now in charge, and presented me with a dilemma.

USS *Cole*'s information systems technicians, who operated the ship's radios and associated equipment, knew that we had to get a radio operating in order to communicate with higher authority. Since radio central and its associated power panel were in the forward part of the ship without power, they had approached the engineers in the central control station with an idea. If they could run the emergency casualty power cables from a part of the ship that had power up to the panel for radio central, in the forward area of the ship, they should be able to establish communications using the installed radio equipment.

Chief Newton, standing on the deck by the triage area asked me, "Captain, I would like permission to run the casualty power cables from back aft to radio central. It's the only way we can get power to the forward part of the ship until we know what's been damaged."

"Chief, do it. Make sure you follow EOSS and safety procedures," I replied.

The Navy developed EOSS, the engineering operating and sequencing system, to provide watch standers with technically correct, logically sequenced procedures, charts, and diagrams tailored to each ship's specific configuration. It dictates the process to be followed to complete major and most minor plant status changes with minimal risk of damage to equipment or injury to personnel.

He then looked at me with a concerned expression and told me, "Captain, we've never done this before."

At first, I was almost irritated at this statement. In my mind, I knew that of all the engineering drills and exercises *Cole's* crew had completed in the fifteen months since I had taken command, we had not made time to actually rig casualty power cables to test this vital damage control capability. In an odd way I was thinking to myself, Why is this new chief busting my chops now, in the middle of everything else going on around me?

I looked back at him and with a straight face said, "OK, chief. So what? Follow EOSS, follow the safety procedures, and let's get it hooked up."

Chief Newton looked at me again and with all seriousness said, "Captain, I got it but I don't think you understand. We have *never* hooked up casualty power on *Cole.*"

I was dumbfounded. Here was a ship that had been through the most rigorous and intensive training necessary to successfully commission a new ship into the Navy; it had then done all the workups necessary for her first deployment; then successfully deployed to the Middle East and returned safely; then her crew had gone through a maintenance period and again completed the workups for the current deployment. Now I was being confronted with the fact that this crew might not know how to safely carry out this vital procedure.

Taking a deep breath, I looked back at the chief again and said, "It's OK, Chief. I understand what you are telling me. I know you know how to do it. Follow EOSS, follow the safety procedures, and take your time to get it hooked up without damaging equipment or hurting anyone. You can do it."

I told him of my faith in his technical abilities. With a renewed sense of confidence Chief Newton looked at me and said, "Got it, sir," as he turned and headed back inside the ship.

Unfortunately when Chief Newton attempted to get power to the power panel for radio central, there was a ground in the system, which greatly increased the chances of starting an electrical fire. Chief Newton made the wise decision not to troubleshoot the problem in the dark and later told me he had called off trying to get power to the panel.

He had given me this information and I had just mentally filed it away when Lieutenant Colonel Newman and Major Conroe from the defense attaché office in Sana'a had made their way out to the ship, about an hour after the explosion. As I have already related, at that point, because we had no radio communications, I had not yet been able to send my Front Burner report on what had happened. Some of the communications between Newman and Conroe and their office in the Yemeni capital, which I learned about only much later, gave a sense of how completely surprised the embassy was that terrorists were able to mount an attack of such size and scope.

As their boat left the dock, Newman received a call from Master Sergeant James A. Brown, U.S. Army, the Operations Coordinator and the third person in their office in Sana'a. "Sir, it's Sergeant Brown. We got a call about an explosion on board a U.S.-flagged ship in Aden. Do you know anything about this? The *Cole* is refueling today."

"The explosion was on the *Cole*," he responded. Brown could hear a motor running in the background. "I'm on a small boat trying to get out to the ship now. Major Conroe tried to get to the ship in the boat earlier but not knowing who he was, the crew trained their guns on him and he had to turn back. I've called from the harbor master's office to *Cole*'s bridge and identified myself and told them not to shoot me. Hope this goes well."

In an attempt to gather as much information as possible for the embassy staff, Brown asked, "Do you know anything about the explosion?"

"No," Newman replied, "I was at the pool in our hotel when I heard it. I knew we had a ship refueling today and figured the explosion could only mean trouble, so I came down to the harbor. That's where I ran into Major Conroe."

That was when Newman's tone suddenly changed and he exclaimed, "There's a big hole in the side."

Realizing it was the *Cole* that had blown up, Brown told his coworkers, "It is the *Cole*, big hole in the side of the ship."

Everyone wondered if it had indeed been an accident during the refueling that caused the explosion. "I've got to call Washington and Fifth Fleet and tell them there's a problem with one of our ships," Newman said to Conroe. But it was not until he had tossed me his cell phone that I was able to make the call myself and report that it was an attack that had blown us up.

Sitting at the time in a conference in Bahrain, home of the Fifth Fleet, Commander Lee Cardwell, the Fifth Fleet Cryptology Officer, was enduring a rather lengthy contractor briefing when the Fleet Intelligence Officer, Commander Sam Cox, quietly slipped in. Cox discreetly tapped Cardwell on the shoulder and told him to come out of the meeting. Cox told Cardwell that something had happened to the *Cole* in Aden and to go see what he could find out. Cox was going to talk to their boss, Vice Admiral Moore.

Cardwell went onto the Intel Watch Floor and talked to the staff's cryptological support group, which was assigned there from the National Security Agency (NSA). While no one knew for sure what might have happened to *Cole*, repeated calls to the ship using a satellite communications circuit that the ship was required to monitor went unanswered. Cardwell ordered the group to contact an NSA field office in the United States that gathered and monitored satellite information on unusual infrared events worldwide. He specifically asked them if there had been any detections or "blooms" in the area of Aden, Yemen.

While Cardwell continued his discussion with the watch standers about what may have happened, somebody came onto the watch floor and announced that *Cole*'s CO was on the phone again in the Operations Center. Commander Gordon Van Hook, the Deputy for Surface Operations for Fifth Fleet had taken the call. Seeing Cardwell, Van Hook motioned him over and, as Lee flipped open a small notepad, Van Hook tilted the phone so both of them could hear the report.

The initial report had already been made to Fifth Fleet and this was my second call; I made it about ten minutes after the first voice report notifying them of the attack. The initial report focused on the damage control status of the ship and only indicated there were numerous wounded. There was specifically no mention of anyone killed in the attack.

From their perspective, this report was more specific—it articulated the compartments that had flooded, giving a more detailed overview of the damage control status and the efforts being made to control flooding and possible fires. It also contained the devastating news that six sailors had been killed in action and over twenty sailors wounded in the attack. The report also indicated there were a further number of missing personnel inside the ship with an ongoing rescue and triage effort. The last part of the report included a request that when Fifth Fleet personnel came to the ship, that a chaplain accompany them.

Immediately after this latest report, Lee knew he had to get the information about the attack out to as many higher headquarters as possible. He decided to use a Critical Incident (CRITIC) report designed to get important critical information to the President within ten minutes of a message being released.

In all, such messages go to over a dozen different watch centers worldwide that are part of the National Operational Intelligence Watch Officers Network and includes the White House Situation Room, National Security Agency, Central Intelligence Agency, Defense Intelligence Agency, State Department, Treasury Department, Federal Bureau of Investigation, National Military Command Center, and the Combatant Commanders.

One of the great advantages of a CRITIC message is the fact that responsibility for sending it often rests with midgrade officers like Cardwell, and does not have to be authorized by senior officers in the chain of command. Having gathered all this information from the reports coming off the ship, he tried to convey it to one of the watch standers to have them type out the report. Unfortunately, it quickly became apparent to Cardwell that it was taking too much time for the watch team to get organized and set up the computer to send out the message. Instead, he made an on-the-spot decision, sat down in the chair, typed out the message, and hit the send button without consulting the chain of command. The world now learned that a U.S. Navy ship had been the target of a deadly terrorist attack.

A few minutes after I had completed the first call to Fifth Fleet, at about the one-hour point after the attack and with the brow lowered to the pier, Ann was among the first people to leave the ship as she headed directly to a boat waiting to take wounded crew members ashore. Following close behind her came litter after litter of wounded. Ensign Kyle Turner, the ship's anti-submarine warfare officer, had been in the wardroom eating lunch and, immediately after the explosion, ran, first to the bridge, then to his general quarters station in the combat information center, before ending up on the flight deck carrying the wounded down the brow to the pier from the secondary triage area. On his way to the flight deck, he had made a quick walkthrough of the mess decks area where he had found the remains of Seaman Gunn. Along with Hull Technician First Class Michael Hayes, they carried his body into the passageway, where I would come across it a few minutes later.

Once ashore, Ann talked with the doctors, made an on-the-spot assessment that the Yemeni hospitals were running dangerously low on blood supplies, and got word back to the ship that donors were needed to help. Chief Moser then took a couple of volunteers down into the dark of the main medical treatment area. While undamaged, the area was in complete darkness and disarray from the explosion. Using flashlights, they found medical records of crew members with key blood types, most of them O+ and O-, and then located them and asked if they would volunteer to go ashore and give blood for their shipmates. Despite the danger and fear of going into what was now deemed to be a hostile country, none of those asked refused, and still others came forward and asked to help. Ultimately, about twenty sailors, including Sonar Technician Second Class Charles McPeters, Operations Specialist Second Class Denise Alton, Operations Specialist Second Class Earl Morey, Operations Specialist Third Class Missy Butler, Sonar Technician Third Class Kristen Wheeler, and Electrician's Mate Fireman John Buckley courageously went ashore, some to help Ann with the wounded, others to give blood at the main hospital and visit for a few short moments with their injured shipmates.

Denise Woodfin suddenly walked up to me with a new problem. Behind her, under armed guard, was someone I had no idea was still aboard—the Yemeni husbanding agent who had arranged the supplies for the ship. He had been drinking coffee at the back of the ship with a young petty officer escort when the attack came. Both were knocked to the deck, but as they recovered from the shock and word spread through the crew that we had been attacked, the escort became very nervous about the husbanding agent's presence and had one of the security teams take him into a loose form of custody.

As we were wrapping up the evacuation of the wounded, the agent had asked if he could leave, but he wanted to pick up the briefcase he had left with the quarterdeck watch amidships when he had come on board. When Denise came up to me with him, we didn't know who was responsible for the attack and I was not about to release the agent. His briefcase, left in the custody of the quarterdeck watch team, was clearly visible near what had been the quarterdeck watch area, leaning against the forward superstructure. We immediately cleared the area and told the agent that he would have to walk to the briefcase alone and empty it for us while everyone took cover. The escort security team drew their weapons, and the agent slowly walked forward, bent down, unlatched the flap, and gingerly emptied the contents onto the deck. Nothing but pens, paperwork, and his cell phone slid onto the deck. The collective sigh of relief was almost audible.

Seeing that his bag did not contain anything dangerous, the ship's master-at-arms or chief policeman, Master at Arms First Class Justin Crowe, took the bag and contents away for safekeeping and possible use as evidence. I told Denise that until American legal authorities arrived on board, I was going to continue to detain the agent and keep him separated from his bag, especially his cell phone.

By then it was shortly before 1300.

With the wounded evacuated from the ship, I went to the central control station to Debbie for a brief on how the engineers were doing to keep the ship from flooding further. Things were under control, though the only way the key decision makers and emergency teams could communicate with each other was through the emergency battery-powered radio walkie-talkies we had distributed after the power went out, and she was worried about the kilowatt load on the only operating generator, number 3. Then she motioned to me that she had a private matter to raise with me. "Captain, I think we're doing OK, but your continuing to carry around that pistol is making everyone nervous. Would you mind letting the gunner's mates take custody of it for now? I think it will give everyone a sense of security to see that you are willing to part with it." I hadn't thought about it, but reluctantly agreed, and soon the pistol and three clips were back in my stateroom desk drawer.

By the middle of the afternoon at 1530, a little over four hours after the attack, the damage control effort was still ongoing, but the flooding had been controlled and the bulkheads in auxiliary machinery room 1 and main engine room 2 had been braced against collapse from the tremendous water pressure from the flooded spaces on the other side of these walls. There were dozens of boxes of bottled drinking water stacked on the pier, but we at least had enough water for the crew. Most of the blood donors had returned to the ship. Only Ann and a few other crew members remained at the two hospitals to coordinate care for the sailors being treated there.

"XO, we need to get a muster [roll call]," I told Chris, "I don't care how long it takes—it has to be one hundred percent accurate first time out of the barrel. I don't want 'I think I just saw,' 'I just saw so-and-so with so-and-so,' or 'I just saw him or her a few minutes ago.' I want khaki [officer or chief petty officer] eyes on every single crew member until we know everybody is accounted for." And from this point on, I wanted a buddy system applying everywhere inside the ship—I didn't want anyone else killed or injured in an accident at this point.

It took forty-five minutes to complete the muster report. Ann also had one of the crew members bring to the ship a list of all those being treated in hospitals, and where they were.

In the end, we had the grim tally—four sailors confirmed killed in action, identified, tagged, and in body bags down on the pier; thirty-three sailors wounded and ashore in two Aden hospitals with Ann and a few crew members tracking their status; and—lastly—twelve sailors missing. I knew, because the explosion had blasted inward into the ship, that they were all almost certainly somewhere in the destruction of the mess line, galley, the destroyed engine room, and surrounding spaces, their bodies trapped in the appalling wreckage.

The four confirmed and identified dead at that point were Electronics Technician Chief Richard Costelow, Seaman Craig Wibberley, Mess Specialist Seaman Lakiba Palmer, and Signalman Seaman Cherone Gunn. The missing were Ensign Andrew Triplett and eleven enlisted personnel: Engineman Second Class Marc Nieto, Electronic Warfare Technician Second Class Kevin Rux, Hull Technician Third Class Kenneth Clodfelter, Electronic Warfare Technician Third Class Ronald Owens, Mess Specialist Third Class Ronchester Santiago, Mess Specialist Seaman Lakeina Francis, Information Technology Seaman Timothy Gauna, Information Technology Seaman James McDaniels, Engineman Fireman Joshua Parlett, Fireman Patrick Roy, and Fireman Gary Swenchonis.

As the only officer among the missing, Drew was a real loss to the wardroom, and to me in particular. We had no idea where he might be, but Debbie suspected he was in either the destroyed engine room or the fuel lab. The four engineers, Nieto, Parlett, Roy, and Swenchonis, were presumed to be in the engine room, where they had been directed that morning to change out the filters on the ship's reverse osmosis water filtration system. Santiago, Francis, and McDaniels were last seen working in the galley area preparing and serving lunch to the crew. Clodfelter was last seen working at a computer near the doors to the general workshop just outside the entrance to the engine room and across from the fuel lab; that space no longer existed. Rux, Owens, and Gauna were presumed to be in the area of the mess line getting their lunch, and their remains were possibly trapped in the wreckage.

During the course of the afternoon, Ann, ashore with the wounded, provided a more detailed list that contained the full name of each of the injured, which medical facility they were located in for stabilization and treatment, and the ongoing treatment regimen for each sailor. Some crew had reported seeing bodies trapped in the wreckage of the blast area but couldn't identify them. I kept to myself, for the moment, my certainty that none would be found alive.

Unexpectedly, the injured sailors in the two hospitals in Aden soon got some much-appreciated help from one of our closest foreign allies—the French. A reporter from the French news agency Agence France-Presse (AFP) in the center of town had heard the explosion in the harbor and seen the smoke rising from the ship. When he called in to his office in Sana'a, the capital, they contacted the French embassy and spoke with the French defense attaché, Lieutenant Colonel François Vial-Mir, who called the American embassy, which by that time had heard from Fifth Fleet what had happened and told him that some of the wounded would need greater medical expertise than Yemeni hospitals could offer. After reaching Bob Newman, Vial-Mir took matters into his own hands and contacted the Bouffard French military hospital in Djibouti, which he knew was the best medical facility closest to Aden and had access to a French military evacuation aircraft.

The French had operated through the area for decades, and were aware that hospitals in Aden were not in good shape. The French doctors in Djibouti formed a team and Vial-Mir got authorization for them to fly in. Arriving at the two hospitals, Al-Saber and Al Gamhouria, they linked up with Ann Chamberlain at the latter and began examining the injured sailors. In the end, eleven of them were determined to have injuries serious enough to be transported to Djibouti. When asked, Ann made the decision to go with these and leave the less seriously wounded in care of other sailors from the ship.

Within an hour, all eleven plus Ann were being gently loaded onto the French military aircraft and readied for the short trip. But one of the injured sailors, Timothy Saunders, the man who had told Master Chief Parlier, "I don't feel so good," even after his severely cut leg had been bandaged, unexpectedly went into extreme distress before takeoff and succumbed to the internal injuries Parlier had hoped the hospital would be able to treat. In Djibouti, the remaining ten were prepared for surgery in the French military hospital, though two were in critical condition with a very guarded prognosis.

Far away in the United States, notifications to support a continuing medical evacuation were well under way. The Air Force was directed to prepare two Critical Care Air Transport Teams (CCATTs) to fly into Aden,

Yemen, and Djibouti to evacuate all wounded *Cole* sailors to the Landstuhl Regional Medical Center, in Germany, as soon as possible.

At the same time, however, the Fifth Fleet Commander, with approval from the Central Command Commander General Tommy Franks, placed all naval forces in the region at Threat Condition Delta, to indicate that another attack might be imminent. Once learning about this shift in force protection requirements, the Air Force initially refused to fly aircraft into the region unless their security could be guaranteed. At this point, the security situation had many unknown factors and their safety could not be assured at any level.

Now the race against the clock to get *Cole*'s crew members the urgent medical attention necessary to save their lives was in jeopardy once again, this time because the U.S. Air Force refused to risk their aircraft or crews. Finally, common sense prevailed at the national level, and the secretary of defense ordered the Air Force to fly into the region and get the wounded sailors out. On October 13, two C-9 aero-medical aircraft deployed from Ramstein Air Base, Germany, to Djibouti and to Aden, Yemen.

During the return flights to Ramstein and the Landstuhl Regional Medical Center, the CCATTs had two critically injured patients who required constant monitoring to keep alive. At one point, one patient's blood pressure dropped dramatically during the flight and the CCATT had to perform emergency life-saving procedures on him. Although it was a long and challenging flight, thanks to the teams' superb efforts, not one of the patients died.

During all this time, Ann had been in almost constant contact with the U.S. embassy in Djibouti. She could have gone with the injured to Landstuhl, but she declined the opportunity and instead coordinated with the embassy to arrange a return flight to Aden and USS *Cole*. Two days later, Ann landed at Aden's airport and made her way back to the ship on a Yemeni boat. I was as proud as any commanding officer could be when she debarked from the boat, crossed the refueling pier, walked up the brow, and reported back aboard for duty. For everyone who knew what she had been through, her actions set a new benchmark for dedicated professionalism in caring for her shipmates.

Earlier, Petty Officer Crowe, standing on the wing of the bridge looking down at the crew working in the amidships triage area, was appalled to see that crew members, with the best of intentions, had taken out brooms and were beginning to sweep up the debris lying all over the exterior surfaces of the ship. He knew that the cleanup could result in the loss of critical forensic evidence that would be needed in the investigation to determine who had carried out the attack. Getting permission to leave his post, Crowe dashed down several stairways to the main deck, littered with small pieces of black fiberglass from the suicide boat, and started explaining why they needed to be preserved, and not to touch them unless they had to move them to treat wounded crew members. Then he went back to his office and grabbed a handful of evidence bags. His training had taught him that odd-shaped pieces would be the most revealing kind of evidence, and he began putting them into the bags, labeling each one with the date, time, and location in which they were found.

One piece momentarily gave him pause—a fin-shaped piece of metal he thought could be from a missile. "Sir, we need to get everybody away from the port side," he told me. "Look at all those ships and piers across the harbor. Who knows where this shot might have come from?" But as we scanned the shore and other ships for a possible threat, and Chief Larson, who was still standing security watch in the amidships area, began to clear people away from the port side, Crowe realized that the fragment was more likely part of the outboard motor that had propelled the suicide boat. Over the next two hours, in addition to pieces of the boat and motor, he and others found pieces of wiring, and, pieces of flesh, bones, and teeth from the bombers themselves. All of this crucial evidence was taken to the quartermaster's chart room near the bridge and placed under constant watch by the bridge security team.

By Thursday late afternoon, Fifth Fleet had informed us via cell phone that they had dispatched a small team from Bahrain to help coordinate support for *Cole*. Working closely with the ship's leading personnelman, Chief Suzan Pearce, Chris secured the personnel records of all of the killed, wounded, or missing crew members and assembled a report that he was able, with extra cell phone batteries and a charger also supplied by the defense attaché, to dictate to Fifth Fleet headquarters so that the Navy could begin notifying family members.

The assistance team from Bahrain arrived in Aden in early evening, about 1930. Led by Captain Jim Hanna, the commodore or senior officer of Destroyer Squadron Fifty, it included a master chief supply clerk, four Marines to form a small force protection unit, three Navy SEALs who had recently been training local forces in Yemen, a chaplain, and an investigator from NCIS. Arriving at the civilian/military airport in Aden dressed in civilian clothes to avoid offending Yemeni sensitivities, though heavily armed, they stepped out onto the tarmac in the still, hot, and humid night and saw the French medical team with their evacuation aircraft tending to the wounded in preparation for their flight to Djibouti. Hanna walked over and introduced himself to the French doctors and was impressed to find that the seriously injured sailors had been stabilized to the best possible extent, given clean bandages, and obviously provided with first-class medical care.

Hanna and one other member of the team made their way to the port to get out to the ship. The Yemeni military and police forces had set up numerous checkpoints, and Hanna felt that he might have been able to get through them more easily if he had been wearing a uniform. Somehow he managed to persuade each one to let them through, and soon he was on the harbor master's bridge-to-bridge radio communication system telling the watch team on *Cole* that he was on his way out via a Yemeni small boat.

Stepping onto the pier, Hanna was struck by the overpowering smell of fuel. It permeated everything. He walked up the brow and was met there by Petty Officer Crowe, but again, Hanna felt that being in civilian clothes lowered his credibility, since no one on the ship could immediately recognize that help had truly arrived.

When I met Captain Hanna, other than the obligatory salute to a senior officer, there were no formalities or pleasantries extended by either of us. We got down to business straightaway. He was quickly but thoroughly debriefed on what had happened throughout the day, the status of the damage control effort, and the latest information the ship had regarding the wounded ashore. He also received my assessment of how the crew was doing and what security and other watches were manned.

An exceptionally sharp officer, Hanna quickly absorbed this information and told me that he was going to establish an initial headquarters in the Aden Mövenpick Hotel downtown. Most important at that moment, he said he could see that because the galley area and food stores had been destroyed in the attack, we had no ability to feed the crew. The first thing he was going to do was to arrange for food to be brought out to us. He walked down the brow and, just before midnight, called the bridge watch and told them he was on his way back to the ship with meals for the crew cooked by the Mövenpick. A Yemeni boat glided up with him aboard, and its crew began to unload Styrofoam boxes of sliced roast beef, rice with brown gravy, bread rolls, apples, and more water onto the refueling pier.

The food was brought up onto the ship under the tarp covering the forward part of the flight deck, but when told to queue up to get the meal, the crew balked. They wanted nothing to do with meals that came from the Yemenis, who had in their minds attacked them or at least allowed an attack to happen. There was even talk that the food might be poisoned. So we quickly assembled all hands for a frank talk.

I told them how Captain Hanna had been dispatched by Fifth Fleet to help us deal with the aftermath of the attack. He had personally overseen the preparation of the food by the Mövenpick Hotel. It was safe for them to eat, and they would need it for the hard work they needed to keep doing to prevent the ship from sinking or being attacked again. They could not subsist on Slim Jims and Snickers; they needed real food. And though I didn't really know whether we could trust the Yemenis either, I took a Styrofoam box meal and some plastic utensils, and sat down to eat. With the XO and CMC queuing up next, only then did the crew relax and follow suit.

Captain Hanna checked in with me before leaving the ship and told me that the U.S. ambassador to Yemen, Barbara Bodine, was expected to return from a trip to Washington, D.C., during the night and would probably come down to the ship with him the following morning. There would also be more support personnel coming from Bahrain, including additional NCIS agents, as well as divers who would assess damage to the ship below the waterline.

It was now already early Friday morning, October 13. The ship's engineering force was continuing to work on *Cole*'s vital systems. Two of the three 750-gallon-per-minute eductors—devices that depend on water pressure in the main drainage system and operate something like powerful siphons—were operational, keeping the leakage of water from the flooded sections of the ship under control. With workarounds to isolate sections ripped apart by the explosion, the fresh water and wastewater disposal systems were also operational in the aft berthing compartments. Although everyone was dirty and tired, adrenaline kept us all pushing forward. But the fans and air conditioning units for the crew's berthing spaces were shut off to conserve power, and it was over 100 degrees inside. I had told the crew we would be sleeping under the stars until we could get to the point where those systems could be safely operated, and as I looked at the deck it seemed that every piece of horizontal space on every level was now covered with sailors lying down and trying to sleep. And, about 0130, Chris and Command Master Chief Parlier came up to me and told me that we all needed to take some time to power down and get some sleep as well. We went to a small area at the very back of the ship to try to rest, and I closed my eyes with no real intention of sleeping.

Even if I had tried, sleep proved to be impossible. The images of the day kept replaying, even with my eyes shut. My mind raced with the many questions of what I needed to do next to keep USS *Cole* afloat. Chris and the master chief soon fell into rhythmic breathing, but I could not follow suit. I raised myself up quietly and got up to walk around the ship alone, my first chance to get a really good look at what had happened to us.

I checked in with the quarterdeck watch at the brow and told them I had my handheld radio walkie-talkie. Walking up the stairs to my cabin, I found the table still lying on its side, the rug stained and damp from spilled coffee and water. The paperwork that had dominated my world a little over twelve hours ago lay scattered on the desk, singularly unimportant now. The pistol and three clips that had been returned to my cabin were in my desk drawer. I walked into the bedroom, opened the weapons key safe, and locked them away. I hoped I would not need them again anytime soon.

The bridge area was relatively undamaged, but looking back at the face of the forward engine exhaust stack, I could see that the dome for the ship's satellite phone antenna had been blown away, and on the mast, all the antennas for the radios appeared damaged, and one had been sheared off. Back inside, I walked down the ladder from the bridge and then forward up a port side passageway by combat system maintenance central towards Repair 2, crossed to the starboard side, and entered the combat information center, where the radars were dark and the space lifeless. I crossed through and went back into the port side passageway, going aft to where it was blocked by bent and twisted metal. At the entrance to the chiefs' mess was the large hole cut by the rescue teams. I stepped inside, where the sight I met took my breath away. The entire space had been crushed, the aft wall on the right side smashed and bent and folded over the edges of the tables, the seats shoved underneath so forcefully that they had bent the table supports. It was obvious that anyone sitting there when the explosion hit would have been cut in half.

I continued just behind the chiefs' mess entrance to look at the watertight hatch leading down to the destroyed fuel lab, engine room, and general workshop. My flashlight shone down into oily water. The ladder frame and handrails were twisted and deformed with several steps sheared off and missing from the force of the explosion. No wonder Petty Officers Lopez and McTureous had chosen to crawl through a tear in the wall near the waterline and swim out of the hole in the side of the ship. Crossing forward again by Repair 2, I paused to see the locker again restored after the pandemonium that had earlier defined our day. Continuing on to the starboard side, I made my way down the starboard passageway before walking down the ladders leading into the auxiliary machinery room forward of the flooded engine room. I descended to below the ship's waterline, and could see from the emergency lights that had been run down into the space that small holes from various places along the bulkhead between the two spaces had been stuffed with rags and wedges to keep water from leaking in, but fuel and water were relentlessly filling the space. Back up in the starboard side passageway, I walked by the damaged Repair 5 locker. At some point in the evening, the Repair Locker Officer, Ensign Jason Grabelle, and members of the locker's repair team had pried open the door to Repair 5. Damage to the storage lockers and the crushed and bowed-in walls of the space had made it unusable. Rather than abandoning everything inside, however, the crew had completely emptied it of every bit of damage control equipment. Initially refilling the stocks used by Repairs 2 and 3 in saving the ship, the rest of the parts, pieces, and equipment had been neatly staged on the flight deck near what had been the second triage area.

Rounding the corner, the odd-shaped splatters of a blood-stained deck in front of me reminded me again of our situation as I found myself staring into the Command Master Chief's office along the mess line. The walls had been pushed toward the starboard side, and the whole space appeared to be cocked at a ten-degree angle. The desk was shoved against the filing cabinet. Amazingly, a picture of Master Chief Parlier's daughter was still taped to the distorted and crushed wall adjoining the destroyed galley, covered in a film of fuel oil, explosive residue, and dust, but it seemed clear that if he had been in his office, he would have been killed. Without his skills as a medical corpsman, many injured sailors probably would not have been saved.

I found myself once again standing at the edge of the blast hole. Faint light flickered off the harbor waters, the smell of fuel still hanging thickly in the dank air. Exiting through the small vestibule and across the mess line, I peered into the darkness of the blocked port passageway and around the corner at the end of the mess line. As my flashlight slowly traced the overhead, where a piece of the deck had blown up and toward the back of the ship, my heart froze. Just down the passageway from where I was standing, crushed in the mangled metal, the remains of a sailor stuck out from the bent wreckage of the ship—part of a head, a broken arm, some of a leg, and, barely visible in a fold of metal, a cold, lifeless hand.

Farther back down the passageway there was even worse. The explosion had picked up a sailor whole and violently propelled his body off the deck. His head and upper body were pinned into the overhead, and his body hung there against the aft wall. I could almost recognize who it was, but dared not guess for fear of wrongly alarming an anxious family back home.

I was staggered by the sight. Why my ship? Why me? What had I done wrong? Why had God allowed this to happen to us? What about my crew? How are we going to get through this? What would happen next?

Anxiety and a feeling of being overwhelmed washed over me as I made my way back to the starboard passageway and continued toward the central control station. Walking into it at 0515, I smelled fresh brewed coffee, which was welcome to me, but as I looked at the coffee pot, I spotted possible trouble—the pot was hard-piped into the ship's fresh-water system, and there were no empty bottles of water around it. This could only mean the engineers had disobeyed one of our key health concerns—they were drinking unsanitized water directly from the pier. The crew saw what I was thinking and the room grew still. They looked at me sheepishly, until someone finally spoke up. "Captain, we're already on our third or fourth pot of the night . . . well, sir, no one has been doing the Yemeni two-step, so the coffee must be OK."

Finally, I forced a weak smile and looked around the room. "Well, all right. Where's a cup for me?" Everyone laughed.

Somehow, we would get through this.

7 | The Bucket Brigade

L EAVING THE CENTRAL CONTROL STATION before dawn at about 0530 Friday, the day after the attack, I walked down the starboard passageway and out onto the flight deck. Everywhere I looked, I saw exhausted and dirty sailors sprawled on the deck of the ship. Some were out cold. Others had not been able to get to sleep, or had woken up and quietly spoke with friends and shipmates. Several looked up as I walked toward Chris and the Command Master Chief at the stern of the ship. Squatting down, I spoke quietly to not alarm either of them, "Hey, XO, good morning." As he woke up, Chris sat up quickly and objected that I hadn't awakened him earlier. Somberly, I said, "Well, I wanted you to get some sleep. One of us needs to be bright-eyed and bushy-tailed to face the day."

I told Chris and the master chief that during the night the engineers had restored the freshwater and plumbing in the aft part of the ship and that they should go get a shave and a shower, and then get the crew up at 0600 to give them the good news that they could do the same. That meant that I could keep the crew on board instead of having to berth them in local hotels. I viewed this as critical to our survival as a group. It was imperative that we all persevere through this ordeal together.

Learning of the attack on *Cole* the day before through their respective military channels, three ships had arrived during the night off the coast of Aden within hours of one another: first was HMS *Marlborough* of the Royal Navy, commanded by Commander Anthony Rix, followed by USS *Hawes* and USS *Donald Cook*, with which *Cole* had been scheduled to rendezvous this day for turnover of Fifth Fleet duties. None of these ships had yet received diplomatic clearance to enter Yemen's territorial waters. The Royal Navy chose to disregard this inconvenience and immediately had *Marlborough* proceed and offer whatever assistance we needed. South Yemen had at one time been a British colony, and they understood the culture well enough to anticipate that this action would command respect—as a show of determination, strength, and confidence in their ability to help and protect an ally. The U.S. Navy, on the other hand, took a much more rigid and bureaucratic approach to such things. Both *Hawes* and *Donald Cook* were obliged to wait until late morning for diplomatic approvals before crossing into territorial waters to offer assistance. Both commanding officers later told me they were frustrated by the bureaucratic red tape and were prepared to disobey instructions if we needed immediate help.

I was heartened when *Marlborough*'s Executive Officer Lieutenant Commander Andrew Webb—emerging onto the refueling pier from a small zodiac-style (inflatable) boat flying the Royal Navy's white ensign—walked up the brow, requested permission to come aboard, and asked if there was anything we needed. With some pride, I told him that while the offer was greatly appreciated, the only thing that might be in need of replacement was aqueous fire-fighting foam; otherwise, the ship was in relatively stable condition. After exchanging a few more details about the attack and its aftermath, Lieutenant Commander Webb offered the immediate aid of *Marlborough* at any point we needed it, and left the pier.

By about 0825, a Yemeni boat carried Ambassador Barbara Bodine, Captain Hanna, and Lieutenant Colonel Newman across the harbor towards the *Cole*. Their boat approached the ship, slowing as it neared a point about 100 feet from the port side as Captain Hanna pointed out the huge blast hole, and then pulled up to the refueling pier. Ambassador

Bodine was the first to walk up the brow. Saluting, I greeted her aboard and then walked them up the starboard side and across the middle of the ship to stand on the warped deck directly above the center of the explosion. Debris littered the area and the snapped lifelines still lay on deck—not the usual protocol for a VIP visit, but these visitors needed to be aware of the vast amount of damage that had befallen us. I also wanted them to be proud of what the crew had accomplished in the time since the attack.

We continued forward to the bow, where the ambassador could look back and broadly view the damage to the exterior, including the superstructure, electronic warfare system and radio antennas, the AN/SPY-1D phased-array radar, and the forward 20 mm CIWS cannon. Proceeding to the darkened interior, with the only visibility provided by a string of bulbs from the ship's in-port decorative lights, I took the ambassador over to the port side of the ship, near the entrances to main engine room 1 and the chiefs' mess, where the twisted deck bent upward into the overhead. I told her how the deck of the galley had been ripped into four sections and what each piece had done to material and people in the area. Ambassador Bodine, after hearing these gruesome details, became increasingly subdued, asking very few questions as we started the walk through the ship.

We walked forward up the port side passageway and crossed in front of the repair locker, now restored and ready for action, before walking down the starboard side to the medical treatment area where we entered the mess decks. Nothing had been touched since the day before and we crunched our way across the broken glass and food to the port side passageway and the end of the mess line.

Squeezing to make room, the ambassador looked at the deck bent upwards against the aft wall of the mess line. After a slight pause to give her time to take in the devastation around her, I pointed out the sailors still crushed and trapped in the wreckage. Her face slightly contorted in pain and we gingerly withdrew back to the mess decks.

As the tour concluded, we stood in the area between the stacks, near the blast center. Ambassador Bodine asked, "Gentlemen, may I have a moment alone with the captain?"

Unknown to anyone else on board, Barbara Bodine and I had been acquaintances for years. Introduced by mutual friends, Rick and Ann Dorman, at Thanksgiving dinner about five years earlier, Barbara and I had maintained contact, seeing each other at various parties and dinners. In 1997, I had enjoyed a Christmas dinner she cooked at her home, a few days after she took the oath of office as President Bill Clinton's ambassador to the Republic of Yemen. Prior to this post she had clocked years of experience in the Arabian Peninsula, among them as Deputy Chief of Mission in Kuwait when Iraq invaded in 1990.

"Kirk," she asked me when the others had moved out of earshot, "how are you doing?"

"Barbara, I'm fine," I answered, choking up, "but you cannot ask me that question again. Please, I need to focus on my ship and crew."

I let the morning air dry my eyes before motioning to Captain Hanna. As a group, we walked back to the brow, where I bade them good-bye and saluted the ambassador as she left the ship.

I was not the only one struggling to maintain control of my emotions. Members of the crew were showing signs of strain. Whispers had already started about bodies being visible in the wreckage of the galley and mess line, which had been put generally off-limits. But in reality, there was no practical way to stop the crew from walking through that area. During morning quarters with the crew before the ambassador's visit, I addressed the issue and told everyone about their shipmates' remains trapped in the wreckage, saying that they would be extricated with dignity and respect as soon as that became possible. There were some in the crew who did not shave or shower for several days—I think because they were reluctant to go back inside and wanted nothing to do with being in there under the circumstances.

By early afternoon, USS *Hawes* and USS *Donald Cook* had arrived off the mouth of the harbor, and each provided us with additional assistance in the form of extra damage control experts. Shortly afterward, Fifth Fleet Commander Vice Admiral Moore, with Captain Hanna in tow, came out to the ship in a Yemeni harbor boat. Our security teams tracked them closely, in spite of the passengers' rank—for anyone not in an identifiable Navy craft, the crew was not exactly in a trusting mood. As earlier with the ambassador, Hanna had the boat slow and circle off the port side to check out the massive blast hole and the topside damage to the ship.

The admiral crossed the refueling pier, walked up the brow, and was welcomed aboard with only a salute and a greeting from me—there was no way to pipe him aboard as "Fifth Fleet, arriving," what with our 1MC and onboard communications system still down. We walked directly up the starboard side to the port amidships area directly above the blast, and then I followed the same path through the devastation as I had with every other visitor, showing the damage and explaining what we were doing to keep the ship afloat. Admiral Moore was especially moved by the sight of the sailors crushed in the wreckage of the mess line.

He and Captain Hanna told me that a Department of State Foreign Emergency Support Team (FEST) that included an FBI criminal investigation team would arrive in Aden later in the day, and an FBI Hostage Rescue Team had been sent to Germany in case it was needed. A Marine Fleet Anti-Terrorism Security Team (FAST) platoon would join us to help provide security, and a Joint Task Force would be set up to coordinate the broad interagency government effort that would be necessary to investigate and take care of *Cole* and the crew. Admiral Moore pulled me aside for a few minutes as we were walking back to the brow, and asked for my honest assessment of how the crew was doing and what we really needed for support and morale. I reiterated my strong feeling that keeping the crew together and on board their ship was the best thing for them.

Unknown to me at the time, Admiral Moore was experiencing a startling absence of clear direction from Washington. A ship of the U.S. Navy had been attacked. This was clearly an act of war. But what was the response to be? It was the day after the bombing, and there was no indication of any next steps, yet.

As commander of the *Cole*, my perspective was much more focused. My crew's chain of command had been severely disrupted. For that reason, I planned to run quarters for the next few days. Each day I would present a basic synopsis for the crew: here's the vision for the day; here is what we are going to do and how we are going to do it; here is what has happened overnight to support us; and here is what we have accomplished to date in restoration efforts. It would be important to keep the crew updated on our progress, so they had some measure of our accomplishments.

Even so, I knew that the process of how we were going to survive this ordeal still had many unanswered questions. What systems did we still need to restore to maintain our ability to stay on the ship as a cohesive crew? How were we going to recover our shipmates from the wreckage? Even though the Fifth Fleet staff's initial cadre had arrived in Aden and provided us with meals, what was going to be the long-term plan for food? How was I going to get the ship out of port, should it appear that we were going to be under threat of another attack? How was I going to be able to defend the ship? Were the terrorists going to attempt another attack and board the ship using small boats? Every one of these issues could drive our fate. I had hours not only to contemplate where we were right then, but also what the future might bring.

Once again on our own for several hours, we continued to make ourselves busy and keep restoring systems on the ship. The engineers continued to assess the damaged and flooded spaces to determine what equipment could be repaired, which spaces might be able to be emptied of floodwaters. A critical requirement to keep the ship afloat was to thoroughly evaluate the areas surrounding the damaged and flooded areas and slow, if not stop, the steady leak of waters into adjoining critical compartments. These leaks were now down to a few steady but manageable streams of water with fuel mixed in.

As part of the habits everyone was establishing for themselves and the ship following the bombing, I had developed my own routine—and my own headquarters. In an area near the aft vertical guided-missile launchers, and strapped to the ship's superstructure, we had two large eight-by-four foot rubber fenders we had purchased to keep between the ship and the pier during the deployment. Now, these fenders became my office. Thanks to the overhanging ledge just above them, they were in the shade most of the day and offered a protected area out of the sun. From here, I was right near the quarterdeck where I could observe the watch and know who was coming on and off the ship, and most importantly, I could be available for the crew.

As evening came, though I considered getting some sleep, I was still operating on adrenaline and the drive to protect the ship and crew. A little after sunset, Chris approached me and said he had just taken a call from the White House on our borrowed cell phone, telling him that I should expect to hear from the President in about twenty minutes. Chris found the situation almost surreal, but also understood that it was a serious moment. "Well, give me the phone and let's go have a seat on the fantail and wait for the President to call," I said.

As we walked back to sit down on a couple of big bitts—two stubby vertical posts welded to the deck and used to secure the thick mooring lines tying the ship to the pier—I checked to make sure the phone's battery was well charged as we continued to catch up on the events of the day and agree on arrangements for the expected Marine security platoon. About twenty minutes later, the phone rang.

"USS *Cole*, Commanding Officer speaking, may I help you?" I asked. On the line was an officer from the White House situation room, calling to verify that he was, in fact, speaking with me. After being put on hold for a few minutes, another person came on the phone, again verifying that I was still there and the commanding officer of USS *Cole*. Chris and I were quietly chuckling at this point. Finally, minutes later, President Bill Clinton came on the line.

"Commander Lippold?"

"Yes sir, this is Commander Kirk Lippold, sir."

"How are you and your crew doing?"

"Mr. President, the crew and I are doing OK. They have done a great job saving the ship and we're working hard to get systems restored."

"On behalf of the American people, I want you to know that our prayers are with you. Each of us is thinking of you. We're working very hard to get this situation back in the box in the Middle East to prevent people from doing things like this to you. Again, I want to thank you for the great job you're doing and let you know that you and your crew are in our prayers. God bless!" said the President.

"Mr. President, thank you," was all I could say back to him. What he had told me may have conveyed his concern, but there was no offer of support or discussion of future action, let alone retaliation.

At that point the phone was handed back to someone else in the White House, and I was told that was the end of the conversation and thanked for taking time from what I was doing to speak with the President.

Looking at Chris, all I could do was take a deep breath and rub my temples. "Grab your pen and copy this down before I forget what he said," I told him, then slowly recounted the words exactly as I remembered the President speaking them to me. "XO, I want to read this to the crew tomorrow morning at quarters," I said. "It will be important for them to understand that this is becoming bigger than any of us can imagine."

Chris nodded in agreement, and we returned to my fender perch for the rest of the evening.

The Marine security team arrived a little after 2230. You could almost hear the crew breathe a sigh of relief—the Marines had landed and were here to help us save the ship. Captain Wesley A. Philbeck, the platoon commander, strode up the brow, crisply saluted the national ensign and requested permission to come aboard the ship. A model image of a Marine, he stood well over six feet tall and cast an imposing figure in his camouflage uniform, flak vest, and helmet, with a weapon strapped across his chest. His self-confidence in his abilities was reflected in his demeanor. "Captain, my team is ready to assume responsibility for your ship's security," he announced.

While not doubting their ability to do a great job, I calmly looked back at him and responded, "Captain, I don't want any of your folks to take responsibility for any security stations until they each stand at least two watch rotations with our security teams. It is going to be critical for them to have clear situational awareness and an understanding of how we are operating in this port." *Cole*'s security teams had become guardedly familiar with how the port operated. The teams also knew how internal communications worked with the bridge watch teams, as well as how and when small boats approached the ship and the pier area. To prevent any misinterpretation of their movements, I knew the Marines had to gain this valuable insight and experience.

"Understand, sir," he replied, and within minutes the Marines began to take up positions shoulder to shoulder with *Cole*'s security teams.

The Marines' arrival in Aden had not been an easy one. The Yemeni military and police forces at the airport felt threatened by Captain Philbeck and his team, who were bristling with weapons. Almost simultaneously another plane landed carrying the Foreign Emergency Support Team (FEST) that had been deployed from Washington. As the Marines disembarked off their aircraft, armed and ready for any confrontation, it was readily apparent the Yemenis felt inadequate and defensive of their capability, and compensated by brandishing weapons in a misguided attempt to appear helpful. They leveled their own weapons directly at the arriving Americans. Ever since the explosion, the Yemeni government had been denying the presence of terrorists in their country and repeatedly claimed that this incident was an accident connected with the refueling. Given this attitude, reinforced by their military superiors, the personnel at the airport could not understand why the arriving U.S. personnel needed weapons.

In the middle of this standoff, a civilian passenger airline packed with German tourists landed and taxied up to the ramp area, passengers pressing their faces to the windows trying to figure out what was happening. The German tourists were taken off in buses to their hotel; the standoff at the airport continued.

Neither American team had diplomatic clearance to enter the country. The Yemeni government's weekend was Friday and Saturday—this was Friday night, so it had not yet been formally contacted. Finally Lieutenant Colonel Bob Newman, the defense attaché, was able to tell the Yemeni authorities at the airport that the government had given permission to let the Marines go to a staging area from which they could launch inflatable boats and get out to the *Cole*. The FBI agents and others on the emergency support team could proceed to their hotel—the same one where the German tourists, now perplexed even further, were staying.

As part of the FEST, an FBI team came on the scene as well. The FBI special agent in charge of the civilian team was Don Sachtleben, an FBI veteran since 1983, with a specialty as a bomb technician. He had been involved in investigating the embassy bombings in Kenya and Tanzania two years previously, and before that had been one of the crime scene team leaders at the World Trade Center bombing in 1993 and the Oklahoma City federal building bombing in 1995. He had cleared the explosives-filled Montana cabin of Ted Kaczynski, the Unabomber, after he had been identified and captured in 1996. Now, as a supervisory special agent in the Forensics and Explosives Laboratory at FBI headquarters, he was running the team that would gather evidence and try to determine who was responsible for the plot to attack USS *Cole*.

By early morning Saturday, a small but growing advance team from NCIS had linked up with the FBI, and around 0930, Don Sachtleben led the small joint law enforcement contingent off the dock and chugged out to *Cole* on one of the Yemeni supply boats. Don had thought, seeing CNN's reports on the attack before he left Washington, "This one can't be that difficult; it's a Navy ship. Probably just a puncture." He had brought a video camera with him, and now, taking pictures of the ship, realized that this deployment would be no cakewalk. The scope of the damage, the dangling piping, the shredded and torn metal, was huge. Making a circle around the ship before docking at the refueling pier, the boat disembarked its passengers, and Don took charge as we started to walk around the ship.

He did not want a repeat of the problems he had experienced at the Khobar Towers, the military housing development in Saudi Arabia where a suicide bomber killed nineteen U.S. servicemen in 1996. In the aftermath of the event, the Saudis had prevented the American evidence collection team from doing its job. In the case of *Cole*, the entire ship was essentially an evidence scene; fortunately, even though we were in Yemeni waters, naval ships are legally considered sovereign U.S. territory. Don gave his group a quick safety briefing and then asked me if he could film the damaged areas of the ship, emphasizing that he would not be filming the crew.

With the XO and Petty Officer Crowe, we started the rounds directly above the epicenter of the blast. From the standpoint of national security, I was concerned about keeping elements hostile to the United States from getting a close enough look to have any understanding about the vulnerability of a U.S. Navy ship to this type of attack, which might enable them to think up ways of producing even more devastating damage in the future. To prevent them and the media from being able to see into the hole and the interior, I had a white tarp tied and lowered from the undamaged deck stanchions above the blast hole to cover the side of the ship from the deck edge to the waterline. Several crew members were rounded up to lift the tarp up and away from the hole, and with Petty Officer Crowe holding his belt, Don leaned over the side to film the blast area, indented metal, and explosive residue spray that covered the side of the ship. Continuing the inspection toward the forecastle, the group saw debris and pieces of all sizes and shapes from the suicide boat still scattered about the deck. Don asked if the ship was normally one color, or painted in different shades. No, it was uniformly gray on the outside; what he was seeing was the residue from the wave of soot and explosive residue that had washed over everything after the blast.

He continued filming the evidence of damage—the radar dome of the forward 20 mm close-in weapons system, crushed and blown off by the concussion; antennas sheared or broken off other pieces of equipment; debris at every level.

Don said he would propose bringing more investigators out to the ship and, with the help of the crew, sweeping the deck clean, noting where the pieces came from. He thought it would take about an hour. "OK, great!" I said, looking forward to getting the ship back under our complete control and jurisdiction. At this point, Chris and Crowe spoke up and told him about the crew finding shards of bone and flesh on the forecastle and other areas of the ship. Knowing these were key pieces of evidence, they specifically showed the agents where a tooth had been imbedded into one of the mooring lines that tied us to the pier. Crowe also told them about the evidence he had collected and how he had maintained a strict chain of custody with it under guard.

We saw in the starboard passageway outside the combat information center how much progress the crew had managed to make in restoring the overhead lighting and even the 1MC announcing system in this part of the ship. Closer to the center of the damage, we warned the team to be careful about where they stepped and what they grabbed onto. The chiefs' mess and the port side passageway were untouched and provided Don with his first real view of the damage done to the interior of the ship. Again crossing up by the forward repair locker and down the starboard side, we made our way back to the mess decks and then through the small passageway that led up to what was left of the mess line.

The full scope of the damage was beginning to come into view. Surveying it for the first time, Don told me later, he thought to himself, "This is going to change everything." He gingerly stepped out to the edge of the blast hole to the same spot I had reached immediately after the attack. As he panned the camera, he asked about where the missing sailors might be. I pointed out that there were up to three bodies trapped further down the passageway where we were standing, and the rest were located in the folds of metal of the galley area and down in what remained of main engine room 1 and the general workshop.

Up to this point, Don figured he and his team would recover parts of a bomb—the wires, batteries and switches, explosive residue, and so on— and be out of there in fairly short order. Looking around now, he knew that was not going to happen. The FBI/NCIS team would have to deal with the recovery of twelve bodies trapped in the wreckage, above and below the waterline. As far as evidence was concerned, parts of the suicide bombers' bodies had been found outside, with more pieces probably located on the interior of the ship. Coordination between the various support groups would have to be worked out to avoid duplication of effort and confusion. The ship would not truly belong to the crew for much longer than anyone could imagine.

As we walked back into the hot sunlight, Don told the group that now that they had an idea of what they were dealing with, they needed to get back to the hotel and brief the rest of the team, as well as the follow-on group that would soon land in Aden. As the group filed off the ship, Don told us to expect another visit that afternoon if we could support them. Of course we could: the work of the criminal investigation took priority over almost everything else.

Two key new members of the next group included Bob Sibert, now the most senior on-scene FBI agent, and Steve Kruger, an FBI chemist. Arriving back at the hotel, Don quickly briefed them and with three to four hours of daylight left, they were soon back on the ship to see what they were dealing with. Sibert then made it clear to everyone that the ship was an explosion crime scene and the explosives experts would have primacy in directing the gathering of evidence. FBI and NCIS would gather and maintain evidence. At the back of the ship, under the flight deck, the ship's classroom and career counselor's office were emptied of non-essential gear and equipment to serve as the law-enforcement coordination center on board the ship. The career counselor's office could be locked and secured, which made it an ideal location to process and store evidence gathered during the course of the investigation.

All evidence gathered on the ship had to stay strictly within U.S. custody. Don also knew he would have to work closely with the Department of State personnel to ensure that FBI members were an integrated part of the Yemeni teams that were expected to gather evidence of the criminal activities of the terrorists who had planned, financed, and carried out the attack from in town, but as much as possible he hoped to minimize the amount of evidence handled by them so as to be able to build the strongest possible case.

Navy divers from Detachment Alpha, Mobile Diving and Salvage Unit Two (MDSU-2) also arrived on Saturday, with repair equipment from the Mediterranean to help assess the damage to the ship. They joined the long list of Americans who had to endure the not-so-helpful hospitality of the Yemenis. Like the FEST, they wasted hours standing with the hot sun burning down on the tarmac, explaining in mind-numbing detail why all the equipment they had brought with them required clearance through customs to be allowed into the country. Eventually, all their equipment was unpacked, physically examined and "x-rayed" by Yemeni customs authorities, and cleared into the country without any further harassment.

Concerned about the security of their equipment, they decided that the only area to stage the Detachment Alpha dive equipment before it could be sent out to the ship was near the security area established by the Marine FAST Platoon, who controlled access to the boats supporting *Cole*. Soon they arranged to load the dive gear onto trucks and have it driven out there. Detachment Alpha's officer in charge, Chief Warrant Officer Frank Perna, along with his divers, shortly loaded themselves onto small hot buses, interspersed with armed Yemeni military personnel, and drove to the staging area.

Before they left, however, they were strictly warned to maintain as low a profile as possible—do not lean out of the bus windows, do not take any pictures, avoid eye contact, and be quiet but courteous at the check points. The staging area was in a very good location from a force protection standpoint, but it was a long thirty-minute drive from the airport through three Yemeni checkpoints and a U.S. checkpoint to get there.

Once at the FAST Platoon security site, the divers unloaded their gear and set it up for movement out to *Cole*. Warrant Officer Perna knew he had to get out to the ship as soon as possible and make that initial assessment on where they could set up dive stations and what the best methods were to access the flooded compartments and dive underneath the ship. It was Saturday night before he and two other senior members of his team, Engineman Senior Chief Lyle Becker and Boatswain's Mate Chief David Hunter, were able to make their first visit out to us.

A third support plane would arrive Sunday morning, carrying one of the FBI's most experienced counter-terrorism experts, Supervisory Special Agent John O'Neill, who had been one of the leaders into the investigation of the 1993 World Trade Center bombing, which led to the capture of the al Qaeda terrorist Ramzi Yousef and his subsequent conviction and imprisonment for that crime. (O'Neill later became head of security for the World Trade Center and died heroically there on September 11, 2001.) With his experience as a supervisory agent in the FBI's New York Field Office, he would now take charge of the investigation.

A couple of hours before Don came out to the ship with his team Saturday morning, shortly after quarters, the commanding officers from USS *Hawes* and USS *Donald Cook* arrived to get their first-hand look at the ship. *Hawes* was an *Oliver Hazard Perry*–class guided-missile frigate, and *Donald Cook* was identical to *Cole*, an *Arleigh Burke*–class Aegis guided-missile destroyer.

First to arrive was *Hawes*, Commander Jeffrey S. "Scott" Jones. Subdued but still upbeat, Scott had brought a thermos of coffee to share with me. Although the coffee pot in the ship's central control station still worked and I had already gone through several cups, I gladly accepted his kind offer and kept up the intake of caffeine. A few minutes later, *Donald Cook*, in the person of Commander Matthew E. Sharpe, arrived as well.

Both Scott and Matt were armed and dressed in flak vests and Kevlar helmets. After being dropped off, they both ordered the boats that had brought them to slowly circle off the stern of the ship and provide security to supplement the Yemeni navy boats that were "patrolling" the harbor area. Each of them had also brought in their own shipboard experts to offer any additional expertise and assistance *Cole*'s teams might need.

Prior to arriving, Scott and Matt had discussed what each ship would be best at providing us and had agreed to a division of duties to avoid duplication of effort. *Hawes* would focus on general damage control and crew amenities, like food and laundry. *Donald Cook*, being similar to *Cole,* would focus on engineering and platform-specific damage control equipment.

It had been with Matt Sharpe that I had quietly exchanged e-mails about the port of Aden before we arrived. He had given me many of the pieces of information describing the port and its facilities that I could otherwise only have learned about upon arrival. *Donald Cook* had been in the port in August to conduct the same type of short-duration refueling stop as *Cole*. Like me, Matt had run into the same issues with the pilot being reluctant to turn the ship around and moor starboard side to the pier. He had also experienced the same lack of communication from the U.S. embassy and Fifth Fleet staff.

In this first meeting, under obviously challenging circumstances, I tried to gain insight into their perspectives. While it seemed as if *Cole* was almost cut off from contact with the outside world, information flow, while as good as the circumstances allowed, came mostly from the excellent updates provided by Captain Hanna and from the few calls I received on the cell phone I was still carrying. It was good to spend some time listening to their views and asking a lot of questions.

Obviously, my first question to them was how they had found out we had been attacked. Each told me that their watch teams had heard some background radio communications that there had been an explosion on a ship in Aden, USS *Cole*. Not knowing the situation and deciding not to wait for direction from either the *Abraham Lincoln* battle group staff, Destroyer Squadron 50, or Fifth Fleet, Scott, as the CO of *Hawes* and the senior officer between the two ships, took tactical command of *Donald Cook* and ordered both ships to proceed south toward Aden at best speed. During the course of the transit, both ships were updated on *Cole*'s status, undoubtedly from my voice reports and later from an assessment provided by Captain Hanna.

En route, Scott and Matt discussed how each ship must now be prepared for any situation, including the potential for further hostile action. After several minutes discussing their readiness, I took them privately aside to give them a status brief. I told Chris that he could update the other individual team members from their respective ships but I was going to give the COs a separate and more detailed update and tour.

The three of us had become good friends and squadron mates in the months prior to deployment. I knew that I needed to be candid and up front with them about what had happened to the *Cole* and her crew. I was also aware, however, that I did not want to paint too grim a picture and risk them misinterpreting the outstanding job the crew had done and how well they had adjusted to their circumstances following the attack. As the commanding officer, I felt obligated to directly share my insight into how the ship and crew had performed throughout the event.

Slowly and methodically, we walked the standard route I had developed for anyone coming aboard the ship. Both Scott and Matt received a detailed account of what had happened before, during, and after the explosion.

They were surprised at the depth of detail I knew regarding support flowing into the region—more than they had learned from message traffic and e-mail.

It gave me a sense of confidence that Captain Hanna had done a great job in letting me know what was going on, which I then freely shared with the crew. We discussed my meeting with the ambassador and the Fifth Fleet commander the previous day. They also considered those meetings to be the most important things I had done, since they would directly impact the breadth and depth of support USS *Cole* could expect in the coming days. I also let them know that the Royal Navy had beaten the United States to the punch in coming to our aid earlier that day.

They were amazed at the amount of debris covering the ship and the conditions the crew were working and living in. They understood why we had to sleep outside of the ship and how important it was for the crew to continue with mechanical and electrical systems restoration efforts. They also completely understood the need to keep the crew on board and not allow them to leave the ship to stay in local hotels, and why this effort would prove critical in the days to come. Also emphasized was the need to avoid disturbing as much of the explosion detritus as possible, since it was considered evidence and the FBI would need it for their criminal investigation.

Finally, we entered the darkness of the ship. Using my flashlight to initially light the way, we slowly made our way into the forward port side passageway near the chiefs' mess. The up-and-over lights had been strung in the passageways but they only provided a minimum amount of light. I needed flashlights to show them key areas of damage, including the interior of the chiefs' mess, the entrance to main engine room 1, and the folded-up deck of the port side passageway that backed up to the galley.

They spoke very little and were clearly taken aback by the extent of the damage. They understood their responsibility to their own ships and crews, but walking around USS *Cole* gave them a whole new outlook and sense of accountability.

We continued up forward and crossed by Repair 2. Standing outside the locker, we paused to discuss in detail the reaction by the crew to the attack and how the damage control organization had been affected by the loss of ship-wide communications. The benchmark of how the U.S. Navy had performed against kamikaze attacks in the Pacific during World War II had quickly become our new operating standard within minutes after being attacked. The crew had fallen back on time-tested methods of communication. As the minutes had progressed, they reestablished not only communication between the repair lockers and the central control station but also between the teams of investigators going out and checking for damage throughout the ship.

Slowly, Scott, Matt, and I made our way down the starboard passageway after stopping into the combat information center. The three of us paused at the access to radio central and auxiliary machinery room 1 and a detailed explanation ensued about how the loss of power in the forward part of the ship had impacted our ability to contact Fifth Fleet. The discussion also naturally led to the decision to rig casualty power cables, how that decision had come about, and the process we had followed to ensure there was some form of power now being supplied in the forward part of the ship.

Walking on, we came to the most challenging part of their briefing, the mess line and mess decks. In greater detail and at a much slower pace, Scott and Matt learned about the heroism of the crew and what they had done in those first few dramatic minutes. Damage control, lifesaving measures, rescue efforts, evacuation of wounded, and communications were all covered and discussed. Lastly, I pointed out the challenge that we faced in how the crew was going to have to find a way to locate, recover, identify, and transfer the remains of the twelve sailors missing in the ship.

Walking the exact same route that I had traced the day of the attack, we made our way through the main medical treatment area, across the debris-littered mess decks, and into the port side passageway just aft of the blast area. As Ambassador Bodine and Admiral Moore had been, Scott and Matt were taken aback by the sight of the bodies in the wreckage. As we stood at the edge of the blast area itself, the briefing continued, but they had grown silent, each deep in thought about what the crew must have experienced and still had to face.

Quiet and somber, the three of us crossed back through the mess decks and walked out the back of the starboard passageway into the heat and humidity of the day. As the three of us neared the area next to the brow and quarterdeck, both Scott and Matt promised that whatever assistance USS *Cole* and her crew needed, we could count on them.

Since each had already discussed their respective ship's contributions, the first order of business was to get food prepared by *Hawes* to *Cole*'s crew. We had had our fill of food from Yemen's Aden Mövenpick Hotel. Of course, we appreciated that they had been kind enough to prepare healthy meals for us, but everyone looked forward to an American-made meal. Both COs knew this would be an important morale booster. They also started preparations for a rotation of watch standers to supplement our damage control and engineering watch teams. Together, the coordination between us was unsaid but clearly understood.

Early in the afternoon, the Yemeni port authority notified *Cole* that a large barge with two tugs maneuvering it would be crossing the harbor and coming out to the refueling pier where the ship was docked. Captain Jim Hanna had made arrangements to deliver a 250-kilowatt diesel generator to the pier as an emergency backup to our only operating gas turbine generator. With our gas turbine generator 3 still running, but slowly deteriorating internally, and gas turbine generator 2 not yet operating, this diesel generator would become a critical backup should we lose power.

Gently and ever so slowly, the tug maneuvered around the mooring lines to dock along the eastern edge of the refueling pier off *Cole*'s stern. Lifting cables were hastily attached to the generator. Carefully, they lifted the generator from the barge and swung it onto the pier near the middle of the ship. In the event we would need to operate it, this location was the shortest run for the cables to provide power to us.

With the generator in place, the ship's engineers worked with the Yemeni company's operators to get it running. Despite language difficulties, they were able to understand how to start and safely operate the generator. With the universal language of mechanics, they showed the engineers how to connect and energize the cables that would provide electricity to the switchboards and equipment. Jim was on board to oversee the entire operation and once complete, he again went back ashore to continue coordination work for the myriad groups that had started to arrive in support of *Cole*.

Later that afternoon, *Hawes* informed us that the U.S. ships had worked out an arrangement to start sending in replacement damage control team members as soon as we were ready to take them on board. That was an easy decision and within an hour, the first teams arrived. These sailors would provide a welcome relief to some of the crew, many of whom were exhausted from the stress and tension that still gripped the ship.

That evening, when dinner arrived, I don't think I had ever seen the crew look as relieved and hungry since the beginning of this whole ordeal. *Hawes* had prepared a standard Navy meal that many sailors consider the ultimate in shipboard comfort food—chili mac. *Cole*'s crew dived into this concoction of elbow macaroni, hamburger, tomato sauce, and spices as if they hadn't eaten in days. Some of them in fact had probably only eaten enough Yemeni-prepared food to keep themselves from starving. This chili mac was real food, cooked by real sailors, and served up in familiar big stainless steel chafing pans. Watching them, it was clear to everyone that this one meal did more to boost morale on the ship than anything else over the past two days.

All had seemed to be going well, until about 2100 Saturday night when a new emergency brought all of our considerable progress to a screeching halt. The ship's engineers had managed to restore the main drainage system, capable of pumping out up to 1,200 gallons of floodwater per minute. The biggest leak that they still faced was the damaged seal that surrounded the starboard propeller shaft, where it passed through the bulkhead between the main engine room 2 and the flooded auxiliary machinery room 2. That leak had so far been staunched the way sailors have dealt with battle damage since time immemorial—with wooden wedges and a tar-soaked rope fiber called oakum, forcefully pounded into place around the shaft by the damage control teams. There was also the threat that the pressure of the floodwater on the bulkhead could cause it to buckle and collapse, flooding still other compartments, and so all the bulkheads around the flooded spaces were braced with wooden four-by-four beams, and later with steel ones.

We had been successfully dewatering the flooded auxiliary machine room for some time, and by late Saturday the water level had gone down almost to the point where we would be able to get into the space and seal the places where water was getting in. With no more than two or three inches of water over the deckplates, damage control personnel could go in safely with repair equipment.

But now, for reasons we did not yet know, the water level had started to rise again. Bringing on one and then two extra pumps did not succeed in bringing it down. To some extent, we were the victims of our own success. Decreasing the flow of water coming through the propeller shaft seal and the cracks in the bulkhead had reduced the pressure on the wooden wedges and oakum, and they had loosened. Now that the machinery room was filling with water again, however, they were being forced out of position, and main engine room 2 also began filling with water at a much faster rate than before. After midnight, around 0130 Sunday, the situation had grown so serious that Chris and Debbie had gone down to the mess decks and the emergency escape trunk to auxiliary machinery room 2, to personally monitor the status of the pumps and the floodwater. As they were standing there, something in the machinery room gave way. There was a loud whoosh of air from inside the space, and suddenly, the floodwaters began rising rapidly. Nobody knew if a bulkhead had collapsed, a pipe had ruptured, or something even worse had happened.

With the waters slowly rising in main engine room 2, the engineers started another pump to help stem the flow of water, but with little effect. Around 0230, Chris briefed me that the machinery room had been lost to the floodwaters. He had ordered the emergency escape trunk door from it to be shut, dogged closed, and not opened again. In the engine room, water was now flowing in at a very worrisome rate—over twenty gallons per minute, by his estimate.

Sensing disaster, I ordered Chris to immediately wake the crew, man the repair lockers, and put the ship back on emergency footing. Everyone sprang into action, but suddenly the ship was thrust into darkness when gas turbine generator 3, the only source of the electric power we had, tripped offline. It was 0305 and main engine room 2 was flooding. In darkness, USS *Cole* started to sink next to the pier.

The generator had been running since our arrival in Aden. There was no way to get fuel to the tanks of gas turbine generator 1 up forward in auxiliary machinery room 1, and the engineers were still trying to figure out why number 2, in main engine room 2, would not run. But the number 3 generator's inner workings had not been left undamaged by the explosion. Metal particles and shavings found in its lubricating oil showed that, while the generator had kept running so far, it was only a matter of time before it would seize up. Now we thought that moment had come. The failure left the main drainage system incapable of pumping out floodwater, and if main engine room 2 flooded, as main engine room 1 and the other spaces had earlier, the ship was going to go down to the bottom of the harbor.

We were enveloped in darkness. Flashlight beams bounced off the bulkheads and decks as people yelled back and forth. I made my way to the central control station, and heard from Debbie that the engineers had found that the generator had simply run out of fuel, burning more than it should have because of the damage it had sustained.

But the ship's gas turbine engines and generators required high-pressure air, at 3,000 psi, to start. We now had no power to operate the high-pressure air compressors on the ship even if they were usable. But there was enough high-pressure air stored in air flasks in the ship to give the engineers three chances to restart the generator.

Half an hour after the shutdown, they made their first attempt. It failed. An hour later, a second try: failure again. Water was flowing almost unabated into main engine room 2, endangering the very fuel-oil transfer and purification units we needed to keep the generator running. If they became submerged, nobody knew whether they would keep operating.

The damage control teams rushed into action with an alternative: P-100 diesel-operated portable pumps, rigged up to pump water out of the lower level of the engine room up to the first discharge port in the side of the ship that a hose could reach. Failure again. The pump, set up in the starboard passageway, was not powerful enough to lift water from the lower flooded levels to the passageway. As the leading uninjured damage control expert on the ship, Damage Controlman First Class Robert Morger thought the engineers could overcome that shortcoming by connecting two P-100 pumps in series, one from the bilges to the engine room's midlevel and the second from there to the discharge port. Yet again, failure. Our $1 billion ship was in mortal peril for the lack of a spare part that probably would have cost only a few dollars—a coupling adapter to connect the three-inch discharge pipe from one pump to the two-and-a-half-inch suction pipe of the second pump. The Navy had not foreseen that P-100 pumps would ever have to be connected in series; no such part was carried on board *Cole* or any other ship. The general workshop, with welding equipment that might have been used to make one, had been completely destroyed.

Even so, there was one more chance to restart the generator with high-pressure air. The engineers suspected that trapped air in the fuel system was the root problem. With only a limited number of access points, the engineers picked the highest and most accessible fuel piping coupling to the generator, disconnected the fittings, and slowly bled what they hoped was all the entrapped air out of the system. At around 0600 Sunday morning, Debbie and her engineering team gathered in the control station for the last and final attempt. With the push of a button, high-pressure air was applied to the starter, and the generator rapidly wound up almost to the point where it should have ignited the fuel, fell 50 rpm short, and slowly wound back to a stop.

We still had a long shot. The 250-kilowatt diesel generator brought out to the refueling pier, near the middle of the ship, now became a critically needed emergency backup and our last, best hope. It had worked well enough in a test on Saturday. Several engineers quickly checked its systems and pressed the start button—after numerous tries, failure again.

By this point, the sun was rising over the harbor as we faced another hot, humid day. Floodwaters were flowing into the ship and there seemed to be nothing we could do to stop them.

I saw Debbie standing alone near the starboard topside shelter with no one around. "How are you doing?" I asked. Utter disappointment was written across her face. "Captain, I just don't know what to do. We've tried everything and I can't get anything to run." I told her I had every confidence in her and walked away to give her the time and space she needed to pull herself together and get back to fighting to save the ship.

At about 0730 Sunday, after several hours of poring over technical specifications and architectural drawings of the ship, Chris and Debbie came to me with a new idea. A P-100 pump operating on the second level of the flooded engine room could pump water from the bottom and over the side at that level—if we cut a hole in the side of the ship, that is, because there were no discharge ports that low in the hull. They thought we could do that with our portable exothermic cutting unit, a device the Navy had adopted as a replacement for heavier and bulker oxy-acetylene cutting torches. The portable unit could be set up rapidly and cut metal at temperatures well over 2,500 degrees Fahrenheit.

"Do it," I said. "Just make sure we measure not once, not twice, but three times, and take the list of the ship into account. If we start cutting and it's below the waterline, we'll be screwed."

Hull Technician Second Class Chris Regal, whom Fireman Jeremy Stewart had implored to "save the ship" after he was rescued from the galley, was the most experienced welder in the crew, and volunteered to do the job. With other members of his division, he set up a portable exothermic cutting torch near the exposed hull and marked the section to cut. Donning his protective gear, Regal picked up the torch and tried to strike a spark. Nothing happened. The batteries were dead. Once again, it seemed that if anything could go wrong it would. We were apparently out of options again. USS *Cole* continued to sink next to the pier.

"Captain, I'm not sure what else we can do at this point," the XO told me after reporting this latest setback to me on the quarterdeck. Looking him squarely in the eye, I told him, "XO, we have over two hundred able-bodied sailors on this ship. I want every one of them to find a bucket. Line them up going down into main two and if we have to use a bucket brigade for the next two hours until I can get a portable torch from *Hawes* or *Donald Cook* and we can make those cuts, that's what we'll do. *We are not going to lose this ship.*"

By word of mouth, the order energized the crew. Everyone swung into motion and the ship seemed to come to life as sailors rushed about the ship gathering buckets and staging them near the entrance to the engine room. By now the floodwaters were four feet over the deck plates in the lower level, and vital equipment needed to get the generator running again was partially or completely submerged. After taking about fifteen minutes to get organized, the crew had established a line that ran from the flight deck, into the starboard side passageway, and down the ladders to the lower level of the engine room. Soon bucket after bucket of water was being handed up and dumped over the side. We were saving our ship.

In what seemed like only a few minutes, a boat from *Donald Cook* raced into the harbor and loudly throttled to a stop at the refueling pier with not one but two portable torches, which were raced aboard *Cole* and straight to the engine room.

The bucket brigade cleared out of the space, and with the smell of the fuel that was mixed with the floodwater heavy in the air, Regal began to make his cut. Slowly and methodically, he cut through the half-inch thick hull plate, making one six-by-twelve-inch cut about a foot above the waterline. Once the steel had cooled to the touch, a P-100 pump was moved into position, rigged, and started.

Floodwaters from the engine room began flowing out the discharge port. Within minutes, the engineers were able to report to me in the central control station that the water level was holding steady but had already flooded to four feet over the deckplates in the lower level of the space. While the level was not going down, it was no longer rising and covering any more equipment. To my enormous relief, it also meant the ship was no longer sinking.

I was sitting at the damage control console, across from the ship diagrams where we had plotted the initial explosion and aftermath of the attack, and I was alone. The space was dark and empty except for the morning sunlight shining hotly through the open watertight scuttle that was right above me. It was about 0830 Sunday morning. Sitting there, I suddenly found myself unable to move. My head drifted closer to my chest. Everything went dark.

I had not slept for over seventy-two hours since docking in Aden. For two nights, I had allowed Chris and Master Chief Parlier to sleep, thinking that I would wake them when I needed some rest. But waking them had never been an option I allowed myself to think about exercising. Now, paralyzed by exhaustion, I found myself overtaken by sleep without warning.

Yet only an hour later, my body was screaming at me to wake up. It felt as if a truck had run over me. I was still alone. I felt personally embarrassed, and angry at myself for leaving the ship and crew vulnerable even for an hour, and I went out into the sunlight of the flight deck to find Chris and Debbie to give me an update.

The bucket brigade and temporary pumps had held the floodwaters at bay. Debbie and her engineers were still racking their brains to find a way to restart the ship's working gas-turbine generator with high-pressure air and reactivate the main drainage system, so that we could fully pump out the flooded engine and machinery rooms. At 1000, the engineers told me that they had put their heads together with the crack Navy divers of Detachment Alpha who had flown in the day before, and come up with an imaginative way to produce a new supply of high-pressure air. By jury-rigging fittings from their diving gear, they could take our two shipboard self-contained breathing apparatus chargers, useful in an emergency to refill firefighting breathing bottles, to get air from the two compressors they had set up on the flight deck to the ship's high-pressure air system and the air flasks that could restart the generator. Could something designed to supply emergency air for shipboard firefighting equipment be effective in restarting a powerful turbine generator supplying electricity to an entire ship?

The engineers and the divers said it could. The portable pumps could produce pressure of 5,000 psi. After spending over an hour tracing system lines, the engineers and Warrant Officer Perna and his divers found a gauge line that, with the jury-rigged fittings, could be hooked up to the air hoses running down through a watertight hatch on the flight deck into the generator room. If they could refill one of the flasks, they estimated that they could try again to restart the generator in about twelve hours.

Around 1030, the compressors started and HP air slowly started to fill the flasks. A bit longer than twelve hours later, at five minutes after midnight Monday morning, the engineers shot compressor starter air from the recharged air flask into the generator. As if there had never been a problem, gas turbine generator 3 smoothly restarted, electrical power was applied to the switchboard, and one by one, pumps and equipment came online and, within minutes, pumped main engine room 2 dry.

It had been a long and tense twenty-one hours. The crew had performed flawlessly under trying and unnerving conditions. They had weathered poor sanitation, an absence of operable toilets on the ship, and no ventilation. There had been an outbreak of abdominal cramps and diarrhea. Several crew members had become dehydrated. In response, Chief Moser instructed the crew to use bottled water to wash their hands and faces before handling or eating food. Those measures, plus Imodium and Ciprofloxacin, brought things under control before we had a crisis on our hands. Illness still affected a number of the crew, but they had persevered. They had kept the ship from sinking.

They were not going to give up the ship—their ship.

8 | Assessing the Damage

I T WAS 0530 WHEN THE ALARM next to my head began once again to beep incessantly, not even four hours since my collapse onto the flight deck in a horizontal pile of flesh and bones. Slowly and with the hazy blur from lack of sleep, the reality sunk in that it was now Monday morning, day four after the attack. The steady high-pitched whine of the generator in the background was still the most comforting noise in the world. Given the implications of its silence, everyone had slept better knowing it was running, providing us with power, and keeping us afloat. But now it was time to get up and start the day.

Over the past three days, the Navy, Department of Defense, and other branches of the U.S. government had deployed a series of people and organizations into Aden. Across the globe, the ripple effects from the attack were being felt, especially in the Middle East where the threat level was raised to Threat Condition Delta, meaning another attack could be imminent. Almost every ship deployed overseas across the world sortied out of port, and security at every military base was markedly and visibly increased.

Less than twenty-four hours after the attack, the Chairman of the Joint Chiefs of Staff, General Hugh Shelton, U.S. Army, ordered the creation of Joint Task Force (JTF) Determined Response to coordinate the U.S.

government response to the attack. Rear Admiral Mark "Lobster" Fitzgerald, U.S. Navy, the Deputy Commander of U.S. Naval Forces Central Command, was designated to head up the new organization. He was immediately dispatched to Aden to take charge of the many disparate groups and organize them to provide support to *Cole* without overwhelming the ship and crew.

The night after the attack, Commander Patrick J. Keenan and Lieutenant Commander Matthew Long, the Officer in Charge and Assistant Officer in Charge of the Navy Ship Repair Unit stationed in Bahrain as part of the Fifth Fleet Staff, had arrived in Aden. They planned to conduct a SCUBA dive under USS *Cole* to see if the ship could eventually be moved to a safer location. They were using the diving gear of a Navy Explosive Ordnance Disposal team that had been helping the Yemeni government remove thousands of mines left over from the civil war in the 1990s.

In the early morning hours of October 13, they had disappeared into the eighty-five-degree water under *Cole* and slowly and methodically swam the length of the ship. A large sheen of oil coated the water, but beneath it there was visibility of about fifteen feet. Taking their time to ensure they did not miss any damage, Keenan and Long worked their way up to the forward part of the ship near the sonar dome, then back along the keel to the stern of the ship near the rudders and propellers. They planned to enter the hole in the side only to the extent necessary to determine the structural integrity of the ship and perhaps take some measurements, because jagged and sharp metal protruded inward around the entire circumference.

While the curve of the top of the hole could be seen above the waterline, the widest part was several feet below water. Carefully, both divers measured the hole's extent down the side and underneath the ship. They were awestruck by the amount of devastation caused by the force of the hydraulic impact from the detonation. Numerous cracks emanated away from the blast hole where the steel had been deformed and torn like thick paper. The bilge keel, a large strake of metal attached to the ship on each side and running along most of its length, had been torn in about a sixty-foot section, although it was still attached at each end. It was clear from the amount of fuel still in the water that the fuel tanks underneath main engine room 1 had been breached by the force of the explosion. These were still leaking fuel into the harbor.

The explosion of the suicide boat had created a massive shock wave, which in the incompressible water of the harbor instantly translated tremendous force in all directions outward and downward—outward into the side of *Cole,* punching through the half-inch hull and inward into the ship, and downward into the seabed to form a crater about twenty feet across and four feet deep, then reflecting upward toward the bottom of the ship and its keel.

The initial damage assessment listed the following:

A 9-meter long by 12-meter high (roughly 30 x 40 foot) hole in the portside shell-plate of the hull extending 5 meters (16 feet) below the waterline.

Significant radial cracking and dished plating emanating from and adjacent to main engine room 1, completely flooded and in free communication with the sea.

Blast damage to equipment extending to amidships in the engine room with significant damage to adjoining main deck and first platform spaces.

Auxiliary machinery room 2 flooded to a level equal to the external waterline via cracks and tears in bulkhead 220, which separates it from the engine room.

Main engine room 2 flooding progressively from auxiliary machinery room 2 through the bulkhead 254 starboard shaft seal (30 gallons per minute).

No electrical power in the forward two-thirds of the ship.

Although the ship's initial list and trim (sideways and longitudinal tilt) immediately after the blast were greater, it settled to a 4.6 degree list to port with a 0.5 degree (1.6 meter) trim down by the bow.

Amidships bank compensated fuel oil storage tanks and port side
    service tank ruptured.
Starboard propulsion plant (main engine room 1) out of commission.
Port propulsion plant status unknown.

The divers estimated that 200 tons of fuel (almost 60,000 gallons) had
been lost from the damaged tanks and that the ship had taken on approximately 2,300 tons of floodwater.

This information was sent to the Naval Sea Systems Command in
Washington. There, experts developed a plan of action to continue the
work the crew had begun to stop progressive flooding, maintain power
and keep the firemain operational, and reduce the list (sideways tilt) and
trim (longitudinal tilt) of the ship caused by the flooding. Later, they developed a plan to move the ship from Aden to a safe location.[1] Our own
next step would be to decide how to begin the recovery of the remains of
sailors trapped in the wreckage of the mess line, galley, and main engine
room 1.

Today there would be no rest for the weary. While the crew had already
seen Ambassador Bodine, Vice Admiral Moore, and several Yemeni government officials come out to the ship to view the results of the attacks,
General Tommy R. Franks, U.S. Army, the Commander of Central Command, was to make a visit (his only one) to the ship. *Cole* was under General
Frank's operational control and this visit, while expected, came sooner
than we anticipated.

A tall and imposing figure, the general arrived by one of the Marine
anti-terrorism security team's zodiac inflatable hull boats. With an armed
security detail in tow, he strode quickly and confidently across the refueling
pier and up the brow. There was no place to mount the ship's bell and still
no fanfare for any visitor, regardless of rank. Chris, Master Chief Parlier,
and I greeted him at the brow. After a quick brief about the stability of
the ship and the welfare of the crew, we started to walk the now standard
visitors' route.

At the epicenter of the explosion, the galley, the general paused and
we talked about the effects of the blast on the ship. He seemed very inter-

ested in how watertight integrity on the ship worked. I explained—in probably more detail than he wanted or needed—how our decision to set modified condition Zebra on the damage control deck and below and to compartmentalize the ship as much as possible was a key factor in our ability to save it. He had also heard how, despite an inoperative 1MC and no one to tell the crew what to do, they had performed magnificently and used their training to respond to the attack with damage control and security measures. He seemed impressed at how well the crew had held up in the days since.

But as we walked about the ship, he repeatedly did something that made me think he was disconnected from the reality of what had happened to us. As we passed crew members going about their work or standing their watches, he would stop them, shake hands vigorously, and slip from his palm to theirs small metal coins. These were called challenge coins, with a red Central Command emblem on one side and a miniature relief map of the region on the other. These were his personal challenge coins, with his name on them, and he seemed fixated on handing them out to crew members right and left.

At first, I thought it was a nice gesture and a measure of his respect for the crew. As we continued to walk around, however, it seemed to me that he thought this was just another peacetime visit to troops in garrison. We still had bodies trapped in the wreckage of the mess line, galley, and the destroyed engine room. The crew, only hours before his arrival, had barely been able to prevent the ship from sinking. Everyone was traumatized and exhausted. Yet here was the commanding general in charge of a major theater of operations, walking about a devastated ship, handing out coins and backslapping the crew as if nothing out of the ordinary had happened.

As we wrapped up the tour and walked back to the flight deck, General Franks asked if he could address the crew for a few minutes. While I looked composed on the outside, inside, my mind was churning with the disbelief about his casual demeanor. As calmly as possible, it was explained to him that the crew was extremely busy preparing for the coming onslaught of support personnel. While they would probably have enjoyed hearing his remarks, it would be disruptive to stop everything. No doubt disappointed, but thankfully accepting my explanation without a clue as to the real reason, he prepared to leave the ship from the quarterdeck. Again without fanfare, he saluted, walked down the brow and across the pier, and quickly faded into our memory as he went ashore, with his security detail in tow.

Back again on my black fender perch, I motioned for Chris to come over. With no one in earshot, I pulled from my pocket a plastic bag of about twenty coins the general had handed me and asked, "Can you believe him? He was totally oblivious to what happened to us. As we were walking around the ship, he kept handing these coins out to the crew like he was on some walking tour of an Army base." Chris just shook his head in amazement. "Captain, do you want me to take those from you and distribute them?" he asked with a smile. I just smirked back at him and said, "No, I'll just hold onto these for now. I don't know what I'm going to do with them but I'll just hold onto them. I just can't believe him."

More pressing matters soon consumed our attention.

Besides the FBI team and the divers (joined by the lead officer from their home unit in Norfolk, Mobile Diving and Salvage Unit 2, Commander Barbara L. "Bobbie" Scholley, USN), volunteer workers and technical experts from the Norfolk Naval Shipyard and the Shore Intermediate Maintenance Activity in Norfolk came aboard to assist in the ship stabilization efforts. Lastly, a Special Psychiatric Rapid Intervention Team (SPRINT) deployed from the Naval Hospital in Sigonella, Italy, plus two Fifth Fleet chaplains, arrived to begin working directly with the crew to start the process of helping everyone deal with the post-traumatic stress from the attack.

Up until this point, Chris and I had, for the most part, mutually coordinated our efforts to organize the crew and work with the lead members from each support agency that came aboard the ship. That approach would no longer work; too much was happening too quickly. Without ever discussing or even acknowledging it, we divided the duties. Chris would handle and deal with the operation and coordination of efforts internal to the crew and ship, while I would deal with the myriad personnel that were coming from ashore. Without even exchanging a word, our relationship as CO and XO had matured and transitioned to a new level. It was one of the blessings of having a great executive officer.

Initially, the FBI's evidence collection teams had planned to work independently of the ship's crew. They did not know how well the crew was coping with the aftermath of the attack, and in their previous experience at post-blast crime scenes, they had not had people who had lived through the attack available to assist them. After the initial assessment survey on Sunday, however, Don Sachtleben, now the FBI lead forensic advisor on the scene, decided to take advantage of the manpower pool available in *Cole's* crew and use them to supplement the evidence collection teams.

This turned out to be the right decision. Working with the FBI and NCIS agents allowed the crew to participate in the vital task of evidence collection, helping to determine who had carried out the attack and bring them to justice. When off watch, crew members would not be left sitting around to bemoan their circumstances or worry about their fate; they would have work to do. Similarly, the FBI benefitted from having skilled experts familiar with the ship, its components, and how things operated in a shipboard environment.

Time was of the essence. The crew knew that the faster the job of evidence collection could be completed, the faster they would get the ship back under their complete control. While it was always their ship, having a team of twenty to thirty law enforcement agents, plus other support organizations, crawling everywhere created a sense that for the time being they had lost ownership. Most just wanted to be done with this work so they could start the process of cleaning up all the debris topside and give the ship a thorough freshwater washdown. It would also mean being able to clean up the area around the mess line and galley, thereby reducing the growing stench of rotting food.

Throughout the day, the FBI/NCIS forensic teams, including key personnel Supervisory Special Agent Leo West (FBI), Special Agent Cathy Clements (NCIS), and Special Agent Mike Martz (NCIS), worked to section off different areas of the ship and systematically gather evidence, which would all be kept aboard ship or transferred to other Navy ships so as to keep it entirely under U.S. control. For these seasoned investigators, the entire ship was covered in question marks. Specific material they looked to gather included pieces of wire, batteries, and other mechanisms to indicate the ignition source for the explosives, the type of motor used in the boat, or any other pieces that might provide a clue that would fit into the massive puzzle they were just starting to work on. They also looked for key components that would give them clues about the size and origin of the boat as well as how the explosives may have been positioned in it.

Another major requirement of evidence gathering was to find pieces of the bombers whose bodies had been obliterated by the explosion. Their DNA would make it possible to identify them and give clues to how the attack had been so skillfully planned and executed. Pieces of bone, flesh, and teeth from the bombers had already been found on the ship and more was being discovered as the day wore on.

Every piece of material that did not appear to come from the ship went through careful examination and review. On the forecastle, shaded by a tarp erected over the MK-45 5-inch/54 gun barrel, several tables held the evidence the crew uncovered. At each table, the investigators carefully pored over the material brought to them in bags and buckets, and then sifted through a screen. It was a slow and detailed process that went on for hours at a stretch before the team members would take a break inside the ship to gain some respite from the oppressive heat and humidity.

Once sorted, bags of evidence were deposited in the ship's classroom under the flight deck, and turned over to the FBI/NCIS team as the central office for evidence collection and documentation. Right next door, the ship's career counselor's office became the initial storage point for evidence. Since this space could be locked and maintained under strict access control, it was the best place for evidence to be received, logged in using evidence collection materials and forms—the FD-192, or green sheet, for the FBI— and secured until it could be taken off the ship.

The crew knew not to walk through or disrupt key areas that might still contain undisturbed evidence. Looking back on the ship from the forecastle, the evidence collection team knew they would be spending days if not weeks getting into every nook and cranny in every possible topside location of the ship. Inside, in the area of the mess decks, galley, mess line, and chiefs' mess, other teams slowly began to pick their way through the debris. Here, the location and sorting process was made even more difficult by lack of ventilation in Aden's stifling heat and humidity, as well as the dearth of adequate lighting.

From the moment Don and other FBI agents came on board, their focus was the collection of evidence. Within hours though, that focus subtly shifted; while evidence would continue to be collected, the recovery of crew remains became the overriding priority for everyone on board. In discussions with Jim Hanna, Chris and I were led to understand that the shipyard workers from the Norfolk Naval Shipyard would help us recover the remains of our shipmates from the wreckage above the waterline, and to brace structures around the blast area so that the ship could be safely and slowly towed out of port. Commander Scholley and her MDSU-2 divers would assess damage to the flooded spaces of the ship, figure out how to stop water from leaking out of those spaces to the rest of the ship, and conduct the underwater recovery of missing sailors. Planning for how to get *Cole* out of port was going on concurrently with these efforts and as the sailors' remains were recovered and the ship was stabilized and readied, the plan to get *Cole* out of Aden and back to the United States would kick into high gear.

That was not going to be easy. The first problem was how to stop flooding from the auxiliary machinery room 2 through the shaft seal into main engine room 2. That had been held at bay by the pumps, but if the ship lost power again, the engine room would flood all over again.

Two divers, Hull Technician Second Class Bret Husbeck and Engineman Second Class Michael Shields, dressed out in full dive gear and helmets, made the first attempt to reenter the machinery room from the mess decks, straight down the vertical escape scuttle that had been shut late Saturday night to control the floodwaters. With their MK 21 dive helmets connected by hoses to their air supply and equipped with lights and a video feed to let supervisors provide guidance, they made their way down into the black hole and disappeared under the oily water.

Surprisingly, they reported, the explosive force of the blast had not demolished the interior of the space or its equipment. Walking carefully on the deck plates above the bilges, they were unable to see any damage and determine how the floodwaters were flowing into the machinery room. But turning to the problem of the damaged seal around the propeller shaft where it passed through the bulkhead to main engine room 2, they were able to jam and wedge a long length of three-inch braided nylon towing line into the crevice surrounding the shaft, and stopped the leak.

Once they were topside again, it was clear that the fuel and oil floating everywhere in the water had wreaked havoc with their equipment. It had started to interfere with the diaphragms built into the regulators inside their helmets, and the slick coating on wetsuits had to be quickly and completely removed to prevent the material from degrading. Also the seals around the connections for air, video, and communications would slowly decompose from exposure to the toxic mixture. This hazard was going to be a continuing problem, as was our power supply, and we needed the help of the divers to deal with that, as well.

Our one working gas-turbine generator, number 3, had appeared to be running well after being restarted that morning, though the magnets in its lubricating oil strainer still were attracting shavings of metal, proof of excessive wear that would inevitably lead to its failure. But gas turbine generator 2, in the engine room we had just saved from leaks through the propeller shaft fitting, could not be restarted at all. An isolation valve somewhere between it and the flooded main engine room 1 was open, and the pressurized air that would be needed to start it was escaping the system. Everything was in order inside the now-dewatered main engine room 2. That could mean the leak was in the flooded supply office or the parts storage area directly above auxiliary machinery room 2—and if we were going to get the generator running, we would need to find it.

Members of the crew had talked with the two sailors who had been working in that area at the time of the explosion—and been since evacuated to the United States for treatment of their injuries—and had learned that the only damage was probably to the port side wall and forward corner of the supply office, not farther back in the area containing spare parts for the ship and the isolation valve.

So down went another set of divers into the murky floodwaters. Stepping up once again, Chief Pelly, who had helped rescue Seaman Lafontaine from the devastation of the galley after the explosion, volunteered to monitor the camera feed with the diving supervisor, to guide the divers to the likely source of the air leak.

As the divers slowly made their way down the ladder near the mess line and into the flooded supply office, a large tear in the metal bulkhead in the forward port corner explained what had happened. At the top corner, that bulkhead had been torn open and forcefully blown into the space, allowing water to flood in through the ripped-open hull. We had been lucky to get everyone out of the now completely flooded supply office alive. Walking through the wreckage of furniture, filing cabinets, and papers floating in the water, the divers went toward the back of the ship to enter the space next door that contained most of the spare parts for the ship. The non-watertight door had been blown off its hinges and partially blocked their access. Initial inspection showed that the space had received only minor structural damage, but the force of the blast had knocked every loose spare part and piece of equipment and tossed it around.

As they picked their way through the clutter at their feet, Chief Pelly carefully guided them to where he thought the valve could be located. Again, working slowly and methodically through the water, the divers quickly found the valve and within a few minutes had shut it off. Hopefully, gas turbine generator 2 would soon be ready to start.

The crew was steadily restoring vital living systems throughout the ship. Air conditioning units were back online for the berthing compartments and workspaces in the back of the ship; the aft sewage system had been running smoothly for hours; and electrical power and lighting were slowly being energized in the forward part of the ship that had been in the dark since the attack. The Norfolk Naval Shipyard workers had quickly communicated their technical skills to the law enforcement and other support groups on board, and the FBI and divers took advantage both of their skills and equipment to build evidence collection boxes for the FBI and ladders for the divers to allow safe entry to the upper levels of main engine room 1.

Things were beginning to look up. Then—*Bang!*

A sharp, loud crack echoed across the aft missile deck and the flight deck as everyone within sight of my perch reacted, heads snapping around and bodies poised to hit the deck for cover. Without thinking, a shipyard worker had opened one of his large metal equipment storage boxes and after grabbing his tools, had let the large lid slam shut. The loud bang was not a noise he considered unusual, but it clearly had put an already jumpy crew on edge again.

With a slight smile, knowing this had to be approached in the right way, I hopped down from atop the fender and intercepted the worker as he was walking forward with his tool bag. "Excuse me, but do you know where I can find the supervisor for you guys? I need to get in touch with him if he has a few minutes."

"Sure, I know right where he is. I'll go get him for you, Captain," he said, as he ambled off toward the amidships area of the ship.

Chris and Master Chief Parlier were standing nearby and knew what I was up to but didn't quite know how I would handle it. A few minutes later, the supervisor, Kenneth Baggett, came up to me.

"Captain, I understand you were looking for me," he said.

"Yes, I was, thanks. I need you to do me a big favor. The crew has been through a lot these past few days and some of us are still pretty sensitive to loud noises. When your workers open their toolboxes, could you please ask them to make sure they gently close the lids? One of them just scared the bejesus out of everyone when he let the lid slam shut like shipyard workers usually do. Right now, I need a little help with this one," I asked.

Ken looked mortified. "Captain, I'll get hold of everyone right away. I'm so sorry. I had no idea. I'm sure he didn't even think about what he was doing. I'll make sure everyone knows. I apologize. I'm sure he didn't mean to do it," he managed to say to me.

I did not want him to think we were all skittish and overreacting, but I had also seen the crew's response to the noise. I looked at him, smiled, and said, "Ken, it's all right. Don't make a big deal out of this. It's just that the noise surprised everyone and if your folks can just take a few extra seconds to carefully close the lids, I don't think there will be any problems. I really appreciate your help."

As he turned to walk away, he smiled, as he said, "No problem, Captain. We'll get this fixed right away."

The crew had been watching. I walked back and hopped back up on my perch knowing that Chris and the Master Chief had observed my interaction with the supervisor. Now, with both of them standing near me, each had a bit of a slight smile on his face as I said, "Well, that shouldn't be a problem again." With the increasing stream of outside help flowing to the ship to assist in every aspect of getting through this ordeal, a deft touch in making them sensitive to the crew and their feelings would be an ongoing process. Confident the crew could handle anything thrown their way, I also knew that beneath the veneer of hardened capability and confidence, they were still very sensitive to the reality and the dangers of our situation.

From then on, Ken and the Norfolk Naval Shipyard workers so effectively blended into the efforts of the crew and support teams that for all intents and purposes they were just another extension of *Cole's* crew.

The day seemed to be grinding on, when our lives suddenly turned on a dime again: at 1424, gas turbine generator 3 suddenly tripped offline without warning. Once again the ship was plunged into silent darkness as the engineers scrambled to find out what happened. Within minutes, they determined the cause to be the same as early Sunday morning; the generator had run out of fuel because it was impossible to monitor the fuel tank level.

The crew was hardened by the past two days of work. Even so, you could feel discouragement creep in. While no one doubted we could keep the ship afloat, these types of setbacks frustrated everyone and kept them on edge.

By 1500 that afternoon, the problem was solved as number 3 again roared to life. Power and lights came on quickly after that, and within minutes a normal routine returned to the ship, although with a heightened sense of anxiousness. Within a few hours, however, a more permanent fix to the fuel problem was made, allowing the fuel system of main engine room 2 to provide a constant flow of fuel to the online fuel service tank for the generator.

Now Commander Scholley and her divers turned their attention to how we were going to get into the destroyed main engine room 1 to continue to gather forensic evidence and begin the search and recovery of the remains of the sailors there. The entrance to the space, just below the chief petty officers' mess and next to the fuel lab, was almost completely flooded. There were at least eighteen inches of water over the deck grating at the upper level of the engine room. The main entrance watertight door was buckled in about twelve inches, looking as if it had been punched at the center. The bolt dogs surrounding the door to hold it tightly shut and maintain the watertight integrity for the space were bent and deformed, as was the latching mechanism on the other side of the door. This access was definitely unusable. Using a cutting torch to gain access was not an option, given the amount of fuel and oil still floating in the water. While we might have been able to control a flash fire on the cutting side, if one started in the engine room, there was no way to effectively fight it. The danger of accidentally starting a fire in a space that could not be accessed was deemed too great.

The next option considered was the escape trunk that led from the engine room up to the destroyed mess line, but a light lowered down into it showed that the trunk was too heavily damaged to be safe. So it was back to the ship's damage control drawings for ideas.

Since innovation and flexibility were now the new normal, the next option was to look at how air entered or left the engine room. Through fortuitous design, on the starboard side was a fan room that contained a ventilation duct providing fresh air to the engine room. A round ventilation motor and fan measuring about twenty-four inches across and forty-eight inches high could be unbolted from its mount to expose the duct, leading directly down to the upper level of the engine room. We had found our access point.

While evidence collection and processing was a priority throughout the day, everybody was steeled for the more sensitive and essential mission that had now become the number one priority in the minds of every member of the ship's crew: the extrication and recovery of our twelve shipmates who were crushed and entombed in the wreckage of the mess line, galley, and the destroyed engine room. Until we finished recovering their remains to begin that long journey to their families, no one could rest easy. Everyone wanted to get our shipmates headed home.

9 | Recovering the Fallen

EACH OF THE THREE MAIN GROUPS working on the ship felt that recovering and repatriating the remains of our dead was now the main objective. The FBI/NCIS team, the Navy divers, and the shipyard workers from Norfolk Naval Shipyard now put one mission first: the recovery of the sailors killed in the attack and still trapped in the wreckage of the ship.

Although the primary mission of the Norfolk shipyard workers was to help enhance the structural stability and seaworthiness of *Cole* to make the ship ready to withstand being towed from port and returned to a stateside shipyard, little more than an hour after they arrived that morning, they discovered that they had become the linchpin that would enable the other organizations to access and recover the dead sailors.

When the shipyard team left Norfolk, their mission was twofold: do whatever was necessary to enhance the structural integrity of *Cole* to allow it to get out of port safely for future transportation back to the United States and support the FBI and other teams on board in their efforts to gather evidence and get the dead sailors out of the wreckage. The FBI needed them to cut access holes in the steel bulkheads. The divers needed them to build a ladder strong enough, yet narrow enough, to lower through the ventilation duct in the starboard brake fan room to access the upper level of the flooded engine room. While it had never been explicitly stated, we all assumed that the shipyard workers' mission would include not only accessing the trapped sailors but handling their remains as well. This erroneous assumption in their mission was about to have a drastic and unexpected impact.

But there was one hitch, as I learned when Ken Baggett came up to me with a very worried expression on his face.

"Captain, can I speak with you privately for a minute?" he asked.

I hopped down off the fender and motioned for him to step forward near the inflatable small craft, where we would be out of earshot.

"Captain, I think there may be some confusion about what the shipyard workers and I can do for you. We came here to help get your folks out of the wreckage and get the ship ready to leave port but we can't handle the bodies. I'm not going to pull a union card on you, but we are not trained or equipped to handle that kind of work and you're going to need to have some of your folks do that," he told me.

We had apparently misunderstood their mission. It was not their fault but now I had to come up with a new plan and quickly. "I completely understand. Don't worry about it, we'll put together a list of my crew and we'll get them down there shortly," I said. "Captain, I don't want you to think we don't want to help, we just didn't volunteer to come here for this," Ken said.

"Ken, don't worry. We'll take care of it. Thanks for letting me know," I said. Without another word, we shook hands and he headed back to his workers.

Sensing that something was amiss, Chris walked up, "Captain, is there a problem?" I explained it to him, and he took a deep breath.

Once again, the frame of reference hearkened back to World War II kamikaze attacks in the Pacific. Those suicide pilots sank more than thirty Navy ships and damaged many more, including the destroyer USS *Laffey*, "the ship that would not die" even after taking five hits in the battle of Okinawa. The carrier USS *Bunker Hill* had suffered 389 deaths in one of the worst attacks, but its crew had kept the ship from sinking and had helped recover the remains of their shipmates. If those sailors before us had done this kind of difficult work, there was no doubt this crew was also capable of handling that necessary but unpleasant task. Taking a deep breath myself, I just looked at Chris and said, "XO, we need a list of five sailors who we think have the mental stamina and toughness to deal with what they will see. While they need to volunteer for this, we have to pick them carefully. I'll let the FBI know what we are doing and that we'll have them ready to go in a few minutes."

Chris looked at me, clearly troubled. Before I walked away, we ran through a few names of crew members both of us felt were capable of dealing with this problem, but we still needed a couple more. This was not going to be easy for anyone, and my gut churned with anxiety. Even with the area in the mess line and galley blocked off, I had seen the deteriorating physical state of the bodies in the wreckage and knew that these five crew volunteers would see things that would haunt them for the rest of their lives. We both knew the Navy would inherit a lifelong obligation to these people. While I knew the divers dealt with the delicate task of remains recovery when it came to aircraft crashes and other at-sea accidents, the recovery effort above the waterline did not fall exactly into their line of work. Still, I felt that if anyone had to do that task, it naturally fell to this crew to handle it. Chris turned and walked away to get the names.

As I stood there for just a moment longer, Don Sachtleben from the FBI walked up to me.

"Captain, I'm working with the shipyard folks down on the mess decks and heard their concerns about having to handle the bodies," he said. Assuming he wanted to get started with the recovery effort as soon as possible, I responded, "That's correct. I already discussed the issue with the XO and we're putting together a list of five sailors as quickly as possible who we think can handle what they're about to do. As soon as we get the list, we'll get them down to you."

He looked at me a little surprised. "You don't need to do that," he told me. "We have folks here that can do that job. We're trained to do this type of work and have agents here who were involved in the recovery efforts at Oklahoma City and some just recently finished up work in Bosnia at a mass grave excavation. We have the Tyvek suits, gloves, facemasks, and scented filters. We'll take care of your sailors for you."

A huge weight lifted off my shoulders. The crew did not have to be exposed to the tragic sight of their shipmates and friends. Somewhat overcome with gratitude, all I could say was, "Thank you, thank you very much. That helps us out a lot." Don just smiled, shrugged his shoulders in his typical no-problem manner, and walked back toward the amidships area to continue his work.

Chris was as grateful as I was when he heard the news.

With their toolboxes staged on the aft missile deck and flight deck, several of the shipyard workers gathered up their equipment and cutting torches and, in company with the FBI, went down to work on the mess decks. There two, possibly three bodies were trapped in the deformed, unyielding metal of the mess line.

There was still no power in this area of the ship and forward. While some up-and-over lights had been strung in the mess decks area, it was still relatively dark. The pungent smell of rotting chicken fajitas and the other remnants of last Thursday's noon meal permeated the air. Combined with the still powerful smell of fuel, it was as close to the putrid smell of hell as one could imagine. Yet, no one complained; no one flinched; no one declined the work. Everyone down there knew their mission and went about it with steely determination.

The problem now became how to get this curved wall of metal away from the sailors. There was no way to pull it away from the bodies since there was nothing on the other side except the large open cavern inside the ship where the general workshop, galley, and engine room used to exist—no way to gain the leverage needed to do the job. The next option was to cut away the bulkhead between the mess line and the mess decks where the remains were pinned into the wreckage.

Before the explosion, members of the crew had been walking down the mess line with food trays in hand. When they rounded a corner to enter the mess decks, they came to the drink line, which formed across the forward bulkhead to their left. They passed sectioned plastic racks holding glasses at the beginning of the line, then machines dispensing a wide array of selections: white and chocolate milk, water, lemonade, various soda pop flavors, and "bug juice"—a flavored water similar to Kool-Aid relished by sailors worldwide for its high sugar content and unique ability to shine brass. This forward bulkhead, with all this equipment along it that had to be removed, was the aft-most wall relatively undamaged by the blast. On the other side were the devastated mess line and trapped bodies.

To gain access to the flat surface of the bulkhead behind what had been the drink line and prepare it for cutting, the machines had to be un-bolted from the deck and bulkhead, and within thirty minutes they had been disconnected and shoved aside to give the shipyard welders unfet-tered access. Mindful of the possibility of a fire, they had a qualified en-gineer test the immediate area where they would make the cuts and check the quality of the air to ensure it contained no explosive gases or vapors. While the hot air hung heavy with the humid stench of decay, it would not ignite from sparks or flames.

After taking very careful measurements of where to cut, the torch popped to life and the slow process of removing a section of bulkhead be-gan. The cut had to be made all the way around, with special care to avoid the bodies of the sailors known to be just on the other side. To access the first of those sailors, a piece of bulkhead measuring four feet wide and five and a half feet high was carefully cut and pulled away.

Three FBI agents, Special Agent Tom O'Connor, Special Agent Kevin Finnerty, and Special Agent John Adams, volunteered for the difficult task of recovering and handling each of the bodies as they were removed from the wreckage. No training or previous experience truly prepared any of them for doing this type of work, yet here they were, doing an extremely demanding job in the knowledge that these were loved ones of American families waiting for them to come home.

It had been about an hour since Don had approached me with the offer to have the FBI handle the trapped crew. Now, around 0900, he came back up to the aft missile deck and motioned that he needed to speak with me. Standing near the inflatable boats, he told me that two sailors had been recovered from the mess line and asked if I wanted to come down, help identify them, and tell him what we planned to do to honor them as they left the ship.

Quickly, Chris learned what was going on as Don took me down to the mess decks. There, carefully arranged on the tables, were the first two recovered missing crew members. Fortunately, their identification was straightforward. But standing there, I became acutely aware of how crew members that had been providing assistance to the FBI in gathering evidence might react if exposed to the recovery of human remains. My decision was quick and immediate. The crew would not be allowed to see their shipmates in this condition. It would be my sole responsibility as commanding officer to be the only member of the crew who would work with the FBI to identify my sailors.

Don told me that this was just the first stage of the recovery effort. Regardless of whether the FBI or the divers completed the extraction process, as sailors were recovered, they had to be taken to a well-lighted staging area where the FBI could examine them for forensic evidence and to the best of their ability verify their identification. The best place to do this was the amidships area between the stacks.

To ensure privacy for the FBI to work uninterrupted, and also to prevent the crew from seeing their shipmates in this condition, I gave Chris the task of arranging to cordon it off. With two white tarps, stretched from the back of the forward stack to the front of the aft stack and hung from lines about eight feet off the deck, we created an accessible but isolated area that no one could look down on. As the recovered sailors were brought up to this area, the FBI examined them for any visible signs of evidence. This included detailed documentation by Special Agent Garrett McKenzie. All aspects of their recovery, including where they were found, and physical features such as nametags on uniforms, identification (dog) tags, armed forces identification cards, and jewelry were used to accurately determine who they were. With the first two identifications complete and the forensic analysis and collection finished, these sailors could begin their final journey home.

I thought it was paramount for the crew to have an opportunity to participate in some type of ceremony to honor their fallen shipmates and friends and say good-bye to them forever. Each recovered sailor's remains were placed into a body bag, sometimes two. As a tribute to the demanding job being done by Special Agents O'Connor, Finnerty, and Adams, I asked them to tape an American flag carefully in place on each body bag. Next, six sailors, either from the individual's division or close friends, were selected to act as pallbearers in an honor guard. We then gathered the honor guard outside the draped area.

Once alerted that the recovery effort was complete and the FBI was ready, at the same time Chris announced on the partially restored 1MC that all available crew should assemble on the aft missile deck and flight deck. The FBI pulled back the drape and the six sailors lined up, three on each side of their shipmate. On command, they bent down, firmly grasped the looped handle on the black bag, and in one smooth motion lifted it off the deck. With one of the Fifth Fleet chaplains and me at the front of the procession, the command to start marching was given and, in lock step, the group marched out from the draped area, turned to the right, and began a solemn walk toward the flight deck and the brow. As the honor guard with our fallen shipmate approached the area where the assembled crew stood at attention, Chris called out, "Hand salute." A few feet from the brow, the chaplain and I broke away from the procession, took up ranks on either side of the brow, and joined the crew in a salute as the remaining members of the honor guard carried their shipmates off USS *Cole* for the last time.

As the last member of the honor guard set foot on the refueling pier, Chris called out, "Ready to," and everyone dropped their salute. With an "About face," all members of the crew turned towards the refueling pier and their fallen shipmate, who was then to be solemnly escorted ashore by the Marine FAST platoon, returning the honor the ship's name itself had given to Sergeant Darrell S. Cole. The ship's honor guard walked across the refueling pier and gently placed each of the dead in the well of the zodiac boat, which gently glided away from the pier. As the zodiac headed toward shore, the American flag at the stern of the boat flapped in the slight breeze as a Marine sat at attention with his M-16 pointed forward as a vanguard and protector. When the boat cleared the stern of the ship, Chris ordered, "Carry on."

When this first ceremony ended, the crew stood frozen in the moment. No one moved. Everyone watched as the zodiac plowed effortlessly through the calm waters of the harbor toward shore. Several crew members openly but quietly cried and turned to seek comfort from their friends nearby. A couple of minutes later everyone slowly dispersed and wandered back to work.

Not everyone was comfortable with how we had handled this ceremonial send-off. After the first two sailors were taken ashore, word came to Chris that some of the crew had been unable to get away from their work or had not known that a departure ceremony had taken place. Several were upset and were very outspoken in their criticism. Quickly, we changed our routine. At the next departure ceremony, work would be stopped throughout the ship to allow the entire off-watch crew and any support personnel who wished to participate, assemble and pay their respects.

Less than an hour later, a third body was recovered from the area of the destroyed galley. This recovery proved especially difficult since this sailor had been standing at the epicenter of the explosion and his remains had been rolled up into the twisted and distorted ball of stainless steel that had been the serving line. Despite their misgivings, the workers from Norfolk Naval Shipyard had worked very hard to unravel the metal and allow the FBI to make the extraction. It was an intense undertaking, but they had done it. It had been underneath this same roll of metal that Fireman Stewart had been initially trapped until freed by Petty Officers Foster and McCarter. This time, Chris assembled every crew member not standing watch to come topside to participate in the honors departure ceremony and a short time later, another of our shipmates left *Cole*.

The divers now turned their attention to the destroyed engine room. While they had access through the ventilation duct, they also wanted to inspect it from the hole in the ship's side, despite the sharp jagged metal from the shredded hull plating that protruded into the space. Even getting a boat close to the hole without damage was a problem. A zodiac-style boat would not work since the inflatable pontoons could be easily punctured. The only metal boat on the ship was the boatswain's mates' aluminum paint punt, fourteen feet long and almost six feet wide, used to paint the waterline while in port and designed to carry up to three people with a capacity of 600 pounds, including gear. The boatswain's mates took *Cole*'s paint punt and tied it off next to the ship just aft of the blast hole with a pilot's ladder lowered over the side, and two divers climbed down to the boat, had their gear lowered down to them, and then suited up. They carefully swam over the thick rubber mats they had placed over the jagged metal around the blast hole, but despite all their precautions, their umbilical cords kept tangling every few feet. It was quickly determined that the divers would be unable to safely access the area of the upper level of the engine room this way, and the ventilation shaft now became the primary entry point.

By early afternoon on Monday, the Norfolk Naval Shipyard workers had constructed a simple but sturdy wooden ladder down into main engine room 1, which had three levels. The upper level, on the same plane as the fuel lab and general workshop, was referred to as the first platform, containing ductwork to support the intake and exhaust for fresh air into and out of the engine room itself, as well as air to support the operation of the gas turbine engines. The normal entrance to this level was through the damaged and dished-in watertight door located between the entrances to the fuel lab and general workshop. The second platform, the next level down, contained the fresh water system's reverse-osmosis and water purification units. The lowest level was the bilge, containing the foundations and support structure for the two gas turbine main engines, the modules that enclosed them, the reduction gear that converted the high-speed turbine revolutions into turns of the starboard propeller shaft, and various other equipment.

The divers had reviewed the engineering diagrams to understand what to expect and find there. But when they went in, they found it barely recognizable, except for the large ducts coming from the tops of the engine modules, which had been dished in and distorted by the force of the blast. And the smell of fuel and lube oil was overpowering. Carefully, they walked around the first platform, testing the strength of the steel deck and gratings to support their weight, until they found several points where they could carefully lower themselves into the floodwaters and dive down farther to search for the missing sailors.

Initially, Commander Scholley and Warrant Officer Perna were very concerned about the quality of the air and asked one of the shipyard workers who was certified to test it to take measurements. Though the air was deemed safe to work in, the support divers who worked in the space for extended periods of time helping out the divers occasionally wore a self-contained breathing apparatus to be on the safe side.

As the divers wriggled down the wooden ladder and ventilation duct into the engine room, they found themselves standing on the starboard side of the first platform. No matter which way they turned, they saw a confusion of shredded steel, twisted beams, bent hull plating, mangled pipes, loose electrical cables, and deformed duct work. Machinery that weighed hundreds or thousands of pounds had been ripped from its foundations and tossed about the space. The water at this level was about eighteen inches deep, and everything below was completely flooded. At the waterline, sunlight flickering off the calm waters of the harbor outside reflected throughout the space through the blast hole, creating spectral shadows that appeared to be moving around.

To prevent accidental cutting and chafing of their umbilical cords, with air, video, and communications feeds, the divers took several fire hoses that were no longer usable, cut off the brass connectors at either end and routed the umbilical cords through the hoses. Once their assessment of work conditions was complete, they began recovering the sailors whose bodies were trapped in the engine room below the waterline.

Within an hour, they had recovered the first one, Don Sachtleben informed me. I went forward to assist in the identification process and Chris quietly prepared the crew for another honors departure ceremony after the FBI team had completed its forensic examination. Thirty minutes later, we rendered full military honors to the fourth sailor recovered from the wreckage as he left the ship.

By the end of the day Monday, as the sun began to set and the crew finished dinner, there was a growing sense of pride in honoring our fallen friends and shipmates.

Tuesday started out hot and humid and immediately got even hotter. By midmorning, the recovery and collection teams were well into the second day of recovery operations. Just as the FBI was about to start their work for the day, the group working in the area of the galley and mess decks approached Don with a potential problem, and when he told me what it was I went down to the galley area with him to see it firsthand. Standing at the entrance to the destroyed galley, what I saw made almost every piece of metal in the surrounding area appear to be slowly moving. The surface of the metal was crawling with the larvae of thousands of flies. The now-decayed residue of the chicken fajitas had been blown everywhere by the blast, and the flies had feasted on it. Chief Moser sprayed down the entire area with pesticide and repeated the process every three days thereafter to prevent another infestation.

Don Sachtleben and I continued the routine we had developed for the recovery of remains. When the FBI had completed the forensic analysis work, Don would come get me for the identification phase behind the white tarps. While the crew was curious, they stayed away from the area, respecting that this difficult work required privacy. As I was soon to learn, not everyone shared this sensitivity.

By midmorning, the divers had recovered a second sailor from the engine room, but just before the FBI started the forensic examination, Don approached me, agitated and upset. "We have a big problem," he told me. "Is there any way you can tell someone not to be involved in our work?" I shrugged and said, "Absolutely. Why? What's the problem?"

"Well, it's the Fifth Fleet Surgeon, Captain something or another, I forget his name," Don told me. "He has been with us during each of the recoveries but he is now interfering with our work and potentially impacting our ability to gather evidence. I didn't mind it yesterday when he wanted to poke his nose into every body recovery we did. We just kind of ignored him as long as he stayed out of the way. He seemed a bit too curious in some ways and kept asking too many questions that we just didn't bother to answer. Today, though, he went too far. He just asked me if he could bring some of his technicians from ashore to watch and help. He thinks this would be a great training opportunity for them. This is not a training opportunity! I don't know what he thinks this is but I just can't have that going on. Is there anything you can do?"

I was mortified. Then, pure anger set in. With barely controlled fury I said to Don, "I'll take care of it. Go back down to the mess decks and tell him I want to see him up here now." Don, clearly surprised by the intensity of my reaction, said, "I'll go get him now."

I grabbed the clip-on microphone to my wireless walkie-talkie and, looking up the starboard bridge wing, called out, "Ops, Captain."

Derek was on the bridge standing watch and keeping an eye on the communications with all the support ships offshore. The inflatable boat from *Hawes* that was supplementing the Yemeni force protection around *Cole* and making the occasional shuttle run ashore was tied up and refueling at the backside of the pier. A second or two after my call, he walked out onto the bridge wing and answered, "Ops."

"Ops, do we have a small boat available to take someone ashore?" I asked.

"Yes, sir. *Hawes's* RHIB [rigid hull inflatable boat] is on the backside of the pier refueling," he said.

"Tell them to stop refueling and get the boat to the loading area to take someone ashore, now."

"Roger, sir," he replied.

I could see Derek shift channels on his walkie-talkie and contact the boat crew. The boat captain looked up at the bridge and acknowledged the order but nothing happened. He and the crew just went back to sitting around as they continued to refuel the boat. This was not a time for delay and the boat was needed in position immediately.

With a very controlled and staccato voice I called back up to the bridge, "Ops, Captain. Tell that boat crew to stop refueling! I don't care what they are doing, I want that boat at the loading area, right now!"

Derek knew from the tone coming through the radio that he needed to get the boat crew in motion, and quickly. Again, he contacted the boat crew on their separate channel. Derek never told me what he said but the reaction was swift and instantaneous. The boat crew sprang to their feet, stopped refueling, and scrambled to jump into the boat. The engine roared to life as they cast off the lines and raced around the corner to the landing area at the back of the pier.

There was no time to tell Chris, who was standing beside me, what was going on; the surgeon had come up from down below and was headed towards me. Chris walked away as the surgeon came up.

"Captain, I understand you wanted to see me," he said.

Working hard to project a calm demeanor, I looked at him and said, "Captain, I have been informed by the lead FBI agent that you are interfering with the investigation. I cannot have that happen. I have made arrangements for a small boat to take you ashore. You will not be allowed back on the ship."

He started to stammer out a reply, "I—I don't understand. I just . . ."

Turning and indicating with my arm that I wished him to walk with me toward the brow, I continued, "Sir, please, this way. The boat is waiting to take you ashore and I do not want you back aboard. Please leave the ship, now."

Clearly confused, he did not argue or question my request. He just started to walk toward the brow saying, "Yes, sir, Captain, but I just don't understand."

In my mind there was nothing to explain. In many ways, the FBI/NCIS team was the most important organization on the ship. They would gather the evidence necessary to capture and hold accountable the terrorists who had attacked the ship and killed seventeen of my crew. They had also done the crew and me a huge service by taking on the unenviable task of removing the dead sailors from the wreckage of the ship. This was my ship and no one was going to interfere with the FBI's operations, period.

As we reached the brow, the captain saluted and requested permission to go ashore. As he walked down toward the pier, he kept glancing back at me with a look of disbelief at what was happening. Thankfully, he continued to cross the pier, got into the boat, and headed towards shore. That was the last time we had to deal with him on the ship.

It was at times like this that it felt supremely good to be the ship's captain. It was my ship and my crew and nothing was going to prevent or interfere with my doing what was in their best interests. Hopping back up onto my fender office, I got back to work, but it took me several hours before I could bring myself to discuss the incident with Chris. When he was filled in on the details, he was as shocked as I had been.

The process of recoveries continued, and later that day the divers brought up two more sailors from the engine room. Trained to deal with these recoveries in a sensitive and respectful manner, they worked very carefully in extracting each one from the wreckage. The effects of salt-water immersion for so long were appalling, but as each sailor was recovered, the divers placed the remains in a body bag before having them lifted gently out of the engine room through the narrow ventilation shaft and taken into the draped-off area for the FBI to do their work.

By now, the crew knew the routine, and, within an hour of each recovery, assembled topside for the honors departure ceremony. After the second one Tuesday, Don told me that, while they had located more sailors in the wreckage, they wanted to wait until the next day because each successive extraction was going to take longer, given the amount of debris and metal surrounding the remains. Everyone knew that families back home were anxiously awaiting news of their loved ones, but accomplishing the recovery properly was supremely important.

Just before departing the ship that evening, Don asked what happened with the Fifth Fleet surgeon. He looked somewhat bemused by my explanation, but thanked me for taking care of the problem so decisively. Later that evening, there was also the inevitable call from Captain Hanna seeking an explanation. Methodically, I walked him through what the surgeon had done and why the FBI had asked for my help. After patiently listening, he used some rather colorful language to emphasize that he would make sure the surgeon never set foot back on the ship the rest of the time we were in port.

The crew of USS *Cole* in formation and manning the rail for a group photo the day before deployment to the Middle East and our rendezvous with destiny. *Photo courtesy of PHCM Charles Pedrick, USN (Ret).*

USS *Cole* crossing the Atlantic en route to Mediterranean port visits at the beginning of deployment.

USS *Cole* two days after being attacked. A ship's life raft blown out of its fiberglass container is hung up on an antenna above the bridge.

USS *Cole* moored at the refueling pier in Aden several days after the attack. Mooring buoys are visible just off the bow and stern of the ship.

For several days after the attack the crew had to sleep outside under the stars since there was no power to berthing compartments in the forward part of the ship.

The view standing along the mess line near what was the galley entrance. Sunlight is shining through the hole in the side of the ship and everything within twenty feet of it is blown inside.

Damaged watertight door, left, to main engine room 1 making entrance impossible. The destroyed general workshop is in the background.

Command Master Chief's office with the picture of his daughter on the wall. Debris and food trays were tossed into the space during rescue efforts in the galley.

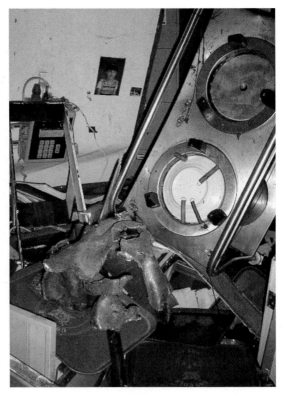

Starboard propeller shaft as it enters main engine room 2. Wooden wedges and oakum slowed the floodwaters coming in around the shattered shaft seal.

Wooden ladder made by Norfolk Naval Shipyard workers and used by MDSU-2 divers to enter upper level of main engine room 1 for the recovery efforts to find missing sailors below the waterline.

The U.S. flag that flew at full mast over the ship, lighted at night, until every sailor killed in the attack was recovered. This Battle Ensign was lowered and replaced only after the memorial ceremony to honor our seventeen fallen shipmates.

The United States Navy Ceremonial Guard honors fallen members from USS *Cole* at Dover Air Force Base, Delaware, after their arrival on October 14, 2000.

USS *Cole* resting on docking blocks on M/V *Blue Marlin*.

The 40-by-40-foot hole in the port side of USS *Cole*. Personnel on the deck of M/V *Blue Marlin* give perspective to the size of the hole and force of the explosion.

USS *Cole* at the refueling pier, as viewed from the al Qaeda safe house where covert observation and planning for a small boat attack on a U.S. warship took place.

USS *Cole* Memorial to honor the seventeen sailors killed in the al Qaeda terrorist attack and the valiant crew who never gave up and saved their ship from sinking.

On Wednesday morning, Don and the FBI/NCIS team approached Commander Scholley and the divers with a request. In the middle of the cavernous area blown away by the explosion, a sailor's "boondocker" boot along with some clothing hung by a shred of cloth from the overhead. There was no easy way to reach these partial remains except by sending the aluminum paint punt back into the engine room with a team member who could then step out carefully where there was good footing and use a pole to unhook the remains of this sailor and lower them into the punt.

Within about an hour Commander Scholley and one of her divers crawled down the ladder that was still hung over the side of the ship to the paint punt and then slowly maneuvered to enter the ship from the hole in the side. Carefully, the diver stepped out of the boat and up onto a narrow piece of bent deck. Using a long six-and-a-half-foot boat hook and holding onto a piece of twisted steel to steady himself, the diver leaned out into the middle of the cavern and slowly stretched out to get the boat hook into position. At the same time, members of the FBI recovery team were working from a piece of narrow ledge at the edge of the blast hole in the middle of the galley. Using the same technique as Commander Scholley and the diver below, John Adams and Tom O'Connor slowly leaned out over the edge with another boat hook. As both groups leaned out, Commander Scholley tried to steady the punt and maneuver into position. The diver's boat hook could not quite reach, but the hook from the FBI found its mark as the sailor's remains fell straight down into an open body bag set out in the well of the boat.

Shortly afterwards, the crew assembled for another honors departure ceremony. Later that afternoon, the pace picked up with the recovery of two more sailors' bodies. The difficult task of identification continued within the draped-off area and by the end of the day, only three sailors remained in the wreckage.

The next day, Thursday, was a day of extreme highs and lows. At the start of the day, the crew was increasingly upbeat about the pace of recovery of their shipmates. Everyone hoped today would be the last day for rendering honors in the remaining three departure ceremonies. These last recoveries, however, would prove the most difficult. To date, all the sailors found by either the divers or the FBI recovery team had been relatively easily extricated.

The FBI had located two more remains in the galley, but access was extremely difficult. They were pinned between the bulkhead and the overhead in the area separating the galley from the chiefs' mess, with large pieces of unrecognizable debris blocking any easy path to reach them. These last two recoveries were so difficult, they could reasonably have been put off until the ship returned to the United States, but by now, all the FBI and NCIS agents on board *Cole* had developed an unspoken bond with the crew and knew that no one should be left behind.

Once again the Norfolk Naval Shipyard workers were called into action to cut away the pieces of mangled rubble in the galley. John Adams, dressed in full protective gear, slowly worked his way up into the small area where he could reach the remains of the two sailors trapped there. There was no way to pull either sailor straight out; both would have to be dragged across his torso and handed out to the waiting team. It was dark, hot, and humid. Portable lights only partially illuminated the area and cast odd shadows as other FBI agents tried to light the crevice. Lying on his back, John slowly and carefully reached over himself and slid each of the two sailors across to Tom O'Connor and Kevin Finnerty, waiting below him. The honors departure ceremonies for these last two sailors were held about an hour apart to allow the FBI to complete their forensic analysis work.

But one sailor was still frustratingly missing somewhere in the engine room. The MDSU-2 divers began a detailed and methodical search. Time ticked by with agonizing slowness. Although work and watches continued normally, the crew grew increasingly anxious. By mid-afternoon the sailor's remains were found. Commander Scholley and her divers notified everyone that a body had been located trapped under machinery that had been blown on top of it by the explosion, but that it would take some time to pry it out. Word quickly spread and an air of tense anticipation took hold.

Over the past four days, the crew had endured the emotional toil of knowing friends and shipmates were dead and trapped in the wreckage on the inside of the ship. Most had seen the bodies in the wreckage of the mess line, and everyone had struggled to understand how they had escaped death. In their own way, every one had gone through the mental exercise of wondering what their own families would think if they had been killed, wondering how and where they were trapped and what was being done to get them out. The crew worked hard to come to terms with what had happened to them. They intuitively sensed that the recovery of the bodies would naturally lend a degree of closure. They anxiously looked forward to the recoveries, to be able to say good-bye, but also to know that a family back home could begin to deal with the unimaginable tragedy of losing a loved one.

Finally, the moment came when Don Sachtleben motioned for me to come up to the staging area to help with identification. Minutes later, Chris assembled the crew for the last honors ceremony.

The ship cast a growing shadow on itself and late afternoon sunbeams streamed across the harbor. And as the final zodiac with the Marines slowly departed the refueling pier carrying the final casualty ashore, I could almost hear the crew breathe a collective sigh of relief. It was not lost on anyone that there had been thirteen departure ceremonies, for twelve missing shipmates, but the last of the seventeen USS *Cole* sailors killed in the attack had begun their journey home. We were all emotionally drained and exhausted, knowing that our shipmates had paid the ultimate price for our freedom. But we would not let them down in the days to come.

It had been a trying week in many other ways, as well—the most trying week of my life.

10 | Recovering From Stress

T HE SPECIAL PSYCHIATRIC RAPID INTERVENTION TEAM (SPRINT) that was mobilized by the Navy the day of the explosion to provide help to us was led by Lieutenant Commander John Kennedy, a Medical Corps psychiatrist. The team, including a Medical Service Corps administrative officer, a family physician, an inpatient ward nurse, a substance abuse counselor, two independent duty hospital corpsmen, and two other hospital corpsmen, one a specialist as a psychiatric technician and the other a patient administration specialist, had some difficulty getting diplomatic clearance to Aden but had finally been able to board the ship on Sunday evening, at the height of the crisis caused by the loss of electric power.

Walking up the brow, all of them were struck by the darkness. Crew members lay about the ship in a tense state of rest, ready for the next crisis that seemed sure to come. The portable JP-5–fueled air compressors were running loudly in the background to recharge the high-pressure air flask that would be used to restart the generator that had failed.

Commander Kennedy requested permission to come aboard, and I warmly greeted him at the brow. "What can we do to help you?" I asked.

John was stunned by the question. He was here to help the crew, not the other way around. Nevertheless, I grew up with a father who was a psychologist in the field of stress management. I viewed the team's arrival as a force multiplier, not a distraction from our mission to save the ship and the crew. Soon Commander Kennedy and I were on first-name terms. He had trained with experts from Walter Reed Army Hospital in Washington and the National Naval Medical Center in Bethesda, Maryland. He had had access to Army combat stress training and to lessons learned from ground combat in World War II, Korea, and Vietnam. "Shell shock" trauma was not something the Navy had to deal with often, but he was an expert on it and that was exactly what *Cole*'s crew had experienced.

John laid out the mission of the team for me: minimize stress symptoms, foster unit cohesion, and facilitate normal grieving. The primary focus would be the well-being of the crew, and John was well aware at the time he first came aboard that twelve bodies were still entombed in the wreckage of the ship. We worked out an approach and he went back to the Aden Mövenpick Hotel, where his team was housed, to consult with the two Fifth Fleet chaplains who had also come to do counseling on the ship, Commander George S. Ridgeway, a Protestant minister, and Lieutenant Commander Michael Mikstay, a Roman Catholic priest.

When the crew was briefed on the team's visit, some of the officers openly expressed skepticism about how a "bunch of touchy, feely types" could "help" them work through their traumatic experiences. As delicately but firmly as possible, it was patiently explained to everyone that the Navy didn't send teams like this to help each individual get in touch with his or her inner self. Their job was to enable the crew to get back to normal and to the work that needed to be done—and that included us officers as well. We were still Navy professionals, and standards of performance, cleanliness, and grooming would be adhered to.

But things were not anywhere near normal. In the heat, a powerful odor of putrefaction lingered in the air, especially in the blast area. To avoid the awkward complication imposed by military rank, the team members walked around the ship on Monday wearing civilian clothes to encourage open communication. *Cole*'s career counselor, Navy Counselor

First Class Christina Huber, escorted the team on their way. They found an organizational structure of the ship that had been dramatically altered by the blast. Between deaths and injuries, there were personnel missing in almost every division. Coping with the loss of power on Sunday and the flooding further disrupted what semblance of organization had reinstituted itself since the blast. Huber told the team members that the crew was functioning more as a mass group that performed tasks in randomly assembled groups, not by division, as a military unit should.

We were finding ways of providing relief for the crew. Thirty sailors per day were receiving nights of "liberty" on one of the ships that had come to support us—*Camden*, *Hawes*, and *Donald Cook*. This way, they had a chance to take a hot shower, get into clean clothes, enjoy fresh chow, and spend a few precious moments without the stress of responsibility or the odor of the attack. John helped Chris select those who seemed most urgently in need of the option to decompress and recenter themselves.

Commanded by Captain John L. "Turk" Green, *Camden* was a favorite for these liberty visits. After stepping off the boat and climbing the accommodation ladder, each *Cole* crew member was greeted with a "welcome" corridor of four sailors on each side. Two strokes of the ship's bell sounded and the Boatswain's Mate of the Watch announced, "*Cole* hero, arriving." Many wiped tears from their eyes after these demonstrations of support and sympathy. Some felt guilty at being immersed in the attention and "luxury" of normal shipboard life, and volunteered to stand a watch on the ship hosting them.

Hawes and *Donald Cook* continued to provide excellent Navy food and support personnel to us, and by late Monday evening the air conditioning, lighting, and sewage systems had been repaired enough to allow most of the crew to use their own personal bunks to sleep at night. But some showed signs of anxiety about returning to the inside of the ship, preferring to sleep outside. We had survived the weekend and kept the ship from sinking, but crew members still seemed distrustful of the ship's overall structural integrity. Some wondered aloud if we could survive until it was time to get the ship out of port.

On Monday, at the end of the team's first day aboard, John stayed behind to share some of their observations with Chris and me:

The crew was growing increasingly frustrated at the lack of news from their chain of command and felt they were getting more information from the sailors on other ships and the SPRINT members who just arrived on board.

The crew was similarly frustrated by the disrupted command hierarchy. Many felt that because of the amorphous grouping of the entire crew together, work was being done more by volunteers and not evenly shared. A defined chain of command would better distribute the workload. The Command Master Chief should be reengaged into his traditional role.

The crew had compartmentalized the ship. Many felt anxiety about going near the mess decks or the forward part of the ship. A few still did not want to enter the ship, even after they returned from their liberty aboard the other ships.

Grooming standards were becoming lax, even given understanding of the conditions of the past thirty hours. Simple personal sanitary standards like shaving, showering, and changing clothes were not being consistently followed after the return of power to the ship.

The Liberty Program could stand to be improved. It was an excellent chance for the crew to be removed from their surroundings but would only be beneficial if the time away provided the opportunity for support and counseling while on the other ships.

Admittedly, both of us were quietly defensive as we listened to him. But while we felt embarrassed, we both knew he was right. After John left, we gathered up Master Chief Parlier and put our heads together to plan the next day.

Given the extraordinary circumstances, since the explosion I had been holding morning quarters, announcing general instructions for the day. Traditionally this is the XO's responsibility, and we decided that Chris should take it up again. Normally, he would hold an Officers Call with department heads, division officers, and chief petty officers in attendance, and the department heads would then assemble all their divisions and brief them. In the wake of the bombing, and with so many chiefs missing or injured, Chris had the crew assemble by department. They needed to realize that they were part of a division, not just a large amorphous mass. Chris also resumed issuing a formal Plan of the Day, a schedule of events and notes of interest to the crew, including liberty call arrangements on the support ships. At quarters, he announced that the crew would be expected to sleep in their own racks inside the ship and grooming standards would be strictly enforced henceforth. While there was some grumbling, the crew now knew we were back in business as a group of combat-hardened professionals.

We knew the crew felt they were not getting enough news from the chain of command. To address this issue, I decided to share a key piece of information with them at a special Captain's Call, with all crew members not standing a watch assembled on the flight deck. I told them that we had learned the previous afternoon that a ship, the Motor Vessel (M/V) *Blue Marlin*, was confirmed as being available for hire for possible use as a transport platform to take *Cole* back to the United States for repair. M/V *Blue Marlin* is a semisubmersible heavy lift ship designed to transport very large drilling rigs and other outsized equipment, and it had just delivered two Navy minesweepers to Fifth Fleet in Bahrain. It was currently pierside in another Middle East port undergoing routine maintenance with no immediate follow-on contracts. M/V *Blue Marlin* would be available in about three weeks.

This news had the exact opposite effect I had hoped for. The idea of having to face another three weeks in this port was devastating. Most of the crew looked down with expressions of discouragement. One started crying out loud. I might as well have told them the ship was sinking again. Sensing their mood, I backpedaled with a promise to find out more information as soon as possible.

What was going on here? This intrepid crew had just saved their ship. Couldn't they see they were bonded to it? What was their problem? As professionals, why couldn't they just toughen up and realize that we were in a combat situation? My World War II frame of reference wanted this crew to reflect those same heroic values as they continued to valiantly fight to keep their ship afloat and save themselves. For the sake of history yet to be written, we too needed to live up to that standard. Darrell S. Cole, awarded the Medal of Honor posthumously after the Battle of Iwo Jima, would have expected nothing less.

At sick call Tuesday morning, the Fifth Fleet surgeon had seen the few remaining members of the crew who were still suffering from diarrhea and other gastrointestinal problems and brusquely recommended that the entire crew be evacuated off the ship. Calmer heads prevailed and that action was not taken. He may have been a good doctor but as a naval officer, he just didn't get it. Later that morning the issue became a moot point when I threw him off the ship for interfering with the FBI's investigation and crew recovery efforts.

Even Chief Moser, a key leader and informal counsel to the crew, began to suffer from the stress of what he had been through. While hesitant, he recognized his condition and was reluctantly convinced to turn his duties over for a day to another senior corpsman who had arrived from the Naval Support Activity in Bahrain. By the end of Tuesday, the crew was beginning to realize the value of the psychiatric support team. A series of shipwide, divisional briefings were held, and 85 percent of the crew were in attendance.

John told us he thought they needed a clearer sense of what their mission was to be over the coming days and weeks. Up to now, it had been a matter of saving the ship, and keeping it from becoming a trophy for the terrorists at the bottom of the harbor. Now the mission was to prepare the ship to leave port, and the crew to depart for home once *Cole* was on M/V *Blue Marlin* and ready for transport back to the United States.

The growing Joint Task Force Determined Response support infrastructure supporting *Cole* greatly expanded in the pre-dawn hours of Wednesday morning when the *Tarawa* Amphibious Ready Group arrived off the harbor in Aden and prepared to take over the support role for us. The USS *Tarawa* is an amphibious assault ship, specifically designed to conduct combat operations using landing craft, helicopters, or both to transport Marines ashore. Two other ships in the ready group, USS *Duluth*, an amphibious transport dock, and USS *Anchorage*, an amphibious dock landing ship, accompanied *Tarawa*. In charge of this group of ships was Commander, Amphibious Squadron Five, Captain Bob Wall.

After its arrival was reported to Admiral Fitzgerald, the Commander of Joint Task Force Determined Response, *Tarawa* took charge of all logistical support from the ships offshore. This meant laundry services, meals, and mail and e-mail support to families back home, and sailors who began to stand many of the watches previously supplemented by crew members from *Donald Cook*, *Hawes*, and *Camden*. Their crews had been an absolute godsend to us, and while they would now work under *Tarawa*'s direction, for the most part they were ordered into an indirect support role.

In addition to basic crew service support, there were other significant changes. The security for *Cole* was shifted from Captain Philbeck and his Marine FAST platoon to a Marine rifle company deployed with the *Tarawa* amphibious ready group. The rifle company, along with other security-related forces like the Navy SEALs who had joined us, significantly increased our force protection posture. It was a much-appreciated deterrent to any plans the terrorists might have to attack again. And intelligence was picking up signs that they might be getting ready to do just that.

Another welcome development was the setup and installation of more robust communications, including a portable radio and satellite telephone with the ability to send and receive classified and unclassified transmissions. After days of my reliance on a cell phone, a key link from the ship directly to the Joint Task Force headquarters was in place and operational.

On Wednesday, October 18, we pressed for more detailed information about what was going to happen to us and when, and were told that M/V *Blue Marlin* might be available as soon as the end of the month—a lot shorter than three weeks. This was great news. But no sooner was one morale problem solved than another completely unexpected one took its place.

Some of the laundry that had been sent out to *Tarawa* for cleaning had come back stripped of the USS *Cole* patches sewn onto the crew's uniforms. Additionally, *Tarawa* sailors who had come aboard to supplement the damage control and engineering watches that had been manned by *Donald Cook* and *Hawes* were also suspected of stealing patches off uniforms, as well as ball caps and belt buckles from the berthing compartments.

For sailors at sea, the most corrosive force is a thief in their midst. On Thursday morning, Chris kept the crew assembled after morning quarters, where the issue was addressed head-on. I tried to convince them that the problem would be swiftly dealt with, and to stand tall and know that they were better than the sailors on the other ships who had done this to us. All they wanted, albeit quite wrongly, was to have a piece of history and, unfortunately, we were the victims of their perverse admiration.

While logically that might sound like the right thing to say and do, the words that came out of my mouth felt sour and disingenuous. I was just as mad as the crew and spoke critically of the other ships and their apparent toleration of this behavior. Despite my best effort, this attempt to buck them up went over very poorly—a bad start to a long day of challenges that soon got even worse.

A couple of days earlier, the Commander of Naval Surface Forces, Atlantic Fleet, Rear Admiral John "Jay" Foley, had called to find out about the explosion and how the crew and I were faring, and he had asked me if there was anything we needed that he could provide. I had told him that cellular phones that would allow everybody to communicate with families back home had been promised, but that nothing had happened. Getting those would be the single biggest boost I could think of to crew morale. Admiral Foley had delivered. The arrival of the phones on the pier, provided free of charge by AT&T and converted to operate on an analog rather than digital voice signal that would not work on the cell phone system in Yemen, was announced after I had wrapped up my remarks. At first, only two phones were activated and worked; the rest were expected to become operational later that day. Nothing seemed to be going quite right yet, but two phones were better than another day of no phones at all.

Two small draped-off areas were created on the ship to ensure absolute privacy for these sensitive conversations, which were initially limited to five minutes. Chris, Master Chief Parlier, and I agreed that the calls would be done in reverse rank order. The most junior seaman and fireman would call first, and the CO and XO would make the last two calls.

Over the course of the next several hours, every sailor signed into the call log and took a phone behind the curtain. Five minutes later, almost to a person, they walked out wiping their eyes but smiling with a sense of relief that they finally reached home. It was the phone call they had been waiting for days to make, the good news call that had been promised to them. The few who did not get through to someone were given first priority for another chance to reach family later in the day. By the end of the day, all the phones were working, and everyone had an opportunity to make a call home every few days.

That morning was also the last morning for *Hawes* and *Donald Cook* to deliver our meals to us. *Tarawa* had informed the Joint Task Force Determined Response commander that they had taken over those duties as well. It was a shift that everyone would soon regret. As noon approached and a hungry crew, as well as the support teams, prepared to take a meal break, a boat from *Tarawa* moored to the back of the pier. Box after box was then passed onto the pier and loaded onto *Cole*'s flight deck. As soon as the boat was empty, its crew hopped back in and left to go back out to *Tarawa*.

As the boxes were still being opened, Chris came up from the flight deck and got on the communications satellite telephone. For several minutes he engaged in a rather pointed conversation, then hung up and walked over to me with a look of exasperation. Lunch from *Tarawa* was not a lunch. All that arrived were boxes of tuna fish snack packs with crackers. Chris contacted someone in the Supply Department from *Tarawa* who bluntly informed him that that was all we would be getting for lunch; there was nothing more coming in for us. Chris had explained to him that we needed lunch, not snacks. The individual he spoke to then off-handedly informed him that we could expect better at dinner.

This was unacceptable. Ever since their arrival, most of the people from *Tarawa* had been acting as if their support to us was an imposition on their day. Now they were not even properly feeding the crew and everyone else on board. How could anyone in their right mind expect me to keep not only *Cole*'s crew but the FBI, NCIS, the divers, the Norfolk Naval Shipyard workers, and the supplemental watch standers nutritionally sustained with only a small tin of tuna and a meager stack of crackers? In no mood to accept this, I hopped down from the fender and headed straight to the phone. On top of the theft problem, this was not something to leave festering.

Dialing the number to the headquarters element of the Joint Task Force, I got Captain Hanna on the line. "What can I help you with?" he asked. Taking a deep breath before I spoke, I curtly replied, "Captain, the *Tarawa* just delivered lunch to the ship. All we received was a load of snack packs filled with tuna fish and crackers. They did not deliver lunch."

"What do mean they didn't deliver lunch? That's all you got?" he testily replied.

"Yes, sir. The XO contacted the ship but they just told him that was all that was coming in and that the chow line was secured until dinner. Sir, I can't keep a crew going in this environment unless I can keep them fed and tuna snack packs just don't cut it," I told him.

"Dammit! I'll take care of the problem right now. Don't worry; we'll get food out to you as soon as possible. I'm sorry this happened," he snapped back at me.

I knew he wasn't angry with me but he was clearly frustrated.

I went back to work and told Chris that we should expect to get some chow sent out to us soon and that Captain Hanna had the situation well in hand. Chris said he would get word out to the crew and tell everyone to stand by for more food to arrive soon. Less than an hour later, the *Tarawa* watch team manning the communications equipment took a call. It was Captain Hanna with an update—and the news wasn't good.

"Kirk, Commodore Hanna here. I contacted *Tarawa*. I don't know what their problem is but I'm sorry; no more food will be coming out to you until dinner. I know that's a lot to ask of your crew but can you hang on until then?"

Not that we had a choice. I tried to be as upbeat as possible, "No problem, sir. We can wait 'til dinner. The crew's hungry but we'll get the word out and just deal with it. Thank you for your help, sir."

"I'll be coming out to the ship with Admiral Fitzgerald. He just wants to get out to the ship and see how you and the crew are doing."

"Sounds good, sir. We'll be standing by for your arrival."

He again expressed his own frustration with how the support logistics were unraveling but was just as adamant that everything would be solved, and in short order. Like me, when I shared this news with Chris, he expressed the same resigned frustration. Given everything else we had been through, more pressing issues overshadowed this inconvenience. It was an unusually hot day, but it was also the day that we expected the last of our crew to be recovered from inside the ship by the FBI team.

Admiral Fitzgerald had visited almost every day since Sunday. Since he was responsible as the Determined Response commander for our overall safety and welfare, as well as the coordination of all the U.S. government elements that had flown into Yemen in response to the attack, it was important for him to keep tabs on how we were doing. John had already briefed him back at the Aden Mövenpick Hotel on the psychiatric team's assessment of the crew's mental state, but there was nothing like actually spending more time with the sailors to get a true sense of their feelings and morale.

This time the admiral would be bringing some high-ranking dignitaries: FBI Director Louis Freeh and Ambassador Bodine, as well as Captain Hanna and about twenty other people. Around 1300, the launch from *Tarawa* pulled up to the back of the refueling pier as the ambassador and Director Freeh, followed by a gaggle of officers and civilians lead by Admiral Fitzgerald, clambered out of the boat and headed toward the brow. Still without fanfare, they were welcomed aboard with only a perfunctory greeting and introductions to the leadership of the ship before we started out on the standard tour route.

As we walked by the amidships area and up to the forecastle, Director Freeh greeted the divers still working down in the destroyed engine room, as well as the FBI and NCIS agents involved with remains recovery and evidence collection—in fact, a forensic analysis of a recovered sailor was in progress. Director Freeh and I slipped behind the draped off area for a few minutes to speak with Don Sachtleben and the other agents and get a quick briefing on their work. Once we were back out from behind the curtained area, everyone walked up to the forecastle where the director specifically commented on how many sailors were busy helping out the FBI/NCIS evidence collection groups.

Clearly, Director Freeh was pleased that the crew was so well integrated with the FBI's work and apparently happy to be contributing to their efforts. Like everyone else at first exposure to the site of the explosion, he was taken aback by the utter devastation. As we paused at each major area, the specific acts of heroism and hard work that had followed the attack were explained in detail. In the mess decks, the cuts in the forward bulkhead behind the drink line were stark reminders of how hard we were working to locate and retrieve the remaining dead sailors.

After about an hour walking around, I asked Director Freeh if he would be willing to address the assembled crew. It would mean a lot to them to hear from the director himself that the FBI was going to find the terrorists responsible for the attack and hold them accountable. He understood the importance of the moment and within minutes, the crew was assembled on the flight deck with a temporary sound system set up with a microphone. His speech was short and to the point. He thanked the crew for their valiant effort to save the ship and their continuing work with his agents and those from NCIS. He emphasized that they would find those responsible for this heinous act and bring them to justice.

Until that moment, we had not heard that assurance from any American official, yet it was probably the thing most important for us to hear. An American ship of war had been attacked in an act of war, and we needed to know that the blow would not go unanswered.

After the director and the ambassador returned to the task force headquarters in the Aden Mövenpick Hotel, Admiral Fitzgerald remained aboard for another hour or so to walk around by himself and chat with the crew. Perfect. Petty Officer Crowe was designated as his escort and Chris and I turned our attention back to the routine of managing and running the ship.

A short time later, the admiral came up to speak with me. We briefly discussed a number of issues that had arisen and been dealt with over the past six days. He told me he was pleased with not only the progress of everything on the ship and the level of cooperation and support given to the crew but also the attitude of the crew in wanting to help the FBI and NCIS agents, and the divers. He then broached a sensitive subject.

He told me the crew was "tender" right now and that I needed to take their emotional state into account when making critical decisions affecting them. Coming from an admiral, this was unexpected enough; then he told me he was not sure they could "take another hit." I held my emotions in check, but this was hard for me to swallow. My answer was very frank. The crew did not have a choice, I said; they had to be ready to take another hit. We were battle-hardened professionals and the crew needed to act like professionals. This was serious business. We had been attacked and from my vantage point, we were still in combat.

Even as we were speaking to each other, I learned later, intelligence analysts determined that the terrorist threat had increased to a point that the task force was starting to shift all personnel out of the Mövenpick and out to *Tarawa* for security reasons. While I heard and understood what Admiral Fitzgerald was telling me, inside, my feeling was: "Tender?" What did that mean? This wasn't the time for a feel-good game of patty-cake. If another attack came, I had absolute confidence in the crew. Yet here was this admiral questioning our ability to survive another hit. While not outwardly disrespectful, in my mind I was thinking, "Thank you for your advice and concern, Admiral, but please go away and give us the support we need to let us continue to get this ship ready to leave port."

As he prepared to leave with his entourage, Captain Hanna came up to me to thank me for having everyone on board. It was only then that I shared with him the morale-busting problem of the thefts by *Tarawa* sailors. I truly felt sorry for him as I saw the expression of shock and frustration on his face. Evidently, there had been a number of other issues that we were not privy to regarding the support and behavior of the recently arrived amphibious ready group. He promised to look into this issue and, like the noon meal problem, fix it.

As he was about to turn away and join up with Admiral Fitzgerald, Captain Hanna said, "Admiral Moore is going to come down tomorrow and would like to visit the ship again. Is there anything you need from him?"

This was a golden opportunity. I could ask for anything. Given how well the crew had been holding up in the heat and humidity and the stress of recovering our dead shipmates from wreckage, the satisfaction of seeing the crew embrace the psychiatric support team's mission, and who knows what else, maybe just plain hunger after subsisting on a lunch of tuna fish and crackers, I knew exactly what to request. With the impending recovery of the last of our shipmates, I told him, "Captain, I think it would be a nice treat if the crew could have some ice cream."

Looking at me as if I must be out of my mind, he just smiled and replied, "I'll see what I can do."

Maybe the stress was getting the better of me. Over the past several days, the Fifth Fleet chaplains and some of the psychiatric team members had given the crew the impression that they were going to be evacuated from the ship and sent home in just a few days. Whispers and rumors filled the passageways as wisps and tidbits of unfiltered information also trickled out from the support ship sailors. It seemed to the crew that everyone knew what was going to happen next—everyone except the captain.

This background chatter made me feel as if my crew and command were slipping away from me. My judgment and decisions were being second-guessed. Some of the task force staff were questioning how the crew was being managed in support of the FBI/NCIS investigation and evidence collection efforts; the psychiatric team leader briefed the task force commander on the crew's status without giving me any direct input into his comments; and now, the chaplains and other sailors were telling the crew they were going home as soon as a replacement crew from Norfolk, Virginia, could be organized to relieve them. There is nothing more important than unity of command. I had a growing sense that the crew I commanded through a horrific terrorist attack was being pulled away from me from several directions without consultation or forethought about the repercussions.

These feelings now led to the most significant meltdown of my career.

Two of my officers sheepishly approached me midafternoon with some disturbing information. Command Master Chief Parlier had privately met with the chief petty officers. They had urged him to approach me about letting the crew go home as soon as possible. As a group, many of them had talked themselves into believing the ship was unsafe, and that they needed to get out of there. During that discussion, my officers said, the Master Chief changed his view from support for me to support for them. He, too, also began to question the structural integrity of the ship. The chiefs had also expressed their fears about the known and growing threat of another attack. To add fuel to the fire, the Master Chief had allegedly questioned my judgment in understanding the risk of a follow-on attack and ability of the crew to respond effectively.

To my mind, this confirmed the unsubstantiated rumors I had heard. One of the three key leaders on *Cole* could no longer be trusted to back Chris and me in our decisions about our future. The ship and crew could not afford this. Decisive action must be taken. Pacing back and forth near the inflatable boats, I summoned Master Chief Parlier.

"Master Chief, I understand you have been going around the ship questioning my authority," I confronted him. "I heard you don't think the ship is safe and that the crew can't handle another attack. How dare you undermine me in front of the crew? Why didn't you come talk to me? Why didn't you come tell me about this before?" I loudly and heatedly demanded.

The look on his face was one of complete disbelief. He just stood there with his eyes wide and mouth hanging open. After a few seconds of tense silence between us, he spoke softly. "Captain, I never said any of those things. I know the crew is still nervous about the ship but I would never say any of those things about you."

I didn't believe him. The stress of the attack and body identifications, lack of sleep, the possibility of a follow-on attack, and growing paranoia that I might be relieved of command at any moment all converged viciously in fury aimed right at the man standing before me.

"Master Chief, if I ever hear of you undermining my authority on this ship again, I will relieve you of your duties and send you home on the next plane out of here. Do I make myself clear?" I tightly said to him, leaning menacingly forward into him.

In a voice cracking with emotion, his eyes pleading for me to understand and have faith in what he had told me, he just said, "Yes, sir. I understand, but, Captain, I didn't do it."

I felt as if I were in a vise. My breaths were coming short and shallow. My temples thumped with the rhythm of a runaway heart. I wheeled about and stormed toward the quarterdeck and my makeshift office. Rather than going back to work, I grabbed my flashlight and announced to no one in particular that if anyone needed me I would be walking around the ship. I needed to cool down and try to make sense of what just happened. I didn't need to worry about surrendering my command to anyone; I was doing a fine job of losing it all by myself.

The walk around the ship was intense and hurried. The overload of adrenaline slowly dissipated, but only after an hour of struggling to burn it off. Eventually, my dark and overheated cabin in the forward superstructure became my refuge. Long since abandoned and left undisturbed for the most part since the explosion, it seemed like a faded memory that now haunted me. Sitting in a chair with the back to the desk, I surveyed my dark, unpowered, and unlit surroundings.

The flashlight pointed straight up at the overhead and cast a faint light about the dark room. Odd shadows with soft edges highlighted some features while others disappeared into the inky darkness. The round table once centered in the room and toppled over by the flexing of an exploding ship stood upright and shoved to one side. A slight dusty haze slowly floated in the air. As my head sunk down into my chest, the large coffee stain on the dark blue carpet stared back at me as if to say I had created a blot that now soiled the ship, my command.

This issue could not fester. My reaction, without absolute concrete proof, was not that of a leader. The crew deserved better and certainly, the Command Master Chief deserved better. Slowly, with a tired sense of failed resignation, I pulled myself up to go find Chris and talk with him about it. Composed but unsure what to do next with the Master Chief, I walked down the ladder and back out into the brilliant heat of the day. The sun burned my eyes. Hopping back up onto the fender, Chris was already clearly aware of what had passed between Master Chief Parlier and me. He cut straight to the point: he did not know of any instance nor had he heard any circumstances where the Master Chief had purposely challenged my authority. His meeting with the chiefs had not gone as well as it could have, and while he may have said some things that were best left in private, he was still loyal to the ship and us. Still on edge and slightly defensive, I just listened intently. He told me that Master Chief Parlier was devastated by the accusation and even more by the threat of being fired.

Not more than a few minutes later, the cell phone in my pocket rang persistently for attention. It was Master Chief Greg Pratt, the Fifth Fleet Commander Master Chief, who told me that he and Master Chief Parlier had just spoken about the incident. True, the discussion with the chiefs may not have gone as planned, but Master Chief Pratt was adamant that Master Chief Parlier was absolutely supportive of what I wanted to do with the ship and crew. That gave me a lot to think about. Perhaps I had been wrong. This incident with the Master Chief had to be addressed but I wasn't ready to face it again—at least not yet.

Near the end of the day, everyone—the crew, the FBI/NCIS team, the divers, and other support groups—was mentally spent. As the day wrapped up, the grumbling in our stomachs returned with a vengeance as everyone looked forward to an overdue hot meal. By 1830, though, nothing had arrived for dinner. A few minutes later we heard over the radio on the missile deck the announcement of a boat puttering into the harbor from *Tarawa*. With the bridge security team notified of its approach to the pier, it slowly swung in a gentle and unhurried arc to a stop at the landing area. The crew again hopped out and unloaded a stack of several large boxes onto the pier. Just as quickly, they motioned that the boxes needed to be brought on board. Quickly they were stacked on the flight deck as the boat crew cast off their lines and headed back out into the harbor on a return trip to *Tarawa*.

Chris and I watched from the aft missile deck as both of us thought the same thing. This can't really be happening. Sure enough, when the crew opened the boxes, dinner was served: tuna fish snack packs with crackers. This was almost too surreal to comprehend. What was the crew on *Tarawa* thinking—or were they thinking? Chris started to head toward the communications suite when I stopped him.

"I'll handle this, XO," I told him. The day had already gone through a number of highs and lows, so what the hell; let's just express our frustration with a pointed radio transmission.

Captain Hanna was going to go through the roof when he found out, but a more forceful and direct approach was needed to get my frustration across to *Tarawa* and the support from the amphibious ready group. Clearly, they just didn't get it. Instead of the telephone, I picked up the radio handset. Chris looked at me with surprise but said nothing. The Joint Task Force Determined Response headquarters, as well as every ship and command element operating off the coast of Aden in support of USS *Cole,* could hear everything that was said on that radio circuit. They were about to get a blunt lesson in Navy communications and chain of command etiquette.

With everyone in earshot listening to me, I took a deep breath, cleared my throat, and keyed the microphone, "JTF Determined Response, this is *Cole* actual, over."

"This is JTF Determined Response, roger, over," came the quick reply.

"This is *Cole* actual, request to speak with Commodore Hanna, over."

Only a couple of seconds passed before Captain Hanna was on the radio. He must have been standing nearby and jumped up to answer my call, "This is Commodore Hanna, roger, over."

Without giving even a second to pause, I waded in, speaking in a very clipped tone that, while maybe bordering on disrespectful, was even so hardly adequate to express the dissatisfaction and annoyance at my crew's not being fed, again. "This is *Cole*, roger, break. Commodore, once again we did not receive a meal from *Tarawa*. All we got from them for dinner was another load of tuna snack packs with crackers," I said. After only a momentary pause, I continued, "If this is the level of support we can expect from *Tarawa* and the ARG, request you detach them to proceed on duties assigned and bring back *Donald Cook* and *Hawes* who at least know how to take care of this crew, over."

The words seemed to hang in the airwaves for what seemed an eternity as the slight hiss and crackle from the radio penetrated my ear. The commanding officer, executive officer, and amphibious ready group commodore were all senior Navy captains; several years in seniority and experience to me. But they had rolled into Aden with an arrogant attitude that did not measure up anywhere close to what I felt my crew needed for support and sustainment. To ask the commodore to "detach them to proceed on duties assigned" not only publicly embarrassed them by calling them out over the radio, it was a blunt request to have them fired from their mission. They were failing my crew, and after what we had been through, I was not going to let anyone do that.

Expressing little tolerance for what my tone just expressed toward senior officers but flush with his displeasure at the *Tarawa*'s failure to feed us, Captain Hanna just as curtly replied, "I will take care of the problem, out!"

Putting down the handset, I recognized that this could mean more trouble for everyone. In this instance, I didn't care. This crew had done too much, sacrificed too much, and had endured too much not to get something as simple as a hot meal delivered by one of the most capable and robust support platforms within 1,000 miles of Aden. If *Tarawa* and the other ships in its group thought they were so good, let them prove it by doing their job right.

The evening did not get much better. Word came back to us that *Tarawa* had refused to feed us. Even after the radio transmission, no food was expected for the crew until morning. I was furious and in a foul mood. Staying upbeat and positive was my job but this tested the limits of even my tolerance. If the crew was tender, the incidents of this day had done nothing to prepare them for another hit.

Shortly before sunset, it was time for me to set things right with Master Chief Parlier. Seeking him out, I asked him to walk with me up to the forecastle. It started as a long, silent stroll. Inviting him to sit down next to me on a set of bitts, we both looked back down at the ship for a few moments before either of us spoke.

"Master Chief, I'm sorry that I said what I did to you earlier today," as I started what was sure to be a difficult conversation. "You are too valuable to this ship and crew to send home. I'm not sure what caused me to doubt you but it seems like no one understands what we need to do here. This crew has been through a lot and I just want to do what's right for them."

It was now his turn, "Captain, I feel like I've let you down. When I met with the chiefs, I just wanted to do what was right for the crew but it didn't come across right. I'm sorry."

We spent the next half hour in a deep and sometimes emotional conversation. While I had never intended to hold anything back, there was a lot of information that he had not been aware of that suddenly opened his eyes to the myriad issues going on outside the crew's view. In detail, we covered the complete spectrum of problems and challenges that we had faced over the past week but also the prospect of what lay ahead for us. It was as much an emotional "Come to Jesus" meeting as it was an opportunity to lay out the plan for our remaining time in port.

In the end, I just looked at him and said, "Master Chief, this crew deserves the honor and privilege to get this ship out of Aden and, once that mission is done, to get on a plane together, meet our loved ones on the tarmac and give them a hug, and show them we're OK, and what we did together."

With these words, we became forever bonded together not only as professionals but as two lifelong friends. Through a crucible defined by the attack and its aftermath, we each passed through a transition point that defined our relationship for the rest of the time in port. Trust was not only reestablished, it was reinforced, and became an unbreakable bond.

Sensing that most of Thursday had been a day of emotional extremes and complex work, John had stayed aboard after his team left for the day. In the early evening, he patiently listened to my explanation of the episode with Master Chief Parlier and the climactic conversation between us on the forecastle. Thinking that maybe the captain himself was long overdue for some counseling, he asked how things were going. I said I thought that with a few minor exceptions, such as today's debacle of not getting fed, the crew was holding up remarkably well. We discussed the plans for getting the ship ready to leave port and where the crew would be going. We also touched on how I was handling my own exposure to the recovery of remains, but he could see I wasn't responding to the point of his question. This conversation was not about what was being done for the ship and crew, it was about me; I knew it and was doing an artful job dodging any discussion. Growing up with a psychologist for a father has its advantages and disadvantages.

John finally got to the point by asking me what I thought about the task force commander's assessment that the crew was too "tender," could not "take another hit," and my subsequent reaction to that judgment. I stubbornly stood by my assertion that as a crew in harm's way, we did not have a choice; we had to be ready to fight and save the ship if we were attacked again. He then hit me with a hammer blow. "Well, sir, maybe you're right," he said. "*A* crew might be ready for another hit, but not *your* crew." Looking at him with a growing sense of what was coming, I challenged him, "Please elaborate, I don't understand."

"I think your crew could 'take another hit' if *you* were a better leader," John said.

This simple but blunt observation brought my actions of the past week into sharp focus. He didn't say it directly, but implicitly he was saying I had to recognize my shortcomings and possible failure as a leader and commanding officer. He knew he had to keep going with me, and he continued on, pointing out the growing disconnect between my expectations for the crew and their ability to live up to and achieve those objectives. I was preoccupied with the idea of being commanding officer in charge of a ship in combat. But the crew had been inadvertently influenced into misconstruing their circumstances, becoming overly concerned with their immediate safety, and seeing it unnecessarily jeopardized by my keeping them so long in Aden.

The crew had also expressed an almost universal frustration, he told me, at my seeming detachment from how they had experienced the disaster and how they were dealing with it. They felt that I was insensitive, too mission-oriented, and that I was growing more and more angry. With example after example, John patiently walked me through my perceptions and the reality of how I was dealing with the issues affecting the crew and me. Slowly, the truth of what he was saying dawned on me.

As commanding officer, it was my duty and obligation to be the strongest member of the crew. I had to be the strongest for everyone, so that each of them could have those precious moments to take a step back, reflect on what had happened to them, and then stand strong as a crew again. While everyone had had that opportunity, for me it was a luxury that I felt I could not afford to take right now. My time would come when the ship was safely out of port and the crew headed home to their families. It was not that the crew failed to understand me; I failed to understand their perception of me.

Inside, I was hurting just as much as they were. I had already judged myself knowing that seventeen sailors had died and thirty-seven more were wounded while under my command. Accountability may be a harsh master but command of a ship is an unforgiving profession. The crew needed to better understand who I was as their captain. It was now up to me to share what I had been through. It was going to be a long night of thinking about how to lead forward from here. Before long it was dawn, the first boat arrived, and John went ashore to meet with his team back at the Aden Mövenpick Hotel.

At quarters that morning, following Chris's standard litany of announcements and assignments, I addressed the crew. What I shared with them that morning was a part of me they had never seen before. As directly as I could, I told them I felt an immense sense of loss for our shipmates killed in the attack. I viewed them as my sailors and my responsibility, as a group and as individuals. I also expressed the almost indescribable pride I felt for the job their shipmates, the crew standing before me, had done over the past week. They had saved the ship not only once but twice. They had persevered through incredibly hot and humid days and toiled for hours on end standing watches and working to help the divers and the FBI retrieve our shipmates from the wreckage, so that they could return home to their families. In my eyes, each of them was a hero, just as much a hero as each of their dead shipmates, and I would forever be in their debt for what they had done for our Navy and the nation. It was solely because of them that *Cole* was not going to become a trophy for the terrorists.

A short time later, a large landing craft from *Tarawa* pulled up to the pier. With no small amount of surprise, Chris and I watched as the Commanding Officer of *Tarawa* strode up the brow and introduced himself, as his supply officer and a crew of about ten sailors unloaded breakfast supplies. Within thirty minutes, a smorgasbord of breakfast choices lay ready for the crew to enjoy. The day was off to a great start. By midmorning, John and his team were back on board. But today was different. Their overnight assessment was that the crew did not need much more in the way of intervention. From John's perspective, even after our intense conversation of the previous night, the command was functioning well. The team planned to operate in an "as-needed" mode and conduct one-on-one interventions only as required.

Standing at quarters with us for the first time was one of the most welcome guests to come on board the ship since the attack, Chaplain Loften C. Thornton. Chaplain Thornton, "Chaps" as we liked to call him, was one of the crew's favorite officers. He was the chaplain for Destroyer Squadron 22, *Cole*'s squadron in Norfolk. Throughout our time in Norfolk during workups before deployment and during every extended underway period at sea, the crew always looked forward to have Chaps helicopter on board, not just to minister to them but to listen sympathetically to whatever they wanted to say to him outside the chain of command.

Chaps had been embarked on USS *George Washington* in the Mediterranean when the attack occurred, and patiently worked on the chain of command to allow him to fly into Aden, so he could get out to "his" crew, some of whom had also asked when he could get to the ship. Fortunately, he was going to be with us the rest of our time in port.

With the last of the sailors recovered out of the wreckage the previous afternoon, we had immediately begun planning for the memorial service we would hold this evening, and Chaps was to preside over it.

Later that morning, the task force headquarters radioed us that the Fifth Fleet Commander, Admiral Moore, was on his way out to the ship and that a working party was needed to quickly unload a cargo of ice cream. Through some miracle, Captain Hanna had come through for the crew. Knowing the ice cream must be melting quickly, Chris rapidly got the flight deck ready—for the admiral and the ice cream. We had also received word that *Hawes* had baked a large cake for us. Today, after a seven-day delay, we were going to celebrate the Navy's birthday! (October 13, 1775, was the day the Continental Congress in Philadelphia voted to fit out two sailing vessels as the start of the Continental Navy.)

Admiral Moore was in a good mood as he quickly crossed the refueling pier and spryly strode up the brow onto the ship. I greeted him at the quarterdeck and we spent a few minutes just catching up on the events of the past week. He had been closely monitoring the reports coming in from the Joint Task Force headquarters, as well as from other ships; but there was nothing like actually seeing a crew in action to get a real sense of the morale and attitude of everyone on board.

John Kennedy joined us for a few minutes on the aft missile deck and the admiral warmly greeted him. He had been providing Admiral Fitzgerald and the Joint Task Force Determined Response staff daily updates on the crew's mental health and outlook, which the staff had forwarded to Admiral Moore. Out of the blue, as Admiral Moore stood looking over the flight deck and the crew as it was assembling, he looked at both of us and asked, "What's happened? This is not the same crew I saw a week ago. I don't know what has happened but this is amazing."

John just modestly grinned and replied, "Well Admiral, I think you are seeing a crew who has been through a lot and knows what they are capable of surviving."

Within a few minutes, Chris had the crew assembled back on the flight deck for several events. First, the admiral was asked to preside over our delayed celebration of the Navy's birthday; and second, to participate in a reenlistment ceremony for one of the crew, Fire Controlman Chief Thomas Cavanaugh. Despite the circumstances the crew had survived under during the past week, they had a sense of victory and pride that had been missing over the previous few days. Now, as they went about their watches and helped the FBI and the divers, there was a quiet sense of confidence in their demeanor.

The Navy birthday celebration had to come first—the ice cream was rapidly melting in the hot midday sun. Following longstanding Navy tradition, the oldest crew member, Chief Moser, and the youngest crew member, Petty Officer Foster, would together cut the Navy's birthday cake and help serve it to the crew. As the first slice was made, the crew cheered. Everyone had big smiles plastered on their faces. The admiral and I took our rightful place behind the large tubs of now soft ice cream and started to dish it out. It was quite a sight—a three-star admiral in his pristine Summer White uniform and a commanding officer in his combat-stained blue coveralls, standing side by side scooping out heaping mounds of ice cream and plopping big globs onto Styrofoam plates filled with yellow cake and thick, creamy frosting.

After a hundred or so scoops, the admiral and I were relieved of our duties for a few minutes and went for a short walk. "I need to speak with you privately for a few minutes," he said. When we were alone and sitting near the ship RHIBs, he said, "Kirk, your crew has been through a lot this past week and I would like you to consider something. The Navy has assembled a team of about a hundred people from Norfolk who have volunteered to come over here and relieve your crew. Most have served on guided-missile destroyers and are familiar with this type of ship. Now, anyone you think you need to keep the ship going will stay behind, but I would like you to consider allowing half or more of your crew to go home."

I leaned forward on my elbows, my hands clasped in front of me, my chin dropped into my chest as I stared at the non-skid deck that had suddenly become a sea of intense gray ridges and valleys. Inside I knew I had to stay absolutely calm, but I was in total disbelief. Everyone knew the crew had been through a lot and the emotional toll was tremendous, but without warning, the world collapsed around me again. All I could think to myself was, "This is the Commander of Fifth Fleet, a vice admiral in the United States Navy, and he's asking me to allow my crew to abandon ship because what we've been through has been 'hard' on them!?" I was utterly astounded that the Navy's leadership would even consider such a thing. The historical roots of the Navy clearly meant nothing to the admirals running the Navy today. They appeared ready to make decisions that flew in the face of generations of sacrifices by others who had also suffered at the hands of the enemy. The leaders and commanding officers throughout the history of the Navy, from John Paul Jones to Chester Nimitz, would never have even contemplated such a decision, and I wasn't ready to, either.

I was on thin ice. How and what I said next to the admiral would probably make the difference whether or not the crew stayed with their ship. Slowly, carefully, and with great emphasis, I looked up directly into his eyes and said, "Admiral, I could not disagree with you more. This crew saved this ship; this crew saved their shipmates; and, this crew, as a crew, will get *Cole* out of Aden and onto *Blue Marlin*; then, as a crew we will go home. Together."

Now it was the admiral's turn to think about what had just been exchanged between us. He paused, looked down at the deck himself for a few seconds; then, as if to redeem himself in the eyes of history, he looked at me and with a confident tone, said, "OK, you've got it."

Longstanding Navy tradition held that no crew surrendered to the enemy or abandoned their ship without a good fight or unless it was absolutely impossible to keep the ship afloat. This was best memorialized at the Battle of Lake Erie when Captain James Lawrence, who was mortally wounded while furiously battling a British frigate, cried out, "Don't give up the ship." History was about to cast its shadow on us. The crew of *Cole* and I had fought to keep our ship afloat from the moment of the attack until now. They could not be seen as giving up because of a lack of courage on the part of the Navy's leadership or for the sake of political pressure or expediency—it would have cast a pall of shame on the crew and their captain for time immemorial.

For just a few brief seconds, the history of the crew of *Cole* and the United States Navy had hung in the balance. It was the right decision and for the right reasons. Standing, I extended my hand to shake his and thank him for supporting me. Both of us knew it would be a difficult decision to maintain back in Washington. We also knew, however, that eventually the Navy would back us; too much was at stake otherwise.

As the admiral and I walked back to the flight deck for the reenlistment ceremony, it was apparent that another change within the crew had taken place. With a growing sense of pride, many contemplated their commitment to the nation and their future in the Navy. Already, a dozen people had approached the ship's career counselor, Petty Officer Huber, to adjust and modify their reenlistment dates so as to fall, with symbolic significance, during our time in Aden. Concerned that this life-impacting decision could be misinterpreted, every sailor who reenlisted had to speak with me about the decision, and only after calling home to discuss it with family. Their decision to reenlist would extend an irrevocable vow to continue a life of service to the country, and I did not want the emotions of the moment to blind them to the broader, long-term implications this decision would have on them.

Just before walking onto the flight deck, the admiral mentioned that he would like to address the crew. Unlike General Franks, Admiral Moore was not about flash, pomp, and circumstance. He had done more to ensure the survival of the ship and crew than anyone else. It would be an honor for the crew to hear from him, just as it had been with FBI Director Louis Freeh.

Under the bright sun, the admiral reenlisted Chief Cavanaugh, and as he addressed the crew, he hailed them as heroes for what they had done to save the ship. He made no mention of the discussion he and I had just had, but he said the ship would soon leave port and be taken home on M/V *Blue Marlin*.

While some of the crew had clearly hoped Admiral Moore would confirm the rumor about getting off the ship early, most were grateful for the recognition of what they had achieved as a team. The crew applauded his remarks and shortly afterwards, he left the ship to go back ashore. It was a great visit but from my perspective, it had been fraught with the potential for disaster. Later that afternoon, rumors began flying that he had come with an offer to let them leave, but that I had quashed the opportunity. This time, however, the undercurrent of discontent seemed to be limited to a shrinking number of the crew.

The flight deck needed to be prepared for the memorial ceremony. As a working party of boatswain's mates set up the cots recently used as beds in row after row of benches, Debbie came up and asked if she could brief me on several items in the central control station. As we walked down the starboard passageway, still dark in the area of the galley and mess decks, just as we were about to turn the corner to walk into the control station, a young petty officer, Engineman Third Class John Thompson, confronted me. Agitated, his voice rising with each word, he said, "Captain, I don't understand why you're keeping us here. We had a chance to go home and you just don't seem to care about our safety." Debbie, who had been walking behind me, was not about to brook even the slightest hint of disrespect to the captain, and immediately tried to move around me and throttle this upstart. Sidestepping in front of her, I raised my right hand to signal her to keep the wrath that was about to escape her lips buttoned up. Thompson continued, "I think you're going to get us all killed. We've been through a lot," he stammered. In a pleading tone, he blurted out, "I just want to see my wife and kids again."

Overcome with my own emotion at seeing his pain and the heartbreak of knowing we were not going to send anyone home early, all I could do was step forward and give him a hug. Stepping back and holding both his upper arms, I looked him squarely in the eye and told him, "We're going to get everyone home safely but first, we are going to get the ship out of port, onto *Blue Marlin*, and then we're going to go home; together, as a crew."

He nodded his head up and down, unable to say another word. While he probably did not fully embrace what I was telling him, at least he had been able to say his piece to the captain. Now it was time to get back to work and get everyone ready for the memorial service to honor our fallen shipmates.

The quartermasters calculated sunset that evening to be at 1738. At 1720, the ceremony began, the air perfectly calm and the flag still, hanging from the flag staff at the aft end of the flight deck. The crew was quiet and introspective as they solemnly took their seats. A hush fell over the crowd. Up on the aft missile deck, the investigators from the FBI and NCIS, the MDSU-2 divers, the Norfolk Naval Shipyard workers, and crew members from ships that had been supporting us, as well as staff from Fifth Fleet and the Determined Response Joint Task Force, stood quietly looking down.

A single microphone on a stand stood near the back of the flight deck. As if on cue, "Chaps" Thornton approached the microphone and the crew stood up from their seats.

Taking a deep breath, he intoned, "Let us pray." He invoked God's blessing on each of our shipmates with an invocation spoken from his heart. At the conclusion, the crew took their seats. One crew member would speak for each of the ranks we had lost—officer, chief petty officer, enlisted. Lieutenant Derek Trinque spoke for the officers, Senior Chief Pam Jacobsen for the chief petty officers, and Petty Officer Randall Butte for the crew. At the conclusion of the remarks, Chaplain Thornton again approached the microphone, asked the crew to stand, and sang the first note of "Amazing Grace," the crew quickly joining in:

> *Amazing grace! How sweet the sound, that saved a wretch like me!*
> *I once was lost, but now am found, was blind, but now I see.*

As always with this song, the power of the melody and words worked with and against everyone. The crew drew close together, in comfort and support:

> *Through many dangers, toils, and snares, I have already come;*
> *'Tis grace that brought me safe thus far, and grace will lead me home.*

I wanted to look out and see their faces, but my eyes had welled up with tears.

As the song ended, Chaplain Thornton paused for a brief moment before asking everyone to once again bow their heads in prayer for the benediction. At the conclusion, everyone involved in the ceremony stood back as Petty Officer Crowe and Petty Officer Butte slowly but precisely marched up to the flagstaff and untied the halyard. Understanding the importance of the moment, each of them paused to look up at the flag.

Slowly they lowered the flag and unhooked it from the halyard. Tightly holding the corners at each end, Crowe and Butte precisely, and with great care and deliberation, folded the flag into the traditional triangle shape. When they had finished, only the dark blue background and smudged white stars were visible. With his right hand firmly resting on top, Crowe took the flag and confidently strode to the starboard side of the ship.

Seventeen sailors had silently lined up and stood at attention along the starboard side of the flight deck. Crowe stood at the head of the line as the first sailor saluted the flag and held his hands out to accept it. With the flag passed to the first person, Crowe then paused and saluted. As his hands fell slowly and evenly back to his side, the ship's bell pealed out two distinct strokes, then Chaplain Thornton called out the first of seventeen names of our shipmates killed in the attack.

The sailor then smartly executed an about-face to the next in line. The same short ceremony was then executed: salute the flag, pass it on to the next in the line of seventeen, return the salute, ring the ship's bell, and announce the name of a fallen shipmate.

Seventeen times.

At the end of the line was Master Chief Parlier. As the seventeenth sailor finished accepting the flag and turned to face him, he saluted it, took it in his hands, and marched to the back of the flight deck and presented it to me for safekeeping until the day when we would all come home.

That flag was our battle ensign. Stained by the black residue of the explosion, it had proudly flown over *Cole* since the moment of the attack. It had sustained us during our darkest moments immediately after the explosion; it was streaming still when *Cole* almost sank next to the pier on Sunday; and over the past four days it had honored us as we said good-bye to our shipmates for the last time. We had survived under that flag. It had been a symbol of our determination not to give in, not to be intimidated by a cowardly act of terrorism. I had refused to lower it until we had recovered every one of the crew who had given their lives. Now the flag was a stark reminder of the price of freedom, a part of our naval heritage and a proud emblem of our country's history.

11 | Underway Again

THE NEXT EIGHT DAYS went by in a continuous whirlwind of activity. The oppressive weight of recovering our shipmates was lifted from our thoughts, and by Saturday, October 21, we could finally allow ourselves to look forward. The fallen were on their way home to their families, and the crew now turned fully to the task of getting *Cole* out of port.

Commander Pat Keenan, the resident technical expert on the ship's structural integrity, and Commander Bobbie Scholley and her divers expanded their assessment to include the undamaged spaces and the hull, to determine as clearly as possible how the ship would bear up under the load and stress of movement at sea and onto the docking blocks on M/V *Blue Marlin*. Some of the Norfolk Naval Shipyard workers had returned home, but the remaining workers and the engineers set about determining which areas needed support braces welded into place to ensure the bulkheads did not collapse when the ship was towed out of port.

Their work might have been easier if we had been able to contract to conduct repairs at the nearby Aden Container Terminal, which had two berths that might have accommodated *Cole* and five forty-ton-capacity gantry cranes. However, when the U.S. Navy approached the Yemeni-owned company that owned it and the Singapore company that was operating it, the request was flatly refused. The growing political tensions, coupled with intelligence indications of an increased threat of a follow-on terrorist attack, were considered too problematic.

The FBI/NCIS evidence collection team, with *Cole's* crew still providing help, continued to sift through evidence up on the forecastle, but the piles had been growing smaller every day. The evidence gathered so far had been easily accessible but a follow-on plan was already being formulated at FBI Headquarters and the FBI's New York Field Office to have another evidence collection team meet the ship when it arrived back in the United States. Already, the FBI/NCIS evidence team anticipated that once the ship was up on M/V *Blue Marlin,* the area inside the flooded compartments at the center of the explosion needed to be examined in detail for additional evidence that had been blown into the ship by the force of the explosion.

Additionally, many areas of the galley and the spaces surrounding it would remain inaccessible until the folded and mangled metal could be pried or cut away in a safe environment.

In addition to evidence, Don Sachtleben informed me that his FBI team members had spotted pieces of crew remains they could not reach or safely retrieve. Those areas had been identified, and the remains would be removed upon the ship's arrival in the United States. This news was of particular concern. When Captain Hanna and the Joint Task Force Determined Response staff were briefed on this, they clearly understood. Back in Norfolk and Washington, however, it seemed as if the leadership of the Navy could not grasp what the enormity of the explosion had done to the ship and how that force had physically torn apart some of the sailors nearest the epicenter of the blast. The families of the deceased were not immediately told of this new development.

We wanted to be able to get the ship underway on its own power to leave port, and Debbie and her engineering team determined that the gas turbine modules in main engine room 2 were intact and capable of operating the port shaft. The port reduction gear and its lubrication system would work properly, and there were no obstructions in the engine's air intakes. Days of checking remained, but the engineers were buoyantly optimistic. By midmorning Sunday, the FBI/NCIS team had completed their external sweeps for evidence, and at last we could hold a freshwater wash-down of the exterior of the ship to remove the disfiguring streaks of greasy, black explosive residue left over from the blast.

As the Sunday work day drew to a close, the ship was starting to look shipshape again—until, at 1618, the engineering officer of the watch announced over the partially restored 1MC system, "Fire, fire, fire. Class Charlie fire in number 3 switchboard. This is not a drill." Number 3 switchboard was in the same engineering space as the crucial gas turbine generator 3, and moments later the high-pitched whine from the generator slowly wound down and stopped, as thick smoke billowed out of the space. A power failure meant that the ship would start sinking again, if more slowly than a week before because of all the repairs and reinforcements that had been made. With the interior of the ship now in darkness, the FBI team prepared to wrap up for the day, and the crew steeled themselves to save the ship once again.

Don would later tell me that when the fire broke out and the crew started reacting to the alarm, he was amazed at how calm they seemed. Normally, a Class Charlie fire in a switchboard is a momentous event on any ship. This battle-hardened crew took it in stride, reacting with a focus that left no doubt that they would handle the situation efficiently and effectively.

Fortunately, the electrical fire in the casualty power terminal in number 3 switchboard was quickly contained. Many of the electrician's mates and engineers surmised that water we had used to clean the exterior of the ship after the FBI had finished gathering evidence had seeped into electrical outlets and circuits damaged by the blast, causing the system to ground and short out. Gas turbine generator 3 could not be reconnected to the switchboard, and we began to start generator 2, but did not want to take unnecessary risks by immediately reenergizing the electrical system and put power back to the switchboard. The ship again began to take on water, but reinforcements over the previous week had made the leaks into main engine room 2 and auxiliary machinery room 1 far less dangerous than they had been during the previous bout of flooding. The engineers started generator 2 at 1625 but waited to complete a set of system checks to ascertain that there were no electrical grounds in the system that might further damage the switchboard or the ship before placing the generator online at 1709. As everyone dipped into reserves of physical and mental strength, we again refocused our energies on getting *Cole* out of port and onto M/V *Blue Marlin* successfully. We were not about to give in now.

In order to determine if the ship could be safely maneuvered out of port and docked onto M/V *Blue Marlin*, the engineers at Naval Sea Systems Command back in Washington needed a series of critical measurements taken to determine how much the keel of the ship might have been bent and flexed. Over the weekend, the divers had rigged two ratchet hoists attached by the sonar dome at the bow of the ship and at another point between the two rudders at the stern. A Kevlar mooring line was then attached between the two points and slowly drawn taut. Approximately three tons of pressure created a straight line underwater to measure any deflection in the keel. It was innovative and creative, but it worked. Measurements by the divers were made every twenty feet, and in the end the keel was deemed undamaged.

The divers then carried out a number of surveys to locate every crack in the hull plating emanating from the blast hole. At the end of every crack, they drilled a hole into the hull plating to stop the crack from spreading when the ship twisted and flexed while being towed at sea.

On board M/V *Blue Marlin*, the calculations of how *Cole* would fit on the deck mandated that several strict requirements be incorporated into the docking plan. In order to keep the center of gravity low, the normal height of the wooden docking blocks that the ship's keel would rest on had to be greatly reduced from a normal height of thirty-six to sixty inches, down to a nominal height of fifteen inches. Since the ship would rest low on the blocks, the blades of the propellers would not fit without hitting the deck. Measurements indicated the blades would extend at least 1.65 meters into the deck. Here was the choice: either remove the lower blades on each shaft by unbolting them from the hub or cutting them off, or cut two holes in the deck of M/V *Blue Marlin* big enough for the blades to slide into as the deck came up and met the keel when the ship was docked. It was determined that two large cutouts into the deck could be made without damaging M/V *Blue Marlin*. The propellers on *Cole*, however, had to be centered over the holes with the blades in exactly the right position, or they would not fit. On a 505-foot ship, the margin of error was down to inches on either side of the blades as they slid into the holes during docking.

Another major concern was maintaining the position of the blades on the starboard shaft. *Cole* used controllable-reversible pitch propellers. In this arrangement, the shafts always rotated in the same direction, outboard when viewed from the stern. To change the direction of the ship, the propeller blades are hydraulically rotated to either face forward or backward. While the blades on *Cole* were in the neutral position now, if they could not be locked into place, there was a possibility that while under tow, the hydraulic force of water flowing over the blades would cause them to rotate out of the neutral position. This in turn might cause the starboard shaft to rotate, prying out the wooden wedges around the shaft seal in the engine room and causing the ship to flood and sink. If the blades did rotate and the ship did not flood, the blades might not fit into the slots cut into the deck of M/V *Blue Marlin*. Ultimately, the problem was solved as MDSU-2 divers donned their gear again, went down into the darkened depths of the destroyed and flooded main engine room 1, and located the shaft-locking lever on the reduction gear. With some difficult effort, they were able to shift it into the locked position to prevent rotation of the starboard reduction gear and shaft.[1]

The next issue was how to position the ship on M/V *Blue Marlin*. The greatest concern by the engineers was the height of the center of gravity of M/V *Blue Marlin* once an 8,400-ton ship was docked on it. The route planned for the return was still under discussion. M/V *Blue Marlin* would either transit to the United States via the Suez Canal or, if force protection and security requirements could not be guaranteed, go around the Cape of Good Hope at the southern tip of Africa. In either case, the possibility of running into storms at sea that could cause M/V *Blue Marlin* to roll excessively from side-to-side was a worry.

The ultimate solution was unique and elegant at once. Two large metal stanchions currently welded to the deck of M/V *Blue Marlin* could be moved and reconfigured to serve as alignment towers for *Cole*. These towers would hold the ship, canted off-center and docked bow to stern at a 17.5-degree angle. This off-axis alignment was necessary to put the sonar dome hanging over the port aft side. Since the dome was the deepest part of the ship, this would allow for smaller docking blocks of only 0.4 meters high to be used, lowering the center of gravity once the ship was docked. Although the ship would be facing backwards on M/V *Blue Marlin*, that would have little to no effect on its seaworthiness or stability.[2]

The next challenge the engineers faced was how to position *Cole* exactly, relative to the propeller holes cut into the deck on M/V *Blue Marlin*. Using the original technical drawings from when the ship was constructed at Ingalls Shipbuilding in Pascagoula, Mississippi, precise measurements were calculated to weld a steel beam marker to the port side of the ship back near the flight deck (at frame 338). The marker measured about three feet across and four feet long and was shaped like a steam locomotive cowcatcher. With the pointed end facing toward the bow, as *Cole* contacted the alignment towers and slid along them into position, the back, flat side of the cowcatcher would stop movement of the ship at the rear-most post. To account for any slight miscalculations in the measurements, six one-by-six-inch wooden planks were bolted into place and could be removed to ensure precise propeller alignment over the deck holes. If pulled off, this would truly be an engineering feat of incredible proportions. Up to this point, M/V *Blue Marlin* had been in port in Dubai, United Arab Emirates, undergoing routine maintenance and contract negotiations with the U.S. Navy. On October 24, all work necessary to dock *Cole* was complete and the vessel set sail for Aden.[3]

The end was in sight at last. The date for leaving port was set for October 29. As the task of collecting evidence and talking with potential perpetrators continued ashore, the level and intensity of credible and specific intelligence warning of a follow-on attack had been building for days. The most detailed information clearly indicated that the Aden Mövenpick and Gold Mohur hotels where the FBI and support forces, such as the MDSU-2 divers and the Norfolk Naval Shipyard workers, were housed had become prime targets for a car bomb, similar to the attack on the U.S. Marine Barracks in Beirut in 1983. Already the Determined Response staff and the Navy divers had moved out to *Tarawa* and other ships in the ARG as much safer and better protected platforms to operate from. Now, despite protests by Ambassador Bodine that this movement was exactly the wrong signal to send to the Yemeni government, the FBI and NCIS also moved their teams out to ships offshore.

This move infuriated the ambassador. Although she had been pressing for a smaller and more nimble footprint in Aden, now that she was getting her way, she did not want it, and clashed over this and other issues repeatedly with the FBI Supervisory Special Agent, John O'Neill. It was a subdued but heated point of discussion on the ship that the ambassador seemed far more obsessed with representing Yemeni interests to the United States than being the President's representative as our ambassador to Yemen. The FBI team was as leery of the Yemeni government's commitment to our safety as the crew and I were. Already incidents involving the ambassador's handling of evidence and intelligence, as well as her dismissive treatment of not only the FBI but many of the support forces that were helping us, had become common knowledge, even at my level.

Within days after the attack, I was ordered to turn over the husbanding agent's cell phone. With that turnover, precious evidence was lost that may have given the investigators insight into how far al Qaeda had penetrated local commercial, law enforcement, and military operations. This was one of many frustrating developments that would continue for months, but with my focus on the ship and crew, I was grateful not to be in the middle of those heated discussions and decisions.

Every day, I was briefed on the evolving intelligence picture. On more than one occasion, I was asked to make a trip up to the bridge to view a ship anchored in the harbor or a house in Aden that might have been used by the terrorists to plan attacks. It was good to know that progress was being made on determining how, where, and by whom the attack against us had been carried out, and I began to hope that soon those responsible would be held to account.

As part of the concern for our safety and in light of the growing threat, the Marines from *Tarawa* brought sandbags on board, and built up reinforced fighting positions around each of the .50-caliber machine guns to reduce their exposure to potential hostile fire. On the area directly above the bridge the Marines, and the SEAL detachment with them, also had a rotating team of snipers that constantly scanned nearby ships and the shoreline. The tension level on the ship slowly began to rise as the crew observed these actions, and while no specific briefings were held, everybody clearly understood that the danger had not passed and we were far from being out of the woods.

Four Yemeni tugs were contracted to tow *Cole* out of port, and two of them would continue to escort the ship to the docking point twenty-three miles down the coast. Even at this point and despite the assistance provided by the FBI, NCIS, and the U.S. embassy, frankly no one really trusted the Yemeni government. To highlight this distrust, the Determined Response task force arranged for each tug to have an armed military sentry posted on board ostensibly to provide protection for them while underway. While this statement was true, the other plain fact was that if one of the tugs tried to do anything that would damage the ship or pull it aground, swift and forcible action could be taken to safeguard us.

As our in-port towing and docking preparations continued, a group of thirty engineers and technical experts, half active-duty Navy and half government civilians, flew to Dubai to meet M/V *Blue Marlin*. Already underway and en route, the group was completing the last-minute preparations and measurements to ensure the vessel was ready to dock our damaged ship.

The Determined Response commander, Admiral Fitzgerald, had paid one last visit to *Cole* on Monday, October 23. With his operations now completely shifted to *Tarawa*, he provided Chris and me with one last update on the plan for the ship's movement, crew transfers to *Tarawa*, and the closeout of the mission from our end. Initially, the plan called for me to stay with the ship with a handful of key technical experts, all *Cole* crew member volunteers, who would ride back to the United States with the ship on M/V *Blue Marlin*.

Chris would remain with the rest of the crew and facilitate their arrival back in Norfolk. Almost as quickly as this plan was formulated, however, the Navy's leadership changed its mind. With one notable exception, the crew would come home together. Whether I would come home with the ship or stay with the crew was left entirely to me. Surprisingly, the Navy at that point was putting no pressure on me one way or the other. Regardless of what my decision would be, a lot of naval history and tradition would be riding on it, and many in the Navy had already formed their own opinion of the right answer.

The psychiatric support team planned to come out one final time on Tuesday morning, October 24, to give them an opportunity to bid the crew farewell and for us to recognize their hard work. The leadership team of *Cole* felt it was very important to publicly recognize their contributions, and many of the crew had bonded with the team members. As part of the closeout of their mission, one person had proved particularly important to me and, by extension, to the crew—Dr. John Kennedy. I asked Admiral Fitzgerald if John could stay with the crew until their return to Norfolk. His presence and knowledge of the intimate details of the crew's mental state would help Chris during the trip, and with any post-arrival care and treatment that may be required. Without a second thought, the admiral agreed to the proposal.

At the farewell ceremony, the team marched up in uniform for the first time in the crew's experience. Some crew members were amazed to discover that these people who had been so open and sympathetic all this time were all active-duty Navy personnel, including some officers. At the conclusion of my remarks thanking them for their work and the comfort and counsel they had given us, the entire crew applauded, and many went up to individual team members they were close to and shook their hands.

Later that afternoon, the constant companion cell phone in my pocket startled me with a sharp ringing and buzzing. On the line was the Chief of Naval Operations in Washington, Admiral Vern Clark. He asked how the crew was doing and if we were getting all the support we needed prior to leaving Aden. I filled him in on the status of the ship, the plans for M/V *Blue Marlin*, and for the crew's transportation back home. He probably already knew most of the information, so the details were less important than giving him my perspective on the crew's performance and morale. Near the end of the conversation, he told me, "Kirk, the decision of whether you stay with the crew or come home with the ship is entirely up to you."

"Admiral, thank you very much, but I have to be honest with you, sir; I need some guidance from someone with over thirty years of experience and who has had at least ten commands in the Navy. If you were in my shoes, what would you do?" I asked him. Without any hesitation, he answered, "Kirk, if I was in your position, I would stay with the ship."

"Then, Admiral," I answered after a slight pause, "I've made my decision. I will stay with the ship and bring it back home."

"Kirk, I know that's a tough decision but I think it's the right decision," he replied.

It was done. For all intents and purposes, in a few days, Chris would be in command of the crew while I stayed in command of *Cole* during the transit. It might be difficult for people who have never had the opportunity to be in the Navy and serve on board a ship to understand why: a commanding officer *is* the ship, and the ship reflects the commanding officer. When coming aboard his or her ship, the commanding officer is announced with a striking of the ship's bell followed by the pronouncement of the name of the ship, not the individual: "*Cole*, arriving," or "*Cole*, departing" in my case. This has been tradition with the Navy since 1781. I had no intention of breaking with tradition.

I was very concerned about getting the ship into international waters by the most direct route, and as soon as possible. Chris, Derek Trinque, and I spoke at length about how we would implement the emergency destruction plan all Navy ships had been required to have since 1968, when the North

Koreans captured USS *Pueblo*, if the ship began to break up and sink under tow. The first goal was to prioritize the material to be destroyed and then to walk through Derek's plan step by step and down to the minute. The biggest fear was sinking in Yemeni territorial waters, which extended twelve miles out from shore. If that happened, the Yemeni government could prevent the United States from regaining access to the ship and its contents. In international waters, we would be free from any such restrictions.

By Wednesday, October 25, Derek completed the final reviews and adjustments to the emergency destruct plan and the team was ready to either destroy or lock up everything. Ensign Jason Van Foeken, *Cole's* communications officer and communications security material system (CMS) custodian, had successfully accounted for and transferred all cryptographic equipment and material off the ship to the CMS custodian on board *Tarawa*. All of the excess paper cryptographic material that did not need to be transferred was dumped into a barrel on the flight deck and, with a small team nearby in case of an uncontrollable fire, burned to ashes. I don't think I had ever seen a happier officer than Jason was after that burden was off his back.

Later that morning, the ship achieved another benchmark with a successful rotation of the port shaft and reduction gear and test of the 2A gas turbine engine in main engine room 2. The sense of satisfaction and confidence that came with knowing USS *Cole* could get underway from Aden on her own power if need be was almost overwhelming. We had come a long way in the past thirteen days.

That evening, John still had one outstanding point of business that he needed to deal with as leader of the psychiatric intervention team: how to get the crew some convalescent leave upon our return. He asked if he could meet with the department heads and solicit their ideas of how to best deal with the crew once they were back in Norfolk. During the course of the meeting, the department heads wanted to know if convalescent leave could be arranged for the entire crew. Initially it did not seem possible. After a thorough review of Navy instructions and rules, we concluded that only a doctor, after conducting a thorough diagnosis and certifying a medical need, could authorize this type of leave. It only took a few seconds for Debbie, with a big grin, to point out to John that he was a doctor and was, in fact, empowered to grant this type of leave. The next day, with Admiral Fitzgerald's blessing, John authorized thirty days of leave for the entire crew.

Finally, it was Sunday, October 29, time to get *Cole* back underway, out of port, and under tow headed down the coast of Yemen toward M/V *Blue Marlin*. The plan called for *Cole* to be towed twenty-three miles south, where M/V *Blue Marlin* would be positioned in a four-anchor moor ready to dock the ship. Why so far? The Navy's leadership was still concerned about how it would look if anything happened to the ship leaving port or while underway. Should the ship begin to sink, it must not happen in view of Aden or any of the growing and increasingly curious media. Consequently we would dock out of sight of everyone.

The sea and anchor detail was stationed at 0815. Although we had no way to determine our position with absolute accuracy, Lieutenant Ann Chamberlain had laid out the navigation charts for the transit and manned a navigation watch to at least monitor our progress. While many of the normal checklist items could not be completed, it was important for the crew to go through the routine of following all the standard procedures. On a very good note, the engineers had managed to shift fuel and water around within their tanks and now, the list on the ship's inclinometer registered only a two-degree list to port. On the other hand, even despite a tremendous effort by the engineering and combat system personnel, many systems still did not work; the alarm system for the ship, including the general quarters alarm, was still not working, only 70 percent of the 1MC announcing system worked, and the ship's whistle could not be operated because of a lack of low-pressure air in the superstructure. Getting underway was shaping up to be a strangely quiet affair.

At 0843, four Yemeni tugs, *Almahrah, Dhu-Hirab, Mayoon,* and *26 September,* approached the ship and began to pass their towing lines up to the crew on deck. The Aden harbor pilot, who had come aboard at 0825, spoke quietly into his walkie-talkie with the tug masters and within a few minutes, he informed me they were ready to work and start to move us away from the pier and out of port. At 0848, Derek, as the Officer of the Deck, ordered all lines singled up. Cautiously we took our time, and minutes later he ordered all lines to be cast off from the pier. One by one the crew retrieved the mooring lines from the U.S. Navy sailors on the pier who had been specifically brought in from *Tarawa* to see us off.

At 0915, USS *Cole* was underway again. The ship's large battle ensign waved proudly in the breeze, sending an unmistakable signal: we had not been defeated.

Slowly, almost imperceptibly, the ship moved away from the pier. For those standing on the bridge, in complete silence, the tension was thick, hanging in the air like a dense fog. This was the moment of truth about the structural integrity of the ship. The crew was manned in a modified general quarters posture with the two functional repair lockers, Repair 2 led by Ensign Greg McDearmon and Repair 3 led by Ensign Robert Overturf, fully manned and ready to respond to the first indication of flooding or damage. The crew would be able to hear the ship breaking up or flooding long before they might be able to see it. Every engineering space below the waterline was manned, and extra watches were posted to check on other spaces to ensure they were not flooding or experiencing damage from the movement.

The ship held together, rock solid. Within minutes, *Cole* was in the middle of the harbor basin as the Yemeni tugs swung around to the bow and began to tow us down the channel out of port. There was not even the slightest indication of expanding damage or flooding. The quiet tension on the bridge began to subside as Chris, Derek, Ann, and I looked at each other and collectively breathed a sigh of guarded relief. At that point, it was time to send a signal.

Looking around the bridge and at last letting out a deep breath, I smiled at Chris and said, "XO, play the first song."

Grinning back in his subdued way, Chris acknowledged with a clipped, "Aye, aye, sir," as he quickly spoke into his walkie-talkie and gave the order.

Prearranged between a group of crew members back on the flight deck and the two of us on the bridge, the ship's stereo system for picnics was set up to play songs during the initial phase of the transit. It was directly connected to the 1MC announcing system and within seconds of the stereo operators being notified, the first strains of "The Star Spangled Banner" boomed out from the speakers and echoed across the harbor.

With our national anthem playing loudly, we were leaving Aden with our heads held high despite what had happened to us. USS *Cole* was now a symbol of American might and resolve.

Now only one tug steadily pulled on the towline at the bow as we left the harbor. The other tugs had retrieved their lines and were chugging alongside as escorts in the event of an emergency. As the national anthem finished playing, we noticed to our left there were two Yemeni Navy patrol craft moored to a pier jutting out into the harbor. Wearing their dress uniforms, the crews from both ships had assembled on the pier to see us off. Just before the bow of the ship came even with the pier and the patrol boats, their commanding officers called them to attention and as we slowly and quietly glided by them, they saluted us and rendered full military honors.

With pride, the crew came to attention and returned the honors.

The governments of Yemen and the United States still had differences on how the attack occurred and why terrorists had been able to conduct such a brazen operation without any reaction from the Yemeni government, but that was beyond our control. All we knew was that as fellow sailors, those exchanged salutes signified the bond that had been passed between navies for centuries.

Really smiling now for the first time in what seemed like weeks, I turned again to Chris as I said, "XO, let's play the second song."

With the same swift precision, Chris called back to the flight deck and within seconds the next song boomed across the waterways. Once again, we played "The Star Spangled Banner"—only this time, the Jimi Hendrix version. It was somehow a fitting transition for what came next. As Hendrix finished ripping, I turned to Chris and told him, "XO, the crew has earned it. Let them play whatever songs they want to."

Chris looked a bit surprised, but within seconds he told the flight deck crew to cue and play their next song.

The screeching noise that then began emanating from the buzzing and vibrating speakers on the bridge and out on the bridge wings—at the loudest possible volume, so the Yemenis watching us leave would be sure to hear it—made me think I had made a huge mistake.

"XO, what the fuck is that noise?" I was beside myself. "That's not music. I don't know what it is, but it's not what I wanted for music. Get it stopped right now," I thundered out. It was the first time since the attack that I had used foul language, and as soon as I said the words, I regretted it, but it was too late to take it back now.

Chris was shocked at my reaction, but when he yelled into his walkie-talkie, the music was so loud the flight deck crew couldn't hear him telling them to turn it off. I gestured toward the back of the ship and said, "Get back to the flight deck right now and get that noise shut down!"

Within seconds, Chris hustled out the port side watertight door and headed down the ladders on the exterior of the ship. By this point, Derek and Ann were too surprised to do anything but get away from me as fast as possible. They found some safety on the starboard bridge wing and pretended to scan the harbor for unseen dangers.

Within less than a minute, Chris was on the walkie-talkie for me. "Captain, the song is almost over, do you still want me to shut it down? They're playing Kid Rock, 'American Bad Ass.'"

Out of the corner of my eye, I could see Derek and Ann, who had overheard the conversation on their own walkie-talkies, working hard to suppress laughter. Shaking my head, I finally understood the amusement of the moment in the calm part of my brain as I responded to Chris, "No, just let it go, XO. Just tell them that a better selection of music would be appreciated in the future." While I may have wanted to send a signal by playing the national anthem on behalf of the American people, the crew wanted to send their own signal in a way that only a sailor could appreciate—up yours, Yemen!

Minutes later, the bow of the ship slowly swung left as we headed down the channel to the open sea. About three miles offshore, the Yemeni tugs cast off their lines as USNS *Catawba*, a U.S. Navy ocean-going tug, maneuvered into position just off our bow. With the disciplined effectiveness of a well-trained crew, a new towline was passed up to the boatswain's mates and by 1154 we were under tow again and headed down the coastline.

Off in the distance, Commander Matt Sharpe on USS *Donald Cook* hoisted a clear message on her signal flags—EN10-17, meaning "the enemy is in retreat."

So far, so good, despite a surprising amount of drag created by the large hole in the port side. It took thirty degrees of right full rudder just to keep the ship on a straight course. On several occasions, probably because of the wind and current, the *Cole* would slowly drift off to the left of *Catawba*. The only way to very slowly recenter it at the end of the towline was to order thirty-five degrees of hard right rudder. Since we had no idea of the complete dimensions of the hole at this point, it was difficult to comprehend why so much drag was being created on the port side of the ship.

Starting around 0300 the next morning, October 30, *Catawba* began the long process of slowing *Cole* as we approached M/V *Blue Marlin*. By 0415 the ship was dead in the water, the rudder was ordered to amidships, and preparations for the crew to disembark began. Landing craft sent over from *Tarawa*, who had shadowed us as we came down the coastline, temporarily tied up alongside the stern and, with the exception of a small number of crew left on board for the docking or an emergency, everyone else mustered on the flight deck to leave. Each crew member was allowed to take one duffel bag on the trip home. The rest of their personal gear was left on board to be retrieved and shipped to Norfolk once the ship returned to the United States.

Emotions ran the gamut as, one by one, *Cole*'s crew left their ship. They had lost their friends, saved their ship, and stayed the course through an unbelievable tragedy; all in the finest traditions of the United States Navy. Most would never set foot on the ship again.

12 | M/V Blue Marlin and USS Tarawa

A S THE FINAL LANDING CRAFT PULLED AWAY, two of the Yemeni tugs maneuvered into position alongside us, and a pilot/docking officer from M/V *Blue Marlin* was escorted to the bridge. It was a few minutes until sunrise, and the clear sky was alight with the glow of the morning. The sea was calm, almost as flat as glass. Only an occasional gently rolling swell drifted by the ships. M/V *Blue Marlin* was ballasted and sunk down almost sixty feet, as far as it could go. Even from the height of the bridge wings, the deck where *Cole* would dock was invisible beneath the water.

Mooring lines from the M/V *Blue Marlin* were placed onto our bitts, the Yemeni tugs cast off their lines, and the ship was steadily pulled into position. With a slight clang, the port side made contact with the two large towers, and we slowly slid backwards towards the bow. Inch by inch, the cowcatcher moved towards the aft-most pole, and at last it made contact. Navy and Marine divers then jumped into the water to verify the position of the ship as the M/V *Blue Marlin* started to deballast and rise up toward *Cole*'s keel. There was a short-lived problem when the blades on the starboard propeller made contact with the forward edge of the pit they were supposed to fit in, and the removable planks on the cowcatcher turned out to be permanently installed, but we hoisted several members of the crew over the side with an axe to chop them away. At one point, someone asked over the radio whether there was concern whether the docking process might scratch the hull. We all looked at each other and pointed out that we already had a huge hole in the port side, and had cut a small hole into the starboard side ourselves; a few scratches at this point would not make a difference in the repair bill.

Slowly, in position, the ship rose out of the water, and by late afternoon, with the sun just above the horizon, the docking was complete. As the water spilled off the flat deck, the Master of M/V *Blue Marlin* invited me over to meet him. After exchanging greetings and meeting some of the caretaker crew that would board *Cole* for the long voyage home, the Master offered to put me in a basket attached to one of the two yellow cranes and lower me to the deck to walk out and see my ship resting on the keel blocks. I gladly accepted his offer.

Minutes later, I walked across the deck of M/V *Blue Marlin*. Water still swirled about the deck as it chased low points to drain off the sides of the vessel. Having been in ship dry docks before, I found the sight familiar, remembering seeing the underside of *Arleigh Burke* as part of the commissioning crew that built that first ship in the class. *Cole*'s hull was no different; it was only lightly coated with a routine buildup of marine life and moss after sitting essentially still for two and a half weeks alongside the pier in Aden.

Carefully, I made my way between the two rudders and twin propeller blades. The shadow cast by the hull made me feel as if the ship was pressing down on me. The blade pits were still full of water and the blades from each shaft were at slightly different angles as they dipped into the dark waters. Walking steadily forward and not knowing exactly what my reaction was going to be when I saw the full extent of the damage, I came out into the sunlight and strode up the port side. I wanted to look up but was also anxious. Out of the corner of my eye, I could see I had reached the point near the center of the blast hole. I slowly turned and stared up at the opening in the side.

Instantly, my throat tightened as my mind tried to grasp the sight before me. It was hard to believe how huge the hole actually was. I took several steps backwards in an attempt to better absorb the shock to my senses. Water mixed with oily residue continued to drain from inside what was left of the destroyed main engine room 1 and dribble out along the numerous ripped sections under the ship. A rainbow-colored film of oil ran by my feet as it headed over the side. The bilge keel, while still attached at either end, had been ripped away from the ship in a sixty-foot section and was strangely rippled and bent.

All along the edge of the blast area, the metal that had once been the hull was torn and bent inward in bizarre shapes. From just above the fuel tanks at the lowest level in the engine room to the overhead in the remnants of the galley, the inside of the ship was exposed. Wires, cables, mangled pipes, bent structural beams, and crushed equipment was visible at every level. The scope of devastation was staggering.

Yet a feeling of total awe and amazement overtook me. My crew had saved USS *Cole*. Looking up at the deck edge along the side of the ship, several faces peered down at me, probably wondering what I was seeing and thinking. My eyes grew moist and I lowered my head. A tear slowly rolled down my right cheek as I looked back up again at the hole. Though seventeen of my crew were dead and thirty-seven more were wounded and hospitalized, 240 sailors had survived this ordeal. While this crew had accomplished what many deemed impossible in saving their ship, the burden of my responsibility as commanding officer now seemed to weigh even more heavily on me.

Back on board, Chris had already begun to assemble the remaining crew as the landing craft from *Tarawa* made their way toward us. It would be another couple of hours before the last of the crew was loaded onto the boats. As each group prepared to leave, they were given the opportunity to walk up the port side and behold the hole as they, too, gained an appreciation for what they had accomplished together. Many let their emotions openly show as they stood on the deck of M/V *Blue Marlin* and looked up. Like the group that morning, they now faced leaving their ship for the last time. Through blood, sweat, and tears, they had accomplished history.

An hour past nightfall, Chris, the last of the crew to leave the ship and M/V *Blue Marlin*, was ready to join them on *Tarawa*. "XO, for all intents and purposes, you are the captain of this crew," I told him. "Take care of them when you get back to Norfolk and I'll see you in six and a half weeks. If anything comes up and you need to reach me, you know where to find me."

We exchanged a firm handshake. Neither of us was capable of saying any more. I was too overcome by emotions put on the backburner for the past two weeks. We just nodded at each other as he turned and got on the boat. Seconds later, it disappeared into the night seas.

That evening, I moved into a small cabin on M/V *Blue Marlin* and prepared to hunker down for the long transit home. The next day was Halloween and that afternoon I passed out to the caretaker crew some small snack packs of M&Ms that I had received in a care package delivered by mail; they were touched by this reminder of home. An updated set of communications equipment had been installed on *Cole*—a satellite radio that served as our primary link to the outside world, and now a more robust secure telephone unit that allowed us to make calls and send faxes that were of a classified nature.

Later that evening, the satellite radio crackled to life with Commander Scott Jones from *Hawes* requesting to speak with me. "*Cole*, this is *Hawes*. I am going to send my boat over to you to pick you up. The admiral would like to speak with you in person on board *Tarawa*, over," Scott told me. I was confused by this request. *Tarawa* was already miles away up the coast and the only way to get to her would be a flight in a helicopter. It was already dark, and an over-water night flight was only permitted in time of critical operational necessity. To my knowledge, there was no pressing need for this flight.

"This is *Cole*, roger, over. Request advise [me] why the admiral can't just speak with me via radio? We can go secure if required but a night, over-water flight is not really necessary, is it?" I asked. "This is *Hawes*, roger, the admiral would like you to pack up your luggage, fly to *Tarawa*, and come home with the crew, over," he replied.

I shook my head in irritation. I had already had a very detailed and specific conversation with the chief of naval operations himself about the decision to remain with the crew. I just assumed that everyone knew about that discussion. I was not about to leave the ship without his knowledge.

"This is *Cole*, roger. Please inform the admiral that the CNO and I discussed this issue and based on his recommendation, I am staying with the ship. Over," I replied with just a hint of annoyance.

Scott now clearly understood my reluctance to go, "This is *Hawes*, roger. Ummm, I was unaware of that conversation and will let the admiral know about your decision. Over."

"This is *Cole*. Roger, out," I replied.

Scott would be back in touch a few minutes later. Since their arrival, the caretaker crew established a radio watch to continuously monitor communications. Knowing this might be a drawn-out process, I plopped myself down into one of the chairs brought out from inside *Cole*. Less than five minutes later, the radio popped back to life.

"*Cole*, this is JTF Determined Response, over," came the voice from *Tarawa* that I recognized immediately as the admiral himself.

"This is *Cole*. Roger, over," I replied, sitting up.

"Kirk, this is Admiral Fitzgerald. Scott is going to send one of his boats over to you and pick you up. We're closing your position now and are going to fly you on board so you can come home with the crew. Over," he told me.

Smiling slightly, I quickly replied, "This is *Cole*, roger, break, Admiral, I had a very specific conversation with Admiral Clark a couple of days ago and we discussed my decision to either stay with the ship or come home with the crew. He and I agreed that I should stay with the ship and that was my decision. Over."

After only a slight hesitation, he replied, "This is Determined Response. Roger, I was unaware of that conversation. I'll get back in touch with you shortly. Over."

"This is *Cole*. Roger, out," I replied.

This situation was about to get real interesting. I leaned back in the chair and tried to contemplate what was going on and what had caused this sudden interest in getting me off M/V *Blue Marlin* to join the crew headed home. Something was up and no one seemed anxious to explain what was going on. Once again, about five minutes later, the radio crackled to life.

"*Cole*, this is Fifth Fleet, over," came the call for me. "This is *Cole*. Roger, over," I replied.

"Kirk, this is Admiral Moore. I want you to get on the boat from *Hawes* and fly out to *Tarawa*. You are going home with the crew. Over," he said in a manner that clearly implied this was not a request.

I took a deep breath and replied, "This is *Cole*, roger, break, Admiral, I understand what you are asking me to do but I had a very specific conversation with Admiral Clark a couple of days ago and we discussed my decision to either stay with the ship or come home with the crew. He and I agreed that I should stay with the ship and that was my decision. I am concerned that the CNO is expecting me to stay with the ship and now I'm being told to come home with the crew. Over."

The curt reply clearly belied a bit of irritation with my response, "Kirk, I wish you had told me about that conversation. Over," replied the admiral.

"Yes, sir. I apologize for not telling you. I have had a number of conversations with people in my chain of command over the past few days and I just assumed you were aware of my discussion with the CNO. Over," I told him with the heartfelt humility of a commander who had just been chastised by a senior three-star admiral.

"I'll get hold of the CNO and talk to him about this situation and will be back in touch shortly. Fifth Fleet, out," he answered and with that the conversation abruptly ended.

How was I supposed to know Admiral Moore was out of the loop on the discussion and my decision? I had taken everyone in the chain of command at face value when they told me it was my decision to make whether to stay with the ship or come home with the crew. This was all the more reinforced after my conversation with the CNO. Something was up; and clearly, I did not have all the pieces to completely understand what was happening. It was about thirty minutes before the radio snapped back to life again.

"*Cole*, this is Fifth Fleet, over." Admiral Moore, sounding calmer this time. Still, I steeled myself for an awkward conversation, "This is *Cole*. Roger, over." The admiral sounded genuine and sincere in what he said next.

"Kirk, this is Admiral Moore again. The CNO is on travel, which is why it took me so long to get back with you. He and I talked about this situation and he now thinks it would be best for you to come home with the crew instead of staying with the ship. Over."

For a second, I had to ponder my situation. On one hand, to leave the ship was to break with longstanding Navy tradition; on the other hand, the crew really was the heart and soul of *Cole* and my loyalty to them was now an unbreakable bond for life. If the CNO wanted me to change my mind, it must be for a good reason. Clearly the time to make a different decision was upon me. While a decision either way would be lauded by some and criticized by others, there was no more time to question why the senior leadership of the Navy wanted me to come home; I just had to trust in their judgment.

What I did not know at the time, but found out years later, was that at the highest levels of the Navy, there was a growing twofold anxiety about how they would look if I remained behind. First was the concern that as commanding officer, I would appear to be "conveniently" unavailable to the media during the course of an ongoing investigation into my actions and the actions of the crew leading up to the attack; and second, the unknown status (to them) of my mental stability. Apparently, there was concern that, essentially alone for six weeks during the transit stateside with *Cole* on M/V *Blue Marlin*, left to contemplate my role as commanding officer in the fate of my ship and crew, I might succumb to depression. With the Navy's leadership unwilling to risk the public scrutiny that would surely follow if I did something like commit suicide, the CNO then recommended that regardless of historical precedent or my feelings in the matter, I should come home with the crew.

I could certainly understand the first concern, but doing harm to myself was the furthest thing from my mind. Despite what had happened, I was confident of my actions and those of my crew. *Cole* had suffered a brutal suicide terrorist attack of a type that the Navy of no other country had ever experienced. Even with training, intelligence, and forewarning, no nation had yet effectively been able to stop suicide bombings anywhere in the world. Surely, I would not be made a scapegoat for what had happened to us.

"This is *Cole*. Roger, sir. In that case, I've changed my mind and I'll get my things packed and head over to *Hawes*. Over," I replied with just a hint of humored resignation.

Thirty minutes later, a boat from *Hawes* pulled alongside M/V *Blue Marlin* and shortly afterwards I found myself strapped into an SH-60 helicopter thundering toward *Tarawa*. All of a sudden, strapped tightly into a seat in the back of a warm helicopter that was vibrating and shaking in a manner that only an aviator can love, I found myself drifting off to sleep. The next thing I knew, we were in a hover over the flight deck of *Tarawa*, and seconds later we jostled to a solid landing on the deck.

Within minutes of my arrival, Admiral Fitzgerald and his staff sat me down to brief me on the plan for a change of command. In coordination between Admiral Moore and Admiral Fitzgerald, the lawyers at Fifth Fleet had found that Navy Regulations authorized a temporary change of command in these unique circumstances. Within less than an hour, the paperwork was prepared and with two signatures, I turned command of USS *Cole* over to Commander Richard J. Abresch, who would ride the ship back to the United States. Somewhat tongue in cheek, both of us kidded each other that when the ship finally arrived, I really did expect him to give it back to me.

Now I was without a ship. But I was still with my crew of heroes.

The plan called for *Tarawa* to transit up the coast of Yemen and Oman for the next two days. The crew would fly into Thumrait Air Base, a joint

U.S. Air Force and Omani facility, where a chartered DC-10 would pick us up and fly to Germany for a brief layover before continuing the next day to Norfolk for the crew to be reunited with their families.

Our routine on *Tarawa* was in many ways similar to what we had established the past week on *Cole*. Chris held Officers' Call with the chiefs and officers, who would then meet by department with the crew. We then convened an XO/Department Head meeting to go over the plan for our return to Norfolk and for the crew's care once home.

On November 1, the second day of the transit, *Tarawa* held a "steel beach" picnic for the crew. It was a great event, especially since a special dispensation had been authorized for each of *Cole*'s crew to consume two beers. Ever since July 1, 1914, when Secretary of the Navy Josephus Daniels outlawed the consumption of alcohol on ships, the fleet made only a few exceptions to this policy and the crew now thoroughly enjoyed one of those exceptions.

The next day, early in the morning on November 2 at 0517, *Tarawa* went to flight quarters in preparation for transporting *Cole*'s crew ashore. As several CH-46 Sea Knight helicopters noisily idled, the crew assembled on the flight deck in groups. Everyone was dressed out in float coats (inflatable life preservers normally reserved for a flight deck crew) and hearing protection. One by one the groups boarded the helicopters and lifted off for the forty-minute flight into Thumrait. All our baggage followed separately.

At the base, it was several hours before the DC-10 was scheduled to arrive, and a large open-bay building was made available for the crew to get snacks and sit in air-conditioned comfort. Admiral Fitzgerald had flown in to pay one last visit with the crew and see us off. Already, the tension level with the crew was slowly easing as they realized they were only one day away from seeing their loved ones.

With every crew member accounted for and the bags stacked outside, I had a few minutes alone. Outside in the blazing hot sun, not a cloud was in sight and the bright blue sky seemed to stretch forever from the sandy hills surrounding the base. Sitting down on top of a cream-colored picnic table, I leaned back on extended arms to enjoy the quiet expanse around us. There was not as much as a whisper of a breeze. The dry heat was a welcome relief to me. After two and a half weeks of oppressive humidity in Aden, I was slowly drying out. It felt absolutely wonderful.

I heard the door open and someone walk outside. Glancing over, I saw the admiral walking toward me and was halfway to coming to attention when he motioned me to sit back down. He came over and sat down next to me on the table.

"You doing OK?" he asked.

"Yes, sir. I'm doing great, why?" I replied.

"Just making sure you're all right. Some of the crew is a little concerned about you being out here by yourself, that's all," he answered with a voice of genuine concern.

I couldn't help but smile as I told him why I had stayed out here as long as I had, "Admiral, I grew up in the high desert of Carson City, Nevada, and have never quite adjusted to humidity. I'm just soaking up the wonderful, dry desert air and enjoying every minute of it. I'm fine and will head back inside in a minute."

"OK, sounds good. I'll see you back inside," he said as he hopped down from the table and headed toward the door.

His sincerity deeply touched me, and less than a minute later I went back inside to circulate slowly among the crew, to let them know they had nothing to worry about with me and to ask them how they were doing themselves.

Less than an hour later, everyone had piled outside to watch the plane land and taxi up to a slot on the tarmac. After refueling, it was finally time to board and put some distance between us, Aden, and the Middle East, and the memories that would be with us forever.

After several hours, the plane landed at Rhein-Main Air Force Base outside Frankfurt-am-Main, Germany. The airbase was collocated with Frankfurt's civilian airport, but the base was locked down in a heightened state of security while we stayed in quarters overnight before continuing on the next morning to Norfolk, Virginia. The entire crew was keyed up during the flight and while some slept, most were exchanging one-upmanship stories about their intended exploits during their well-deserved convalescent leave. During the flight, Chris and Master Chief Parlier also raised the issue of whether the crew would be allowed to drink in Germany.

My first reaction was blunt. No. I had observed that during the steel beach picnic on *Tarawa*, unfortunately, some of the crew had taken the opportunity to gather up more than the two beers allotted to them and several had become mildly intoxicated. While that was somewhat understandable after a harrowing two-plus weeks in Aden, I was very apprehensive about having crew members hungover upon arrival in Norfolk. Every major news network and most other flagship news organizations across the country would be covering our arrival on television, radio, internet, and in print. The last thing the crew and the U.S. Navy needed was to have a wobbly sailor stumble down the stairs and slur words of thanks to the assembled dignitaries. No.

The reaction was exactly as expected. "Captain, you don't trust the crew." "Captain, these are adults, not children." "Captain, the crew deserves the chance to show they can handle themselves like the heroes they are." I patiently listened to all of the quite reasonable explanations but was still hesitant. Even John Kennedy tried to intervene on their behalf. Finally, everyone was told to back off and leave me to think about it. Word spread quickly through the crew and many were not happy. My thinking had been, better pissed and sober, than hungover and regretful. But after what they had been through and survived, the crew felt entitled to be treated better.

After about an hour, it was time to readdress the issue. Five of us huddled together: Chris, the Master Chief, John Kennedy, and Chaplain Thornton, who also accompanied the crew on the return voyage home, and me. Master Chief assured me that the ship's chiefs would take full responsibility and keep an eye on everyone. No one would be allowed to drink to excess. Once again, it was time to face up to my responsibility as the commanding officer and make a decision. OK, they can drink, I agreed finally, but I implored them to please make sure the crew understood that if the drinking even started to look like it was getting out of control, the bar had to be shut down. The nation's eyes were going to be on us.

Thank God I made that decision. Because that evening, after we landed and the crew checked into their rooms at Rhein-Main, each room had been pre-stocked by the Air Force with a six pack of beer. The Base Exchange even stayed open late to give the crew a chance to shop for alcohol, and at the non-commissioned officers' club, a free keg of beer kicked off an evening of celebration. It was almost funny that I had even considered trying to control this one.

But the crew did great. There was not so much as even one incident or alcohol-related problem. The heroes of USS *Cole* understood how to responsibly celebrate, knowing what was at stake the next day.

At the airport the next morning, the crew boarded the same DC-10, and leave chits were handed out. The Public Affairs Officer at Rhein-Main had delivered a letter outlining how the crew should interact with the media after our arrival. With an FBI/NCIS criminal investigation, the USS *Cole* Commission investigation, and a U.S. Navy Judge Advocate General command investigation all ongoing, the Navy not only wanted to reduce as quickly as possible the ongoing media exposure that naturally followed the attack but also to ensure that no classified information leaked out by accident. No one was prohibited from speaking with the press, but it was highly encouraged that prior to any interview, each person should contact the Navy Public Affairs office. There was also a very nice letter cosigned by the secretary of the Navy and the chief of naval operations welcoming the crew home and congratulating them for saving USS *Cole*.

After an uneventful flight lasting just over eight hours, the plane touched down at the Naval Air Station in Norfolk. At the first solid thump and squeal of the wheels on the runway, the crew let out a huge cheer, with whistling, clapping, and high-fives. It was good to be home.

As the plane taxied up to the brand new terminal building, the crew craned their necks in a valiant effort to see their families. The sight outside was amazing. Families were lined up behind a rope line about 200 feet from the bottom of the accommodation ladder being wheeled into place at the aircraft's forward door. Once in place, the lead flight attendant gave a thumbs-up, and the aircraft door swung open. The cool air of fall gently blew past as I stood up front to be the first to walk off the airplane. Stepping outside, I paused for just a moment to survey the crowd. The band played patriotic marching songs and the crowd cheered wildly. Hopefully, no one would notice my misted eyes.

At the bottom of the ladder was a welcoming party that amazed me: Secretary of the Navy Richard Danzig; Chief of Naval Operations Admiral Vern Clark; Commander in Chief of the Atlantic Fleet Admiral Robert Natter; and Commander Naval Surface Forces Atlantic Fleet, Rear Admiral "Jay" Foley were all looking up at us as we descended the ladder to the tarmac. They shook everyone's hand and personally welcomed each home. At first, the crowd and the families held back, but soon, overcome with emotion and joy, every family was able to rush forward to meet their sailor at the end of the official greeting line. Within minutes, it was gleeful pandemonium. With hugs, kisses, tears, backslapping, and handshakes, a grateful Navy and nation welcomed home a ship of heroes.

13 | Investigation and Responsibility

U PON GETTING WORD OCTOBER 12 of the huge jagged hole unknown terrorists had blown in the side of USS *Cole*, the U.S. Navy had immediately launched what had to be a thorough investigation into the actions of the commanding officer and crew of the ship. The Navy's Judge Advocate General Manual is the governing document for investigations of this magnitude, especially when the death of service members is involved. The other military services have very similar documents based on legislation passed by Congress and defined in U.S. law. These same laws also form the basis for the Uniform Code of Military Justice.

On October 14, Vice Admiral Moore, dual-hatted as Commander, Fifth Fleet, and Commander, U.S. Naval Forces Central Command under the combatant commander, Central Command, signed a memorandum appointing Captain James W. Holland as the investigating officer for a command investigation.

In *Cole*'s case, we had been under the operational control of Fifth Fleet but reported directly to Commander, Task Force Five Zero (CTF 50), the battle group commander embarked on the USS *Abraham Lincoln;* the aircraft carrier battle group that had relieved USS *George Washington.* Our mission in Fifth Fleet had principally been to operate in the North Arabian Gulf and enforce United Nations Security Council sanctions and maritime intercept operations against Iraq as a result of the first Gulf War in 1991. These operations were expected to consist of Visit, Board, Search and Seizure measures against suspected smugglers, mostly oil tankers that operated in Shat al Arab waterway and the international waters bordering Iran, Iraq, and Kuwait.

Such operations were risky but routine. They involved Navy ships stopping a suspected smuggling boat or vessel based on its location, cargo manifest, maneuvers, and other intelligence information, and boarding it with a security and inspection team to determine if it was truly in compliance with the sanctions. The Navy had been conducting these operations for years without incident, and despite a well-documented lack of proper equipment and adequate training, fortunately, no major life-threatening incidents had occurred.

Since we had not received our in-theater operations, threat, and security briefings before pulling into Bahrain on October 17, it was assumed that even with our limited 56 kbps download capabilities, we would draw our necessary threat briefings and port security information directly from the Fifth Fleet web sites with supplemental information from the staff of the *Abraham Lincoln* battle group.

In his letter to Captain Holland, Admiral Moore gave him the formal task of inquiring into the facts and circumstances surrounding the actions of USS *Cole* in preparing for and undertaking a Brief Stop for Fuel (as the Navy officially classifies it) at Aden Harbor, Yemen, on October 12, 2000. The investigation completion date was initially set for November 13, 2000. Admiral Moore directed that the FBI and NCIS would investigate the actual act of terrorism. The command investigation team was required to cooperate with them as necessary, but Captain Holland was not to inquire into the facts and circumstances of the explosion or the persons who may have been involved in that explosion.[1] This directive limited the scope of the investigation to internal command actions, but the limitation also removed it from the full context of how the attack occurred.

During Admiral Moore's visit the day after the explosion, he and I briefly discussed his decision to appoint an investigative officer. We both knew this was not going to be an easy or quick process. Every fact would be checked, every qualification verified, and every measure and process *Cole* had put into place to protect and defend the ship would come under intense scrutiny. While the investigation was tasked with ascertaining facts, it was understood that given human nature, there would also be a tendency, unfortunately, to assign blame, given the nature and extent of the attack.

A command investigation creates an atmosphere of intimidation and anxiety, since no one can be sure not to be found to have failed in some manner and subsequently assigned blame, or cited for a failure. Informally meeting with *Cole*'s officers and chiefs on Friday afternoon, I made it clear that whatever the investigating team needed, it would get. Complete and total cooperation was expected from everyone, regardless of personal feelings or impressions. If one of the crew were needed for an interview or to provide a particular piece of evidence or page of documentation, watch schedules would be adjusted to accommodate the investigation requirements. The crew was expected to give their unwavering cooperation.

Captain Holland and Lieutenant Command Thomas Copenhaver, a Navy lawyer appointed to assist him with legal advice, arrived on board Saturday morning, October 14, two days after the attack, to start the investigation. As with almost everyone who arrived on the ship, they were unfamiliar with our unique circumstances following the attack and appeared to have an expectation of office spaces, working computers, and administrative equipment readily available to support them. Although the forward two-thirds of the ship was still without power, Chris quickly adapted our limited resources and set the team up in a Combat System Department space near the back of the ship.

This small space with a couple of computers, desks, and a copier would provide them with at least some degree of privacy for interviews. While it was an awkward arrangement, since the crew often needed to access the space for technical information, drawings, and equipment manuals, it worked for their purposes. This space also served as a central location for them to collect the reams of data that would be incorporated into the body of the investigation.

As the investigation started, one of the first questions they addressed was how *Cole* came to be in Aden in the first place. A Navy oiler, USS *Arctic*, made the first port visit to Aden in 1997 following the 1990 Yemen Proclamation that, after years of war, initially unified North and South Yemen into one country. That was subsequently followed by port visits, not brief stops for fuel, by two Navy ships in April and May 1998. The Navy and Department of Defense, in consultation with the Department of State, assessed that the security situation and evolving political and military ties warranted greater involvement with Yemen. Consequently the Navy, in coordination with the Defense Energy Support Center, negotiated a fueling contract for the port of Aden. The contract ran for a five-year period from June 9, 1999, to June 8, 2004. By the time the contract was signed, six ships had already pulled into Aden to refuel. Over the next fifteen months prior to *Cole* pulling into Aden, twenty more ships pulled into Aden for brief stops for fuel. *Cole* was the twenty-seventh ship to pull into Aden for a brief stop for fuel.

After the attack on *Cole*, national security officials in Washington expressed bafflement that the Navy had ever allowed ships to enter the port. Ali Soufan, the Arabic-speaking special agent who had been in the FBI team on the ship, later wrote, "Yemen was well known in the intelligence community to be full of radical Islamists, including al-Qaeda members." He said that the NCIS's Multiple Threat Attack Center had even described security in Aden as "tenuous," and that though the government of President Ali Abdullah Saleh had turned a blind eye to radical Islamic activities, the Clinton administration, wanting its cooperation, decided to trust Yemen with hosting U.S. ships. None of this, of course, was known to me or anyone else aboard *Cole* as we sailed unsuspectingly down the Red Sea.[2]

Before pulling into port, *Cole* had submitted the mandatory force protection plan with sixty-two measures required for Threat Conditions (THREATCON) Alpha and Bravo (Appendix). We also reviewed messages that contained lessons learned about the port from other ships that had pulled into Aden to refuel. None of them commented on either the threat conditions or force protection measures implemented during their time in port.

It was not until October 11 that *Cole* received approval of the force protection plan by Commander, Task Force 50, with no deviations authorized, and early on October 12, we received the message from the U.S. embassy granting us diplomatic clearance to enter Aden. The message was addressed only to *Cole* and did not contain any updates to either intelligence for the port or a change to the expected threat environment.

At 0546, according to the timeline that would be established in the investigation report, *Cole* stationed the sea and anchor detail watch team to enter port. At about 0740 we arrived at the first navigation buoy outside the port to pick up the harbor pilot who guided us into the inner harbor and pier. By 0851 the ship was twisted around with the starboard side next to the pier with mooring lines being worked by the deck crew to securely moor us in place. The ship was finally ready to start the in-port refueling checklist by 0940 when we secured the Sea and Anchor detail. The in-port watch team, consisting of an officer of the deck, petty officer of the watch, and messenger, was shifted from the bridge to the amidships quarterdeck area between the stacks and on the starboard side where they could better communicate with the Yemeni fuel workers and coordinate the activities of the husbanding agent. The engineers commenced refueling the ship at 1031.

Although the ship's deck log had entered a time of 1115 for the explosion, that entry was written in during the post-blast period, after the quarterdeck watch standers had been injured by the force of the explosion and evacuated to local hospitals for treatment. The blast was recorded in the engineering log at 1118, and the investigation report ultimately determined that time to be the most accurate estimate, given that the engineering officer of the watch, who was uninjured by the explosion, was maintaining the log in the central control station.

For two and a half weeks, Captain Holland and a growing team of Navy lawyers interviewed crew members, gathered up the ship's deck log, engineering log, and messages exchanged between *Cole* and Fifth Fleet, CTF 50, and others, as well as key shipboard documentation on qualifications and training. When it was all analyzed and put together, the team hoped to build a picture of our force protection mindset and posture prior to the attack. Most of the officers, as well as key members of the crew, were brought in for interviews or asked to provide statements for the record. Almost immediately, however, the command investigation team ran into a legal issue that put them in conflict with the criminal investigation headed by the FBI.

Initially, crew members were read their legal rights and signed an acknowledgment form under the Uniform Code of Military Justice (UCMJ), article 31(b), prior to being questioned by the command investigators. The problem that arose was that once a person has heard UCMJ legal rights read to them as part of any legal proceeding, if another agency needed to interview the individual, each crew member had to be given a "cleansing" statement about their rights, as well as be afforded the right to have an attorney present during any further questioning. While the crew was blissfully unaware of this issue, in the eyes of the FBI and NCIS investigators, it could severely complicate their criminal investigation of the terrorists.

Almost immediately, the lead FBI and NCIS investigators, after consultation with John O'Neill, approached me about this issue. They specifically sought to assure me that neither organization had any intention of pursuing criminal charges against the crew for what had happened. While that was good to hear, everyone remained somewhat guarded since no one knew exactly what the Navy's investigation might try to do regarding my actions and those of key crew members responsible for force protection. But the matter appeared to be quickly resolved when Captain Holland and his legal advisors chose to take unsworn statements from the crew without reading them their UCMJ legal rights. Complications from this decision would arise later, however.

At the end of the two and half weeks in port, the command investigation team left the ship and returned to Fifth Fleet headquarters in Bahrain to finish the investigation and reach their conclusions. At the same time, however, another investigative team arrived with a mandate from the secretary of defense. A week after the attack, on October 19, Secretary of Defense William Cohen had assigned retired Army General William W. Crouch and retired Navy Admiral Harold W. Gehman, Jr. as co-chairs to head up a commission to carry out an investigation from the perspective of the Department of Defense into the circumstances surrounding the attack on the USS *Cole*.

The *Cole* Commission was specifically tasked with taking a larger perspective view to determine the circumstances surrounding the attack on *Cole* and what the implications were about the possible vulnerability of any military unit in transit around the world. General Crouch and Admiral Gehman visited the ship while pierside in Aden and were taken on the standard tour of the ship that other visitors had received. There were also shown the areas where the crew had been recovered from the wreckage of the mess line, galley, and main engine room 1.

When speaking privately with me, they both reiterated their desire to know the mindset and procedures the crew followed as we entered port. This was a national-level report that would drive a number of force protection changes throughout the Department of Defense and had ramifications far beyond the attack on us. Without a clear understanding of what processes were followed by not only the ship and crew but also those within the chain of command, as well as other government agencies and departments, General Crouch and Admiral Gehman would not be able to adequately determine just how vulnerable U.S. military units were during transit periods like our move from the Mediterranean to the Arabian Gulf. Following a short few hours on the ship speaking with Chris, Joe Gagliano, and me about force protection issues and the status of the ship and crew, the *Cole* Commission team left the ship to continue their investigation.

Back at Fifth Fleet headquarters in Bahrain, the command investigation team spent long days organizing and collating all the information and interviews gleaned from the crew. Poring over the material, they confirmed that once *Cole* moored to the refueling pier, we had waived a number of the sixty-two force protection measures we had agreed to follow because of the physical surroundings of the ship.

Since the pier was located in the middle of the harbor and not pierside, there were no fewer than nineteen measures that did not apply to our circumstances (see Appendix, THREATCONs Alpha and Bravo: 6, 8, 10, 12, 13, 14, 15, 17, 22, 24, 27, 30, 31, 32, 33, 45, 56, 57, 60). These force protection measures included actions that pertained to vehicular access, vehicle barriers, liberty boats, conducting searches under the pier, and placing armed sentries on the pier (as there would be no liberty calls ashore, and we were moored at a refueling station in the middle of the harbor, no brow or gangplank was put down to the pier), and so on. In statements submitted to the command investigation team, all the officers involved in force protection said that we had completed all remaining measures—our assessment was that we had taken all the precautions that were applicable, in light of what (little) we had been told to expect.

One issue that directly impacted the investigation was the damage sustained by the electronic data system the ship used to store information about personnel qualifications, which by Navy-wide mandate had replaced the old-fashioned paper filing system for crew members' service records that had to be submitted to the Bureau of Personnel in Washington. The shipboard electronic system thus was the only official record of their training and watch qualifications. Located on the refrigerator decks, however, it was now mostly underwater. The magnetic drives were damaged and deemed unsalvageable, and there was no backup or off-ship storage of the training and watch qualification material. Consequently, the command investigation team felt they had no choice but to determine that all qualifications were not officially verified. All the hard work we had done before leaving Norfolk to get the crew qualified to stand all watch stations while entering or leaving port was thus ignored in the command investigation report.

The team also conducted interviews with personnel other than those assigned to *Cole*. These included the commanding officers of *Hawes* and *Donald Cook*, as well as staff members, force protection officers, and intelligence officers assigned to Fifth Fleet, and the *George Washington* and *Abraham Lincoln* battle group staffs. These interviews tended to focus on instances when force protection requirements in a plan that had been approved by higher authority could be waived or not completed. In almost every case, staff officers expected a ship to follow the submitted plan no matter what. From the staff's perspective, at no point would a waiver be considered even if it were clear that the ship could not complete or would be unable to complete measures it had listed because of physical arrangements or conditions that staff members, unlike ship's officers, were aware of in the particular port.

The command investigation team also conducted an extensive interview with Lieutenant Colonel Bob Newman, the defense attaché in Sana'a. He stated that, "during at least one BSF (brief stop for fuel) prior to my arrival (during a period when Fifth Fleet was in THREATCON CHARLIE) [a higher threat level than when *Cole* stopped in Aden for fuel], a USN ship put a small boat (RHIB) in the water for security reasons, . . . and the Yemeni Navy objected to this as a sovereignty issue, even though we believed we had not had any previous problems with this."[3] He further stated that he had addressed this issue with the Yemeni minister of defense and Southern Area commander and considered this issue resolved; however, he was unaware if this information was passed on to Navy ships that pulled into port. The command investigation report determined that it had not been. It also observed that no Yemeni assistance had been offered in ensuring the safety and security of *Cole* while the ship was in Aden.

After weeks of reviewing all the information they had collected, resolving conflicting statements from crew, staff, and other personnel, and piecing together the timeline of events and actions of the officers and crew, Captain Holland submitted his report on November 27, 2000, to Admiral Moore.

Throughout the course of the investigation, I had not had any access to it, nor to the endorsements by senior officers in the chain of command and their conclusions as they made them. I did not learn about any of it until the report and the endorsements were publicly released in early 2001.

When I finally got the report, I saw that Captain Holland, given the narrow scope of his mandate, had clearly sought to place blame for the entire incident squarely on my shoulders, and to varying degrees accused my officers and crew of being derelict in the performance of our duties. It was unfortunately shortsighted, failing to put the attack into the larger context of the then-unacknowledged war being waged by al Qaeda against the United States. But the report was merely the first step in the investigative process, and the chain of command had yet to weigh in with opinions and conclusions that would address and counter the report's assertions of substandard performance.

The key finding was that, of the sixty-two force protection measures listed for completion in the plan that *Cole* had submitted, the ship had waived nineteen and completed only thirty-one.

Of the sixty-two measures, the opinion section of his report concluded, "Nineteen measures could possibly have prevented the suicide boat attack or mitigated its effect. Of those 19 measures, the ship accomplished 7. The remaining 12 were either waived by the Force Protection Officer under the authority [of] the Commanding Officer, or were simply not accomplished."

Six of those twelve unexecuted measures the report considered to be of "particularly high importance." Its assessment of the failure to execute them was starkly critical.

"The collective failure to execute these six measures created a seam in the defense posture of USS *Cole* and allowed the terrorist craft to come alongside the ship unchallenged by those responsible for the ship's protection," it said.

These were the six crucial measures Captain Holland's report accused my command and me of not executing, in his opinion thereby exposing the ship fatally to the attack:

(1) Brief crew on the port specific threat, the Security/Force Protection plan, and security precautions to be taken while ashore. Ensure that all hands are knowledgeable of various

THREATCON requirements and that they understand their role in implementation of measures. Remind all personnel to be suspicious and inquisitive of strangers, be alert for abandoned parcels or suitcases and for unattended vehicles in the vicinity. Report unusual activities to the Officer of the Deck.

(2) Muster and brief security personnel on the threat and rules of engagement.

(18) Water taxis, ferries, bum boats and other harborcraft require special concern because they can serve as an ideal platform for terrorists. Unauthorized craft should be kept away from the ship; authorized craft should be carefully controlled, surveyed, and covered. Inspect authorized watercraft daily.

(19) Identify and inspect workboats.

(34) Man Signal Bridge or Pilot House and ensure flares are available to ward off approaching craft.

(39) Implement measures to keep unauthorized craft away from the ship. Authorized craft should be carefully controlled. Coordinate with host nation/local port authority, Husbanding Agent as necessary, and request their assistance in controlling unauthorized craft.

We had, of course, briefed key personnel on security duties during the refueling stop, but the investigators, doing interviews among the crew at random, found that few others were aware of the security situation, and on this basis, the judgment of the report was that we had not executed measures 1 and 2. As for the remaining measures, 18, 19, 34, and 39, discussed above, I had judged that putting one of the ship's boats in the water to be manned on fifteen-minute standby made little sense in light of what I had been told to expect in the harbor. The boats were stored on the starboard side of the ship, and I had insisted on mooring with the starboard side next to the refueling pier because that would allow *Cole* to get underway quickly under its own power in case of danger; but that also meant that the boats were not deployable after we had tied up to the pier. Even if we had deployed them, the standing rules of engagement under which we were operating would not have allowed us to take a boat under fire unless it fired at us first or showed other signs of imminent hostile action— hardly the case with the suicide boat, whose two occupants were waving and smiling at us right up until they blew themselves to (they hoped) kingdom come.

The command investigation report viewed the force protection plan submitted by *Cole* as a "perfunctory submission," but it also judged the review of the plan by higher authority, the Task Force 50 staff we were reporting to, as equally "perfunctory." Neither Fifth Fleet nor the CTF-50 staffs ever fully reviewed the implementation of the force protection measures that either did not apply or could not be completed due to the physical circumstances of the brief stop for fuel. For the ship's part, the report said, there was a failure to think critically about the force protection posture in view of all the security factors that were unknown to us.

"The crew, while trained, failed to shift their mindset or increase their awareness regarding the new threat environment," the report concluded. The opinions listed in the report found a lack of focus on the importance of strictly executing the plan that was amplified by confusing messages from up *Cole*'s chain of command about the threat level and the nature and danger of the threat. "When USS *Cole* . . . arrived in Aden, Yemen, the threat level was HIGH and the THREATCON was BRAVO," it observed, yet "many of the ship's crew were not attuned to, or even aware of, the heightened threat level." A new four-point system (High, Significant, Moderate, Low) had gone into effect, and Yemen was rated Significant, but Central Command had not implemented it and was still using the old five-point system of "CRITICAL, HIGH, MEDIUM, LOW AND NEGLIGIBLE." "At a minimum this contributed to confusion as to the actual threat environment, as the Commanding Officer and the Executive Officer interpreted this as a 'decrease in Threat Level,'" the report said.[4]

Even though *Cole* had made self-authorized adjustments to the plan based on what we had learned about previous ships' experiences in Aden and on procedures in the Sixth Fleet area of operations, the report's conclusions criticized the ship for not notifying the chain of command that we had done so. There had been a disconnect between the work done by the embassy and defense attaché, the Fifth Fleet staff, and the ships deployed to the region, the report concluded, with information gaps about who was responsible for security on the pier, identification and certification of boats approaching the ship, as well as the latest port security and threat information.

Though the force protection planning system places the onus on individual ships to gather information regarding threat levels and conditions for the areas they deploy to and ports that they visit, the report noted that there was no mechanism in place to ensure that a ship has in fact acquired this information.

The last part of the command investigation report made recommendations for the Navy and the chain of command—lessons learned from this attack:

(1) Increase the emphasis on force protection measures and incorporate them into the training cycle prior to every deployment. Key areas included: specific delineation of responsibilities, clarification of host-nation responsibilities, better coordination with local NCIS threat assessments, and a better process for recommending and reporting force protection measure deviations.

(2) Fleet Commanders must conduct force protection briefings for ships in their area of responsibility before they arrive, thereby encouraging the proper mindset is established for the applicable threats.

(3) The Force Protection Officer should be designated as a primary billet on ships, not a collateral duty, as it was on *Cole*. In other words, it should not be a part-time job, and specific training and experience standards should be set for the designation.

(4) The Navy must initiate dialogue with the Department of Defense, the Department of State and other federal agencies in developing plans for port security of U.S. ships in foreign countries, and ensure the necessary authority is granted to carry out all necessary force protection measures.

(5) There should be closer coordination between individual U.S. defense attachés and ships pulling into their country of responsibility.

(6) Uniform force protections should apply throughout the Navy and other services.

(7) There should be daily backup and preservation of shipboard electronic databases containing watch qualifications.

(8) The Navy should encourage the Department of Defense to develop a system by which threat analysis information is "pushed" to individual units, rather than putting the burden on the unit to "pull" information from individual sources.

But to me as commanding officer, as captain, the most devastating finding—again, in the opinion section of the report—was its conclusion that I and my executive officer, Chris, and two of our subordinate officers had shown "a notable absence of supervision" and "did not meet the standards set forth in Navy regulations."[5]

The report began winding its way up the chain of command for endorsement—in this case, first by Fifth Fleet/Naval Forces Central Command, then by Commander in Chief, U.S. Atlantic Fleet, then by the chief of naval operations, and finally by the secretary of the Navy, and the secretary of defense.

Admiral Moore, the commander of Fifth Fleet and Naval Forces Central Command, rejected its central conclusion in his letter forwarding the report to Commander in Chief, U.S. Atlantic Fleet. He determined that Cole's crew had a robust force protection program incorporating the intelligence assessments that were available, and though he said that he was "disappointed" in the way we had implemented it, he also observed that, "had USS COLE implemented the THREATCON Bravo Force Protection Measures appropriately, the ship would not have prevented the attack. I am convinced THREATCON Bravo Force Protection Measures were inadequate to prevent the attack."[6] It was a stunning admission.

The admiral continued that neither Fifth Fleet nor the ship possessed specific threat information that would have compelled a higher degree of readiness. None of the available information or intelligence included any assessment that hinted of adversaries lying in wait and poised to strike a U.S. Navy ship moored at the refueling pier in Aden harbor. Had it been known that al Qaeda was poised to strike, the ship would not have been scheduled to stop there.[7]

In specifically addressing my actions as commanding officer, Admiral Moore stated that the Navy "cannot use hindsight to penalize a commanding officer for not knowing in advance what has become common knowledge—that a determined, well-armed and well-financed terrorist cell was operating in the Port of Aden. In fact, all of the intelligence assets of the United States and its allies, as well as the U.S. Embassy in Sana'a, did not identify the threat, let alone communicate the presence of that threat to the Commanding Officer of USS *Cole*."[8]

Admiral Moore wrote that because by the time he forwarded his review up the chain of command, at the very end of November 2000, the criminal investigation by the FBI, NCIS, and the Yemeni authorities had identified the terrorists responsible for the attack as close associates of Osama bin Laden. The FBI investigators, including George Crouch and Ali Soufan, discussed their findings with John O'Neill and others up the chain of command in the FBI and believed that bin Laden had ordered his subordinates years earlier to come up with a way to destroy a U.S. Navy ship in or near Yemen, though at this early stage in the probe they were having trouble tying him directly to the actual carrying out of the attack against USS *Cole*.

The Yemenis had interrogated suspects who told them that Tawfiq bin Attash, aka "Khallad," a longtime trainer at one of the al Qaeda camps in Afghanistan who was known to be in constant touch with bin Laden, had supervised the planning. Khallad, easily recognizable because he had lost a leg, tasked one of the jihadists he had trained, Jamal al Badawi, with obtaining a boat from a source in Saudi Arabia and getting it to Aden for an attack against a U.S. Navy ship. The boat, the one that blew up alongside *Cole*, arrived well before the start of 2000.

On-scene planning in Yemen was the responsibility of Abd al Rahim Hussein Mohammed Al-Nashiri, a Yemeni who was another longtime bin

Laden operative and a first cousin of the suicide driver who had attacked the U.S. embassy in Kenya in 1998. An explosives expert, he oversaw the handling, preparation, and installation of explosives into the boat, a fiberglass and wood hull with a centerline console to control the engine. Operating from a safe house with a view of the harbor, he and at least two other Yemeni terrorists, Hassan Said Awad Al Khamri and Ibrahim Al-Thawar, known to the authorities as associates of local al Qaeda operatives, could see when Navy ships came into the port.

Their first attempt had been a failure. On January 3, 2000, as the USS *The Sullivans*, an *Arleigh Burke*–class guided missile destroyer like USS *Cole*, glided into Aden, the boat, mounted on a trailer, was slowly backed down into the water. Although nobody knows for sure, apparently it was backed too far into the water, became stuck with the boat still attached, and could not be freed from the shoreline mud. Despite numerous attempts, they could not free the boat quickly enough and it became swamped and flooded. Unsure whether their actions had come to the attention of the local authorities, the plotters panicked and abandoned trailer and boat. By that afternoon, *The Sullivans* had been refueled and set sail for sea unscathed and, like the rest of the Navy and U.S. intelligence, unaware of how close it had come to disaster. Over the next few weeks it became clear to the terrorists that no one had detected their attempted attack. They recovered the trailer and boat and all the explosives they had placed in the hull, and continued plotting.

A new safe house was picked that was farther out of town, surrounded by a wall, in a quiet neighborhood where people minded their own business—not so different from the one in which bin Laden himself hid in plain sight for so long in Abbottabad, Pakistan, until 2011. The terrorists also selected a small apartment close to the harbor from which they could observe ship movements and film an attack to impress the world with their capabilities and exploits. Here they noted that when Navy ships tied up to refuel, small garbage boats usually came alongside soon afterward.

In September of 2000, bin Laden was reportedly so unhappy with the terrorist cell's lack of success that he wanted to replace Al-Khamri and

Thawar. Al-Nashiri, in response, ordered them to execute an attack on the next U.S. warship to enter the port of Aden—that would be *Cole*—and left Yemen to try to talk bin Laden out of making any changes.[9]

By the time *Cole* arrived on October 12, the terrorist attack boat sported a fresh coat of white paint, with red and black speckled carpet laid in the interior that gave it a clean look. Over months of careful and methodical work, Al-Nashiri had precisely placed blocks of explosives into the hull. As each was placed inside, fiberglass sheets and coats of sealant held it securely in place. The explosives used were blocks of C-4 and Semtex, containing cyclotrimethylenetrinitramine, or RDX, interleaved with blocks of TNT, or trinitrotoluene. TNT is not readily moldable, and as the explosives were built into the boat and slowly filled, it was probably used to line those areas where there were minimal curves and bends along the hull. Batteries built into the boat as part of the bomb provided the charge for the electric blasting caps the attackers used, apparently at least two for each block of RDX-based explosive. It can never be known with certainty how much was used, but the terrorists apparently believed there was enough to sink a ship at the refueling pier.

The suicide bombers themselves—Al-Khamri and Al-Thawar—initiated the detonation, exactly according to the plan. Allah was surely going to bless them when they triggered the switch that morning, which explained why they were smiling and waving at the infidels they thought they were dispatching to hell. No one knows whether the trigger was built into the console or activated by a foot switch, but it did not matter. The ignition circuit closed and their destiny was sealed. A surge of current from the battery raced along the lines to the electric blasting caps. The caps' bridge wires heated white hot and burst into searing flame, igniting the RDX-based explosive that initiated the explosive conversion of the TNT surrounding it as numerous strands of detonation cord extended the blast. In about one ten-thousandth of a second, the chemical chain reaction was initiated and the massive shock wave, travelling at over 25,000 feet per second, began to do its work.

Ultimately, prisoner interrogations and other evidence showed that bin Laden had not only ordered the attack, but also paid for it himself.

None of this, none of this at all, was known. Not to me as commanding officer, nor to Admiral Moore as Commander, Fifth Fleet, nor to anyone in Washington when *Cole* pulled up to the refueling pier on October 12.

The admiral did not know that the Central Intelligence Agency had absolutely no assets in Aden to monitor and assess the terrorist threat there. In reality, without relying on local Yemeni authorities to provide NCIS with information, the United States was essentially blind in its ability to accurately evaluate threats in the port. As the FBI investigator Ali Soufan put it much later in his book, *Cole* was "a sitting duck."[10] The blind leading the blind had led directly to the tragedy that disabled my ship.

In closing out his review of the actions of the leadership on *Cole*, Admiral Moore took a broader view of the events of October 12, 2000, and put them in context. He felt the combination of actions by USS *Cole*, fleet logistic and contingency requirements, the declining number of replenishment ships, intelligence assessments, Task Force oversight, U.S. policy and relations with the government of Yemen, Navy and Joint Force Protection Measures, and the training cycle prior to deployment had all contributed to putting USS *Cole* and its crew in a situation where a successful attack could be ruthlessly carried out by a well-trained and determined adversary.[11]

Admiral Moore concurred with each of the recommendations set forth in the investigative report. Just as damage control is integrated into every facet of a sailor's training, he said, force protection must now assume that same priority. But regardless of what measures were taken to improve force protection measures throughout the Navy, he observed, a ship and its crew must not bear the onus of finding out what the threat was in a theater of operations. That burden should be borne by the upper echelons of the chain of command, which should assume greater responsibility for the coordination and integration of intelligence reports to support commanding officers in making force protection decisions. He also called for closer coordination and a broader intergovernmental effort to provide ships with relevant information about ports. Admiral Moore said he and his staff did not believe an attack in Yemen was any more likely than it would be anywhere else in the region. "The simple fact is that terrorists operate out of most Middle East countries," he wrote.

The United States had been drawn into an undeclared war with al Qaeda, Admiral Moore observed. The attack on USS *Cole* was not a purely criminal deed; it was an asymmetric act of war. While our nation had dedicated billions of dollars towards developing a sophisticated intelligence network and a modern military that could detect, deter, and defend against conventional threats, these resources, tactics, and strategy must now be focused on the global terrorist threat. Clearly, there was insufficient emphasis on waterborne security by the Navy. Unlike land facilities where layered defenses were possible, no such protection existed for ships. His conclusion set the stage for the revolution in the Navy's approach to force protection that the attack on USS *Cole* made inevitable.

Immediately following Admiral Moore's endorsement on November 30, 2000, the entire command investigation package was forwarded to Admiral Robert J. Natter, Commander in Chief of the U.S. Atlantic Fleet, in Norfolk, and Admiral Natter's legal team, headed by Captain Larry McCullough, JAGC, USN, started an independent internal review process.

The document was classified Secret, with the special caveat NOFORN attached, meaning not for release to foreign nationals because the information contained in it was so sensitive that it could not be shared with any of our allies. When it arrived at Atlantic Fleet headquarters on December 6, Admiral Natter was adamant that only a limited number of personnel could have access to it.

But the media were continuously pressing the Navy for updates on the status of the investigation. Once the crew returned home on November 3, the drumbeat picked up considerably. Given the public attention being devoted to the investigation, the hunt was on to find a scapegoat, someone who must have been responsible for ordering *Cole* into the port of Aden and leaving the ship open to attack. It was only a matter of time until someone in the Navy leaked the investigation still in progress. On December 9, the *Washington Post* published a front-page article citing the failure of *Cole* to fully execute its classified force protection plan. The article also noted that while some of the crew had assumed the attacking boat was a garbage scow, they were unaware of any attempt to challenge it.

In response to the bad press, the head of the Navy's public affairs office, Rear Admiral Stephen Pietropaoli, warned against a "rush to judgment" against the crew or me, stressing that the inquiry was continuing. The damage, however, was done.[12] I took the leak as a violation of the trust I had assumed existed between the Navy's leadership and me.

The morning the article came out, I debated for a couple of hours before deciding to telephone a Naval Academy classmate of mine, Commander Frank Thorp, the public affairs officer of Admiral Vern Clark, the Chief of Naval Operations. I felt betrayed and set up, and said precisely that. "Frank, the only way the *Post* could know about the status of what security measures I did or did not complete could be if someone familiar with the investigation purposely leaked it to the press," I told him.

Frank was an exceptional officer. Calm and focused, he had been working the halls of the Pentagon for years. As the public affairs officer for the CNO, he was a candidate for eventual promotion as the Navy's Chief of Information. "Kirk," he said, "you know as well as I do that these kinds of leaks happen. I don't know who did it but there is nothing we can do about it now."

"Well, Frank, let me put it to you this way," I told him. "That investigation is classified Secret–NOFORN. If the Navy is casually leaking classified information to the press in an effort to create the appearance that I'm going to take the fall for this, they better stand by. I have been completely loyal to the Navy to date and have yet to say anything to the press while the investigation is ongoing. You know as well as I do that the Navy's instruction for handling classified information calls for a signature by anyone that checks out or handles classified information at the Secret level or above. That means the Navy knows who has had access to the investigation and that means we have a limited group of people that could leak it to the press."

Frank tried to calm me down. "Kirk, come on now. You know that this stuff happens. You saw it all the time when you were working for SECNAV (Secretary of the Navy). There's nothing we can do about it."

I was stunned. If the Navy was going to try this case in the court of public opinion through leaks to the press blaming me, it would look self-serving and vindictive. Unwilling to let this slide, I continued, "I'll tell you what, why don't you let the CNO know that I am going to go to the press and let them know that since the Navy can't seem to control access to classified information, perhaps that same lackadaisical approach compromised the intelligence I had available to me and now seventeen sailors are dead as a result of the Navy's approach to safeguarding this type of material. That investigation is classified Secret and I will not tolerate any more leaks or I will call into question the ability of the Navy to protect its ships and sailors. Is that what you want?"

For a number of seconds, Frank was silent, thinking about what to say next. Finally, he took a deep breath and pleaded with me, "Kirk, please don't go to the press. Let me see what I can do, but don't do this. I'll take care of it, I promise."

Frank and I were still good friends and had worked together on a number of projects over our time together at the Pentagon and with that, I too took a deep breath and in a very measured tone replied, "OK, you've got it. I won't go to the press, but these leaks have got to stop or I have no choice. I am not going to tolerate this investigation being tried in the press when the Navy expects me to keep my mouth shut. That investigation is classified Secret–NOFORN and it better be handled that way from this point on."

Almost immediately, the leaks seemed to diminish considerably. Whether our conversation made the least bit of difference didn't matter; the media would have to wait until the investigation was done before drawing any more conclusions. Adding to the pressure of the investigation was a larger national issue; the country had become consumed with the outcome of the presidential election. Butterfly ballots and hanging chads became the talk of the day, and a suicide bombing in Yemen lost the interest of the press and public.

On January 4, 2001, Admiral Natter forwarded his second endorsement of the command investigation to the Chief of Naval Operations. He viewed it as his responsibility to ". . . assess whether Commanding Officer,

USS *COLE* (DDG 67) or any of his officers or crew should be held accountable for actions taken in regard to the terrorist attack of 12 October 2000."[13] And his view was clear and unambiguous. "After careful consideration of the matter of personal accountability, I am firmly convinced, and conclude, that the Commanding Officer, Executive Officer, Command Duty Officer, Force Protection Officer, and other officers and crew of *COLE*, were not derelict in the execution of duty. Further, they did not act in violation of any regulation, order or custom of the Navy. Accordingly, no disciplinary or other adverse administrative personnel action is warranted."[14]

From the beginning of his endorsement, Admiral Natter concisely addressed the issue of the decision not to put a boat in the water on fifteen-minute standby for picket duty. He pointed out that the presence of a patrolling boat would not have caused the crew to suspect the approaching boat was anything other than the third garbage barge. Even if *Cole* were operating under the more robust THREATCON Charlie procedures and patrolling around the ship, he noted, the rules of engagement *Cole* was operating under did not allow for any meaningful engagement since the boat did not give any indication of hostile intent or commit a hostile act against the ship until it detonated. By his assessment, there would have been no justification in U.S. or international law for USS *Cole* to use force, deadly or non-lethal, against a vessel or individuals in a vessel making an apparently benign approach.[15]

The endorsement then addressed the issues of crew knowledge and the planning process for the refueling in Aden. In both cases, Admiral Natter found more than ample evidence through the actions of the crew that they had been briefed on the heightened level of awareness required in a port operating under THREATCON Bravo, and he rejected the investigation report's assertion that they had not been. The crew had shown this to be the case by controlling access to the ship by unknown personnel from one of the garbage boats, and in the way the husbanding agent had not been left alone but escorted around the ship.

Regarding the actual execution of the force protection plan for Aden, Admiral Natter took specific issue with the investigating officer's opinions:

In distinct contrast to these statements [by the investigating officer], I find that USS *COLE* was cognizant of force protection concerns, employing an active and knowledgeable team. *COLE*'s performance during the interdeployment training cycle and her aggressive pursuit of force protection training and information is well documented in this investigation. Beyond the force protection performance of the ship, and fully consistent with that performance, were the extraordinary successful and effective damage control and medical efforts undertaken by the ship after the attack. . . . These exceptional, and in many instances heroic, life-saving efforts reflect the ship's character. Read in its entirety, this investigation conclusively demonstrated a taut, highly capable ship—well-trained and well-led.[16]

His endorsement was also not without criticism of my performance, nevertheless. "I am not completely satisfied with the Commanding Officer's performance," he wrote, adding that he was "troubled" that I had not pressed harder before we entered port in Aden for information about where the ship would be moored, whether we would be authorized to deploy small boats, and so on. But in addressing several key measures that we had not implemented, his endorsement specifically refuted the opinion that their omission had created a seam in the defensive posture of the ship that allowed the terrorist boat to approach.[17] Admiral Natter viewed the seventeen men and women of *Cole* who gave their lives in defense of their country as casualties in a continuing conflict between the forces of a free nation committed to protecting the liberty and lives of its people and ruthless bands of highly organized terrorists, bent on destruction and death.[18]

His endorsement, the second, was forwarded to the Chief of Naval Operations, Admiral Clark, who on January 9, 2001, completed his endorsement, the third. Admiral Clark concurred with the Atlantic Fleet commander's recommendation to take no punitive action against the commanding officer or any of the crew for the tragedy. "I concluded, along with the previous endorsers, that the tools and information at the

Commanding Officer's disposal on 12 October 2000, coupled with the lack of any indication of hostile intent before the attack, severely disadvantaged the Commanding Officer and crew of *COLE* in trying to prevent this tragedy. Likewise, I concur that the investigation clearly demonstrates that *COLE* was a well-trained, well-led, and highly capable ship."[19]

In his comments, Admiral Clark maintained that, based on the threat warnings, NCIS Threat Assessment, and other information and intelligence, the ship was focused almost exclusively on a shore-based threat. There was an absence of any specific indication of a waterborne threat. Moreover, an intelligence assessment contended that the known terrorist groups in Yemen had limited operational capability. Given this paucity of specific indications, the Chief of Naval Operations felt that the security measures employed by *Cole* were not unreasonable.[20]

The admiral also agreed with the assessment by both Naval Forces Central Command and Commander in Chief, U.S. Atlantic Fleet, that implementation of all THREATCON Bravo force protection measures would not have thwarted or stopped the attack. Specifically, Admiral Clark stated, "I find nothing in the warnings that would have induced a commanding officer to deploy boats and establish a security perimeter around the ship, the only measure that, in my judgment, would have protected the ship from a suicide attacker. I conclude that THREATCON BRAVO measures were inadequate for the 12 October scenario."[21]

During the course of his review, Admiral Clark also determined that none of the previous ships entering Aden had requested additional security or intelligence information about the port and all had adjusted their force protection posture based on the conditions in the harbor when they pulled in to refuel. Yet while the inadequacy of THREATCON Bravo measures was central to his determination that disciplinary action was not warranted, like Admiral Natter, Admiral Clark was troubled by one shortfall in my performance as commanding officer—my failure to press the chain of command harder before pulling into port in Aden for answers to my questions about the mooring arrangements and other conditions we would find there. That, he said, had contributed to inadequate formulation of the force protection plan.[22]

In the end, the command investigation, limited to examining the actions taken by the ship's commanding officer and crew, did not address the conduct of others higher up in the chain of command for their degree of accountability and responsibility for what happened. Admiral Clark indicated that he would address this issue separately.

More broadly, Admiral Clark's endorsement addressed the issue of the Navy's force protection program. The measures then in force were written to be applicable in all situations, but gave insufficient guidance to commanding officers, for example, as regarding the requirement to keep unauthorized craft away from a ship. Without benefit of picket boats specifically trained in what to look for, or trained linguists to be able to interface with the local police and populace, what commanding officers should do was not clear. Admiral Clark was particularly concerned that the scope of the measures for each threat condition must also be reassessed to determine their adequacy in addressing waterborne and other threats.

Additionally, he concurred with Admiral Moore's recommendation that ships should be provided with more assistance in formulating force protection plans for particular ports. Ships should not be required to draw information and intelligence from the "system"; higher headquarters should ensure that information is provided to ships as they develop their plans. While the nature of naval operations might preclude a briefing as soon as a ship reported for duty in a particular theater of operations, some information had to be provided before they entered that area of operations.

The Chief of Naval Operations deemed the performance of *Cole*'s crew in damage control effective. The CNO remarked on the investigation's findings of brilliant and determined leadership and demonstrated that when significant damage occurred to the ship, the *Cole*'s crew immediately and aggressively fought for their ship and the lives of their shipmates, relying on their countless hours of training.

The crew's heroic actions, both individually and as a team, saved the lives of many shipmates and ultimately saved the ship. His pride in the actions of the individual sailors was apparent with his comment, "This tragedy demonstrated the courageous character and resourcefulness of our service members, many of whom risked their lives to save their shipmates and their ship. Their heroic lifesaving and damage control efforts upheld the highest Navy traditions."[23]

As he put it in a press conference when the command investigation report was released a few days later, "The investigation clearly shows the commanding officer of the *Cole* did not have the specific intelligence, the focused training, the appropriate equipment and on-scene security support to effectively prevent or deter such a determined, such a pre-planned, assault on his ship. So in short, the system—and that's all of us—did not equip this skipper for success, and if you look at my statement, you will see those kinds of words. If you look at my endorsement and my assessment of the . . . and conclusions about the investigation, we did not support him in this kind of an environment, the kind he encountered, when they pulled into Aden on October the 12th."[24]

As the chief of naval operations was preparing to deliver his endorsement to the secretary of the Navy, the Department of Defense released the USS *Cole* Commission Report prepared by General Crouch and Admiral Gehman. It went beyond the focus of the command investigation, to find ways to improve the U.S. policies and practices for deterring, disrupting, and mitigating terrorist attacks on U.S. forces in transit. The recommendations in their report were to create a form of operational risk management applied at both the national and operational levels to balance the benefits against the risks of overseas operations. Ultimately, the report focused on five functional areas—organization, anti-terrorism/force protection, intelligence, logistics, and training.[25]

As has been true in the aftermath of other tragedies of this nature, the report called for greater unity of effort among the offices and agencies in the Department of Defense to provide resources, policy, oversight, and direction and gain the initiative over a very adaptive, persistent, patient, and tenacious new kind of terrorist. This unity must also extend across other U.S. government agencies, the Defense Department report said, including developing security capabilities of host nations to help protect U.S. forces.[26] Force protection considerations were broken down into national level policy and procedural and resource improvements to better support anti-terrorism and force protection for units in transit.

The recommendations called for a number of initiatives and changes, including designating a unit's Force Protection Officer as a full-time billet [the command investigation report had also recommended this]; augmenting individual units during transits through high-threat areas; fully funding service anti-terrorism and force protection programs to support threat and physical vulnerability assessments; assessing and funding anti-terrorism and force protection physical security requirements during the budget cycle; initiating a major unified effort to identify near-term anti-terrorism and force protection equipment and technology requirements, field existing solutions, and develop new technologies to address shortfalls; and giving geographic combatant commanders sole responsibility for assigning threat levels for a country in its area of responsibility.[27]

In the realm of intelligence, the report was blunt in its assessment that intelligence priorities and resources were only making progress at the margins in the shift from a Cold War mentality to the new and emerging threat of terrorism. Once again, it called for reprioritization of resources for collection and analysis, including from human and electronic sources, of intelligence against terrorists. Intelligence production should be refocused and tailored to keep watch over transiting units to mitigate the terrorist threat, it said, and it also endorsed an increase in counterintelligence resources dedicated to combating terrorism and development of clearer counterintelligence standards.[28]

As far as logistics were concerned, the report concluded that the number of refueling oilers operated by the Navy was sufficient to meet the requirements of national security. Although no resource requirements were identified in this area, the report did urge the secretary of defense to ensure that enhanced force protection needs were addressed in the logistics planning and contract award process. It also called for the Defense Logistics Agency to incorporate anti-terrorism and force protection concerns into the entire fabric of logistics support.[29]

In addressing the last area, training, the report called on the U.S. military to create an integrated system of training so that units had a level of anti-terrorism and force protection proficiency on par with their other primary mission areas, including primary combat skills, such as anti-air and anti-submarine warfare tactics. It was incumbent on the Department of Defense to develop and resource credible standards of deterrence against terrorism: tactics, techniques and procedures, and packages of defensive equipment.[30]

With the release of the USS *Cole* Commission Report to the public, the secretary of defense had a number of specific recommendations for review and action. The command investigation report remained as a piece of unfinished business. With the endorsement of the chief of naval operations now complete, the investigation and all three endorsements were delivered to Richard Danzig, the secretary of the Navy. A brilliant lawyer and strategic thinker, Secretary Danzig meticulously embraced his role. Since I had briefly worked for him prior to taking command of *Cole*, he knew me, but I also knew that his views regarding the investigation, endorsements, and my accountability would not by swayed in the slightest when he rendered judgment on the investigation and accountability for the attack.

Unfortunately, politics was beginning to cast a shadow on the question of accountability.

Both the command investigation report and the USS *Cole* Commission Report were scheduled for simultaneous release on January 10, 2001. The Clinton administration wanted to finish both investigations before it left office. On one hand, the President understood the need for a thorough and complete investigation into the attack and its causes. On the other hand, there was immense political pressure not to leave an incident as controversial and public as the attack on *Cole* as an outstanding piece of unfinished business for fear that the Bush administration would use it politically against them. So the Clinton administration was pressing the Department of Defense to find a single individual or organization that could be pointed to as responsible for allowing the tragedy to occur. While the temptation to blame the commanding officer looked like the quickest and easiest way to close out the investigation, the senior political and military leadership of the Department of the Navy strongly resisted it, for the reasons given in the endorsements that had been made.

Secretary Danzig and Admiral Clark stood firm; no one individual would be singled out to take the fall for the attack. They understood the larger and more strategic nature of the conflict with terrorism that had been brought to the fore by this event and blame was not an option. Frustrated with this intransigence, Secretary of Defense William S. Cohen ordered the release of the investigations decoupled. Only the USS *Cole* Commission Report would be released on January 10, 2001. The command investigation could wait and perhaps the Navy's leadership could find it in themselves to come up with the "correct answer" to a perceived thorny political problem. The Navy leadership's unwillingness to single out fault for the attack resulted in the sliding of the release date until late Friday afternoon, January 19, 2001, the day before the inauguration of President George W. Bush.

It was ugly, hardball Washington, D.C., politics. If the Navy was going to be stubborn and affix blame to the entire chain of command instead of one individual, then the service would be made to pay a price. The perception that the Navy was trying to sweep the entire incident under the rug was sure to go over badly with the American public and, more importantly, Congress.

Eight days after the release of the USS *Cole* Commission Report, Secretary Danzig, in a January 18, 2001, memorandum to the secretary of defense, organized his comments on the command investigation report into three main areas—the issues that concerned him; the implications requiring action within his responsibilities for training, organizing, and equipping the Department of the Navy; and finally the implications of the analysis for the commanding officer of the *Cole*.

Secretary Danzig noted that although there had been substantial intervals between successful terrorist attacks, they were happening again and again, and succeeding. He cited the Navy as a whole for six failings:

(1) *Coordination of intelligence efforts and policy decisions.* While intelligence can never be perfect, in the three months since the attack on *Cole*, the intelligence community had ascertained that more than a dozen people had participated over eighteen months

in a plot against Navy ships in Aden; yet, the intelligence community had failed to detect this ongoing terrorist operation.

(2) *Operations risk assessment.* The original decision to use Aden for brief refueling visits had been carefully weighed, but Secretary Danzig could find no indication that any organization compared the risk associated with limited intelligence about terrorist activity in Aden against the alternative risks to the *Cole* of proceeding with less than a 50 percent fuel supply, or conserving fuel by proceeding at slower speeds, or by refueling elsewhere or at sea. While THREATCON BRAVO measures may have been deemed appropriate for those permanently stationed in Aden, there was inadequate consideration of raising the THREATCON level for the short duration of *Cole*'s visit.

(3) *Security cooperation with host nations.* The Yemeni authorities did not provide significant inport protection and the commanding officer was not well informed about the support to expect.

(4) *Navy Force Protection Training.* Even in light of the lessons learned from the attack at Khobar Towers, force protection training still placed too much emphasis on known scenarios—the kinds of attacks, like truck bombs and car bombs, that had taken place before. There was a tendency to focus force protection plans and assets against attacks like that rather than against a kind of attack that had never happened before.

(5) *Counter-terrorist equipment.* Despite robust research and development efforts directed towards defense against familiar forms of military attack, the Navy and Department of Defense were underperforming in the development of equipment that could detect, thwart, or insulate units against terrorist attack.

(6) *Maintaining situational awareness.* The commanding officer could reasonably alter force protection measures to account for the unique circumstances in Aden. While some had been vigorously implemented to minimize risk, others were not, which resulted in a reduced level of situational awareness. That said, even if all measures had been implemented, the attack would not have been thwarted.[31]

As he put it in a press conference the next day:

> In general, I am in many respects impressed by the conscien-
> tiousness of the commanding officer with respect to thwarting
> certain kinds of terrorist attacks. The challenge lies in the words
> "certain kinds." I believe that our training program sensitized him
> in many ways, but may have produced the disadvantage of a some-
> what blinkered vision. When this commanding officer underwent
> his training program, and the *Cole* as a whole did, it was com-
> mended for its work in countering land-based attacks on the ship.
> When it went to Slovenia, the CO instituted particular force pro-
> tection measures that were highly successful, again, against land
> attack, and were substantially beyond what may be the norm. Go-
> ing through the Suez Canal, he was diligent with respect to a num-
> ber of issues. And when he was in Aden, in my view, he vigorously
> protected against attack that might come from the dolphin at
> which he was refueling. The problem, I think, is that by focusing
> so intently on that particular set of scenarios that he had been spe-
> cially trained for, he may have lost some situational awareness with
> respect to other kinds of scenarios, like attack from the sea. We need
> to make sure that uncertainty is broadly appreciated by our com-
> manders, and that in fact, we recognize that we're not training—
> inevitably, there will always be a risk out there that we will not
> train for some scenario that some people will think of. And we
> need to become more muscular with respect to expecting that kind
> of level of surprise and being prepared to deal with it.[32]

Secretary Danzig's memorandum addressed the Navy's, as well as USS
Cole's, force protection training as required by his responsibilities under
Title 10 of the U.S. Code. *Cole*'s force protection measures implemented
in the Mediterranean, during the Suez Canal transit, and even in Aden
before the attack were diligent, but the ship had not trained to defend
itself against a small boat attack of this nature while in port. He ordered
Navy training immediately expanded to include a broader range of scenarios

and to make commanders aware of the need for higher levels of alertness and vigilance in situations where uncertainty is high.[33] He specifically cited the need to do better in risk assessment and management, and to balance that process against the available intelligence. He stressed the need for the chain of command, which typically possessed experts with greater experience, to use their talents and supplement the needs of commanding officers and force protection officers in the protection of their units. He stressed that "one size does not fit all" and that each force protection plan must receive the benefit of being specifically tailored to the circumstances encountered by each individual ship or unit.[34] Investments specially crafted to thwart terrorist threats must receive high priority to improve both lethal and non-lethal weaponry and improved methods of surveillance, threat identification, interdiction, and physical protection.[35]

Finally, he made his assessment of my accountability as commanding officer. In his view, command of a U.S. Navy warship was the greatest privilege the Navy can bestow on an individual. In Navy regulations, the responsibility of command is cleanly and simply defined: the responsibility of the commanding officer for his or her command is total; the authority of the commanding officer is commensurate with that responsibility. It rests—whether for success or failure—squarely on the commanding officer's shoulders.[36]

But, he continued: "This does not mean that it follows inexorably that when bad things happen to, or on, a ship, the commanding officer must be punished. Terrorists are attempting to wage war on Americans. We will suffer additional casualties as a result of their criminal acts. If commanders were regularly sanctioned whenever we suffered casualties, we would compound the injuries to our crew by crippling the will, and, for that matter, the willingness to serve, of our commanders. Furthermore, those commanders we retrained might be more concerned with preparing for the aftermath, than with preventing the occurrence, of an attack."[37]

He agreed with the three admirals' comments in their endorsements of the command investigation report that the conduct of *Cole*'s officers was not so deficient as to warrant criminal punishment by courts-martial or other measures. The additional investigation into the post-attack damage control measures that saved the ship, he found, established that the commanding officer was exceptional both in training the crew in damage control measures and in leading them through the horrific hours and days after the attack. But the Navy had not provided the ship with the information and training that might have prepared it to deal with the attack it had sustained. And, Secretary Danzig wrote, while I as commanding officer was keenly focused on the threats I had trained for and understood, I had fallen short in anticipating the unexpected and adjusting the level of preparedness to deal with the unknown.

In closing, the secretary said, in order to adequately judge my suitability for future assignments and promotions, the sum total of my performance must be considered. Consequently, in consultation with the Chief of Naval Operations, he took the unusual step of ordering that the investigation, his memorandum, and any other memorandum the CNO chose to write should be included in my permanent service record.

The last person to comment on the investigation prior to its release was Secretary of Defense William S. Cohen. He took a much broader and strategic approach in his comments. In a memorandum to virtually every level in the Department of Defense, including the service secretaries, undersecretaries of defense, and the chairman of the Joint Chiefs of Staff, he delivered his assessment of accountability arising from the attack on USS *Cole*.

From the start, he assumed responsibility for the Department of Defense's failure to fully appreciate the danger posed to in-transit naval forces by waterborne threats in restricted waters, such as during a port call or refueling stop. It was the terrorists' exploitation of a "seam" in our force protection efforts that allowed the attack to succeed.[38]

"Both the JAGMAN [command] investigation and the *COLE* Commission make clear that force protection was indeed a priority issue both at the shipboard level and above," Secretary Cohen wrote. "Nonetheless, all of us who had responsibility for force protection of USS *COLE*—including the Secretary of Defense, the Secretary of the Navy, the Chairman, the CNO, CINCCENT, CINCLANTFLT, COMUSNAVCENT, and CTF-50, as well as the Commanding Officer of USS *COLE*—did not do enough to anticipate possible new threats."[39] He enjoined the Department to seek to identify, in advance, the potential vulnerabilities where a determined adversary is most likely to strike. Commanders at every level should continually test and probe every aspect of our force-protection plans, including the assumptions underlying those plans, in order to identify the "seams" that make the United States vulnerable to terrorist attack. He also pointed out one other aspect of this incident as deserving special mention—namely, the extraordinary professionalism and heroism of the *Cole*'s captain and crew in the aftermath of the attack. Noting the earlier comments of the Chief of Naval Operations, he paid tribute to the crew's heroic actions that had saved the lives of many shipmates and the ship itself.[40]

In the last paragraph, he closed with these words: "Finally, I join the endorsers of the Navy's JAGMAN investigation in paying tribute to the seventeen men and women of USS *Cole* who made the ultimate sacrifice in service to their country. Their performance of duty was in the highest tradition of the U.S. Navy, and their sacrifice a vivid and somber reminder of the traditions and heritage of the United States Armed Forces. I extend my deepest sympathy to each member of every family whose loved ones were lost or injured in this act of terrorism. Our nation shall not forget their sacrifice, and we will not rest until all the perpetrators are identified and held accountable."[41]

After all this, however, the official U.S. government response to the attack was far from quick or decisive. Instead of ordering retaliation, officials in Washington deliberated inconclusively. As the staff of the National Commission on Terrorist Attacks Upon the United States, the 9/11 Commission, reported several years later: "After the attack on the USS *Cole*, [White House] National Security Adviser [Samuel ("Sandy")] Berger asked General [Hugh] Shelton for military plans to act quickly against bin Laden. General Shelton asked General Tommy Franks, the new commander of CENTCOM, to look again at the options. . . . Documents show that, in late 2000, the President's advisers received a cautious presentation of the evidence showing that individuals linked to al Qaeda had carried out or supported the attack, but that the evidence could not establish that bin Laden himself had ordered the attack. DoD prepared plans to strike al Qaeda camps and Taliban targets with cruise missiles in case policymakers decided to respond. Essentially the same analysis of al Qaeda's responsibility for the attack on the USS *Cole* was delivered to the highest officials of the new administration five days after it took office."[42]

Apparently, even bin Laden was frustrated by the long inaction after the attack on *Cole*, according to the 9/11 Commission's final report: "In February 2001, a source reported that an individual whom he identified as the big instructor (probably a reference to bin Laden) complained frequently that the United States had not yet attacked. According to the source, bin Laden wanted the United States to attack, and if it did not he would launch something bigger."[43]

14 | The Long Journey Home

B
Y EARLY DECEMBER, the crew had been back almost a month, including the well-deserved period of convalescent leave. Many had given media interviews, but now they were less interested in talking to the press than in refocusing their minds on their shipmates and the future. The crew also understood that an intensive investigation into their actions was ongoing. While some worried about what that might mean for them, we made a concerted effort to assure everyone that the focus was not on the actions of the crew at large, but on the senior leadership of the ship, and especially on my actions as commanding officer. Admiral Natter and Rear Admiral Foley had made recently renovated barracks available, which was a great way to welcome home the crew. But since there was no ship, there were no offices or duties for the crew to focus on for work.

A small contingent attended to routine administrative duties. This group was comprised of *Cole* personnel who had been injured in the attack, evacuated stateside, and were recovering from their wounds, led by the supply officer, Lieutenant Denise Woodfin. Although seriously wounded herself, she had recently been discharged from Portsmouth Naval Hospital and taken charge of all matters related to the ship and crew until our return.

As wounded crew members were discharged, she ensured they were able get some leave to visit with their families and assumed command of everyone as they reported back in for duty.

Stacked in numerous plastic post office boxes were letters, cards, and notes written by Americans wishing them well, the thoughts and prayers of a nation, including letters from grade-school children using their best penmanship on thick, recycled paper, double-lined to help them print their letters as perfectly as possible. Every day, crew members would come in just to sit and read. From my office, you could occasionally hear the laughter as they passed the letters around. Some were more thoughtful and many brought the crew to tears. There were also small gifts and tokens of appreciation from small businesses around the country. One company donated over 100 singing white teddy bears adorned with a flat straw hat whose red, white, and blue headband made them more suitable for a political rally than as homecoming gifts for a battle-hardened crew. Nonetheless, the crew eagerly took them home, for themselves or their children.

Within days after our arrival, a once-in-a-lifetime opportunity arose. The White House Military Office, on behalf of President Clinton, extended an invitation to visit the White House for a Veterans Day reception, followed by the annual wreath-laying ceremony at the Tomb of the Unknown Soldier at Arlington National Cemetery. Thirty sailors with one guest each could attend the service. Funding was already arranged, as were buses to transport those who could not drive.

In putting together the list, Chris and I both felt it was important to have as many crew as possible attend this event, so we excluded ourselves from the trip to give the opportunity for two more crew members to possibly meet the President. We specifically received permission for several of the wounded who were ambulatory and up to the rigors of the trip to attend as well. Within a day, we put together a list of attendees and forwarded it to the White House. A few days later, Chris took a call from Navy Captain Phil Cullom, director for Defense Policy and Arms Control in the National Security Council, who said he was very concerned that none of the leaders of the ship—not the commanding officer, the executive officer, nor the command master chief—were on the list. Chris explained our thought process to him but he was not satisfied with the answer and asked us to rethink our invitation list, which, of course, Chris readily agreed to do.

Chris gave me a call at home that evening to discuss our predicament. My reasons for not wanting to attend were clear, at least in my mind. I knew that the command investigation was still ongoing at that point. I did not want to embarrass the President by attending such a visible national event only to possibly be found negligent later by an exhaustive investigation. At one point, I told Chris that he would attend, as the command representative. He insisted that I was the commanding officer; I had led the crew in saving the ship and numerous members of the crew.

Then the absurdity of what we were doing struck both of us. We were blowing off the President of the United States. That was totally unacceptable, and we quickly agreed that all three of us should offer to attend the event. The White House cheerfully added three additional invitees to the list—the CO, XO, and command master chief.

On November 11, the invited crew members filed through the security checkpoint at the East Entrance to the White House. Once everyone was through, we were not escorted to the reception area where everyone else was gathered but were instead led to the Blue Room, where we were told the President himself would visit privately with us.

As we casually stood in a large circle, the crew took the opportunity to look around. Some had brought their spouses; others, their boyfriend or girlfriend. One sailor, however, was clearly working to improve his luck at this gig by inviting two female friends from his college days in the D.C. area as his guests. The three of them were wide-eyed.

A door opened and Secretary of Defense Cohen entered the room, but his arrival hardly caused a ripple in the flow of conversations. No one immediately recognized him. Quickly, I went over, introduced myself, and made small talk for a few minutes. As we were standing there, suddenly there was an audible gasp from the assembled crowd. I quickly turned my head expecting to see the President. Instead, it was Tom Hanks. He was in town to promote the building of the World War II Memorial. After the recent release of his latest movie, *Saving Private Ryan*, his presence added a rock-star quality to the day. He kindly took time to walk around the room and meet every one of the sailors and their guests, and then pose for pictures with anyone who asked. Given the reputation of many Hollywood actors, it was clear that he was in a class of his own.

Almost as if on cue, President Clinton walked in just as Tom Hanks reached the last sailor. The President's personal secretary, Betty Currie, escorted him. Lines of worry were deeply etched into his face, and he looked tired and haggard from lack of sleep. Immediately, I stepped forward to introduce myself to him. We spoke only briefly, to give him more time with the crew. Slowly and deliberately, he walked around the gathered circle, shook everyone's hand, and posed for pictures by the White House photographer. As the President finished circling the room, he thanked all of us for the great job we had done to save the ship and expressed the heartfelt appreciation of a nation he said was justifiably very proud of us. It was hard not to get choked up with emotion.

As he left the room, we thought we would be able to join the group outside but instead, Betty Currie asked the group if we would like a tour of the Oval Office. This was almost too good to be true. Access to the West Wing of the White House and especially the Oval Office was strictly controlled and this would be a very special treat. Slowly, everyone filed out of the Blue Room, down the West Colonnade, and into the Oval Office. At first, everyone stood around as stiff and proper as possible. Sensing the mood, Betty told everyone to walk around and have a look at everything but to please not touch anything.

Everyone spoke only in hushed whispers as Betty explained the history of the room, the Resolute desk, and the large oval carpet in the center. With us on the visit were Senior Chief Keith Lorenson and his wife, Lisa. Keith was still healing from the compound fracture to his right leg and while in a bit of pain, he was grateful for the opportunity to make the trip. Using a cane to get around, he sidled up to Betty and, eyeing the President's desk, said offhandedly that he would like to sit in the

President's chair. Betty laughed, immediately pulled out the chair, and offered him a seat. A look of utter surprise, tinged with fear, graced his face before he broke into a big smile and accepted. No sooner had he sat down than everyone realized how uncharacteristic and unusual this was for him. Lisa had already rounded the corner of the desk and was standing in the middle of the room to take Keith's picture. She was not alone. Within a few seconds of assuming a distinguished pose behind the desk in his service dress blue uniform, his discomfort at even being there set in and he pushed himself back up. He had his picture for the memory books.

At the Arlington National Cemetery Amphitheater, it was a cold, bright morning with only a few clouds in the sky as we were escorted to our reserved seats. Our breath came out as slight wisps of vapor in the crisp fall air. The crowd stole glances at us, knowing what we had recently endured. There were combat veterans from every major conflict spanning the last sixty years—World War II, Korea, Vietnam, Beirut, and the Gulf War. We were standing in the presence of heroes who had also safeguarded our nation's freedoms. At least two people in the crowd near the front wore a thin blue ribbon adorned with small white stars and a star-shaped medal hanging around their neck—the Medal of Honor, our nation's highest medal for valor. It was our honor to be in their presence.

The President's speech was moving and powerful. In the middle, however, he caught the crew and me by surprise when he unexpectedly recognized us and asked us to stand. With the President leading the applause, the audience rose to their feet in tribute to us. Like the crew around me, I felt my throat tighten as my eyes brimmed with tears. My crew certainly deserved this honor but I felt oddly detached from the moment and unworthy to be accorded such gratitude. The command investigation, even with this moving recognition and sign of support from other heroes, was still hanging at this point like a sword over my neck.

At the conclusion of the ceremony, several members of the crowd approached the crew, talked about their experiences, and expressed how proud they were that we had saved the ship from sinking. My sailors reveled in the moment and clearly enjoyed sharing their own experiences with sailors from conflicts past.

Back in Norfolk a day later, there was still some discussion about what to do with USS *Cole* when it returned stateside—whether to decommission it for manning reasons, making it inactive, or to leave it in commission during what was expected to be a one-year repair period. Already, a plan was being formulated for a significant number of the crew to be rotated to other ships or transferred to shore duty. Relying on my experience commissioning USS *Arleigh Burke*, I approached Admiral Foley about the ship's personnel and manning during the repair period.

This final manning decision was to allow enlisted personnel of the ranks of petty officer first class and higher to remain assigned to the ship through the rebuild period, but only if they agreed to stay with it for at least one year after the ship returned to service. Officer assignments would be handled on a case-by-case basis to ensure junior officers met their qualification requirements and senior officers would not have their careers adversely impacted by an extended shipyard period. All other personnel would be reassigned to other ships throughout the Navy. The Bureau of Personnel agreed that given the unique circumstances surrounding the attack, *Cole* personnel could choose any available assignment, regardless of its fill priority. Crew members who were within six months of rotating to shore duty could opt to have that time waived and pick a shore duty assignment immediately.

Ultimately, just over forty people met the criteria and elected to remain with the ship. They formed the core group that would report to the shipyard in Pascagoula, Mississippi, and manage the influx of new personnel assigned to the ship as it neared completion of repairs in about a year.

At the same time, the command investigation was continuing up the chain of command, and the criminal investigation of the terrorists, headed by the FBI, continued to make progress. While I was on leave, however, the FBI contacted me at home in Nevada. George Crouch, the special agent in charge of the criminal investigation under John O'Neill, had been directed to interview me. A day later I found myself with him in the local

Carson City, Nevada, FBI office, expecting to spend an hour, two at the most, with him.

George was a former Marine officer, and a lawyer. As we sat down and started to talk, we slowly became immersed in the minute details of the attack. Question by question, he slowly drew out my recollection of events, from before our arrival in Aden, until days after the attack as we feverishly worked to prevent the ship from sinking. Time flew by and when it was over, it was dark outside and well past 5 o'clock in the evening.

It was during these precious days at home visiting my mother and father that I discovered how the Navy had informed them of the attack and whether or not I had survived. Like every family with crew members on *Cole*, they had a heart-wrenching wait to learn my fate—and the Navy had not exactly handled its responsibilities with aplomb.

Prior to deployment, every crew member was required to verify and update what is commonly known as a Page 2—Record of Emergency Data. It contained the important information—full name, address, phone number—that the Navy would use to activate a Casualty Assistance Calls Officer in the event of the death or serious injury of a crew member. Once the entire crew had verified their entries, the data was transmitted to and maintained by the Navy's Bureau of Personnel. I, too, had dutifully verified and signed my sheet prior to deployment. Then it became the primary tool the Navy was using to contact all the families of the crew assigned to *Cole*, but my parents' experience told me it wasn't being used effectively.

My father and mother had divorced years before and my father was remarried; I listed my mother as primary next of kin and father as secondary, knowing each of them was living in Carson City, Nevada. By 0730 on October 12, my mother, who was using her maiden name, Staheli, had learned of the attack on the ship from Nicole Segura, who had already received several calls of support from friends and relatives wondering about my fate. A bit later my mother received a call from another informal source, U.S. Army Lieutenant Colonel Marshall Harper, who had been renting my Washington condo since just before I took command of *Cole*.

At work that morning in the Army's Command Center buried in the bowels of the Pentagon, Marshall had received some of the first intelligence reports that a U.S. Navy ship, USS *Cole*, had been attacked by terrorists in the port of Aden, Yemen. I had provided him with my mother's contact information as part of our rental agreement, and he promptly got in touch with her to pass along the breaking news. At this point, all he knew was that the ship had been attacked, but he did not know if I was alive. In speaking with my mother, Marshall was astounded to learn that he was the first person in the military to contact her and let her know about the attack on the ship. Nicole had since called my mother again to let her know that she had received similar news from Lieutenant Commander Rick Miller, my former Combat System Officer, who had since transferred from *Cole* and was also assigned to the Pentagon. Thankfully, Rick had provided an additional piece of good news—I was alive. Since I was making the initial voice reports off the ship, he deduced I had not been killed in the attack but did not know if I had been injured. As the minutes ticked by that morning, the Navy had yet to react and contact my mother or father.

Around 1000, however, the phone rang again; finally, the Navy was on the line. "Mrs. Staheli?" a polite young officer asked. "Yes, this is she," replied my mother, her heart pounding in her chest, wondering what he was going to say next. Positive in his demeanor that delivery of this good news would surely find a happy family member on the other end, he confidently told her, "Yes, ma'am, I just wanted to inform you that your son, Kirk Staheli is not on the USS *Cole*." My mother was aghast. Of course he is, she thought, and in a very polite but firm tone, she replied, "Young man, my son is Kirk *Staheli* Lippold, and he is on the *Cole*. He's the commanding officer. Please call me back when you have your facts straight." And with that, she hung up on him. She stared at the phone for a moment, dismayed and wondering how many other families would have to go through a similar form of bureaucratic torture because the Navy was so ill prepared to carry out such a simple task in reaction to this disaster. Sadly, it would be the only call she received from anyone in the Navy throughout the entire event.

Thankfully, my father's experience was slightly more positive. His wife, Kathy, had a son in the Navy, Don Nutting. That morning, Don called to tell them to turn on the news, where they learned that *Cole* had been attacked. Shortly afterwards, Nicole also called them to confirm that the ship had been attacked, but that I was at least alive and making voice reports off the ship. Shortly after that, a Navy admiral called to give them an updated status report on the ship. Over the next several days, my father would get periodic updates, which he shared with my mother. In many ways, it was still disconcerting to learn in my short visit home that the Navy appeared to be struggling to keep the families informed about what was going on, even with a crisis of this proportion. What would the Navy do if the nation went to war and other ships came under attack? Despite their reputed and best-stated intentions to always look out for the families back home, clearly there was work to be done to live up to that standard.

A few days later, it was back to the grind at the USS *Cole* offices. A number of the crew had drifted back to Norfolk from convalescent leave early and checked in with Denise. Many of them had found that the experience had changed them in ways they were only beginning to understand; they felt as if no one could quite relate to or comprehend what they had been through. Their shipmates understood what their family and friends could not, and they sensed a certain comfort in being together.

When the crew arrived back in Norfolk there was still a great deal of concern about their psychological well-being. Dr. John Kennedy, who had flown back with us along with Chaplain Thornton, briefed the head of the Portsmouth Naval Hospital psychiatric intervention team and brought him up to date on our status and those crew members he felt would need additional support and counseling. At first, the Portsmouth team wanted to come over to the detachment offices, schedule debriefing sessions with each of the crew members, and create a new intervention plan for us. But after talking it over with Chris and the Master Chief, we all agreed it was an overreaction. Instead, we proposed there be no scheduled appointments, and team members would visit every day and just hang out with the crew. Within days after the crew's arrival as a group, the team found relatively few who needed any additional intervention. It was important to continue to destigmatize the post-traumatic stress interventions, since John and the original team had done a great job in Aden. The crew's mental well-being showed in their resilient behavior.

The nation continued to pour out its support. Many people, entertainers, and businesses across the country donated funds for the families who had lost loved ones in the attack. To organize and deal with this influx of charity, the Navy-Marine Corps Relief Society agreed to become the collection manager and trusted agent to oversee the fund. Two entertainers held benefit concerts for the crew and families to help raise money for it. In December, Faith Hill and Tim McGraw held a concert that raised a stunning $375,000, and in January, the crew was treated to the rocker whose "American Bad Ass" they had chosen as their departure song—Kid Rock, who held a concert in Norfolk that raised over $75,000. Prior to the concert, Kid Rock paid a visit to the detachment offices, signed autographs, and visited with the crew for a few hours. It was the highlight of their month.

The fund expected to collect a total of $1,000,000 by the cutoff date of March 15, 2001. Three main groups were ultimately designated as recipients. In the first category, surviving children, spouses, and parents or guardians, with most of the money designated for the children. As an additional benefit, the Navy/Marine Corps Relief Society agreed to pay for any child's college education at any institution in the United States, from a community college to an Ivy League university. It was an amazing gift.

In the second category, funds would be used to design and construct a permanent USS *Cole* Memorial. Initially, the Navy planned to build it in a public place, but persistent public relations concerns about the Navy's responsibility in allowing the attack to happen relegated its location to a secluded area on the Norfolk Naval Station.

In the third category, funds went to the Veterans of Foreign Wars and the White House Commission on Remembrance for each organization to ensure that over the next twenty-one years (reminiscent of a twenty-one-gun salute) an arrangement of flowers would be placed at the gravesite of each of the fallen sailors.[1]

As the middle of December approached, so did the return of the *Cole* itself to the United States. Based on weather and M/V *Blue Marlin*'s transit speed, the ship's scheduled arrival date was finally set for December 13. That morning, the sky was overcast as the chilled, humid mist of winter air drifted across Pascagoula Bay. M/V *Blue Marlin* with *Cole* riding on top was expected to arrive around ten o'clock that morning as crowds from the local area gathered on a nearby public beach to watch. Slowly, the outline of M/V *Blue Marlin* with *Cole* docked in the center and cocked off to one side came into view, and several tugs chugged out of the harbor to meet the ship and guide it into port. M/V *Blue Marlin* turned and made her way toward the pier where the vessel would remain for the next eleven days. At the offices of Ingalls Shipbuilding, everyone stood quietly looking out the window at *Cole*, a proud but battered and beaten ship. A gray tarp covered the large hole in the port side. Hardly anyone spoke. Seventeen sailors had died in the explosion that had caused that damage.

A few minutes later I walked down to stand on the pier as the mooring lines were doubled to secure M/V *Blue Marlin* as a brow was lowered into place. As the temporary commanding officer, Commander Rich Abresch had taken good care of the ship and the caretaker crew. They had accomplished a lot during the past six and a half weeks. Damage assessments were mostly complete and the ship was almost ready to enter the shipyard for repairs. We shook hands as he handed me the paperwork to execute the change of command. Without fanfare, pomp, or circumstance, I was back in command of USS *Cole*.

Earlier that morning, I had met with a team of investigators from the FBI. Supervisory Special Agent Don Sachtleben was again in charge of the group, with some old team members from our days in Aden, as well as some new faces, including the agent who would eventually inherit the USS *Cole* case for the FBI's Explosives Lab, Special Agent Mark Whitworth. Don explained that during the transit, the caretaker crew found several items of interest for the criminal investigation.

They had also found additional remains of crew members.

Before leaving Aden, I had briefed key people in my chain of command, including members of the Fifth Fleet command, Joint Task Force

Determined Response, and Naval Surface Force, Atlantic Fleet, of the strong possibility that this might happen. It was going to be very tough on the families, but the nature of the explosion and the twisted and mangled metal of the destroyed galley and main engine room 1 made it almost inevitable. After speaking with Don about what the caretaker crew had found, plus the additional evidence that was exposed as the shipyard workers began to cut away metal, I left the ship to make a call and confirm to the Navy what had been found and the status of this new crew recovery effort.

When I reached Admiral Foley's chief of staff, he was initially dumbstruck by the news, and instead of reacting calmly, filled the line with invective and anger. Obviously, he had either not been briefed or had forgotten this information. The questions poured forth in a stream of criticism. "How could this happen?" "Why didn't you tell us about this?" "You told us that everyone had been recovered and now this?" "What are we supposed to do now?"

All I could do was stand there and listen to him rail on. Finally, I had had enough. Pointedly, I told him that, in fact, I had informed the chain of command of the strong possibility that additional remains would be found during the transit and subsequent deconstruction period. Faced once again with yet another officer who just did not get what had happened to the ship and crew, I was in no mood to be yelled at by an uninformed senior officer.

As respectfully as possible, I told him the FBI would handle the remains with the greatest care and dignity. They had already assumed custody of the remains until forensic analysis and identification could be completed. A key point many people still did not understand was that pieces of the bombers had also been found during the recovery process and the last thing anyone wanted was their loved ones commingled with those murderous terrorists.

Given this reaction by my chain of command, I had to assume it also represented the views of the Navy's senior leadership. I thought it was time to put forward a bold proposal: I wanted to visit the families of the seventeen sailors killed in the attack. Several days later, while still at the shipyard in Pascagoula, I broached it with Admiral Foley's staff. Following the release of the command investigation report to the public, I would personally contact each of the families of the seventeen sailors killed in the attack and if they were willing to host me, visit each of them in person.

I viewed this as a paramount duty as commanding officer of USS *Cole* when it was attacked. Those sailors had died on my watch, and their families deserved the right to sit down with me and ask the hard questions: Why was USS *Cole* in Aden in the first place? Why didn't the Navy refuel the ship at sea or at another port? Why didn't you follow all of the security measures you said you were going to follow? These families had the right to hear answers directly from me, not just read about my decisions and those in my chain of command in some antiseptic, detached investigation that could not begin to address the depths of grief and anger they felt over the loss of their loved ones. It was absolutely the right thing to do.

The Navy, however, thought otherwise. No, absolutely not, was the answer from Admiral Foley's staff. It was inappropriate for a commanding officer to contact the families. The Navy, through the Casualty Assistance Calls Officer assigned to each family, would handle any questions of this nature that might arise after release of the command investigation report. It was the wrong answer and I was not about to let it go. Given the recent "revelation" about recovered remains on the ship, it was best to just let the issue die down for a few days and to approach it again during my next visit to Norfolk. I was not about to give this up.

The ship, meanwhile, was ready to be floated off M/V *Blue Marlin*. A Naval Academy classmate, Commander Stephen Metz, was assigned to the Navy's Supervisor of Shipbuilding Conversion and Repair, Pascagoula, at Ingalls Shipbuilding, as the Destroyer Project Officer for the Aegis destroyers being built there. Exceptionally capable, he had been tapped to oversee the reconstruction of *Cole* and was personally involved in every aspect of its planned repair. While in transit to the shipyard, he had been provided with very accurate measurements of the size of the blast hole and the extent of damage radiating away from it, and had overseen the

construction of a large, forty-ton, two-section, sixty-by-eighty-foot reinforced patch to weld to the side of the ship and cover the hole. It took
days of welding and adjusting, but by December 23, the patch was securely
in place.

The Navy, in coordination with Ingalls Shipbuilding, had dredged out
the center of the harbor area just off the basin where new ships were constructed and launched. *Cole* needed a launching in reverse. Early on the
morning of Christmas Eve, M/V *Blue Marlin* gracefully maneuvered away
from the pier and firmly anchored herself over the middle of the dredged
area. The water depth gave the ship the room to ballast down and allow
Cole to gently refloat off the docking blocks and support beams that had
held her in place during the long transit back to the United States. Throughout the entire process, teams of shipyard workers patrolled the engine
rooms and spaces below the waterline to ensure the ship remained watertight and its structural integrity held fast.

Once *Cole* was floating on her own above the keel blocks, M/V *Blue
Marlin* took in the lines holding her in position and, seconds later, several
tugs attached lines to the ship and gently towed her across the basin back
to a pier where she would stay for the next eight days. The remainder of
the year would be spent making preparations for the weapons offload at the
Pascagoula Naval Station and transition to the Ingalls Shipbuilding reconstruction area. It was almost 2100 before the evolution was complete, but
USS *Cole* was back afloat again.

Once *Cole* was secure and a watch established for its security, it was
time to get on the road. That night and through Christmas Day, it was a
long drive to Norfolk and straight back to work for me. Although it was
a holiday period for most of the Navy, many people at Naval Surface Forces
Atlantic Fleet and the Bureau of Personnel worked right through it to chart
the future of the crew. Once again, I broached with the admiral's staff the
subject of visiting the families and was again rebuffed, but they were beginning to see that perhaps there might be some merit in my request. Not
wanting to overplay my hand, I left things where they were for the moment
and drove back down to Pascagoula and the ship in preparation for the
weapons offload.

On January 2, *Cole* was towed from the pier at Ingalls Shipbuilding, across the bay to the Pascagoula Naval Station. In coordination with the combat system officer, Lieutenant Commander Anthony Delatorre, Lieutenant Joe Gagliano, the weapons officer, drafted a detailed and comprehensive offload plan putting together a fully qualified weapons onload/offload team that flew down from Norfolk for the project. Numerous support personnel from the Naval Weapons Station at Yorktown, Virginia, helped complete the offload inventory and equipment checks. Although none of the ammunition appeared to be damaged by the explosion, all of it had sat in the magazines for weeks under the hot sun in Aden and during the transit back to the United States. All missiles, torpedoes, and five-inch gun rounds were individually inspected prior to being moved. Early on January 3, the offload began, and with unparalleled speed and efficiency the entire offload of every round of ammunition along with all weapons was completed by late that same day. The next two days were spent cleaning up the magazines and surrounding areas in preparation for entering the shipyard.

Several days later, the ship was towed back across the harbor to Ingalls Shipbuilding as final preparations were completed to float the ship onto a dry dock for movement onto the land facility for deconstruction and rebuild. Taking advantage of the tides, *Cole* was eased out of her pierside berth and slowly towed into place over the middle of the dry dock. Once positioned exactly in place with mooring lines extending from the wing walls of the dock, water was slowly pumped out. Just like M/V *Blue Marlin*, which had departed a few days after *Cole* was floated off, the dry dock pumped water out of its ballast tanks and slowly the keel blocks rose to meet the bottom of the ship.

Within a few hours, *Cole* was lifted completely out of the water again. With the ship resting comfortably on the keel blocks, the dry dock with *Cole* in the center was towed to a docking area next to the land facility. For the next six days, the shipyard prepared the ship for the move back onto land and into the building yard, using a marine railway transfer system. Initially resting on keel blocks, the ship was slowly raised up with wedges pounded under the keel to provide room for a series of small, electrically powered railway cars. With blocking material on top of each car, specifically designed to uniformly distribute the weight of the ship, the wedge material was slowly removed and the ship then rested on the railway cars.

The dry dock used at Ingalls Shipbuilding could have the wing walls removed in sections and using proper ballasting, the rail section in the dry dock could be exactly aligned with the rail sections that lead up to the land facility where *Cole* would be rebuilt. It was a tremendous engineering feat. A new ship is usually driven off the land facility and floated for the first time weighing in at about 60 percent of its final operational tonnage. *Cole*, even with all the weapons offloaded, would test the imbedded rail system to its limits.

On January 14, *Cole* began the slow journey from the deck of the dry dock. At first, the hum of the electric motors was almost imperceptible, and then slowly one could hear the power being uniformly and steadily increased to the individual motors. There was only a slight hesitation, and then with a low grinding rumble, the ship started to move. It was hundreds of feet before *Cole* would be in position and the journey was expected to take hours; nonetheless, the ship was still my responsibility and I stayed to watch the entire event.

Standing with me was one of the senior shipyard supervisors, Lewellyn "Sparky" Butler. He had been handpicked to lead the workers who would soon rebuild *Cole*. Slowly, the ship cleared the edge of the dry dock and was solidly driven up onto the concrete pads and rail lines leading up the ever so slight incline. With the ship moving less than one foot per minute, this was going to take some time. Just making small talk as the railcars slowly ground their way further into the yard, Sparky commented that on such occasions it was sometimes customary to take a penny, place it on a rail, and let the electric cars flatten it. Almost any kid that lived near railroad tracks had done the same thing with a passing train.

I reached into my pocket and discovered I was carrying no change whatsoever. Sparky just laughed, dug into his pockets, and pulled a penny out for me. As I bent down to put it on the rail, I noticed the year—1981, the year I graduated from the U.S. Naval Academy. The car wheel slowly hit the edge of the penny and began, inexorably, to crush it. The symbolism of the moment was not lost on me, but I continued to hope for the best.

By the end of the day, the ship was in position, and soon became a beehive of activity as scaffolding and workers descended to start the repairs in earnest.

It was during this same time that Admiral Natter, commander in chief of the U.S. Atlantic Fleet, forwarded his endorsement of the command investigation to Admiral Clark, the chief of naval operations. Shortly thereafter, on January 17, he, along with Admiral Foley and FBI Director Louis Freeh, was going to meet with the families in Norfolk to discuss the status of the command and criminal investigations. Now, Admiral Foley's staff contacted me and said they wanted to take me up on my offer to meet with the families. They proposed that when everybody was gathered at the base auditorium for the meeting, I could stand up and take questions. But this seemed like a setup to me. The command investigation was not yet finished, and the Navy leadership had yet to render judgment on my actions and accountability. This was the wrong venue and the wrong time, and I declined to do it. All along, my proposal was to meet with the families after, not before, the command investigation was complete. I thought it was imperative for my visit with each family to take place in their home or some other place of their choosing, where they would feel comfortable and I would be an outsider invited in. My vision for the visits had also evolved in the few short weeks since I had first proposed it. I felt it would also be important for the command master chief, Master Chief Parlier, to be at my side during the visits, since he represented the enlisted members of the crew in *Cole*'s leadership team, and that the casualty assistance calls officer personally assigned to each family should also be in attendance. Intuitively, I knew the families had formed a special bond with these people as the Navy's representatives to them. Admiral Foley reluctantly agreed that the Norfolk meeting might not be the best venue for me to appear before the families. I was told to remain in Pascagoula.

But before the January 17 visit in Norfolk, Admiral Natter wanted to come to the shipyard to better acquaint himself with the ship and with the damage it had suffered in the attack, and I took him and a small entourage around *Cole* on the tour route I had followed for the other distinguished visitors in Aden. The admiral asked a number of questions about the events and decisions leading up to the attack as well as our actions in its immediate aftermath. As the tour ended after well over an hour on board, we walked toward the back of the ship and the flight deck. At the same back passageway in the ship where only three months earlier the crew had tirelessly worked to save their shipmates from dying, Admiral Natter requested a moment alone with me.

As we walked away from the group, he asked me what I wanted to do next. I could not help but smile and told him that decision would depend on the outcome of the command investigation, which would determine whether or not I had a career left in the Navy to even worry about a next assignment. He very directly told me not to worry about the investigation; I would be fine at the end and could live with its conclusions. After a few minutes of discussion, we agreed that an assignment to the Joint Chiefs of Staff was exactly the career move needed to keep me on track in the Navy, and he even offered to intercede if the Bureau of Personnel did not support my request. This was the first indication of how the investigation might render its judgment of my actions and accountability. Finally, there might actually be light at the end of this nightmare tunnel.

Back in Norfolk, the admirals' January 17 meeting with the families did not go well. It was an emotional and pointed gathering, and many of those present were filled with anger, feeling that they had not been given the truth about what had led up to the attack and its aftermath. Some family members were quite vocal in their demands for accountability and blame to be affixed to someone in the chain of command for even allowing USS *Cole* to be in Aden.

The day after the meeting, I flew back into Norfolk to await the release of the command investigation, and learned that the Navy had finally agreed to allow me, unfettered, to contact each of the families directly and to arrange a private visit with any that wanted one.

Since *Cole*'s detachment offices did not have television, I stayed at home the afternoon of January 19, waiting for the press conference with the secretary of defense to start. With the command investigation finally released to the public, I listened intently to the chief of naval operations and the secretary of the Navy explain their findings as part of the investigative process. The press was still asking questions as each of the networks shifted to other news. The attack on USS *Cole* was becoming history.

But I still had work to do. I drove back into the ship's detachment offices to meet with a chaplain and go through the list of family members to start making calls. It took a week to reach them all. Seventeen sailors did not mean just seventeen calls. I contacted thirty-one separate family members, many late in the evening from home, the only time their work schedules made it possible for us to talk. During each call I expressed my condolences and quietly offered to contact them again in a week to arrange a visit.

In the end, every family but one agreed to host me in their homes. Knowing that emotions would run very raw, I asked them to agree to a few considerations.

I wanted to meet with immediate family only—husbands, wives, mothers, fathers, sons, daughters, brothers and sisters, and guardians. I asked that the command master chief and the casualty assistance calls officer be allowed to attend with me, and that no media be invited—these were to be private meetings between the families and me.

When the command master chief and I set out on the road to visit each of the families, there were twenty-nine family groups on the schedule over four weeks. Each visit was scheduled for two hours but could be adjusted depending on the circumstances and requirements of each family.

In some homes, I was welcomed with open arms and embraced by a family who appeared grateful and appreciative of my efforts to save the ship and lead the crew out of danger after the attack. Other families greeted me with outright hostility and anger. As I had predicted, the decision to go to the families' homes, where they felt comfortable and in their element and I was the outsider and guest, encouraged them to hold nothing back.

After the introductions and the invitation to my visiting group to sit down, every family cut right to the point with numerous questions about what had happened and why. The vast majority of questions pertained to why the Navy had USS *Cole* refuel in Aden. Many turned to Master Chief Parlier and wanted to know what the crew thought, or if they had any insight into why this had happened.

During each visit with the families, these questions typically lasted well over an hour. It was very important to be consistent and diligent in the answers. These families had suffered an unimaginable loss of their son, daughter, wife, or husband. They deserved the truth, no matter how painful or difficult to hear. I spoke from my heart, as did Master Chief Parlier. If I did not know an exact answer, the casualty assistance officer took a note to get it later. At the end of an often trying and emotional hour, the questions became less pointed and a subtle shift in the tone of the conversation took place. The families wanted to know about the life their sailor had lived aboard *Cole*.

This was always the most heart-wrenching part of the visit. I was fortunate enough to have been in command of *Cole* for fifteen months before the attack. I knew every sailor on the ship. Even the new sailors that had reported aboard during the deployment met personally with me and I had tracked their integration into the ship's company and routine. In doing this, I was blessed by being able to interact in some small way with each of them during their time on board. With every sailor who had died, I was able to share a story about them with their families and make them come to life again in our eyes, for a brief instant. More often than not, everyone listening interrupted these stories with tears and expressions of overwhelming loss. From small boat rides, to lasagna preparation, to expressive language in following a checklist, to approval of a request chit to attend a school, each account was a delicate memory of a life lost in a senseless attack. With each story, the families also shared their own memories, and in most visits I was afforded the privilege of a lifetime as the families shared their sailor with me.

Often with tears running down my cheeks, I turned the pages of a life captured in family photo albums, wedding albums, and montages created by friends and given to the family. In some cases, pictures were taken down from the mantle and handed to me as if to forever impress on me that while I was in command of *Cole*, their loved one had been killed. This was a burden no one could share with me; I had to bear it alone. The images of those sailors will remain with me forever. I will always feel honored and privileged to have known each of them, to have served as their captain, and to have been allowed to visit with each of those families.

The last visit took place just a week before the change of command on March 9, 2001.

Commander Kevin Sweeney reported to the ship as my relief two weeks earlier, and we spent some time aboard in Pascagoula before finishing the turnover process in Norfolk. Kevin was very unhappy with his situation. Just days before he was to take command, the Navy had completed the final estimate of time and money to repair USS *Cole:* fifteen months and $250 million. He had hoped to be back at sea in less than a year. Now it appeared as if most of his command tour would be spent rebuilding the ship, not sailing it on a deployment.

It was also during this final week that we had to complete the last bit of unfinished business from our time in Aden—the personal awards for the crew. After our return from convalescent leave, Chris and I had gathered the department heads to discuss the criteria for each award we expected to bestow. From the beginning, we planned to make combat, not peacetime awards. While every sailor on *Cole* was a hero, the difficult task now was to single out those whose exceptional performance under fire warranted additional recognition.

Just before the change of command, we completed all the awards packages and forwarded them up the chain of command—initially to Commander, Fifth Fleet, for review and adjudication, and from there to the chief of naval operations and the secretary of the Navy's Board of Decorations and Medals, which would make the final award determinations. This would turn out to be a long and drawn-out process fraught with internal Navy politics and public affairs concerns.

In the meantime, since there was no way to realistically conduct a command turnover ceremony on the ship in the shipyard, on March 9, the crew assembled in the Norfolk Naval Station base theater to witness the ritual. It was a high-profile event with numerous admirals and dignitaries, including my former boss, Secretary of the Navy John Dalton, and his wife, Margaret, as well as local media attending.

The Navy, however, was worried about what I might say or do during the ceremony.

Unfortunately, a few disgruntled outgoing commanding officers had unprofessionally used their change of command speech as a bully pulpit to lambast their superiors and blame the Navy for failing them and their ship. Even with my leadership being praised in the command investigation and after my just-concluded visits to the families, I was required to submit my change of command speech to my Destroyer Squadron commodore, Captain Gary Holst, who then forwarded it to Admiral Foley's staff for review. Needless to say, it was a patronizing and somewhat humiliating condition, but by this point I did not care.

Adding insult to injury, the Meritorious Service Medal I was to get for my accomplishments throughout my command tour would not be presented at the ceremony, supposedly because aggrieved family members might take it amiss. Instead, it would arrive by mail, unceremoniously stuffed into a padded envelope, several months later. Lastly, as if to also hedge their bets, Captain Holst's staff called to inform me that in another break with protocol, my fitness report would not be reviewed and signed prior to the ceremony but only later that afternoon. They claimed it had not been finished in time. Trust was clearly a one-way street as I prepared to hand over the reins of leadership on USS *Cole*.

In my change of command speech, while the attack on *Cole* would be a significant highlight, I planned to talk about events throughout my entire time as commanding officer. When the time came, I spoke about a crew that had attained remarkable achievements; from our scores on numerous inspections to getting the ship underway for deployment with an all-enlisted watch team. In the words that summarized their time on *Cole*, they had been there and done that. Finally, I broached the subject of the attack, observing that on October 12, 2000, the Navy and the lives of every sailor on board had been forever altered in less than three milliseconds. I spoke of the valiant and heroic efforts of the crew as they tirelessly worked to save their ship and shipmates. I had barely uttered those words when John Dalton jumped up from his seat, turned toward the crew, and led the entire audience in a thunderous standing ovation. The crew appeared humbled and thankful for the recognition. Thank goodness it took more than a few seconds for everyone to sit down; for a moment, I was unable to speak with the lump in my throat.

At the end, following a centuries-old, time-honored tradition and in accordance with Navy Regulations, I read my orders to the crew and turned to my relief. Commander Sweeney rose from his chair and walked to the center of the stage. We faced each other and rendered sharp salutes.

"I am ready to relieve you," he said.

"I am ready to be relieved," I said in a very clear voice.

"I relieve you," came his reply.

"I stand relieved."

In the days that followed the change of command, I could finally begin the process of reflection and comprehension of what had happened to my life. With orders to the Joint Chiefs of Staff, in the next few months I would complete the Senior Officer Course at the Joint Forces Staff College in Norfolk. When classes started in April, I felt refreshed and on the road to achieving a sense of balance again with my life and career. Even though I was no longer the commanding officer of USS *Cole*, there was a lifelong connection and bond with the crew, the ship, and the families.

But their awards had been relegated to the back burner. This became clear by comparison with the handling of awards that same spring to the crew of a Navy EP-3 surveillance aircraft who were detained for eleven days by the Chinese after the plane had to make an emergency landing on Hainan Island. It had been damaged by a Chinese fighter jet that had been harassing it and came too close, colliding with it and then crashing into the South China Sea with the loss of the pilot. The Chinese government reacted by fanning anti-American hostility, detaining the twenty-four members of the crew, and seizing all the classified radio and electronic equipment and sensitive cryptographic material on the plane. When they were eventually released and allowed to come home, the crew received a heroes' welcome, and on May 18, just over a month later, President Bush presided over a very public awards ceremony at Andrews Air Force Base. The awards for *Cole*'s crew, however, continued to languish. At this point, some of the families expressed irritation at the delay and with the Navy's failure to recognize what their dead sailors had been through. It fell on deaf ears. Everyone continued to wait.

While it was technically no longer my responsibility, I continued to also monitor the status of the FBI's ongoing criminal investigation into the terrorist attack, out of a sense of obligation. Without regard to the consequences, at the end of April I queried the office of the chief of naval operations on the status of the unidentified remains recovered off the ship. Even during the ongoing deconstruction process, additional remains had been recovered and added to the growing amount of material found when *Cole* returned to the United States in December 2000. The CNO's office did not provide an immediate answer. I continued to follow up with queries over the next two months, to no avail. It was as if the Navy had already put the attack, the crew, and the families in the rearview mirror and was moving on as quickly as possible to distance itself from the event. Even the crew had felt a sense of being cut off when the Monday immediately after the change of command, the new commanding officer, Kevin Sweeney, walked into the ship's detachment offices and announced that the pity party was over, and suddenly all the letters, gifts, and posters from local schoolchildren and patriotic Americans across the nation, everything, was ordered disposed of by the end of the day.

At the end of July, duty on the Joint Chiefs of Staff started my education in the ways of the most professional military staff in the world. The officers in this organization were the best from every service. The hours were long, but the work was incredibly rewarding and never dull.

Even in the midst of this intense environment, my thoughts turned again and again to the crew and the families I had visited with only months ago. Over the next few months, the FBI made several trips to USS *Cole* to recover evidence as the ship was disassembled. Additional remains were recovered by shipyard workers and respectfully turned over in January, February, March, and June 2001.

The unique circumstances of the explosion and the ongoing criminal investigation required a complete chain of custody throughout the recovery process. As remains were retrieved and turned over to the FBI, they would send them within days to the Armed Forces Institute of Pathology (AFIP) to determine their morphology—whether or not that material was human or not. Usually within about two weeks the remains were turned back over to the FBI for forensic and DNA analysis. The Navy leadership seemingly did not believe that there was a possibility that remains of *Cole* crew members could be comingled with those of the terrorist bombers. They viewed the remains only in terms of the sailors being victims and insisted that AFIP should conduct the identifications.

Fortunately, the FBI and AFIP understood the importance of keeping the remains segregated and properly identified. Another complicated and time-consuming factor was the requirement to have only one investigator assigned to the case to ensure continuity of the work and maintain the chain of custody. After months of detailed work, the remains of *Cole* crew members received identification to FBI standards and by September 25 were classified into three groups: *Cole* crew members, terrorist bombers, and unidentifiable material. The *Cole* remains were turned over to AFIP on October 4 to conduct some additional detailed DNA analysis and co-ordinate disposition with the Navy.

Throughout the process, the Navy remained publicly silent on the issue of the additional crew's remains, despite repeated queries. The longer the wait, the more difficult it was going to be for the families to deal with a continuing tragedy as many sought a degree of solace and closure in the healing nature of time. Months had gone by with no word as the families waited in silence.

On a good note, over the summer, the Navy finally completed work on the crew's awards. Regrettably, the attack on *Cole* was still not viewed as an act of war. The crew would only receive downgraded peacetime awards instead of what many families and I felt they deserved—combat awards.

Almost one year after the attack, Admiral Foley held the ceremony on September 5, 2001. With USS *George Washington* on one side of the pier and with the opposite side flanked by USS *Hawes* and USS *Donald Cook*, the crew finally received the long-deserved recognition of having the medals they had heroically earned pinned on their chests. The eleven months it took to get to this point paled in comparison to the happiness everyone displayed. One person in particular showed incredible grit and determination, Seaman Elizabeth Lafontaine. Despite shrapnel wounds, compound fractures to both legs, several surgical operations, and weeks in the hospital, when her name was called to receive her Purple Heart, she rose from her chair and, with only minor use of a cane, proudly strode up to receive her award. Lieutenant Jim Salter looked on from the audience, remembered her rescue, and marveled at the moment.

Only a few days later, with the attacks on September 11, the country became consumed by the Global War on Terror, and once again, anything related to USS *Cole* became relegated to a lower priority until a year after the attack. As part of the distribution plan for funds given to the USS *Cole* Fund, the portion set aside to build a lasting memorial came to fruition. Many families, including those who had lost loved ones in the attack, wanted a ceremony, open to the public and easily accessible to the media and others who wished to pay homage to and celebrate the crew's accomplishments. Once again seeking to downplay and distance itself from the attack, the Navy chose to strictly control media access and prevent the public display many families and the crew had hoped for. Nonetheless, at least there would be a lasting memorial to the seventeen sailors and the heroic crew who had given so much to save the ship.

October 12, 2001, was a beautiful fall day in Norfolk, Virginia, but a tense calm fell over it like a chilled blanket. It had only been thirty days since the September 11 attacks and now the nation was at war. Security and access to the naval base was tightly controlled and force protection measures were at an all-time high. As the ceremony got underway, a helicopter crisscrossed over the bay as armed patrol boats circled in the waters just offshore. All roads leading to the monument were blocked off and admittance was strictly controlled. The attack on *Cole* fundamentally changed how the Navy viewed force protection and with the attacks on September 11, the nation felt vulnerable.

Over the previous months, several local contractors throughout the Norfolk area had donated time and money well beyond the funds set aside and built a beautiful ten-foot-tall monolith of mahogany-colored granite, encircled by seventeen smaller granite slabs inlaid into the ground. A tree-lined pathway leads to the site and is surrounded by tall pine trees, providing a natural seclusion and quiet area for visitors to reflect and contemplate the sacrifices made for our freedom. The site chosen by the Navy overlooks Willoughby Bay, where ships leaving and returning from sea pass by. At its top, the granite slopes forty-five degrees, a symbolic salute to passing ships and the names of the seventeen sailors killed in the attack inscribed on two brass plaques. A third plaque in between reads: "In lasting tribute to their honor, courage and commitment."

It was an emotionally charged day as the crew and families gathered to honor their shipmates, who had paid the ultimate price only a short year earlier. The official unveiling of the monument occurred precisely at 1118 as the names of all seventeen sailors were read aloud. There was not a dry eye in the crowd.

Immediately following the event, as everyone was spending some time visiting with each other, a young sailor and his family approached me alone. Engineman Third Class John Thompson humbly walked up to me and introduced me to his wife, Heidi.

Looking me in the eye, he started to choke up as he said, "Sir, I owe you an apology." While somewhat surprised, I knew what he was talking about—the moment when he had confronted me in Aden and said I was going to get everybody killed because I wouldn't let them go home sooner—and immediately set about downplaying it. "No apology necessary. It was a unique time in our lives and you did a great job over there." "Well, thank you, sir, but I still owe you an apology," he continued. It was a self-conscious moment for both us before he quickly continued, "I never should have said what I did to you. It was disrespectful and, well, I guess what I'm trying to say, sir, is that what I didn't realize then, but I do now, is that when we were over in Aden, you had more faith in us than we had in ourselves."

For a moment, I couldn't think of the right words to say, and even if I had had them, I would not have been able to get them out. His words seemed to linger in the air before we finally exchanged a solid handshake, then paused before giving each other a big hug—again. I was honored beyond words.

While the memorial may have been dedicated, an uncertain wait continued for some of the families. An unforeseen consequence of the September 11 attacks was that the Armed Forces Institute of Pathology shifted their focus from *Cole* to the remains of those who had been killed in the Pentagon. The process of identifying the final fragmentary sets of *Cole* remains dragged on for over two months more, until finally the Institute informed the Navy on December 10 that the identifications were complete. The remains would be turned over to their families, and the fragmentary remains of the terrorists that had been found with them inside the ship were turned back over to the FBI.

When I learned that the identification of my sailors was complete, a new fear settled into my gut when the Navy decided to notify the families just before Christmas. It may not have been my place to do it, but I pleaded with the staff of the chief of naval operations to wait until after the holidays, so the families could at least get through one Christmas without the Navy disrupting it. My thought process was that it would be better for the families to be angry about a delay in being notified than to have their holiday spoiled once again with tragic news. As I would learn from September 11 families years later, thankfully my request was rebuffed and by mid-December, the casualty assistance calls officers were knocking on doors and asking the families to decide what they wanted to do with the remains. The sense of helping them achieve closure and deal with the knowledge that their loved ones had been finally identified was more important than any holiday.

The families, however, were not told that the Institute still retained a mass of genetic material that could not be identified because it was too heavily contaminated by fuel, oil, salt water, and exposure to the elements during the transit back to the United States. There was no way to isolate individual DNA material based on current technology and these remains undoubtedly contained some of the remains of the bombers.

Since World War II, the Navy had followed a long-standing tradition of taking commingled, unidentifiable remains and burying them together in a common casket or urn at one gravesite at Arlington National Cemetery. This pattern was consistently followed as remains were repatriated from excavation sites around the world. On September 12, 2002, Secretary of Defense Donald Rumsfeld presided over a burial service of unidentifiable remains from the Pentagon rubble at Arlington National Cemetery. In a single flag-draped casket, cremated remains from the Pentagon rubble that could not be identified, symbolically representing all 184 victims of the attack on the Pentagon, were buried with full military honors. After hymns, Scripture readings, and speeches from military leaders, relatives and friends paid their respects as the casket was carried by a horse-drawn caisson to a hill within view of the repaired Pentagon. A four-foot five-inch granite marker bearing the 184 names was eventually placed over the shared gravesite.[2]

Meanwhile, the Navy could only discuss the issue of the similar remains from *Cole*. Later that month, a proposal slowly worked its way up the chain of command toward Secretary of the Navy Gordon England. Initially, the proposal called for a ceremony, similar to the one just completed at Arlington National Cemetery for the victims of the Pentagon attack. But the military leadership of the Navy became concerned about having to deal with additional negative publicity—about the attack on *Cole*, the delay, the lack of communication with the families, and the future cost of identifying the remains should it eventually become technologically feasible to do so. To avoid and resolve these prickly issues, the remains would be buried at sea.

It was two months later, in November of 2002, over two years after the attack on USS *Cole*, that the families of the victims of the attack were finally informed of these additional unidentified remains. None expressed any reservations over the Navy's plan for their burial at sea, and on December 9, they were consigned to the deep.

Seventeen sailors ruthlessly killed, thirty-seven more injured and scarred in unimaginable ways, and one of the most modern twenty-first century destroyers crippled by a devastating terrorist attack costing $250 million to repair: October 12, 2000, irreversibly changed the way the Navy conducts its operations across the globe. While many view the attack on USS *Cole* as a professional embarrassment, something that should not have happened, the heroism of the crew speaks to how well they were prepared to face evil in its purest form and defeat it. The crew denied the terrorists the victory they sought. The crew of USS *Cole* saved their ship and their shipmates. All of them are my heroes.

Epilogue

DURING MY VISITS IN EARLY 2001 with the families of the sailors killed in the attack, I was often asked why no one was being punished. Why, despite what President Clinton had promised the nation, did the government appear to be doing nothing to hold the terrorists accountable for killing their loved ones in a brutal suicide bombing? I tried as best I could to answer the questions; sometimes to their satisfaction and at other times to their great frustration, because there really were no clear-cut answers that would temper their anguish or relieve their utter sense of loss.

I was as troubled as they were. Why did the attack against USS *Cole* go unpunished?

Richard A. Clarke, the White House official in charge of counterterrorism under presidents Clinton and Bush from 1998 to 2003, attempted to explain the inaction at the end of the Clinton administration by writing: "Neither CIA nor FBI would state the obvious: al Qaeda did it. We knew there was a large al Qaeda cell in Yemen. There was also a large cell of Egyptian Islamic Jihad, but that group had now announced its complete merger into al Qaeda, so what difference did it make which group did the attack?" In discussions with senior administration officials,

Clarke wrote, "It was difficult to gain support for a retaliatory strike when neither FBI nor CIA would say that al Qaeda did it."[1]

Clarke's statement about the reasons senior officials did not order action was later confirmed by the staff of the National Commission on Terrorist Attacks Upon the United States, the 9/11 Commission, in a report published in 2004: "Neither the Clinton administration nor the Bush administration launched a military response for the *Cole* attack. Sandy Berger and other senior policymakers said that, while most counter-terrorism officials quickly pointed the finger at al Qaeda, they never received the sort of definitive judgment from the CIA or the FBI that al Qaeda was responsible that they would need before launching military operations."[2]

William S. Cohen, the Clinton administration's secretary of defense, said just before the Bush administration took over, "With respect to what action will be taken, we have to be very careful and deliberative and sure of identifying those who . . . were responsible for this act of terrorism, be-cause any action that we take at that time must be responsible. And I think that you would be the first to be critical of the administration if we should simply lash out and say we have a number of suspects and then take mea-sures that would inflict punishment upon them in addition to bringing them before the bars of justice if we, in fact, were not very prudent and responsible in making those determinations. So we'll have to wait for more factual analysis, more investigative work by the FBI. And then that will be the responsibility of the new administration to decide what action should be taken."[3]

But, as the 9/11 Commission staff later reported, "The new team at the Pentagon did not push for a response for the *Cole*, according to Sec-retary of Defense [Donald] Rumsfeld and Paul Wolfowitz, his deputy. Wolfowitz told us that by the time the new administration was in place, the *Cole* incident was 'stale.' The 1998 cruise missile strikes showed UBL and al Qaeda that they had nothing to fear from a U.S. response, Wolfowitz said. For his part, Rumsfeld also thought too much time had passed. He worked on the force protection recommendations developed in the after-math of the USS *Cole* attack, not response options."[4]

Clarke, in his book, recalled watching limousines head back to the Pentagon, after a White House meeting on *Cole* just after the attack, with his State Department counterpart, Mike Sheehan. "What's it gonna take, Dick?" Sheehan demanded. "Does al Qaeda have to attack the Pentagon to get their attention?"[5]

As I prepared to turn over command of *Cole*, the handwriting was clearly on the wall. President Clinton had been briefed on the *Cole* investigation on December 21, 2000, but unwilling to risk military action based mostly on their intelligence, the CIA would not definitively say it was bin Laden that was behind the attack, even though they had ample evidence to draw that conclusion. Ali Soufan and other FBI agents directly involved with the investigation in Aden, however, were quickly convinced that al Qaeda was responsible for the attack on the ship, but their leadership and the senior administration officials the FBI was reporting to remained unmoved by the growing body of evidence they were developing, paralyzed by fear of the political costs of either retaliatory action, or of its failure.[6] Other terrorist actions immediately after the attack, confirmed through various government intelligence channels, provided further proof of al Qaeda's complicity. Many in government were surprised that the President did nothing. An act of war had been committed and as the months went by, even with two ongoing investigations, the Clinton administration was interested only in wrapping up the enquiries. The Bush administration was just as dismissive toward the attack, taking a "we're forward-looking, not backward-acting" attitude. The standard of evidence required to take action kept getting raised and then sidestepped. No one appeared interested or eager to view this attack in the larger strategic context of what it might mean for U.S. national interests.

CIA Director Tenet later said he was surprised that Clinton did not think he had enough information, and that Sandy Berger never told him the President wanted more. It appeared to most that this was a situation in which they were trying to build a case that would stand up in a court of law, not meet a standard for a military strike. And nothing changed after the Bush administration took office, for all George Bush's tough talk during the election campaign about terrorism.

Not until September 11, 2001, that is, when al Qaeda got the attention of the President, the rest of the U.S. government, and the whole country. As I had told Charles Allen at the CIA headquarters in Langley the morning of that day of infamy, I feared it would take an attack that killed thousands of Americans to make us realize we were in a war with terrorism that would not end until we started striking back in a meaningful manner. Now it had happened, and soon we did strike back. But it would take almost ten years for Osama bin Laden to be finally brought to summary justice, and it would be even longer before Abdul Rahim al Nashiri, the on-scene coordinator of the *Cole* attack, would face a military tribunal in Guantanamo Bay for his actions.

Back in the Pentagon immediately following the September 11 attacks, I focused on my work on the Joint Chiefs of Staff (JCS). The United Nations and multilateral affairs office of the JCS that I was assigned to became the lead office for a new mission: detainee policy.

The nation, or at least the Pentagon, was definitely on a war footing, and the feeling around the building was one of dedicated and focused intensity as the military prepared to finally respond to Osama bin Laden and al Qaeda's attacks on the U.S. mainland. The USS *Enterprise* battle group, commanded by my former commanding officer, Rear Admiral John G. Morgan Jr., had recently concluded operations in the Middle East and was preparing to return to the United States when, on the day of the September 11 attacks, he took the unprecedented step of turning the battle group around and steaming at best speed toward the coast of Pakistan in preparation to go to war.

Days later, military strikes would commence. At some point in those initial days, he had the commanding officer of *Enterprise*, Captain James "Sandy" Winnefeld, send me a photograph of a 2,000 pound Joint Direct Attack Munition with writing scrawled on it by the ordnance handlers on board: REMEMBER THE COLE. It brought a big smile to my face as I passed it on to Chris Peterschmidt and several other members of the crew.

In the Pentagon, while everyone knew it, no one outwardly spoke of the fact that already the United States was inserting Special Operations forces and other government paramilitary forces into Afghanistan to attack and topple the Afghan government, headed by the Taliban, which had given unfettered sanctuary to Osama bin Laden.

In our Joint Staff office, everyone understood that combat operations would result in enemy combatants being taken prisoner. Very quickly, the Department of Defense lawyers, in consultation with the Departments of Justice and State as well as the White House, determined that members of the Taliban and al Qaeda would not merit all the privileges of prisoners of war under the Geneva Conventions because they did not meet all of the necessary criteria required under the provisions of the treaty. Those criteria recognize members of regular military forces carrying arms openly and wearing uniforms, war correspondents and supply or maintenance contractors with them, and civilians resisting invasion by an occupying force—not terrorists operating without insignia or any association with a government or state.

Since neither the Taliban nor the terrorists belonging to al Qaeda met these criteria, their capture put them in a unique legal category not clearly defined by either treaty or international law provisions. Eventually, the Bush administration chose to call them unlawful enemy combatants, and within a few weeks determined where to house them—the U.S. naval base at Guantanamo Bay, Cuba.

The unique irony of my working detainee policy issues on how to fight, detain, and interrogate the same terrorists and their supporters who had launched the attack on *Cole* was not lost on me. I found a great deal of solace and satisfaction in my job as I focused on doing the detailed and thorough staff work necessary to support the chairman of the Joint Chiefs of Staff, General Richard Myers, in his role as the principal military advisor to the President and secretary of defense. It was a common joke around the office that we were expected to toil at least a half-day on the job—0600 to 1800 at a minimum—initially six and sometimes seven days a week as the war effort got organized and kicked off. The enemy was not resting and neither were we.

As the relationship of our office and those working the detainee mission became better defined over the ensuing months, I became exposed to the true nature of the enemy we were fighting. They were ruthless, well trained, patient, and had no moral restraint in how they brutally carried out their version of warfare. My crew and I had already been exposed to the cruel and amoral nature of the way these terrorists operated under the guise of a religious banner. Now, those who had experienced the September 11 attacks began to comprehend what we had lived through in Aden. The destroyed section of the Pentagon, the obliterated Twin Towers in New York, and the smoldering hole in the ground in Shanksville, Pennsylvania, served as stark daily reminders that we had been a nation at war for years, but only now had come to grips with it and were finally taking action. While I was glad to see the nation finally doing something, it was equally apparent that *Cole* and the crew had rapidly fallen into the shadow of this larger national event, and that the Navy was all too pleased to finally be out of the news as the most recent victim of a terrorist attack.

It was in early 2002 that a Naval Academy classmate of mine, Captain Neal Kusumoto, contacted me about traveling to Newport, Rhode Island, to discuss the aftermath of the attack on *Cole* with those who were preparing, like me just two short years earlier, to assume commanding officer and executive officer positions on ships. These prospective CO and XO courses were taught five times a year. Initially I demurred, with the excuse that I was too busy with Joint Staff work to take time off to impart lessons learned. In reality, I was not yet ready to face discussing the matter in any detail. It was still too painful a reality, and in many ways, I was still debating if I wanted (or needed) to ever talk about the attack again.

Finally, after missing three classes, Neal called me up and in a humorous but blunt manner informed me that he was smarter than me and therefore had graduated higher in the class standings than me, which therefore naturally made him senior to me regarding this outstanding request to teach these new COs and XOs. Sensing where the conversation was headed, I laughed and in August 2002 arrived at the Surface Warfare Officer School in Newport to teach not only the CO/XO course, but also the damage control assistant class held just across the street from the main building. In the future, it would be those young ensigns and lieutenants (junior grade) that would set the damage control standards for their ships. They had best be prepared, just like Nat Fogg and Sean Dubbs, for what might happen in an instant of time. For the next four and a half years, covering twenty-three classes, I never missed the opportunity to spend several hours with each of those two groups and discuss in detailed and sometimes graphic descriptions what the crew and I did to prepare for and then respond to that terrorist attack. Over time, the department head classes were also included, with those valuable lessons learned gladly shared with them as well.

During the eleven months following the attack on *Cole*, the Yemeni government became more and more recalcitrant and unwilling to cooperate with the FBI in providing evidence and access to suspects, such as al Badawi and a new suspect, Fahd Mohammed Ahmed al Quso, who were in custody for their suspected involvement in the plot. Almost immediately after the September 11 attacks, however, the Yemenis became more compliant and offered the FBI unprecedented access to the al Qaeda terrorists in their custody. It was also during this time that the file on exactly who the principal conspirators were in the attack was narrowed down to five key individuals: [Khallad] bin Attash, Jamal al Badawi, al Nashiri, al Quso, and Abu Ali al Harithi. Later interrogations by Soufan and others clearly established that Khallad had also been one of the organizers of the September 11 hijackings. At the end of 1999, he had personally taken two of the hijackers who would crash American Airlines Flight 77 into the Pentagon to a meeting in Bangkok, where he also collected $36,000 he had ordered al Quso and Ibrahim al Thawar to bring him, ostensibly to finance the planned attack on a Navy ship in Aden. Al Quso later confessed to Soufan that he had been ordered to videotape the attack when it took place, and al Thawar was of course one of the two suicide bombers who blew up *Cole*. But the $36,000, Soufan later concluded, "had in all likelihood been used for the 9/11 attack, probably paying for tickets for two of the hijackers" who carried it out. The attack on *Cole*, like the attacks on the embassies in Africa in 1998, was absolutely central to what happened in Washington and New York City on September 11, 2001.[7]

The *Cole* families continued to undergo a series of highs and lows as the war dragged on. While those responsible for attacking the ship were being killed or captured, it was usually seen as being done in conjunction with the larger picture of September 11 taking the stage, front and center. Given the overwhelming publicity surrounding the September 11 families, along with the extensive benefits and financial compensation received by them, the *Cole* family members were put in an awkward position. They did not want to be seen as whiners but they also did not want to be forgotten by the nation, while the Navy had urged them to move on. The crew and families never complained, but it was always a source of friction, especially because they were kept at arm's length and at times ignored by the Navy in the process.

On a good note, the FBI meticulously continued to build their case and make steady progress so that eventually justice and accountability could be meted out to the perpetrators. Among the first apprehended by the Yemeni government was al Badawi, who had bought the truck and trailer used to launch the boat full of explosives and transported them to Aden. It was a particularly hard blow to all the crew and their families to learn that al Badawi had escaped from custody in Yemen in April of 2003. Many took the news of his escape as a sign that the U.S. government was unwilling to pressure President Saleh to hold al Qaeda terrorists in his country accountable for their actions.

Unknown to the crew and families but related to my work on the Joint Staff, I was quietly briefed in early 2003 that in a highly classified operation, the CIA, operating under a Presidential Finding by President Bush, had conducted a targeted operation in Yemen that had killed al Harithi, along with five other al Qaeda operatives, in an RQ-1 armed Predator remote-controlled drone strike with a Hellfire missile. It was the first operation of its kind, and while the crew and families could not learn of this blow for vengeance for several more years, I certainly enjoyed the deep sense of satisfaction that action was finally being taken on our behalf.

Unfortunately, the Yemeni government continued to prove its ineptness as a reliable partner in the War on Terror. Al Badawi was recaptured in March 2004, and at his trial by a Yemeni court in September 2004, along with other participants in the plot to carry out the attack, he and al Nashiri (in absentia) were convicted and sentenced to death by Yemen. The other four defendants were sentenced to five to ten years' imprisonment. After hearing his sentence, al Badawi was allowed by the Yemeni government to declare, "This is an unjust verdict, this is an American verdict. There are no human rights in the world, except for the Americans. All the Muslims in the world are being used to serve American interests."

Another key piece of information not readily available to the families was the fact that the U.S. government had been—quietly and not so quietly, as in the case of Khalid Sheikh Mohammed—rounding up key leaders of al Qaeda and removing them from the global battlefield. One of those was al Nashiri, who had been captured by U.S. forces in early 2002 and was being held by the CIA at an undisclosed location when that trial in absentia took place in Yemen. It was not until September 6, 2006, that President Bush announced that fourteen "high-value" detainees being held in CIA custody, including bin Attash and al Nashiri, were transferred to the intelligence and detention facility at Guantanamo Bay, Cuba, to await justice.

Unfortunately, politics once again intruded into the process of holding terrorists accountable for their acts, and the families' sense of justice was again delayed. In 2006, Congress passed the Military Commissions Act of 2006, which was subsequently updated in 2009. Although al Nashiri and bin Attash had been held in U.S. government custody for years, when President Obama took office, he upended the entire process on January 22, 2009, his first full day in office, by signing three far-reaching executive orders:

(1) Close the intelligence and detention facility in Guantanamo Bay, Cuba, within one year.

(2) Conduct a review of every individual being held at Guantanamo Bay, Cuba, to determine his or her suitability for release, transfer, or referral for prosecution.

(3) Halt all actions associated with Military Commissions until the review process was completed with a plan to dismantle them and try all cases in the Federal court system.[8]

The *Cole* families were devastated. The entire process of military commissions came screeching to a halt and was to be held in abeyance until the "review" was completed over the course of a year, continuing a series of blows for the long overdue justice for their loved ones. With many delayed proceedings, after being at times seemingly ignored throughout the Bush administration, they felt justice would be even further jeopardized with the very real possibility that now the Obama administration might dismiss charges entirely against those who had so ruthlessly killed their sailors. That was precisely what seemed to be happening when Attorney General Eric Holder, in a tortured twist of legal maneuvering, dropped all charges against al Nashiri in an effort to stymie the Military Commissions process.

In a feeble effort to mitigate the political damage and fallout that was rapidly building from the *Cole* and September 11 families, who had already suffered multiple setbacks and delays in the intervening years, President Obama offered to host a meeting on February 6, 2009, in an attempt to explain the rationale for his recently signed executive orders. With no idea of how to contact the September 11 and *Cole* families, the White House initially relied on contacting only those families who had been supportive of the President's campaign. At first, there were not even families of firefighters who died at the Twin Towers invited to the meeting. The *Cole* families were a much more bonded group and all that could be reached, given the short notice, were invited.

The press, however, had already gotten wind of the fact that the administration was planning to drop charges against al Nashiri as a prelude to abandoning the Military Commissions process and trying all the terrorists in the Federal court system. In order to exercise as much control over the attendees as possible and minimize adverse media exposure, the White House waited until there was less than forty-eight hours before the meeting to extend invitations. Oddly, the Navy, which had been tasked with maintaining the database of family contact information, was unable to provide it to the White House when asked. Apparently the Bureau of Personnel had failed to maintain an up-to-date list. Thankfully, the Military

Commissions prosecution team had been in recent contact with the family members to keep them informed about the impact of the President's executive order, and was able to provide the contact information to the White House. Although I had not suffered the direct loss of a family member, I too was extended an invitation to attend the meeting.

It was scheduled to start at 1530 and last one hour. Although every attendee processed through the North Visitors Entrance and was walked toward the North Portico, the meeting was actually held in a conference room across the street on the second floor of the Eisenhower Executive Office Building. Given the purposefully short notice, only families within a few hours' drive of Washington, D.C., were able to attend. In total, about sixty *Cole* and September 11 family members attended. From *Cole*, eight families were able to attend: Wibberleys, Gunns, Clodfelters, Saunders, Tripletts, Kate Brown (Fireman Roy's mother), Ruxs, and Parletts.

In the conference room, tables were placed end to end to form a large rectangle with chairs around the perimeter. The President arrived twenty-three minutes late but took time before speaking to walk around the entire table to introduce himself to every family member, shake their hands, and accept the occasional hug of appreciation. Talking for only fifteen minutes, he devoted the remaining thirty-five minutes of the meeting to answering questions. While everyone was respectful and deferential to the President in what they said and asked, there was clearly an underlying tone of anger and frustration at the decisions he had unilaterally made without consulting those who were directly affected by it—the families who had lost loved ones at the hands of the terrorists. At the end of the meeting, the President pleaded for patience to allow the review process to work, and for understanding of his reasons for wanting to close Guantanamo Bay. For the most part, most families remained unhappy with his decision and over the coming weeks expressed their frustration in the media. In their eyes, the politics of the moment were once again delaying justice.

Over the next year, the process slowly played out as country after country refused to accept most of the detainees held in Guantanamo, especially after they learned the true nature and background of the individuals they were being asked to integrate into their societies and provide a new life for outside of Guantanamo Bay. I found myself speaking out on every media outlet that would host me on the poorly conceived decision to close Guantanamo Bay. On the Joint Staff, I vividly remember why we had created this particular facility in the first place: as the United States and its allies fought this new type of warfare, it would serve as "an intelligence center of excellence," where terrorists captured from around the world could be held so that we could learn how they recruited, equipped, trained, and financed terrorists, and could conduct planning and operations across the globe. It was obvious to any military person that if you understand your enemies and how they operate, only then can you adequately plan and target them for defeat; otherwise, the old methods of warfare would not work against them. It was a clear shift in how warfare would be fought, and Guantanamo Bay would now be a key pillar in how the nation put itself on a war footing. The President and his new administration clearly thought otherwise and from the view of many, including me, were effectively undermining our nation's ability to fight the war.

A year later, when Obama's plans should have shuttered the facility at Guantanamo Bay, the public outcry and political firestorm created by the President's executive orders resulted in the facility's staying open, but essentially wasted on the purpose for which it was envisioned—a crown jewel in the world of intelligence—now unused. It had become essentially just a detention facility for the worst of al Qaeda's operatives, despite over $300 million invested in state-of-the art intelligence-gathering facilities being built there. On a positive note, however, the process of using Military Commissions would slowly begin to grind forward again. Despite Attorney General Holder's attempt to subvert the will of Congress and the American people by bringing the Guantanamo Bay terrorists to the United States for trial, eventually there was no choice left; Military Commissions would become the de facto legal mechanism for holding terrorists accountable for their actions.

On April 24, 2011, the charges against al Nashiri were sworn: terrorism; attacking civilians; attacking civilian objects; intentionally causing serious bodily injury; hazarding a vessel; using treachery or perfidy; murder in violation of the law of war; attempted murder in violation of the law of war; conspiracy to commit terrorism and murder in violation of the law of war; destruction of property in violation of the law of war; and attempted destruction of property in violation of the law of war. The process of moving toward a hearing and trial started once again in earnest. Someday, the families will see justice; I just hope it happens in their lifetime.

The work of capturing or killing those responsible for the attack on *Cole* went on for years after the attack, but life for the crew also moved forward. With the inexorability of time, many would promote and retire, including some of the key leaders on the ship: Chief Larson, Master Chief Parlier, Master Chief Jacobsen, Master Chief Lorenson, Master Chief Abney, and Petty Officer Butte. Retirements are always a good time to remember the exploits and achievements of a career of service to the nation. There is also the equally important aspect of seeing your officers, those who had performed so brilliantly to prepare the ship for combat or endure the aftermath of a terrorist attack, achieve their own opportunity to excel in command, including John Cordle, Chris Peterschmidt, Rick Miller, Frank Castellano, Derek Trinque, Debbie Courtney, and Joe Gagliano. As any former commanding officer will tell you, nothing is more gratifying than to see the achievements of those who served under you as they become the next generation of leaders in the Navy.

My opportunity to continue my career and contribute to the nation came while on the Joint Staff. My work involved the creation of policy and long-range strategy out of whole cloth and without any real legal or historical references for fighting al Qaeda and bin Laden's followers. New challenges arose constantly. Despite the long but very satisfying hours with this work, there were other *Cole* issues that I kept attending to: awards for the crew, disposition of crew remains, talking with various crew members as they adjusted to new ship and shore assignments where their peers could not begin to relate to their experiences . . . and, of course, wondering what my own long-term prospects were in the Navy.

After spending a career in the Navy, I always held in my heart that at its core, my Navy and the U.S. government would ultimately decide what is best for those who choose a life of consequence in service to the country. Integrity had always been the bedrock of my existence and now, with the nation at war, it was more of an imperative than at any point in my life short of my experiences leading *Cole*. The leadership of the Navy had recognized me with the award of the Legion of Merit, the second highest peacetime award that can be bestowed, for my service and actions while in command of USS *Cole* during the time of the attack in its immediate aftermath. I had been given a career-enhancing staff assignment on the Joint Chiefs of Staff. Although not officially sanctioned by the Navy, I had been sharing the lessons I had learned on *Cole* with the future leaders of the Surface Warfare force in Newport, and now the litmus test for all that work and my future as a naval officer was rapidly approaching. My career in the Navy had developed in me an odd philosophical outlook: I was a professional pessimist (always plan and train for the worst) and a personal optimist (work hard and hope for the best). Quietly, several admirals assured me that while no one can ever predict how a promotion board will ultimately choose those who will lead the Navy into the future, they had every confidence I would be among those selected.

After being on the Joint Staff for about a year and a half, the annual selection board for my year group's promotion to captain met on January 10, 2002, to select those officers who would be promoted during fiscal year 2003. Prior to every board, Secretary of the Navy Gordon England issued a precept to the officers who would be reviewing records as part of the proceedings. In it, he stressed,

> A judgment of the whole person and the whole record is required to determine whose future potential will serve the Navy best. You may conclude that particular adverse information undermines an officer's ability to serve successfully in a position of increased authority and responsibility, despite an otherwise outstanding record. On the other hand, you may find that an officer's overall outstanding performance demonstrated such potential for future service that it outweighs any deficiencies noted in the record. Some officers

will have learned from their mistakes in ways that make them stronger; others will have strengths that outweigh relative weaknesses in the records.[9]

In addition to a career's worth of fitness reports, including my time as commanding officer of *Cole*, the entire JAGMAN command investigation had been ordered by the chief of naval operations and the secretary of the Navy to be made part of my officer record to be considered by the promotion board. I had requested that a message on accountability, issued by Admiral Clark, the chief of naval operations, to the entire U.S. Navy outlining his standards for accountability and personal responsibility and his reasons for handling the *Cole* investigations in the manner he did, also be included as part of my record.

The board convened and met in early January 2002. It was led by a vice admiral and included thirteen one- and two-star admirals. After months of review of each selected officer by both the military and civilian sides of the Navy, Secretary of the Navy England released the FY-03 Active Duty Captain Line Selections results on June 12, 2002. I was on the list! Within the Navy, many of my friends sent me notes of congratulations, seeing my selection as a vindication of the finding that nothing the crew or I could have done would have prevented the attack. As with any controversial decision, there were some disgruntled senior Navy officers less than enamored with the result who saw it as a lowering of the standard of accountability that, in their view, set our service apart from the other military services.

Regarding any officer promotion, the U.S. Constitution is very clear about the process and delineates it in Article II, Section 2:

The President shall be Commander in Chief of the Army and Navy of the United States, and of the Militia of the several States, when called into the actual Service of the United States; he may require the Opinion, in writing, of the principal Officer in each of the executive Departments, upon any Subject relating to the Duties of their respective Offices, and he shall have Power to grand Reprieves and Pardons for Offenses against the United States, except in cases of Impeachment.

He shall have Power, by and with the Advice and Consent of the Senate, to make Treaties, provided two thirds of the Senators present concur; and he shall nominate, and by and with the Advice and Consent of the Senate, shall appoint Ambassadors, other public Ministers and Consuls, Judges of the supreme Court, and all other Officers of United States, whose Appointments are not herein otherwise provided for, and which shall be established by Law: but the Congress may by Law vest the Appointment of such interior Officers, as they think proper, in the President alone, in the Courts of Law; or in the Heads of Departments.

The President shall have the Power to fill up all Vacancies that may happen during the Recess of the Senate, by granting Commissions which shall expire at the End of their next Session.

The promotion list would be submitted by the secretary of the Navy for review and approval by the secretary of defense and the President before submission to the Senate to give their constitutionally empowered advice and consent. But while I was on the list, I was aware that there was a very real possibility that I would never be promoted, having already been informed that several more senior active duty and retired admirals were actively working behind the scenes with politicians on Capitol Hill to ensure that my promotion would never see daylight. In addition, several family members, still distraught at having lost a loved one who had been under my command, reached out to their respective senators and expressed concern that I was going to be promoted to a higher pay grade. Their loved ones had died on my watch and some still sought blame and retribution for their loss.

As the list moved forward, there was a separate addendum included that delineated very specific reasons why my name should remain on the promotion list and why I was deserving of a future in the Navy. Chief of

Naval Operations Admiral Vern Clark, and Secretary of the Navy Gordon England stood firmly in support of my promotion. Over the next two months, both Secretary of Defense Rumsfeld and the Commander in Chief, President Bush, also supported my nomination for promotion by signing off and forwarding the promotion list. By August 2002, the list arrived at the Senate for consideration during the 107th Congress.

Now, politics came into play. The chairman of the Senate Armed Services Committee (SASC), Senator John Warner (R-VA), openly questioned and challenged the Navy on its judgment in selecting me. Coincidentally, he was running for reelection that fall, and at least two Virginia *Cole* families had contacted him and urged him to oppose my promotion.

Senator Warner clearly understood the importance of officer promotion boards and how they directly affected the future leadership of the Navy; he had been a secretary of the Navy during the Ford administration. In short order, he put a condition on the Navy; unless the Navy removed my name from the promotion list, he would convene a full Senate Armed Service Committee hearing, reopen the investigation into the attack on USS *Cole*, afford the Navy the opportunity to explain its views on accountability regarding how the attack was allowed to occur, and now, also include the issue of my suitability for promotion as part of that hearing.

Before the promotion list became an issue, on May 3, 2001, Senator Warner chaired a hearing to obtain statements and information from Admiral Clark, the CNO, and General Shelton, the chairman of the Joint Chiefs of Staff. Throughout the hearing, Warner emphasized over and over the point he had already made abundantly clear in several conversations with the CNO and other Navy leaders: accountability was lacking in the Navy for not finding me responsible and punishing me for allowing the attack to occur. In his opening statement, he openly questioned whether the Navy and the Department of Defense, in not finding someone to blame for the attack, had abandoned their long-held principles of accountability, saying, "we run the risk of repeating such tragedies and sending the wrong message to our commanding officers and all their subordinates. If we are to expect commanders to demand the highest standards of themselves and those serving in their command, do we not have to ensure that institutional values and expectations are consistently and fully applied?"

As he had emphasized over and over again, the CNO patiently reiterated that a proper and just accountability determination had been made, with the firm conclusion that nothing the commanding officer or crew had done or not done would have prevented the tragedy. Although there were issues identified in the JAGMAN investigation, review by some of the most senior officers in the Navy, with years of at-sea command experience, as well as the civilian leadership within the Navy and Department of Defense had determined that punishment was not warranted. Inherent in every endorsement by the chain of command was the belief that there was a fundamental difference between accountability and blame. Senator Warner remained unwilling to see the difference.

By early September 2002, the promotion list had been languishing at the Senate Armed Services Committee for two months without any action being taken. Finally, with the Navy unwilling to punish anyone for the attack, Senator Warner informed the Navy Chief of Legislative Affairs, Rear Admiral Gary Roughead, who had been relieved as *Cole*'s battle group commander and was now assigned to Washington, that unless the Navy removed my name from the promotion list, the entire list would be held up, no officers would be allowed promotion to captain, and the previously threatened SASC hearing would be convened to again reopen the *Cole* investigation where a suitability determination on my promotion would undergo additional public scrutiny.

The Navy had already shown over the intervening time since the attack that it wanted to distance itself at every opportunity from the attack and its aftermath. The attack was an institutional embarrassment, which only reinforced their unwillingness to undergo this very public political spectacle. Admiral Roughead called me in my cubicle on the Joint Staff on September 16, 2002, and calmly informed me that my name was being removed from the promotion list for the good of the service to allow the rest of the list to move forward and be confirmed by the Senate. I could tell he was very disappointed in this development as he reiterated the Navy's support for me; but at the same time, the Navy's leadership was unwilling to publicly stand behind my promotion. Two days later, on September 18, the Senate confirmed the promotion list. My name was not on it and almost immediately all the media ran articles about how I had been denied promotion to captain.

It was a powerful punch to the gut. While I always knew in the back of my mind that a future in the Navy might be nothing more than a mirage, the denial of my promotion was the toughest professional setback of my life, second only to losing my seventeen sailors in the attack. In very real terms, however, the very Constitution that I had served under throughout my career and was even willing to give my life for was being blatantly undermined and subverted by a single senator, John Warner. It was nothing short of a political ruse that he continued to claim, under the guise of holding Senate Armed Services Committee hearings, that he would allow my name to be submitted to the Senate for confirmation. He wanted someone to blame for the attack. Since bin Laden and the other terrorists were not readily available, in his eyes, the commanding officer must be the person held to account.

For the next few weeks, I was disheartened and went through the motions of work only for the sake of the predictability it provided me. Still, my officemates and I continued to craft detainee policy that would have a positive and lasting effect on our nation's ability to fight the expanding Global War on Terror. By early spring 2003, the Navy informed me that it intended to support my promotion again and forward it up the chain of command for submission to the Senate during the 108th Congress. I was very happy that I continued to enjoy the Navy leadership's support as they stood behind me in the aftermath of the attack and investigations. Once again, I stayed focused on my work on the Joint Chiefs of Staff while a new promotion list was generated that contained only one name, mine, and slowly worked its way up the chain of command.

While Admiral Clark and I never spoke, his staff informed me that on several occasions, he had approached Senator Warner about his insistence that I be held "accountable" for allowing the attack to occur. At every turn, the senator refused to budge. Knowing the single-item promotion list containing just my name now sat on the desk of the secretary of defense, Senator Warner sent a letter on April 13, 2004, to General Myers, chairman of the Joint Chiefs of Staff. In that letter he openly questioned the professional judgment of the CNO: "Given the adverse findings of the JAGMAN investigating officer, which were concurred in by Commander, United States Naval Forces Central Command, I questioned whether full accountability, which I view to be at the very heart of command at sea, was enforced. Admiral Clark stated that, despite some shortfalls in performance on the part of Commander Lippold, Admiral Clark concluded that nothing Commander Lippold did or did not do would have prevented the attacker from succeeding." He then continued: "I believe that promoting an officer to the rank of captain, who, in his present capacity as a commander demonstrated questionable qualities of judgment, forehandedness, and attention to detail in complying with security regulations, is worthy of thorough review. I seek your guidance. Quite simply, has Commander Lippold, in your view and the view of the other Chiefs, exhibited the basic values that we have come to expect from our military officers?"

The letter then went much further: "I request that you carefully review the entire investigative file compiled within the Navy and by the Crouch-Gehman [USS *Cole*] Commission and share with me directly your views about Commander Lippold's qualifications in light of a full review of the facts. I also ask that you make arrangements to have the other members of the Joint Chiefs of Staff fully briefed on this matter. I believe that this is a situation in which all members of the Joint Chiefs of Staff should be consulted, and the impact it could have on the officer corps of all services considered."

The threat and expectation had now reached the highest level of the U.S. military. Senator Warner wanted to pinpoint blame and was willing to call out the entire military leadership of all the services to get it. Within days, the chairman of the Joint Chiefs ordered a "tank meeting" attended by all the service chiefs, the director of the Joint Staff, and the vice chairman. In the meeting, Admiral Clark specifically addressed the threat environment leading up to the attack on *Cole*, the JAGMAN investigation findings including the subsequent endorsements, and the issue of my accountability for my actions before, during, and after the attack. Lastly, he explained why a promotion board considered me, in light of all these facts, suitable for promotion.

On April 29, 2004, Chairman Myers responded back to Senator Warner with a short, to-the-point letter. In it, he affirmed that he had thoroughly reviewed the *Cole* investigative files compiled by the Navy and Crouch-Gehman commissions to assess my suitability and qualification for promotion. He solidly affirmed the promotion board's findings, answering Senator Warner, "The Joint Chiefs met and carefully reviewed these investigations. We all concluded that Commander Lippold is fully suited and qualified for promotion, and unanimously recommend that Commander Lippold be promoted to Captain." Each service chief had combat experience, and all understood the responsibility of the action they were taking in affirming support for my promotion.

Senator Warner would not be deterred, and once again my nomination was stalled, this time at the White House as the political theater of the 2004 election gained momentum. Ultimately, my nomination would once again not be forwarded to the Senate and it slid into the 109th congressional session for action.

On July 22, 2004, while I was still assigned to the Joint Staff, the 9/11 Commission had concluded its findings into the attack on our nation and issued its report, finding that "the plot, we now know, was a full-fledged al Qaeda operation, supervised directly by bin Laden. He chose the target and location of the attack, selected the suicide operatives, and provided the money needed to purchase explosives and equipment." No one in the military was held singularly or collectively responsible for allowing the attack to occur.

In November 2004, I finished my assignment to the Joint Chiefs of Staff and was transferred to the staff of the Deputy Chief of Naval Operations for Information, Plans and Strategy (N3/N5), once again working for Vice Admiral John G. Morgan Jr., who had been my commanding officer on USS *Arleigh Burke*. Since the immediate aftermath of the attack and throughout the intervening years, Admiral Morgan had provided me with a unique level of insight and professional mentorship as someone I could turn to for advice and counsel in how to best approach the now contentious idea of continued service in the Navy. He had been the keynote speaker at my change of command and still continued to keep me apprised of what the senior leadership of the Navy was doing in support of my promotion. But by this point, while I still maintained an impeccable work ethic, I knew I no longer had a career in the Navy; now I was on a quest for vindication of the finding my superiors had made, time after time, that nothing I could have done would have prevented the attack on my ship.

Senator Warner's attitude contrasted sharply with his approach to an earlier case, a celebrated historical instance of naval injustice in which he had intervened, years later, to rectify: the court-martial and conviction of Captain Charles B. McVay III, the commanding officer of the cruiser USS *Indianapolis* (CA-35) when it was torpedoed by a Japanese submarine in the waning days of World War II on July 30, 1945.

In mid-1945, *Indianapolis* received orders to carry to Tinian Island parts and nuclear material to be used in the atomic bombs soon to be dropped on Hiroshima and Nagasaki. After delivering its top-secret cargo, the ship was en route to other duties when early in the morning of July 30, 1945, she was attacked by the Japanese submarine I-58 under Commander Mochitsura Hashimoto. Commander Hashimoto launched six torpedoes and hit the *Indianapolis* twice, the first removing over forty feet of her bow, the second hitting the starboard side below the bridge. *Indianapolis* immediately took a fifteen-degree list, capsized, and sank within twelve minutes. Of the crew of 1,196 men, 879 died. It was the worst disaster at sea of the entire war for the U.S. Navy.

About 300 of the 1,196 men on board died in the initial attack. The rest of the crew, more than 880 men, were left floating in the water trying to survive without lifeboats among sharks until the rescue was completed four days (100 hours) later. It was not until 1025 on August 2 that the few survivors were sighted, mostly held afloat by life jackets, although there were a few rafts that had been cut loose before the ship went down.

A plane on routine patrol sighted them but because of Navy protocol regarding secret missions, the ship was not reported "overdue" and the omission was officially recorded later as "due to a misunderstanding of the Movement Report System." Only 316 men survived.

Captain McVay, commander of *Indianapolis*, was among those rescued. He repeatedly asked the Navy why it took five days to rescue his men. He never received an answer. The Navy long claimed that SOS messages were never received because the ship was operating under a policy of radio silence; declassified records show that three SOS messages were received separately, but none were acted upon because it was thought to be a Japanese ruse.

There was much controversy over the incident. In November 1945, McVay was court-martialed and convicted of "hazarding his ship by failing to zigzag." Several circumstances of the court-martial were controversial: one very obvious circumstance was that McVay's orders were to zigzag at night, at his discretion. Zigzagging would make it harder for an enemy submarine sighting the ship to zero in on it with a torpedo. McVay said he decided that the intermittently poor visibility made zigzagging unnecessary. Incredibly, the Japanese submarine commander who sank *Indianapolis* was called as a witness for the prosecution at the court-martial, and he described visibility at the time as fair (corroborated by the fact that he was able to target and sink the *Indianapolis* in the first place). American submarine experts testified that zigzagging was a technique of negligible value in eluding enemy submarines. Hashimoto also testified to this effect. Despite that testimony, the official ruling was that visibility was good, and the court held McVay responsible for his ship's sinking because he had not continued to zigzag.

But there was also evidence that admirals in the U.S. Navy had been primarily responsible for placing the ship in harm's way. Captain McVay requested a destroyer escort, but his request was denied because the priority for destroyers at the time was escorting transports to Okinawa and picking up downed pilots in B-29 raids on Japan. Also, the naval command assumed that McVay's route would be safe at that late point in the war. Many ships, including most destroyers, were equipped with submarine detection equipment, but *Indianapolis* was not so equipped.

On July 24, 1945, just six days prior to the sinking of *Indianapolis*, the destroyer *Underhill* had been attacked and sunk in the same area by Japanese submarines. Yet McVay was never informed of this event or several others, in part due to issues of classified intelligence. McVay was warned of the potential presence of Japanese subs, but not of the actual confirmed activity. After the torpedo attack, no rescue was initiated, because of the Navy's failure to track the *Indianapolis*; as she was the flagship of the Fifth Fleet, this failure amounted to gross mismanagement of the resource by the Navy.

Some 700 ships of the U.S. Navy were lost in combat in World War II, but McVay was the only captain to be court-martialed, and it was widely felt that he had been a fall guy for the Navy. Despite the fact that McVay was promoted to rear admiral when he retired in 1949, the conviction effectively ended his career in the Navy.

I learned only in early 2005 that on September 14, 1999, Senator Warner had chaired a Senate Armed Services Committee hearing into the conviction of Captain McVay. After hearing testimony from Navy admirals and *Indianapolis* survivors, as well as other evidence entered into the record, he supported exonerating Captain McVay of his court-martial. In the FY 2001 Defense Authorization Act, signed by President Clinton, Senator Warner steadfastly supported a Sense of Congress resolution on his case:

> With respect to the sinking of the U.S.S. *Indianapolis* (CA-35) on July 30, 1945, and the subsequent court-martial conviction of the ship's commanding officer, Captain Charles Butler McVay, III, arising from that sinking, it is the sense of Congress, based on the review of evidence by the Senate and the House of Representatives—(1) that, in light of the remission by the Secretary of the Navy of the sentence of the court-martial and the restoration of Captain McVay to active duty by the Chief of Naval Operations, Fleet Admiral Chester Nimitz, the American people should now recognize Captain McVay's lack of culpability for the tragic loss of the U.S.S. *In-*

dianapolis and the lives of the men who died as a result of the sinking of that vessel; and (2) that, in light of the fact that certain exculpatory information was not available to the court-martial board and that Captain McVay's conviction resulted therefrom, Captain McVay's military record should now reflect that he is exonerated for the loss of the U.S.S. *Indianapolis* and so many of her crew.

The contrasts as well as the similarities were striking. There had been no doubt about the danger and hostility from Japanese forces in the *Indianapolis* case, while *Cole* had been attacked by surprise by perfidious terrorists without any indication of hostile intent. The sinking of USS *Indianapolis* left 1,197 dead, while the attack on USS *Cole* had killed 17. Both tragedies were a great embarrassment to the Navy. In the case of *Indianapolis*, the news was not released until after the Japanese surrender and the end of the war, and it was largely lost to sight; similarly, release of the investigation into *Cole* was delayed until just before the Clinton administration left office. Threat information was not transmitted to *Indianapolis*, just as no specific intelligence concerning an al Qaeda threat was available to *Cole* prior to entering port:

CNO Endorsement: "I conclude, along with the previous endorsers, that the tools and information at the Commanding Officer's disposal on 12 October 2000, coupled with the lack of any indication of hostile intent before the attack, severely disadvantaged the Commanding Officer and crew of *Cole* in trying to prevent this attack."

CINCLANTFLT Endorsement: "Nothing in the [Sixth Fleet Intelligence] message indicated a need for *Cole* to take a heightened security posture beyond the THREATCON Bravo measures directed by the in-theater Fifth Fleet Commander."

"Based on the general threat intelligence available to USS *Cole*, this was a reasonable decision."

COMUSNAVCENT Endorsement: "In fact, all of the intelligence assets of the United States and its allies, as well as the U.S. Embassy in Sana'a, did not identify the threat, let alone communicate the presence of that threat to the Commanding Officer of USS *Cole*."

Captain McVay's superiors in the chain of command and my own both supported no punishment. In the case of Captain McVay, Fleet Admiral Chester Nimitz and Vice Admiral Raymond Spruance, who was McVay's immediate superior, both legendary naval heroes of war, went on record as opposed to a court-martial. In my case, CINCLANTFLT's endorsement stated that I "was not derelict in the execution of duty [and] did not act in violation of any regulation, order or custom of the Navy."

With circumstances mirroring Captain McVay's, I was given discretion to make a judgment. I relied on the best information I had, which did not indicate an imminent attack. He exercised the same discretion in judgment. My chain of command supported me, as McVay's had supported him. A duly constituted promotion board comprised of my fellow officers selected me for promotion (even after reviewing the JAGMAN investigation in my file) and the chain of command, including the President, supported that selection.

The attack on USS *Indianapolis* was a closing salvo to World War II. The attack on USS *Cole* was the first purely military strike by al Qaeda and arguably the opening salvo to the ongoing Global War on Terror. No other military CO has had a promotion halted because al Qaeda fired on their unit.

During the course of the hearing into Captain McVay's court-martial, Senator Warner made a profound statement:

> Now I've had a lifetime association, I'm privileged, with the United States Navy. And when I first went to the Pentagon in '69, the four stars then were the Captain McVays and the commanders of the ships, and they had quite properly been advanced. But in spending endless hours enjoying their stories of the past, and we saw a transition of the Navy from the autocratic, what we call the politics—it was totally rigid—of that era, to the more modern Navy that we have today.
>
> Accountability at sea is just absolutely infallible. That's important. . . . But there could have been an element of politics, and that's where my research is going to continue in this case. I must say that

I've watched with some concern as my dear colleague [Senator Bob Smith (R-NH)] has pushed this issue. But this morning, my ship was righted a little bit back on the very objective, even keel as I look at this case, and I intend to myself some further inquiry.[10]

In the end, Senator Warner supported Defense Authorization Act resolution language expressing a Sense of Congress that Captain McVay's record should reflect that he was "exonerated for the loss of the USS *Indianapolis*." President Clinton signed the resolution. This was a stunning reversal of opinion from a senator who had steadfastly supported the Navy's leadership on matters of command responsibility and accountability. Learning of the senator's change of heart in 1999, I hoped he would see the similarities with my case in 2004 and allow my promotion to move forward.

At the beginning of 2005, I still had the guaranteed support of Admiral Vern Clark, but his term as CNO was scheduled to end that summer. I learned that in April 2005, Admiral Clark met with Senator Warner once again to press the issue of my promotion. It was a contentious meeting, with Admiral Clark pressing Senator Warner with specific, detailed facts surrounding my accountability and suitability for promotion, and urging him to allow it to go forward to the Senate for constitutional advice and consent. Reportedly, Senator Warner was so incensed by this continued pressure to relent that he angrily threatened once again to hold a full hearing into the attack on *Cole*. Days afterwards, I was informed that Admiral Clark would not press my promotion issue any further. If I wanted resolution, I would have to wait until after the change of command and approach the incoming CNO, Admiral Michael Mullen, about the prospect of having him continue support for my promotion.

I did not know with certainty where Admiral Mullen stood, but I was told not to get my hopes up. Following the CNO change of command on July 22, 2005, I waited until August to request a meeting with him. Normally, a request to see a superior in the chain of command is granted within days; in this case it took almost two months. In a short meeting on October 13, Admiral Mullen, who had a very close relationship with Senator

Warner, bluntly informed me that he did not support my promotion, thought it was a mistake that I had ever been selected for promotion, and would recommend to the secretary of the Navy that my promotion not be forwarded to the Senate. He was unwilling to discuss the matter in any detail, and I was ushered quickly out of his office.

It was almost too much to grasp that Admiral Mullen thought he knew better than the previous CNO, secretary of the Navy, secretary of defense, and President. I was taken aback by the sudden reversal of support but rather than give up, decided to wait and see what happened with my paperwork. After all, it was not the CNO's promotion board. Promotion boards are under the purview and control of the secretary of the Navy.

When the entire issue of my promotion started, Secretary of the Navy Gordon England had supported my promotion nomination twice, in 2002 and again in 2004. In May 2005, he was nominated to be the deputy secretary of defense and was acting in that capacity when, the day after my meeting with Admiral Mullen, I requested to meet with him and one week later, sat in his office to review his support for my case.

When I walked in, he smiled, motioned me to a chair next to him, and apologized as he wrapped up signing some letters. He asked if I knew what he was doing, and of course I answered, "No, sir." He chuckled and said he was signing the November birthday cards for members of Congress, "You have to make them feel good, you know."

Immediately after signing the last card, he sat back in his chair and launched into the problem, which centered on Senator Warner and his continued threat to hold hearings into *Cole* and my promotion. Matter-of-factly, he said the Department of Defense and the Navy were unwilling to go through that sort of public exposure in pressing support for my promotion. He was aware of Admiral Mullen's feelings on the matter but demurred as to whether he would press his staunch support for me onto whoever was appointed to be the next secretary of the Navy, the position having been vacant since he became the Deputy. I walked through the talking points on why my promotion should continue to be supported but it was clear that until a new secretary of the Navy was in office, no one would be willing to once again move my nomination forward to the Senate. My wait would continue for the foreseeable future.

Incredibly, an event related at this point only to the September 11 attacks intruded in the summer of 2005 into the growing body of evidence surrounding the attack on *Cole*. A classified data-mining program between the U.S. Special Operations Command and the Defense Intelligence Agency had been created in 1999 as part of an information operations campaign plan against transnational terrorism. The program, called Able Danger, was specifically designed to ascertain whether data-mining techniques and open source material from commercial business interests and front organizations were effective tools in determining terrorist activities and plans. The program had recently received a great deal of media scrutiny and attention because of assertions that several people associated with it had, in fact, detected the key September 11 planner and hijacker who flew one of the planes into the World Trade Center, Mohammed Atta, as early as January 2000 but that the intelligence community had failed to take appropriate action to investigate their findings. Even the 9/11 Commission investigated their claims, which remained unproven.

What caught my attention was that the program had also detected an expanding body of evidence of al Qaeda's presence in Yemen, specifically the port of Aden. I was quietly approached by a member of the team and, within the constraints of the program's classification guidelines and need to know, I was briefed on an important but unknown point of interest. The Able Danger team had been conducting their operations until they reached a point where a routine update of their progress was in order, and they had scheduled a meeting in early October of 2000—as *Cole* was on the way to Aden—to brief the Commander of the Special Operations Command, General Peter J. Schoomaker, U.S. Army. Rarely is the four-star commander of a combatant command briefed on the status of an experimental program. Something in Able Danger had clearly triggered this high-level meeting criterion. In the meeting, a J-2 Special Operations Command Intelligence Directorate analyst whose expertise was Yemen pointedly expressed his concern about the breadth and scope of the al

Qaeda presence throughout Yemen. In fact, his concern was so great that the issue of Yemen was moved up to become the second item discussed as part of this lengthy briefing. While not specifically commenting on the port of Aden, he reiterated again and again to General Schoomaker in the briefing that with al Qaeda already known to have attacked two embassies in the region, there was a growing need for concern and possibly action to prevent an attack within Yemen.

At the end of the meeting, no action was taken, no analysis of the dangers to U.S. forces working in the country or conducting a routine visit was made, and no change to the threat posture was transmitted within either the Department of Defense or the intelligence communities because of the classified nature of the Able Danger program. The meeting took place on October 10, 2000, two days before the attack. It was yet another piece in the puzzle of how *Cole* had been put into harm's way and the intelligence community had again failed to detect and analyze critical information that, if shared, might have given the crew and me the warning to avoid disaster. Already, the members of the Able Danger team who talked with me had been ordered into silence by the Department of Defense over concerns related to the possible detection of Mohammed Atta; the team member informed me there was no way they would be allowed to share what they had known about al Qaeda operating in Yemen before the terrorists tried to sink *Cole*.

In December 2006, yet another unrelated, disturbing development occurred. Several months after the attack on *Cole* and the return of the crew to Norfolk, the Naval Historical Center activated their Naval Reserve Combat Documentation Detachment 206 to interview crew members to capture, for the sake of the Navy's historical files, the actions of the crew following the attack on *Cole*. It was a massive undertaking, principally led by two very compassionate and professional officers, Captain Michael McDaniel and Captain Gary Hall. In late spring 2001, the detachment conducted numerous interviews with the crew, including me. Prior to each interview, the subjects were encouraged to be as open and forthright as possible in an effort to capture the powerful emotions and actions of that horrific time in our lives. Each of us was assured that the Navy would keep the interviews in the strictest of confidence, for official use only, and our most private thoughts would never be shared with the general public without our express permission. Similar interviews had occurred with prisoners of war from the Vietnam conflict and their records had likewise been sealed from release to the public.

Now the Department of the Navy Privacy Act/Freedom of Information Action office under the Chief of Naval Operations informed me that they were acting on a request by an individual to give them access to transcripts of these interviews. After speaking with several other crew members, who were equally mortified and distraught at the prospect of having their innermost feelings and emotions publicly exposed, I took immediate action to have this request disapproved. At first I thought it would be a straightforward disapproval, but was stunned to learn that the promise of confidentiality conveyed to us by the Naval Historical Center had never undergone any legal review, and while given to us with the best of intentions, was not considered binding against a Freedom of Information Act request.

It appeared as if the Navy was conspiring against the crew of *Cole*. The impact on the individual was considered irrelevant, and the Navy seemed uncaring as the legal machinations ground through the approval process. Luckily, when I had been the secretary of the Navy's administrative aide, I worked very closely with the head of the Navy Freedom of Information Action office, Doris Lama. An absolutely wonderful person, she was as concerned over this request as me. While the request was eventually denied, it was because of Doris working with her counterpart at the Federal Bureau of Investigation, who, very concerned that there was still an active criminal investigation open on the attack on *Cole,* ruled there should be no possibility for evidence or potential witness statements to be compromised by public disclosure. It was a close call, but thankfully, Doris proved that at the heart of the Navy, the crew and I had a lot of underlying support.

For me, however, the wait for a final decision on my promotion continued. It was not until the 109th Congress and January 2006 that a new secretary of the Navy, Donald Winter, was sworn into office. Still, I waited.

By midyear, the promotion package had not even made it from the secretary's legal advisor to his desk. It was time, once again, to take matters into my own hands and drive my future. According to Navy regulations, anyone may submit a request to meet with their superiors in their chain of command on matters they consider unresolved at a lower level. In my case, since Admiral Mullen had done nothing regarding my promotion, on May 22, 2006, I requested a meeting with Secretary Winter.

The reaction was swift and unexpected. Within a day of my request, Vice Admiral Morgan called me into his office and, while we might have been shipmates and friends for years, he harshly turned on me: "Kirk, you are never going to be promoted to captain and it's time you accept your fate. If you go through with this request to meet with the secretary, the Navy will turn on you and you will find yourself isolated and alone. Do you understand what I am telling you?"

I literally sat there for a few seconds with my mouth hanging open as my throat tightened in disbelief that one of my most trusted mentors in the Navy was abandoning me. "Admiral, I have stood by my Navy throughout this entire event, and I deserve to have my promotion submitted to the Senate. Please approve my request to see the secretary," I answered. Nothing more needed to be said and within seconds, I was dismissed. But at least my request was grudgingly approved.

On May 31, I walked into Secretary Winter's office. The meeting was scheduled for thirty minutes and started off awkwardly when the secretary announced to me that he was unfamiliar with the background about the attack on *Cole* or my case and would I please take some time to give him that necessary information. Irritated, I glanced over at his legal advisor, wondering why he had failed to properly prepare his boss for our meeting; now I would have to waste precious minutes not talking about my promotion but rather talking about the most critical event to happen to a Navy ship since the Israeli attack on the USS *Liberty* in 1967 and the North Korean seizure of USS *Pueblo* in 1968.

Quickly I summarized the events of October 12 and the aftermath of our time in port. I covered the investigation, its findings, and the fact that

I had never wavered from the principle of accountability—I was the sole accountable officer for the actions of my crew—but there was also a fundamental difference between accountability and blame. I felt that in the long view of history, I was being singled out for punishment in a war that the nation had tragically ignored for years, until the attack on September 11. I was the only officer, in any service, attacked by al Qaeda, who was now being punished for it. I requested his support for my promotion and asked that it be forwarded to the Senate for its consideration. He said he would take my request under consideration, thanked me for my time, and showed me the door out. I knew I had just wasted thirty minutes of my life.

A week later, I was informed that the secretary was unwilling to forward my promotion up the chain of command as long as Senator Warner continued to threaten the Navy with hearings. I was at the end of my professional rope. I had given the military and civilian leadership of the Navy and Department of Defense over four years to resolve my case, and was no further along in dealing with Senator Warner's steadfast desire to see someone punished for the attack than I had been in 2002. I exercised my last resort and on June 27, wrote a letter requesting a meeting with Senator Warner. On August 1, I found myself at the reception desk for the staff of the Senate Armed Services Committee.

I had chosen not to officially inform that Navy of this meeting, but knew they were aware of it nonetheless. As a precaution, even though I had gone into work that day, I took a day of leave to eliminate even the hint of a possibility of being accused of unethical behavior by taking time from work to take care of what the Navy might consider a personal matter. A retired Navy JAG lawyer, Captain Dick Walsh, met me just prior to the meeting. He was part of the Armed Services Committee's professional staff and handled personnel issues. He told me the senator was running late as we walked into a hearing room. As I was ushered in, the spectacle before me was almost comical.

Set up in the room was a large table with three chairs on one side and as many as six on the other. Microphones covered the table pointing in both directions, with wires running down the length of the table and across the floor to where audio equipment and a computer were set up and a woman sat poised, ready to begin her work. As we walked in, Captain Walsh seriously intoned, "Kirk, where is your lawyer and public affairs person? You aren't here by yourself, are you?" I knew this was the beginning of an attempt at intimidation. In my mind, I struggled not to laugh out loud, "Sir, I'm here by myself and don't need a lawyer or a public affairs type. If I can't articulate to the senator all by myself why I should be promoted to captain, then I probably shouldn't be a captain. No, sir, I'm here alone and will speak on my own behalf."

Clearly, this was not the answer he was expecting, but he grandiosely swept his arm toward the tableful of microphones and chairs and stated, with all the seriousness he could muster, "I hope you don't mind this meeting being recorded and transcribed. The senator considers it so important that he felt it best to tape it and have it for the record." This was clearly serious business, but again the humor in their idea of what constituted intimidation almost leaked out as I took this next act in the play in stride and said, "Sir, I think this is a great idea! I welcome the opportunity to have this meeting recorded. I think it's important to capture what we say here today for the sake of history. It's important that what the senator decides be accurately portrayed to the public. So, no, I don't mind at all, it being recorded. May I have a copy when you finish getting it transcribed?" Clearly, he did not expect me to gracefully embrace these actions, and stammered, "Of course. Of course we'll get you a copy."

Senator Warner arrived forty-six minutes late, and the meeting began. I sat on one side of the table, alone, directly across from the senator. On his side of the table, he came well stocked with staff members: Charles S. Abell, Staff Director; Scott W. Stucky, General Counsel; and Richard "Dick" F. Walsh, JAGC, USN (Ret), Counsel. Quickly, I recounted the series of events that led up to *Cole* refueling in Aden, the attack and subsequent investigations, and then got to the point of the meeting, the status of my promotion nomination.

For the next twenty minutes, we went back and forth discussing his immovable stance that should my nomination be forwarded, he would hold a public hearing into my suitability for promotion. Several times, I reiterated that if he continued to threaten the Navy with that condition, they would not forward my nomination; he pointed out that such a decision was the purview of the Executive Branch, over which he had no control. Couching his language very artfully, he obfuscated the point with the claim that the senate had not seen my name submitted for promotion since 2002, and until such a time that it was submitted, there was no action he or the SASC could take on it. It was a clever political stance—threaten the Navy with retribution and a hearing if my promotion was forwarded, and then deny he had anything to do with my nomination not being submitted. Once again the art of hardball politics in Washington reared its ugly head.

At one point, the senator emphatically stressed, "There is no way I can, as a member of the Legislative Branch, force the Executive Branch to take that action [submitting my promotion for advice and consent of the Senate], which starts the process." In reply, I agreed and then specifically addressed his concern about accountability, "Yes, sir. They have to do that on their own and I can go back and try and re-engage with them but the issue of holding hearings, when you look across the breadth and scope of history, what makes my nomination so unique that it would cause one officer to be singled out to have hearings held on this issue? Given some of the other tremendous issues of people involved, whether it has been World War II to as recently as September 11, where when you look at the accountability factor there, no one stood up and said they were accountable for what happened on September 11. And yet, I stand up as a good commanding officer should, and say, I was the accountable officer on that ship. Seventeen lives were lost on my watch but we had neither the intelligence, the training, or rules of engagement that would have adequately allowed me to defend my ship. I'll be honest with you, Senator. Not a day goes by—just walking into the Pentagon today, I get stopped by people who say, 'What's going on?' And it's all services. A one-star Army general, three-star Navy admirals. They tell me what is happening to you is flat wrong because you are being unfairly singled out because of the nature of what happened and it's just wrong. Commanders today, when given the intelligence, the training and the rules of engagement, cannot stop terrorist attacks anywhere in the world. While life may not be fair, I've never bought into that because I look at it and say, one of the greatest things about our country is the fact that when we, as Americans, recognize something is not fair, we do something about it."

"I subscribe to that theory," the senator replied before I finished my statement.

"But too many people in *this* case have chosen to take a path of political expediency rather than doing what is right, and I, subsequently, have to be the one that is left to just be told, 'walk away from it,'" I concluded.

By the end of the meeting, it was clear the senator remained unmoved and unwavering in his threat to hold a hearing should my nomination be resubmitted for the Senate's consideration. It was a disappointing conclusion to a years-long journey. I walked out of the Russell Senate office building and into the hot, humid air of a summer day in Washington. It was time to go home, have a glass of wine, and assess my future.

Seven days later, the political fallout of my meeting with Senator Warner reached its culmination. Admiral Mullen submitted a letter to Secretary Winter recommending my name be removed from the FY03 Active Captain Line Promotion List. Six days later, the secretary concurred, and my name was permanently removed, never again to be submitted for Senate consideration. In an odd abdication of his role as the senior civilian official overseeing the Department of the Navy, Secretary Winter did not advise me of my removal from his promotion list but instead abandoned that task to the CNO. Having worked for two secretaries of the Navy, I was struck by the fact that it was not the CNO's role to advise me of my removal from the promotion list. In the end, it appeared that Senator Warner had finally arranged to have a long lingering problem eliminated and Admiral Mullen's future would be richly rewarded for his loyalty.

Immediately following the meeting with the CNO, Admiral Morgan summoned me to his office. We had not spoken about the issue of my promotion since our heated meeting several months earlier. As he motioned me to sit down across from his desk, he sat back and said, "Kirk, I just don't know what to say. I am as shocked by this development as anyone. Is there anything I can do for you?" My reply was clipped, "No, sir." He then asked, "What are your plans?" clearly trying to infer what my reaction was going to be. I was done dealing with the political niceties of the Navy's leadership, and respectfully and politely replied, "Admiral, thank you, but I think I'll keep my own counsel when it comes to my plans for the future."

A tense silence filled the air for a few seconds before he extended what I felt was a heartfelt offer from a friend, "Kirk, if you need anything, please let me know." The meeting quietly ended, I rose from my chair and thanked him, leaving his office to go back to work; the nation was still at war.

Nine months later, on a brilliantly sunny day, May 24, 2007, I retired after twenty-six years of service to the Navy and nation. Over 150 people, including a dozen flag and general officers, attended the ceremony, held publicly in the outside courtyard of the Navy Memorial in downtown Washington. A long-time friend and former Executive Officer on *Arleigh Burke*, Admiral Ray Spicer, honored me as the guest speaker with my chaplain, "Chaps" Thornton giving the invocation for the ceremony. I was also honored with the presence of someone from every at-sea and shore assignment I had in the Navy; from my roommate at the Naval Academy, Commander Bill Lewis, to Lieutenant Matt Fleisher, who worked for me in the Navy's International Strategy division and organized the ceremony. I was even blessed to recognize in my remarks a special attendee and the parent of one of my sailors—Tom Wibberley, whose son Craig was killed in the attack. Several of my crew from *Cole* also attended, including a few who had been wounded in the attack. After the conclusion of the ceremony, all of my former chief petty officers surprised me by presenting a bronze CPO statue. Once again, the chiefs proved themselves the backbone of our Navy. Just as *Cole* had left Aden harbor, I left the Navy proud and undeterred. I knew what the crew and I had accomplished and nothing that happened to me in the intervening years could ever take that pride away from me.

Four years later, more than ten years after the attack on *Cole*, I sat in my living room in Nevada on a quiet Sunday evening, watching nothing in particular on TV. The first day of May 2011 had been quiet and filled with the mundane routine of household chores—laundry, grocery shopping, and preparing for the upcoming busy workweek. Suddenly, the local station announced that the President was going to address the nation at 2230. Immediately, I sensed trouble. For the President to address the nation on a Sunday evening that late at night, it could only mean one thing—tragedy or disaster. Without warning, text messages began to inundate my phone as speculation ran rampant.

Within minutes, the word was out—Osama bin Laden was dead. It was no tragedy but rather long-overdue justice and miraculously good news. As the President's news conference was continually delayed, the minutes seemed to creep by. Finally, the President strode up to the podium and made his announcement:

> It was nearly 10 years ago that a bright September day was darkened by the worst attack on the American people in our history. The images of nine-eleven are seared into our national memory—hijacked planes cutting through a cloudless September sky; the Twin Towers collapsing to the ground; black smoke billowing up from the Pentagon; the wreckage of Flight 93 in Shanksville, Pennsylvania, where the actions of heroic citizens saved even more heartbreak and destruction. . . .
>
> For over two decades, bin Laden has been al Qaeda's leader and symbol, and has continued to plot attacks against our country and our friends and allies. The death of bin Laden marks the most significant achievement to date in our nation's effort to defeat al Qaeda.
>
> Yet his death does not mark the end of our effort. There's no doubt that al Qaeda will continue to pursue attacks against us. We must—and we will—remain vigilant at home and abroad. . . .
>
> So Americans understand the costs of war. Yet as a country, we will never tolerate our security being threatened, nor stand idly by when our people have been killed. We will be relentless in defense of our citizens and our friends and allies. We will be true to the values that make us who we are. And on nights like this one, we can say to

those families who have lost loved ones to al Qaeda's terror: Justice has been done.[11]

While there was no mention, once again, of the attack on *Cole*, I knew we had been avenged. I watched as the scenes of revelers flooded into the streets of downtown New York near Ground Zero and many more celebrated on Pennsylvania Avenue along the fence surrounding the White House. While I wanted to immerse myself in the joy of the moment, instead I got up out of my chair, turned off the television, and walked outside. The night was quiet as the stars brilliantly shone in the crystal clear Nevada sky. Out there, in homes across the country, I prayed that the families of the sailors killed in the attack on *Cole* and those who had survived and continued to rebuild their lives, as well as the entire nation, would hopefully sleep a little easier this night.

There was no feeling of happiness or celebration, only a deep sense of vindication and satisfaction. It was almost too surreal to comprehend that finally we had achieved this elusive victory. Before I left the still night air, I paused to remember those dark days in Aden and a crew that had reached into the deepest recesses of their souls to fight for their ship and shipmates. We lived up to the motto of USS *Cole* and its namesake, Sergeant Darrell S. Cole, USMC—*Gloria Merces Virtutis*—Glory is the Reward of Valor.

APPENDIX

COMUSNAVCENT/COMFIFTHFLT OPORD 99–01
Force Protection
Tab B to Appendix 1 of Annex M
Threat Condition (THREATCON) Measures

THREATCON Alpha. This condition is declared when a general threat of possible terrorist activity is directed toward installations, vessels, and personnel, the nature and extent of which are unpredictable, and where circumstances do not justify full implementation of THREATCON Bravo measures. However, it may be necessary to implement certain selected measures from THREATCON Bravo as a result of intelligence received or as a deterrent. The measures in this threat condition must be capable of being maintained indefinitely.

1. Brief crew on the port specific threat, the Security/Force Protection Plan, and security precautions to be taken ashore. Ensure all hands are knowledgeable of various THREATCON

requirements and that they understand their role in implementation of measures. Remind all personnel to be suspicious
and inquisitive of strangers, be alert for abandoned parcels or
suitcases and for unattended vehicles in the vicinity. Report
unusual activities to the Officer of the Deck.

2. Muster and brief security personnel on the threat and rules of
   engagement.

3. Review security plans and keep them available. Retain key personnel who may be needed to implement security measures
   on call.

4. Secure and periodically inspect spaces not in use.

5. Consistent with local rules, regulations, and Status of Forces
   Agreement (SOFA), post qualified armed fantail sentry and
   forecastle sentry.

6. Consistent with local rules, regulations, and SOFA, post qualified armed pier sentry and pier entrance sentry.

7. Ensure sentries, roving patrols, response force and the quarterdeck watch have the ability to communicate. If practical, all
   guards will be equipped with at least two systems of communication (e.g., two-way radio, telephone, whistle, or signal light).

8. If available, issue night vision devices to selected posted security
   personnel.

9. Review pier and shipboard access control procedures.

10. Coordinate pier and fleet landing security with collocated
    forces and local authorities. Identify anticipated needs for mu-
    tual support (security personnel, boats, and equipment) and
    define methods of activation and communication.

11. Tighten shipboard and pier access control procedures. Posi-
    tively identify all personnel entering pier and fleet landing
    area—no exceptions.

12. Consistent with local rules, regulations, and SOFA, establish
    unloading zone(s) on the pier away from the ship.

13. Deploy barriers to keep vehicles away from the ship. Barriers
    may be ship's vehicles, equipment, port provided barrier sys-

tems, marine containers, or items available locally. Consistent with local conditions, 400-foot standoff from the ship is preferred.

14. Request husbanding agent arrange and deploy barriers to keep vehicles away from ship (400-foot standoff from the ship preferred).

15. Inspect all vehicles entering pier and check for unauthorized personnel, weapons, and/or explosives.

16. Inspect all personnel, hand carried items, and packages before allowing them on board. Where available, use baggage scanners and walk through or hand held metal detectors to screen packages and personnel prior to boarding the ship.

17. Direct departing and arriving liberty boats to make a security tour around the ship and give special attention to the waterline and hull. Boats must be identifiable night and day to ship's personnel.

18. Water taxis, ferries, bum boats, and other harbor craft require special concern because they can serve as an ideal platform for terrorists. Unauthorized craft should be kept away from the ship; authorized craft should be carefully controlled, surveilled, and covered. Inspect authorized watercraft daily.

19. Identify and inspect workboats.

20. Secure spaces not in use.

21. Regulate shipboard lighting to best meet the threat environment. Lighting should include illumination of the waterline.

22. Rig hawsepipe covers and rat guards on all lines, cable, and hoses. Consider using an anchor collar.

23. Raise accommodation ladders, stern gates, Jacob ladders, etc., when not in use. Clear ship of all unnecessary stages, camels, barges, oil donuts, and lines.

24. Conduct security drills to include bomb threat and repel boarders exercises.

25. Review individual actions in THREATCON Bravo for possible implementation.

THREATCON Bravo. This condition is declared when an increased and more predictable threat of terrorist activity exists. Measures in this THREATCON must be capable of being maintained for weeks without causing undue hardships, without affecting operational capability, and without aggravating relations with local authorities.

26. Maintain appropriate THREATCON Alpha measures.
27. Review liberty policy in light of the threat and revise it as necessary to maintain the safety and security of the ship and crew.
28. Conduct divisional quarters at foul weather parade to determine the status of on-board personnel and to disseminate information.
29. Ensure that an up-to-date list of bilingual personnel for the area of operations is readily available. Ensure the warning tape in the pilot house and/or quarterdeck that warns small craft to remain clear is in both the local language and English.
30. Remind personnel to lock their parked vehicles and to carefully check them before entering.
31. Designate and brief picket boat crews. Prepare boats and place crews on 15-minute alert. If the situation warrants, make random picket boat patrols in the immediate vicinity of the ship with the motor whaleboat or gig. Boat crews will be armed with M16 rifles, one M60 with 200 rounds of ammunition, and 10 concussion grenades.
32. Consistent with local rules, regulations, and SOFA, establish armed brow watch on pier to check identification and inspect baggage before personnel board ship.
33. Restrict vehicle access to the pier. Discontinue parking on the pier. Consistent with local rules, regulations, and/or the Status of Forces Agreement, establish unloading zones(s) and move all containers as far away from ship as possible (400-foot stand-off distance preferred).
34. Man signal bridge or pilot house and ensure flares are available to ward off approaching craft.

35. After working hours, place armed sentries on a superstructure level from which they can best cover areas about the ship.

36. If not already armed, arm all members of the quarterdeck watch and Security Alert Team (SAT). In the absence of a SAT, arm two member of the Ship's Defense Force (SDF).

37. Provide shotgun and ammunition to quarterdeck. If the situation warrants, place sentry with shotgun inside the superstructure at a site from which the quarterdeck can be covered.

38. Issue arms to selected qualified officers to include Command Duty Officer (CDO) and Assistant Command Duty Officer (ACDO).

39. Implement measures to keep unauthorized craft away from the ship. Authorized craft should be carefully controlled. Coordinate with host nation/local port authority, husbanding agent as necessary, and request their assistance in controlling unauthorized craft.

40. If not already armed, arm Sounding and Security patrol.

41. Muster and brief ammunition bearers or messengers.

42. Implement procedures for expedient issue of firearms and ammunition from small arms locker (SAL). Ensure a set of SAL keys are readily available and in the possession of an officer designated for this duty by the Commanding Officer.

43. Inform local authorities of action taken as the THREATCON increases.

44. Test internal communications, communications with local authorities, and communications with other U.S. naval ships in port.

45. Instruct watches to conduct frequent random searches under piers, with emphasis on potential hiding places, pier pilings, and floating debris.

46. Conduct searches of the ship's hull and boats at intermittent intervals and immediately before it puts to sea.

47. Move cars and objects such as crates and trash containers as far from the ship as possible.

48. Hoist boats aboard when not in use.

49. Consider terminating all public visits.

50. Set materiel condition Yoke, main deck and below.

51. After working hours, reduce entry points to the ship's interior by securing selected entrances from the inside.

52. Duty department heads ensure all spaces not in regular use are secured and inspected periodically.

53. If two brows are rigged, remove one of them. Use only one gangway to access the ship.

54. Maintain capability to get under way on short notice or as specified by the Standard Operating Procedures (SOP). Consider possible relocation sites (different pier, anchorage, etc.). Rig brow and accommodation ladder for immediate raising or removal.

55. Ensure .50-caliber mount assemblies are in place with ammunition in ready service lockers (.50-caliber machineguns will be maintained in the armory, pre-fire checks completed, and ready for use).

56. Prepare fire hoses. Brief designated personnel on procedures for repelling boarders, small boats, and ultralight aircraft.

57. Obstruct possible helicopter landing areas in such a manner to prevent hostile helicopters from landing.

58. Review riot and crowd control procedures, asylum-seeker procedures, and bomb threat procedures.

59. Monitor local communications (e.g., ship-to-ship, TV, radio, police scanners).

60. Implement additional security measures for high-risk personnel as appropriate.

61. Inform local authorities of actions being taken as THREATCON increases.

62. Review individual actions in THREATCON Charlie for possible implementation.

THREATCON Charlie. This condition is declared when an incident occurs or intelligence is received indicating that some form of terrorist action against installations, vessels, or personnel is imminent. Implementation of this THREATCON for more than a short period will probably create hardship and will affect the peacetime activities of the ship and its personnel.

63. Maintain appropriate measures for THREATCONS Alpha and Bravo.
64. Cancel liberty. Execute emergency recall.
65. Be prepared to get under way on one hour's notice or less. If conditions warrant, request permission to sortie.
66. Muster and arm Security Alert Team (SAT), Back-up Alert Force (BAF), and Reserve Force (RF). Position SAT and BAF at designated location(s). Deploy RF to protect command structure and augment posted security watches.
67. Place armed sentries on a superstructure level from which they can best provide 360-degree coverage about the ship.
68. Establish .50- or .30-caliber machinegun positions.
69. If available, deploy stinger surface-to-surface air missiles in accordance with established ROE.
70. Energize radar and establish watch.
71. Energize radar and/or sonar, rotate screws and cycle rudder(s) at frequent and irregular intervals, as needed to assist in deterring, detecting or thwarting an attack. Man passive sonar capable of detecting boats, swimmers, or underwater vehicles. Position any non-sonar equipped ships within the acoustic envelope of sonar-equipped ships.
72. Man one or more repair lockers. Establish communications with an extra watch in damage control central.
73. Deploy picket boat. Boats should be identifiable night and day from the ship (e.g., by lights or flags).

74. Coordinate with host nation, local port authority, or husbanding agent to establish small boat exclusion zone.

75. If feasible, deploy a helicopter as an observation or gun platform. The helicopter should be identifiable night and day from the ship.

76. If a threat of swimmer attack exists, activate an anti-swimmer watch.

77. Consider issuing weapons to selected officers and chief petty officers in the duty section (i.e., the Commanding Officer, Executive Officer, Department Heads).

78. If available, issue concussion grenades to topside rovers, forecastle and fantail sentries, and bridge watch.

79. Erect barriers and obstacles as required to control traffic flow.

80. Strictly enforce entry control procedures and searches—no exceptions.

81. Enforce boat exclusion zone.

82. Minimize all off-ship administrative trips.

83. Discontinue contract work.

84. Set material condition Zebra, second deck and below.

85. Secure from the inside all unguarded entry points to the interior of the ship.

86. Rotate screws and cycle rudder(s) at frequent and irregular intervals.

87. Rig additional fire hoses. Charge the fire hoses when manned just prior to actual use.

88. Review individual actions in THREATCON Delta for implementation.

THREATCON Delta. This condition is declared when a terrorist attack has occurred in the immediate area or intelligence has been received that indicates a terrorist action against a specific location or person is likely. Normally, this THREATCON is declared as a localized warning.

89. Maintain appropriate THREATCONs Alpha, Bravo, and Charlie measures.
90. Permit only necessary personnel topside.
91. Prepare to get under way and, if possible, cancel port visit and depart.
92. Arm selected personnel of the Ship's Defense Force.
93. Deploy M-79 grenade launchers to cover approaches to the ship.
94. Employ all necessary weaponry to defend against attack.

NOTES

NOTES TO CHAPTER 8

1. Keenan, Patrick J., Commander, USN, Officer in Charge, Navy Ship Repair Unit Bahrain, *Engineering Duty Newsletter,* January 2001, 1, 18–20.

NOTES TO CHAPTER 11

1. Perna, Frank, Chief Warrant Officer, USN, Officer in Charge, Detachment Alpha, Mobile Driving and Salvage Unit Two, *Faceplate: The Official Newsletter for the Divers and Salvors of the United States Navy* 5, no. 3 (March 2001), 7–8.

2. Keenan, Patrick J., Commander, USN, Officer in Charge, Navy Ship Repair Unit Bahrain, *Engineering Duty Officer Newsletter* (January 2001), 1, 18–20.

3. Ibid.

NOTES TO CHAPTER 13

1. Commander, U.S. Naval Forces Central Command, letter dated October 14, 2000, Ser 00/1082, Subj: Command Investigation into the Actions of USS Cole (DDG 67) in Preparing for and Undertaking a Brief Stop for Fuel at Bandar at Tawahi (Aden Harbor) Aden, Yemen, On or About 12 October 2000.

2. Soufan, Ali H., with Daniel Freedman, *The Black Banners: The Inside Story of 9/11 and the War against al-Qaeda* (New York: W.W. Norton & Company, 2011), 154–156.

3. Newman, Robert, Lieutenant Colonel, U.S. Army, Defense Attaché to U.S. Embassy, Sana'a, Yemen, JAGMAN Investigation Statement, e-mail dated November 22, 2000.

4. Command Investigation into the Actions of USS *Cole* (DDG 67) in Preparing for and Undertaking a Brief Stop for Fuel at Bandar at Tawahi (Aden Harbor) Aden, Yemen, On or About 12 October 2000, passim.

5. Command Investigation report, 60–66, 96–106.

6. Commander U.S. Naval Forces Central Command, First Endorsement on Captain James W. Holland, Jr., U.S. Navy, letter of November 27, 2000, Subj: Investigation to Inquire into the Actions of USS *Cole* (DDG 67) in Preparing for and Undertaking a Brief Stop for Fuel at Bandar at Tawahi (Aden Harbor) Aden, Yemen On or About 12 October 2000, 126–128.

7. Ibid., 128.

8. Ibid.

9. *The 9/11 Commission Report, Final Report of the National Commission on Terrorist Attacks Upon the United States, Official Government Version*, photo reprint (Baton Rouge, LA: Claitor's Publishing Division, 2004), 191.

10. Soufan, *The Black Banners*, 157.

11. Ibid., 128–129.

12. Ricks, Thomas E., and Vernon Loeb, "Cole Security Lapses Found; Precautions Not Taken When Ship Was Hit by Bomb," *Washington Post*, December 9, 2000, Section A, 14.

13. Commander in Chief, U.S. Atlantic Fleet Second Endorsement on Captain James W. Holland, Jr., U.S. Navy, letter of November 27, 2000, Subj: Investigation to Inquire into the Actions of USS *Cole* (DDG 67) in Preparing for and Undertaking a Brief Stop for Fuel at Bandar at Tawahi (Aden Harbor) Aden, Yemen On or About 12 October 2000, 136.

14. Ibid., 141.

15. Ibid., 139–140.

16. Ibid., 145.

17. Ibid., 146–150.

18. Ibid., 152.

19. Ibid., 153.

20. Ibid., 154.

21. Ibid., 153–154.

22. Ibid., 155.

23. Ibid., 157.

24. Secretary of Defense, William S. Cohen, et al., Department of Defense Transcript, USS *Cole* Briefing, January 19, 2001.

25. USS *Cole* Commission Report, Department of Defense, January 9, 2001, 1.

26. Ibid.

27. Ibid., 2, 4–6.

28. Ibid., 7–8.

29. Ibid., 8.

30. Ibid., 9–10.

31. Danzig, Richard, Memorandum for the Secretary of Defense, Subj: Investigation to Inquire into the Actions of USS *Cole* (DDG 67) in Preparing for and Undertaking a Brief Stop for Fuel (BSF) at Bandar at Tawahi (Aden Harbor) Aden, Yemen On or About 12 October 2000, January 18, 2001, 1–3.

32. Department of Defense Transcript, USS *Cole* Briefing, Secretary of Defense William S. Cohen (et al.), January 19, 2001.

33. Danzig Memorandum, 3.

34. Ibid., 4–5.

35. Ibid., 5.

36. Ibid.

37. Ibid., 5–6.

38. Cohen, William S., Memorandum for Secretaries of the Military Departments, et al, Subj: Assessment of Accountability Arising from the Attack on USS *Cole* (DDG 67) on 12 October 2000, 1.

39. Ibid., pg. 2.

40. Ibid.

41. Ibid.

42. Steven Strasser, ed., *The 9/11 Investigations* (New York: PublicAffairs, 2004), 111–112.

43. *The 9/11 Commission Report,* 191.

NOTES TO CHAPTER 14

1. Foley, J. B., Commander, Naval Surfaces Force, U.S. Atlantic Fleet memo to Chief of Naval Operations, December 19, 2000, Ser. N02L/1313, 1–3.

2. www.arlingtoncemetery.net/unidentified-091202.htm, accessed November 17, 2010.

NOTES TO EPILOGUE

1. Clarke, Richard A., *Against All Enemies: Inside America's War on Terror* (New York: Free Press, 2004), 223.

2. Strasser, Steven, ed., *The 9/11 Investigations* (New York: PublicAffairs, 2004), 111–112.

3. Cohen, William S., et al., Department of Defense Transcript, USS *Cole* Briefing, Secretary of Defense, January 19, 2001.

4. Strasser, ed., *The 9/11 Investigations,* 111–112.

5. Clarke, *Against All Enemies,* 224.

6. Soufan, Ali H., with Daniel Freedman, *The Black Banners: The Inside Story of 9/11 and the War Against al-Qaeda* (New York: W. W. Norton & Company, 2011), 218–220.

7. *The 9/11 Commission Report, Final Report of the National Commission on Terrorist Attacks Upon the United States, Official Government Version,* photo reprint (Baton Rouge, LA: Claitor's Publishing Division, 2004), 153–159; and Soufan, *Black Banners,* 239, 294.

8. National Archives, Executive Orders 13492-13493, President Barack Obama, January 22, 2009, http://www.archives.gov/federal-register/executive-orders/2009-obama.html

9. Secretary of the Navy Gordon England, Precept Convening FY-03, Promotion Selection Boards to Consider Officers in the Line on the Active-Duty List of the Navy for Promotion to the Permanent Grade of Captain, January 7, 2002, A3.

10. Armed Service Committee Hearing, To receive testimony concerning the sinking of the USS INDIANAPOLIS and the subsequent court-martial of Rear Admiral Charles B. McVay, III, USN, September 14, 1999, statement of Senator John Warner (R-VA).

11. The White House Blog, Osama bin Laden Dead, May 2, 2011, http://www.whitehouse.gov/blog/2011/05/02/osama-bin-laden-dead

INDEX

Commander Kirk S. Lippold was the commanding officer of the USS *Cole* during Al Qaeda's attack in October 2000. Lippold's personal awards include the Defense Superior Service Medal, Legion of Merit, Meritorious Service Medal, and Combat Action Ribbon, among others. He retired from the Navy in 2007, and serves as president of Base to Peak, LLC, a strategic planning and leadership development firm.